To Peter, 1993.

day - nearing the fin[...]

Newspapers after a li[...]

and dedication to the union.

From Gloria, who benefitted

from your wisdom for 16 of those year[...]

LORDS
OF
FLEET STREET

For my mother

LORDS
OF
FLEET STREET
The Harmsworth Dynasty

Richard Bourne

UNWIN

HYMAN

LONDON SYDNEY WELLINGTON

First published in Great Britain by the Trade Division of
Unwin Hyman Limited, 1990

UNWIN HYMAN LIMITED
15–17 Broadwick Street
London W1V 1FP

Allen & Unwin Australia Pty Ltd
8 Napier Street, North Sydney, NSW 2060, Australia

Allen & Unwin New Zealand Pty Ltd with the Port Nicholson Press
Compusales Building, 75 Ghuznee Street, Wellington, New Zealand.

British Library Cataloguing in Publication Data
Bourne, Richard
    Lords of Fleet Street: The Harmsworth Dynasty.
1. Great Britain. Newspaper publishing industries.
Harmsworth, (Family)
I. Title
388.761070172092
ISBN 0-04-440450-6

Typeset in 11 on 12 point Sabon by Computape (Pickering) Ltd,
North Yorkshire and printed in Great Britain by
Hartnoll Limited, Bodmin, Cornwall

Contents

List of Illustrations   *page* vi
Acknowledgements   viii
The Harmsworth Family   x

Part I   Alfred Northcliffe: The Founder

1   Origins and *Answers*   3
2   From Magazines to *The Times*   19
3   From 1914 to 1922   40
4   Family, Personality, Impact   62

Part II   Harold Rothermere: The Brother

5   The Founder of the *Sunday Pictorial*   77
6   From 1922 to 1929   92
7   From 1929 to 1940   107
8   Dynasty and Impact   121

Part III   Esmond Rothermere: The Son

9   From 1898 to 1937   133
10   From 1937 to the 1950s   149
11   From Coronation Year to 1978   167
12   Family, Impact, Personality   184

Part IV   Vere Rothermere: The Grandson

13   From Birth to 1971   199
14   From 1971 to 1981   208
15   Towards the 1990s   224
16   Epilogue   238

Notes   243
Select Bibliography   247
Index   249

Illustrations

Harmsworth Family Tree (*With the assistance of the Hon. Mrs Daphne Macneil Dixon*)   *page* x

Plates 1 to 14 between pages 84–85

1   A cartoon inspired by the Harmsworth children (*Punch*)
2   Elmwood house today (*Photo: The author; by permission of Mrs Mary Davis*)
3   The first real issue of *Answers* (*British Library*)
4   Alfred Harmsworth aged 20 (*National Portrait Gallery*)
5   Northcliffe in middle age (*National Portrait Gallery*)
6   Four directors of the Amalgamated Press in 1912 (*from a souvenir publication at the opening of Fleetway House*)
7   Northcliffe with Harold, the first Lord Rothermere, and Harold's son, Esmond Harmsworth, MP (*Hulton Picture Co.*)
8   Northcliffe and Wickham Steed, Editor of *The Times* (*Hulton Picture Co.*)
9   Lilian Harmsworth and her three sons, Vyvyan, Vere and Esmond (*Countess of Cromer*)
10 Harold and Lilian at Ascot (*Hulton Picture Co.*)
11 The paper mills at Grand Falls, Newfoundland (*Fleetway House souvenir*)
12 Sir Harold Harmsworth in 1912 (*Fleetway House souvenir*)
13 Nikitina the dancer
14 The first issue of the *Sunday Pictorial* (*British Library*)

Plates 15 to 28 between pages 180–181

15 Esmond as a young MP (*Countess of Cromer*)
16 Warwick House (*Photo: The author*)
17 Esmond Rothermere in his university Chancellor's robes (*Hulton Picture Co.*)
18 Esmond Rothermere dressed for the 1953 Coronation (*Countess of Cromer*)
19 Esmond hosting the Prince of Wales and friends (*Countess of Cromer*)
20 Vere as a child holding a bird (*National Portrait Gallery*)

21 Esme, Vere and Lorna (*Countess of Cromer*)
22 Vere aged about 23 (*Countess of Cromer*)
23 Vere, the morning after becoming chairman of Associated Newspapers (*Hulton Picture Co.*)
24 Patricia, Lady Rothermere, in July 1980 (*Hulton Picture Co.*)
25 Lord Northcliffe's room in Fleetway House (*Fleetway House
   souvenir*)
26 Vere Rothermere in Northcliffe's room formerly at the *Daily Mail*
   in Carmelite House, now at Northcliffe House (*Photo: John
   Minihan*)
27 Vere, the third Lord Rothermere in the foyer of Northcliffe House
   (*Photo: John Minihan*)
28 Vere on the journalists' floor of the *Evening Standard* (*Photo: John
   Minihan*)

Acknowledgements

The suggestion for a new history of the Harmsworths, from Northcliffe to the present day, originated with Peter Shellard and Bill Neill-Hall who were then with Messrs J. M. Dent. I should like to thank them most warmly for starting me on a lengthy but satisfying undertaking.

Since the Harmsworth newspaper proprietors have given rise to periodic controversy it should be stated that this is not an official, authorised history commissioned by the family. I have, however, received valuable help from several members of the family, gladly acknowledged below. My object has been to give a fair and rounded picture of a unique newspaper dynasty which has lasted through three generations, where personal and family history is significantly entwined with press, politics, business and the social evolution of modern Britain.

The only time I ever distantly worked for a Harmsworth was in 1959 when I was a trainee reporter on the *Cambridge Daily News*, briefly owned by the International Publishing Corporation of which Cecil Harmsworth King was then chairman. In 1977, I joined the *Evening Standard* as Deputy Editor just a few weeks before it was the subject of a take-over bid by Associated Newspapers; the attempt was repelled at that time, and I was no longer working for that paper when it subsequently joined the Rothermere group.

In thanking the following individuals for their guidance and help I should stress that they are in no way responsible for my opinions or conclusions: Jonathan Aitken, Tom Baistow, the late Noel Barber, Peter and Christabel Bielenberg, Jeffrey Blyth, Arthur Brittenden, David Cash, Lady Lorna Cooper-Key, Aidan Crawley, the Earl and Countess of Cromer, John Dickie, Granville Eastwood, Sir David English, Miss E. Gilbert, John Gold, Vanessa Gorst, the late Desmond, Baron Harmsworth of Egham, Guy Harmsworth, Lady Harmsworth Blunt, Madeleine Harmsworth, Vyvyan Harmsworth, Michael Herd, David Hill, Andrew Howard (for assistance on the *Daily Mail* coverage of elections), Derek Ingram, Simon Jenkins, William Keegan, Richard Kershaw, Randolph Lederer, John Leese, Campbell Leggat, Brian MacArthur (for kindly reading the draft), the Hon. Mrs Daphne Macneil Dixon, Michael Mander, Jim Markwick, the late Keith McDowell, Norris McWhirter, Eugene Nadasy, Roy Nash, Peter Quennell, Michael Randall, Robert Redhead, Vere, Viscount Rothermere of Hemsted, the family of the late Gerald Sanger (especially for permission to consult the G. F. Sanger diaries), Sir Patrick Sergeant, Professor Colin Seymour Ure (who kindly read the manuscript), David Skan, Bernard Shrimsley, Steward Steven, Adrian and Veronica Stokes, Ferenc Szabo, Walter Terry, Noel Vinson, Gritta Weil (for access to papers of Lajos Lederer), John Winnington-Ingram, Charles Wintour, Roy Wright and Peter Younghusband.

Furthermore, I should like to thank the Trustees of the Beaverbrook Foundation and the House of Lords Records Office for permission to quote from the Beaverbrook Papers; and the British Library (Department of Manuscripts and Colindale Newspaper Library) for assistance and permission to quote, especially from the Northcliffe Papers.

The Harmsworth Family

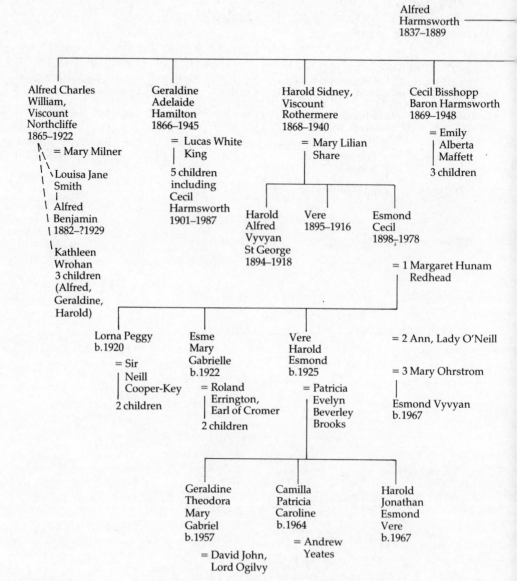

Alfred
Harmsworth
1837–1889

Alfred Charles
William,
Viscount
Northcliffe
1865–1922
= Mary Milner

Louisa Jane
Smith

Alfred
Benjamin
1882–?1929

Kathleen
Wrohan
3 children
(Alfred,
Geraldine,
Harold)

Geraldine
Adelaide
Hamilton
1866–1945
= Lucas White
King

5 children
including
Cecil
Harmsworth
1901–1987

Harold Sidney,
Viscount
Rothermere
1868–1940
= Mary Lilian
Share

Cecil Bisshopp
Baron Harmsworth
1869–1948
= Emily
Alberta
Maffett
3 children

Harold
Alfred
Vyvyan
St George
1894–1918

Vere
1895–1916

Esmond
Cecil
1898–1978

= 1 Margaret Hunam
Redhead

Lorna Peggy
b.1920
= Sir
Neill
Cooper-Key
2 children

Esme
Mary
Gabrielle
b.1922
= Roland
Errington,
Earl of Cromer
2 children

Vere
Harold
Esmond
b.1925
= Patricia
Evelyn
Beverley
Brooks

= 2 Ann, Lady O'Neill

= 3 Mary Ohrstrom

Esmond Vyvyan
b.1967

Geraldine
Theodora
Mary
Gabriel
b.1957
= David John,
Lord Ogilvy

Camilla
Patricia
Caroline
b.1964
= Andrew
Yeates

Harold
Jonathan
Esmond
Vere
b.1967

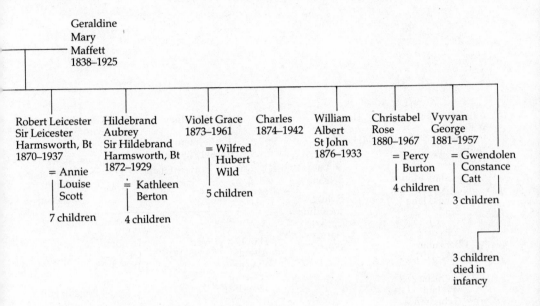

Geraldine
Mary
Maffett
1838–1925

Robert Leicester
Sir Leicester
Harmsworth, Bt
1870–1937
  = Annie
  | Louise
  | Scott

  7 children

Hildebrand
Aubrey
Sir Hildebrand
Harmsworth, Bt
1872–1929
  = Kathleen
  | Berton

  4 children

Violet Grace
1873–1961
  = Wilfred
  | Hubert
  | Wild

  5 children

Charles
1874–1942

William
Albert
St John
1876–1933

Christabel
Rose
1880–1967
  = Percy
  | Burton

  4 children

Vyvyan
George
1881–1957
  = Gwendolen
  | Constance
  | Catt

  3 children

3 children
died in
infancy

PART I

Alfred Northcliffe
The Founder

1
Origins and *Answers*

The future Viscount Northcliffe was born close to two creative fault-lines in the social geology of Britain: he had an Anglo-Irish background, and his parents felt they ought to be middle class but in fact were rather hard up. He was delivered by the family doctor on 15 July 1865 at the family home, 'Sunnybank', in Chapelizod close to Dublin where his father, also Alfred, was then a schoolmaster at the Royal Hibernian Military School. His mother, Geraldine Mary *née* Maffett, came from Scottish Presbyterian stock in County Down; her father, William, had moved down to Dublin and become a tough rich land agent.

The two parents were quite different in character. Alfred Harmsworth, whose family came from Hampshire, was the son of a shopkeeper and a small builder living in what is now St John's Wood, north London. He trained as a teacher at St Mark's College, Chelsea. In temperament he was easy going, self-indulgent and a good conversationalist, with a weakness for the bottle. His wife, however, whom he met when teaching at the Military School in Dublin, was a determined lady who wanted to see her husband become a barrister. Her will power kept what became a large family going in spite of the ineffectualness and limited income of Alfred senior. The wedding had been disapproved of by many of the Maffetts who felt that Geraldine was throwing herself away on a poor schoolmaster. Fortunately, her Alfred had succeeded in charming William Maffett, who insisted that his relations should turn up at the ceremony on pain of being cut out of his will.

Nearly two years after young Alfred was born the family moved to London. There were both push and pull factors at work. The situation in Ireland was not good either politically or in a more personal sense. There was considerable alarm among respectable Unionists at the growth of a revolutionary and nationalist movement, the Fenians. Geraldine Harmsworth heard a rumour in the village that her husband, as an Englishman teaching at the military school, had been targeted by the Dublin Fenians. He commented in his diary, 'Reading law with my sword on my knee. Dieu nous garde.'

For the two parents the death of William Maffett in the year young Alfred was born had been unfortunate. It had exposed them to the unfriendliness of Maffett relatives, and a complicated will which lawyers would fight over had not relieved their financial difficulties. A move to England, where Alfred senior had obtained a salary for nine months as an assistant secretary in the London office of a commission inquiring into the revenues of the established church in Ireland, could also expedite his entry to the Bar.

Baby Alfred, nicknamed Sunny, was sickly, suffering from 'congestion of the brain' and 'fits', with a head that seemed too big for his body. By the time he was taken to London – initially to stay in the house of his paternal grandmother in St John's Wood – he had a baby sister, born in 1866 and called Geraldine after her mother. On 26 April 1868 a third child was born, Harold Sidney, nicknamed Bunny, who was to grow up to be the first Lord Rothermere. The following year, by now with four children, Alfred senior passed his exams and was called to the Bar. But the reality which stretched before him was melancholy: an expanding family, a career of 'devilling' for seniors rather than of forensic triumphs of his own, house moves forced on him for financial reasons, and a corrosive feeling of personal dissatisfaction. He consoled himself with alcohol, his pipe, and the company of friends in the Sylvan Debating Club which he helped to found.

If the father was a bit of a dreamer, and one of nature's losers, the mother was a fighter. Geraldine Harmsworth was tough, with a big physique which permitted her to bear fourteen babies – of whom only three died in infancy – and still to run up and downstairs. With babies coming on average at eighteen-month intervals much of her own existence for twenty years was taken up with child-rearing, and every one but the latest may have been somewhat short on affection. A woman who had been brought up with plenty of money, and able to dress expensively, now had to borrow clothes from friends and relatives; she could not sew or knit. Sometimes her ignorance of the Beetonian skills of household management showed through, as when her husband brought home a three-guinea fee and asked her to buy salmon as a treat for the family – she bought a whole salmon, not knowing it could be purchased by the pound.

The family's difficulties did not, however, upset Geraldine's devotion to her husband or her children's regard for him, even though he did not conceal his disappointments. The children tended to take after him in appearance, but from her they inherited a determination to succeed and a respect for truthfulness. Until her death in 1925, in her late eighties, she exercised a moral authority over children and grandchildren which was classically Victorian. It was not just that she knew right from wrong: she had earned their respect as a mother to so many, often making her own sacrifices in the hard times.

Probably the lowest period occurred when Alfred senior twice lost his voice and was compelled to give up his legal practice. On the second occasion he lost his livelihood for several months. Harold, Lord Rothermere, recalled later that there was often only bread for breakfast and sometimes no Sunday lunch; the younger children were wrapped in newspapers at night for lack of blankets. Young Alfred resolved that he would never let himself be placed in a situation where he had to worry so much about money, and family legend suggested that the mental backwardness of Charles (born in 1874) may have had something to do with the lack of basic nutrition in the household at that time.

How did they survive? The father's Masonic membership – he was for five years a member of the Honor and Generosity Lodge of St John's Wood – may have helped. He sold a Dutch still life at Christie's for £9 15s, and wrote to the butcher postponing payment. He tried to find homes at a cheaper rent – as when he moved from Alexandra Terrace to Rose Cottage in the Vale of Health, Hampstead in 1870, where they stayed for three years before moving again to the terraces of St John's Wood. He made do with a bowl of soup for his lunch. Meanwhile, Geraldine got some support from two of their relations – his talented and attractive sister, Sarah (known in her early twenties as 'the belle of St John's Wood'), and her own niece, Florence Hamilton.

To late twentieth-century eyes, used to the brick expanses of north London, it is not easy to remember that in the last quarter of the nineteenth century houses in St John's Wood had substantial gardens, Hampstead was still thought of as out in the country, and cow-parsley stood shoulder-high on the country road from West Hampstead to Barnet. In spite of other privations, the Harmsworth children had the fun of the great wilderness of Hampstead Heath on their doorstep, and the stimulus of living in a zone where the attitudes of a thrusting city rubbed along with the slower traditions of rural Hertfordshire.

More particularly, for youngsters who were to invent much of popular journalism as it was to be practised in Britain, there was plenty of precept and example near at hand. Their own father was constantly trying to get articles published with indifferent success, and had a respect for words and a gift of wit. Charles Dickens, whom Alfred senior had heard at his last reading, died in the year they moved to the Vale of Health; he noted in his diary that only the previous day a manuscript of his had been rejected by Dickens for *Household Words*, and he and his wife joined the crowd to pay their respects to the dead writer at his funeral in Westminster Abbey.

Nearby then there lived George Jealous, a printer and journalist who had set up his own weekly, the *Hampstead & Highgate Express*, in 1860. He seems to have befriended the young Sunny Harmsworth, giving him a toy printing set with which he taught himself to read, inviting him round to the printing works on press days, and giving him space to escape from the noise of so many brothers and sisters; his wife

recalls the boy sitting in their parlour, in a world of his own, sole pos-
sessor of a kingdom of books and newspapers.

It is possible, too, that Aunt Sarah, who gave readings from Dickens
and talked well, was another inspiration. In 1886 – by which time
young Alfred would be 21 – she set up a weekly paper of her own, the
Kensington Advertiser, which ran for three years. This was a most
unusual enterprise for a woman in this period, and may have been at
the back of young Alfred's mind when much later he sought to launch
the *Daily Mirror* as a daily paper for women.

Finally, although the education of the young Harmsworths was to be
rather ragged until young Alfred was in a position to subsidise it, there
was some genuine scholarship in the family. Two of Geraldine's
Maffett sisters had married Germans. One of them was Albert Maximilian Selss of Westphalia, professor of German at Dublin University, and
a man of presence and learning. He usually called on the London
Harmsworths en route from Dublin to Germany, when he quarrelled
with cabmen and delighted the children by giving them sweets and
inviting them to join him and their father at the Bull and Bush, where
they could drink all the ginger beer they wanted. (In the Franco-
Prussian War the Harmsworths, like much middle-class opinion, had
been firmly pro-Prussian.)

Meanwhile, the family remorselessly expanded and young Alfred,
who hated too much noise, tried to keep control; young Geraldine
ordered and thumped the smaller ones around. There were a lot of
energetic youngsters in relatively small spaces; toys were smashed and
gardens ravaged. After Harold and Cecil had been born in Alexandra
Terrace (Cecil in September 1869), three more were born in the Vale of
Health (Robert Leicester in November 1870, Hildebrand in March 1872
and Violet in April 1873); Charles and St John were born in Grove End
Road, St John's Wood (successively in December 1874 and May 1876).
By 1877 the family had moved to a larger house, 'Burghfield' in Boundary Road, St John's Wood, which was next door to a school run by the
Misses Budd which the children attended. There five more were born of
whom only two (Christabel, who arrived in April 1880 and Vyvyan,
who appeared exactly twelve months later) survived infancy.

As they grew the children became big and assertive. Many had nicknames. Harold, who was good at arithmetic, was Bunny; Cecil was
Bouffles; St John, who was athletic, was known as Bonch. The milieu
encouraged a certain quick-wittedness and ruthlessness. Young Alfred,
warned by his mother that those who ask shan't have, and those who
don't ask won't get, said that it was all right – he just took. (Later on,
Northcliffe would say that those who did not speak up and ask for
things would never get them.) A next-door neighbour in Boundary
Road, fed up with the older Harmsworths scrumping his apples, called
out one morning to them, 'Why don't you come right in and take what

you want? I know you'll have it anyhow – you might as well have it honestly!'

In the Vale of Health days the family inspired a cartoon in *Punch*. Alfred and Harold were having tea with a neighbour. Harold fell silent. His elder brother, perhaps mindful that food at home was not always plentiful, remarked, 'I know what he's thinking about. He's thinking about cake – he's always thinking about cake.' The story came to the ears of George du Maurier, a local inhabitant, who changed the sex of the protagonists to provide an instantly recognisable vignette for *Punch*'s middle-class readers.[1]

Whether for financial reasons, or really as his father claimed because he was against starting formal education too soon, young Alfred did not begin at school until he was 8. At the boys only Academy run by the Misses Budd he began every day with a hymn, learnt some Latin and French, impressed his teachers with his English compositions, and as a new boy himself fought off an older boy who was attacking a small Jewish new boy, Henry Arnholz, who went on to become his solicitor and confidant.

When he was 11, Alfred was sent away as a boarder to Stamford Grammar School in Lincolnshire, then known as Browne's School after a founder. According to his later reminiscences he spent a thoroughly unhappy two years there, being caned three times a week by the clergyman headmaster, Edward Coulson Musson. Life in Victorian boarding schools was notoriously tough, but this was not the spirit he conveyed in a typically inconsequential schoolboy letter dated 15 September 1877 and sent to his mother:[2]

My dear Mama,
    I got your letter telling me of Mr Bacon's death. When did Mrs Bacon come over? Give my love to Mrs Bacon, Sonny and all the others. Shall I wear my school ribbon? You need not wear one if you are in mourning. I went to Mr Stapleton's to dinner and tea. I will get my slippers as soon as I can get the price of them. Papa sent me one shilling. We had a football match. On Wednesday I have a new piece of music called La Petite Fleur by C. Voss. Love to Papa and all the brothers and sisters.
    God Bye
    I am
    Your affectionate Son
    A. Harmsworth

At Stamford he was known as 'Dodger'; there was a fashion among the boys for Dickensian nicknames. What was clearly a bad time for him came to an end when one of his thumbs was split by a caning and he had to spend a term at home. His father decided not to send him back – whether because of the incessant beatings or because the family fortunes were finding it hard to stretch beyond the costs of a day school – and at 13 he was sent to Henley House School, St John's Wood.

Henley House, to which a lot of the children from the Misses Budd had graduated, was much more congenial. The headmaster was J. V. Milne, father of A. A. Milne who created Winnie the Pooh, and a man who had an enlightened and encouraging attitude to youngsters. The young Harmsworth, there known as 'Billy', was made captain of the school cricket and football teams on the grounds that he was a natural leader. With his fair hair, blue eyes and forelock falling over his left eye he stood out as good looking and full of vitality.

He was not a good student, particularly in arithmetic and subjects which bored him, but he was good at spelling and composition and surprisingly well read. He not only knew his Dickens, as his father would have hoped, but he also enjoyed Defoe, Smollett, Oliver Goldsmith and Thackeray. The Henley House experience was to be creative for him not in any strictly scholastic sense, but more broadly. It gave him the confidence to initiate; it set him on the path of journalism; it introduced him to the joys of bicycling; and it launched him on a process that would involve his whole family in attempts to make money.

At 15 he founded the school magazine. It was firmly labelled 'Edited by Alfred C. Harmsworth' on the masthead, professionally printed and laid out by a printer in Kilburn, and was sold for the relatively high price of three pence. (Fifteen years later, when the *Daily Mail* was born, it would only cost a halfpenny). He had badgered Milne to start a magazine for the school; when the head said he was too busy, he offered to do it himself.

Thousands of journalists since have begun by writing for their school magazines. But some of the touches in the *Henley House School Magazine* did prefigure the editor's efforts on a larger stage. One of the nicest, at the head of a kind of editorial gossip column entitled Entre Nous, was in the first number: 'I have it on the best authority that the *HHS Magazine* is to be a marked success.' By the second he commented, 'I am glad to say that my prediction as to the success of this magazine proved correct.' The idea of flattering readers on their discrimination and of blowing one's own editorial trumpet would have wider application: even if they are only schoolboys, people like to feel that they are joining a success story, which then becomes self-fulfilling.

In other ways, too, the magazine gave him ideas and practice for the future. He learnt the value of short, snappy sentences and paragraphs. He harried his printer, who did not regard the production of a school magazine as his top priority, until he got the job done. He drew on his own observations and experience, thus discovering that a good journalist can turn almost anything into copy. And in the magazine's first issue he had a section called, 'Answers to Correspondents' – thus giving him the title and idea for what would be his first outstanding success, and demonstrating that an inventive editor can always provide readable answers even before a journal can legitimately expect to have received any correspondence.

Even though Henley House was stimulating, and for the first time provided him with a society in which he was admired, life was not all school. For a start there were bicycles. At school he got his fag to look after a 48-inch Coventry 'ordinary', with a high front wheel and a smaller one behind, in which he had a half share. Out of school he joined a bicycling club which had a smart uniform and went on club runs round London and down to the south coast. Young Harmsworth prided himself on cycling uphill without dismounting – not altogether easy in the absence of modern gears – and made a number of new friends, including Max Pemberton who would become a journalistic associate. Cycling represented personal freedom: it also inspired in him an abiding thrill for the technological revolution in travel, which in merely a couple of decades would embrace cycles, motor cycles, cars and aircraft.

At home, however, the eldest son could not avoid being aware of the continuing shortage of funds. His father was often depressed, and was kept going partly by his own reputation for good fellowship and the help of his friends; his son, Robert Leicester, had been named for a family friend, George Robinson, a gas company engineer in Leicester who helped with money; later on Robinson would pay the fees of Cecil at Trinity College, Dublin.

It was in this atmosphere that the entrepreneurial instincts of the teenaged Alfred began to burgeon. He played with various schemes to create his own and restore his family's fortune. He tried photographic reproduction and a liquid for reviving silk hats. His most grandiose plan, using a Christmas present of £5 from a rich friend of his father's, was to sell a patent medicine pill largely made out of soap through small shops in the St John's Wood and Hampstead neighbourhood. 'Tonks's Pills – Cure All Ills' was the advertising slogan, except that the customers who tried them were not persuaded. It was Alfred who had called on the shops and got the handbills printed, but he used the labour of his elder brothers and sisters in the packing and dispatch. The concept of Harmsworth family enterprises began to germinate in what everyone afterwards looked back on as a joke.

At Christmas 1881 he left school, aged 16½. This precipitated a crisis in his life. In spite of a brief family flirtation with the idea that he might go to Cambridge, Alfred himself recognised that he did not want to go to university. Instead he wanted to become a journalist, something of which his father disapproved on the grounds that journalism was neither literature nor a profession. He tried freelancing from home. Between bouts of energy and lethargy he made a young family servant, Louisa Jane Smith, pregnant. (A son named Alfred Benjamin was born in November 1882 in Southminster, Essex and brought up by the Smith family.)

The family trauma combined with an attack of pneumonia led his father to prescribe a European tour to get him away from home. Following an advertisement in *The Times* he was packed off to be a secretary-companion to an aristocratic clergyman, the Reverend E. V. R. Powys, who took him on a leisurely journey through France and Germany. Powys commented on his ability to attract all sorts and conditions of people wherever they went and noted his devoted affection towards his mother. It must therefore have been a severe shock to him, on his return, when his mother told him that she would no longer let him live with them at the house in Boundary Road.

He then moved in with a friend, Herbert Ward, who had already lived an adventurous life – he had lived with Maoris in New Zealand and gone round the world as an ordinary sailor – and tried strenuously to make money as a freelance journalist. In fact he freelanced for four years continuously including a short period of staff work when he edited *Youth*. He contributed columns of facts, short stories and serials written round illustrations, and seems to have specialised in publications aimed at young people such as those produced by James Henderson from his Red Lion Square offices with titles like *Scraps*, *Lots o' Fun*, *Young Folks' Tales*. These magazines were aimed at the newly literate teenagers coming out of the elementary schools and they used some talented contributors. Alfred Harmsworth remembered meeting R. L. Stevenson at one of Henderson's editorial lunches, at a time when Stevenson was writing *Treasure Island* as a serial for *Young Folks' Tales*.

When Harmsworth was asked to edit *Youth* for the Ingram family for £2 a week it looked as though his fortunes were on the rise. He had been helping the existing editor, Edward Morton, who wanted to write for the theatre. Nearly fifty years later someone recalled visiting the *Youth* office at that time and seeing a boy with bright eyes and fair hair correcting proofs. 'This is my young friend Harmsworth. He's going to be editor of *The Times* some day,' Morton said.

The experience with *Youth*, part of the *Illustrated London News* group, was valuable in that it introduced him to the responsibilities of editorship, where printing, contributors, budgeting and journalism overlapped. But it was short-lived. The Ingrams were losing money on it and ditched the magazine, selling it over Harmsworth's head and putting him out of a job. Just as freelancing involves all the pains of rejection of copy, so editing impecunious magazines means working hard and never quite knowing when calamity will strike. At *Youth* Harmsworth, who was rather serious in his approach, was amusingly hoaxed by some Eton College boys who invented a bogus custom called 'Slunching the Paddocks': he asked to be invited down to see this pudding-throwing ceremony, and duly wrote it up.

Aged 18 plus Harmsworth faced a financial crisis on losing his steady job at *Youth*. He and Ward were forced to move from lodgings in Hampstead to a cheap single room in Clapham, from which they walked everywhere. They shared most things, including an evening suit, and Alfred Harmsworth was sufficiently back in his mother's graces to be invited home for Sunday lunch.

Ward left Harmsworth to join H. M. Stanley the explorer in the Congo and Max Pemberton, another aspiring journalist, took his place, sharing a couple of other lodgings with Harmsworth. Pemberton had graduated from Cambridge and Harmsworth met him coming out of the British Museum where he had been collecting facts about Robert Burns. 'Nobody wants to read your opinion of Burns. Give editors the kind of thing they want – less British Museum and more life,' he told him.

It was Harmsworth and Pemberton together who made the acquaint-ance of George Newnes, former proprietor of a vegetarian restaurant in Manchester, who had hit the journalistic jackpot with *Tit-Bits*. *Tit-Bits* was vaguely moral and improving, as might be expected from the product of the son of a Congregationalist minister, and it had started out as a cuttings magazine, lifting short, tantalising stories from other newspapers and publications (rather as *Readers Digest* began as a compilation magazine in the twentieth-century United States). But it had cornered a market in 'what' and 'how' information of no great depth for a newly literate mass market.

After Pemberton had written a piece for Newnes on jerry-builders, Harmsworth followed it up with pieces on curious butterflies, how to make a fortune, how QCs are made, and the earnings of organ grinders. Newnes paid a guinea a column and recollected later that Harmsworth was for a time in his office almost daily. Pemberton was sure that, quite early on, Harmsworth saw the possibility of setting up his own version of *Tit-Bits*.

Before he was able to do so, however, he was to have another experience as an editor. Still only 20, in March 1886, he agreed to become editor of the cycling weekly, *Bicycling News*. The offer had not entirely come out of the blue as he had been writing for several of the new cycling papers which had sprung up, mostly in Coventry, to cope with the boom created by the new frames, the new gears and the rubber tyres. He had been urged by his doctor, following an illness brought on by a wet long-distance cycle ride, to get a job outside London. Negotiations were drawn out over a couple of months before Harms-worth signed up with William Iliffe in person, in Coventry, to edit his weekly for £2 10s a week. Iliffe was an entrepreneur thrown up by the manufacturing industries of the west Midlands and his firm came to acquire a dominant position in technical journalism (owning in time *The Motor Cycle* and *The Autocar*) as well as local journalism (the *Coventry Evening Telegraph*).

Although *Bicycling News* was struggling, with a sale of only 300 a

week – far behind Iliffe's flagship *The Cyclist* – it was operating in a
much more competitive and exciting world than *Youth*. Furthermore, it
was Harmsworth's own hobby. This was a world of new inventions, of
cut-throat competition between editors and publishers, of good contributors attracted by the revolution in personal transport. Like all
revolutions it had a social aspect. The better-off carriage driving classes
tended to look down on the young cyclists; in one or two ugly incidents
bicyclists had been horsewhipped. In an age when genteel young ladies
were closely chaperoned, two wheels offered advanced and athletic
young women the freedom of the road.

Harmsworth went to live in Coventry in a house kept by the former
governess of the Iliffe children. In the mid-1880s, William Iliffe helped
Harmsworth by merging two other cycling papers into *Bicycling News*,
but left him with a slight problem in that the former editor and a noted
pioneer and cycling historian, Lacey Hillier, remained as leader writer.
Hillier, who did not like his work being broken up into more readable
paragraphs, complained to Iliffe that his copy was being cut to rags by a
'yellow-headed worm'. The YHW became Harmsworth's nickname to
the Coventry printers.

Throughout his life Harmsworth's energy came and went in spurts,
but the year or so spent in Coventry was undoubtedly one of his most
industrious and inventive. He built up the sale of *Bicycling News* by
making it more readable, making it talked about and by widening the
range of what it covered: it carried articles on photography, cycling
poetry, and had a woman correspondent, Lilias Campbell Davidson,
who had once been president of the Women Cyclists' Association. He
got involved in wars with other cycling papers, which complained that
he did not know enough about the subject and that the *BN* was just a
hotch-potch. He coined an advertising slogan which was adapted from
another product: 'It Comes to a Boon and a Blessing to Men, the
Popular Penn'orth, the Racy *BN*.'

By Christmas 1886, when he was writing to his brother Cecil,
Harmsworth said that Iliffe had given him a rise to £190 a year, and that
he was still freelancing as well. A series for *Young Folks* running over a
couple of years would bring him £70–75 a year, and he was still getting
about £1 a week from Newnes for items for *Tit-Bits*. But in the course of
1887 he resigned from *BN*. From the point of view of William Iliffe he
had become almost too successful: his paper was threatening the sales of
his flagship, *The Cyclist*, and had reached a circulation that was
uneconomic because it was too great for the advertising revenue to
sustain. Rising 22, and falling in love, Alfred Harmsworth was also
impatient to move. Having been an editor twice, he wanted to be a
publisher.

The opportunity arose as a result of a lucky break. A woman friend of
his mother's family was about to marry an Anglo-Irishman named

Dargaville Carr, editor of *The Church of Ireland Gazette*. She was prepared to use her dowry of £1,500 to enable him to come to London from Dublin and set up a publishing house. He called on Alfred in Coventry and persuaded him to become a business partner; a barrister friend of Harmsworth senior named Edward Marwick and his half-sister, Annie Rowley, were the other two partners in Carr & Co. The new company took a room in Paternoster Square, off Ludgate Circus – then a centre for book publishing – and Alfred and Dargaville shared digs in Kilburn.

Coming back to London for Alfred was timely, too, since he was becoming seriously involved with a girl called Mary Milner, usually known as Molly – the eldest of three daughters of a sugar trader, Robert Milner, who lived in West Hampstead. There was also a son, Harry, a friend of Alfred's who regularly quarrelled with his father and who was in due course packed off to Australia. Molly had fine brown eyes, wonderful hair, and was charming and vital. She and Alfred had known each other as children. Even when Alfred had been freelancing, before he edited *Bicycling News*, he had been regularly calling on the Milner household at 'St Vincent'.

The Milners were better off than the Harmsworths, particularly in the mid-1880s when Harmsworth senior was descending into another professional trough, but the West Indies cane sugar business was highly volatile. White planters in the Caribbean and sugar merchants in London rode a switchback from boom to bust, and the new threat of European beet sugar was just appearing on the horizon. Both families occupied the same milieu, with similar anxieties and hopes. Just as the Harmsworths consoled themselves with the thought that a forebear could have been an illegitimate child of a Hanoverian George, so the Milners pursued genealogical inquiries that might link them with the Earls of Rochester.

It cannot be said that Carr & Co. was an immediate success. It published various books and booklets and a handful of magazines including *Recreation* (on behalf of the National Physical Recreation Society, which promoted sport among the working classes), *The Volapuk Journal* (which was pushing a universal language on the lines of Esperanto), and *The Private Schoolmaster* (official journal of the Association of Principals of Private Schools). None of the magazines did well. The books varied between the successful, such as *A Thousand Ways to Earn a Living* by A. C. Harmsworth, and the surprisingly unsuccessful, like *Famous Breach of Promise Cases* and a life of W. G. Grace.

It was a rather struggling firm. Dargaville Carr did not much like office life and Alfred Harmsworth began freelancing again in order to make up his income. A lad on the trade counter, Tom McNaughton, was so underemployed that he went off with his brother to try his hand in a music hall act. Alfred, careful about office punctilio, tried to make the juniors wear Eton suits and top hats, was involved in a fight with a son of his Aunt Sarah who insulted him, and cross-questioned news-agents' reps about the practices of the trade. Some days Carr and Harmsworth did little but stand around and talk. But Harmsworth was confident that the firm would succeed: he was cross when Carr gave a job to the son of their Kilburn landlady, saying that he had several brothers whose livelihoods he was responsible for.

A gleam of light for a concern that gave the appearance of threshing about came when, via the barrister Edward Markwick, it raised a further £1,000 of capital from Captain and Mrs A. S. Beaumont. Beaumont, who had seen service in India, marred a wealthy woman fourteen years older than himself and was living in South Norwood. He used his wife's money – which she continued to control – to support his interests in chess and music, and had an inclination for handsome young men. He was duly impressed by the good-looking and energetic Alfred Harmsworth. The money put in by the Beaumonts was largely spent in promoting an American magazine, *Outing*, which was concerned with amateur sports. Carr & Co. got the agency from Iliffe's and tried gimmicks like dressing up sandwichmen as cricketers and fisher-men to enhance sales. But the magazine was too American for British tastes, and apart from having an influence on the size and make-up of *Strand Magazine* when George Newnes launched that a year or two later, it died without trace.

In spite of some appearances, however, life was accelerating for Harmsworth in 1887–8. His affection for Molly Milner was ripening into marriage and this took place on 11 April 1888. His ambition to set up a magazine which would outdo *Tit-Bits* was given direction when he roughed out a dummy of *Answers to Correspondents*, which he and his best man Edward Markwick carried round on the wedding day. And all this creative excitement was going on against a background of financial gloom in the larger Harmsworth family, where the older Alfred was in a state of considerable depression over his poor earnings and inability to win promotion. It was like a snapshot of Britain in the heyday of the Queen Empress, whose jubilee was celebrated with national rejoicing in 1887, when few of her subjects were untouched by conflicting emotions of optimism and anxiety.

The problems in the greater Harmsworth household were dire and explained why, when Alfred did hit a winning streak, this would be grasped as a miraculous source of employment for his brothers and a hope of income for his sisters. His father celebrated his fiftieth birthday in the summer of 1887 – though curiously Alfred junior was not present – at a time when he went for three months without a brief. There was no money at home to organise a birthday lunch until the 16-year-old Leicester, started in a junior civil service job, came in with his weekly wage of fourteen shillings, of which his mother promptly borrowed ten to buy a cushion of bacon and a large quantity of green peas. His father said how much he enjoyed bacon and green peas, and afterwards retired to read Shakespeare and have a drink.

Watching contemporaries promoted round him, and failing to get county court judgeships or even much devilling work, the 50-year-old Alfred Harmsworth was distancing himself from a family which he felt he had failed. His fecklessness and attraction to alcohol made a strong contrast to the sense of dynamism emanating from his elder son. The younger Alfred Harmsworth, though he too could be lethargic and dreamy, was capable of intense and concentrated industry and at the tender age of 22 had already had a significant journalistic career before becoming a publisher. He showed little sign of being seduced by the spendthrifts of ambition, wine, women and song and, though he respected his father, was also reacting against him. He offered a more enticing, less self-indulgent role model to younger brothers who themselves were looking forward to a lifetime in safe office jobs.

The sense of risk-taking in Alfred Harmsworth at this stage is palpable. Getting married and launching his new weekly paper, *Answers to Correspondents*, were operations he conducted simultaneously. Various people, including his mother, tried to put him off marriage: he and Molly were too young and his income was too insecure. But they were in love. Mr Powys, the clergyman Alfred had accompanied round Europe, officiated at Hampstead parish church and remembered it as a very pretty wedding, made by the youth and good looks of the bride and groom. The family scrimped together clothing and presents for the great day. Alfred and Molly spent their honeymoon at 18 Alexandra Gardens, Folkestone – the beginning of a lifelong affection for the East Kent coast – and he wrote a letter to his mother on the first morning of their stay.

On his honeymoon, Harmsworth continued to work on his plan for *Answers* which he had decided he could launch on a capital of £1,000, aided by credit from William Iliffe in Coventry who would do the printing. *Tit-Bits* was his point of departure editorially, and he roughed out the title of *Answers to Correspondents* (two sections, angled, with 'on every subject under the sun' underneath, and the come-on adjectives 'interesting', 'extraordinary', 'amusing' above the title) on the masthead of *Tit-Bits*. (The full title of *Tit-Bits* was 'Tit-Bits from all the most interesting books, periodicals and newspapers in the world'.)

However, *Answers* was different in conception from Newnes's paper. Although many of the questions to which answers were to be provided were bogus, in the sense that they had been cooked up in the office rather than by readers, Alfred had been haunted by the mixture of authority and reader response involved in providing information for readers since his days with the *Henley House School Magazine*. It had been a feature also of *Bicycle News*. In building a whole paper round this idea he was suggesting to readers that it was *their* paper. A modern equivalent would be the radio phone-in programmes in which listeners ring in and question experts.

Alfred made it clear that he would not accept advertisements for the paper, and initial discussion with trade reps had not been particularly encouraging. On a whim in Folkestone, seeing a piece of orange-coloured paper floating down from an upstairs window, he adopted a colour for the masthead. He and his wife had just seen off Edward Markwick on a cross-Channel ferry. Having failed to raise capital from other sources, Markwick had agreed to call on the Beaumonts in Viareggio in search of the necessary £1,000. When he succeeded he telegraphed Alfred with the one word, JOY.

Launching *Answers* – and the first true number, Number 3, came out dated 16 June 1888 – was bound to be a gamble. In the first year of *Tit-Bits'* existence, twenty-two periodicals attempting to ape its formula had already appeared; most had disappeared pretty quickly. The early issues of *Answers* did not look very attractive: they lacked a cover until the autumn when Harmsworth adopted the bright orange he had admired in Folkestone, which allowed him to describe the paper as 'The Golden One'. Even the name, *Answers to Correspondents*, did not trip off newsagents' tongues, and was shortened to *Answers*. If the paper was not exactly relaunched within six months of its first appearance, it was at least subject to fine tuning.

In the first few months there is little doubt that the editor was writing much of the copy himself, rehashing where he could material he had supplied as a freelance in the past. Items covered the gamut of mystery, horror, health, royalty, women's features, jokes, and interesting facts. Headlines stressed the 'what', 'how' and 'why' of things. Old clothes shops, narrow escapes from burial alive, royal eating habits, electrical flying machines, horseflesh as food, advertising and hangings were all grist to the mill. The style was breezy, the curiosity apparently all-enveloping. The idea was that the reader would end up with a smattering of knowledge on every item under the sun and seem like a walking encyclopaedia: everything you hadn't realised you wanted to know, *Answers* could tell you.

For Alfred Harmsworth, as editor-publisher, this was a period of superactivity. He was having to travel to Coventry once a week, write almost everything, address wrappers for the newsagents – and he had no assurance that the gamble would come off. After giving away a lot of copies of his first issue, the second had not sold over 8,000. His wife Molly and sister Geraldine (known as Dot) were brought into the office to help in various ways. The print bill mounted until it stood at £750 – three-quarters of the initial capital for the venture – and there were rows with William Iliffe over money and the service he was supplying.

Harmsworth agreed to pay off the debt over nine months and switched his printing to the firm in Bouverie Street, off Fleet Street, which had been printing *Tit-Bits*. In the first three months, though *Answers* did not go under, it was not selling more than 20,000 and was losing money. On the other hand, in a year in which 200 new periodicals had been launched in Britain, every month's survival improved the chances of ultimate prosperity.

By early 1889, the sale had reached 30,000 and competitions, mail order offers, and serials were beginning to hit their stride as much as the journalism. In March 1889, Alfred could write to the Beaumonts that he was beginning to breathe more easily, in spite of the effect the snow could have had on sales. The memoirs of an ex-convict, knocked out in instalments by Alfred on his typewriter – whose technological advantages *Answers* plugged editorially, especially to lady readers – were good for sales. Even a relatively uninspired competition to choose the ten greatest advertisers in Britain got a reasonable response – *Answers* was now accepting advertising – and letters were coming into the office at the rate of 2,000 a week.

The competitive battle with *Tit-Bits* added a certain spice to the growth of *Answers*. When Newnes introduced an offer of free insurance for his readers, Harmsworth followed suit. Crucially, on 1 June 1889, Alfred's brother Harold joined the firm as business manager, having resigned his job at the Board of Trade after much agonising. He is said to have wept when he saw the state of the accounts of Carr & Co. and was responsible for a reconstruction of the firm as Answers Co. Ltd, in which Alfred and his wife held a third of the capital.

Judicious promotion of a new *Answers* toy, whereby coloured sweets had to be spaced in a glass-topped box so that they spelled the name of the weekly, pushed the sale to 45,000 about the time that Harold arrived. Travellers were sent out to organise *Answers* puzzle clubs in the major provincial cities. A 14-year-old boy beat all comers to win a prize of £50 for spelling the journal's name in the shortest time. After twelve months of existence Harold told a board meeting that there had been a gross profit of £1,097. It was time to look for bigger offices.

However, the family was struck a blow shortly afterwards when, on 15 July, Alfred Harmsworth senior died suddenly at the age of 52. Like his father the cause of death was given as cirrhosis of the liver. His wife Geraldine was hard hit, although many of her husband's friends recorded their affection for him. Young Alfred wrote to his brother Cecil, now doing well at Trinity College, Dublin, that it would be a bit of a struggle to keep the family in its place, but they would do it. The financial tide had turned: in the week before their father had died *Answers* had sold 57,000 copies.

The real breakthrough came that autumn with the intellectual ancestor of all the get-rich-quick bingo competitions of British newspapers in the 1970s. It was the result of uniting two different good ideas. One was a competition to guess the exact amount of gold in the Bank of England at the close of business on 4 December 1889: this was inspired in Alfred after reading how much gold and silver was held there on a single day earlier. The second was the prize – a pound a week for life. It was suggested to Alfred and Harold by a tramp on the Embankment who had tried to beg money from them, and then given his idea of happiness.

The combination of the topic and the reward was irresistible. *Answers* required every entry to be signed by five other persons and by the time the 'greatest ever' competition was over, a total of more than 718, 218 postcards had arrived. The police were called in to control the crowds in Threadneedle Street when the Bank of England posted up its figures. A young soldier in the Ordnance Survey in Southampton, Sapper C. D. Austin, guessed right to within £2 and married on the proceeds. Over 200,000 copies of the bumper Christmas number of *Answers*, which published the result, were sold.

While Newnes grumbled that guessing games were demoralising, it was clear that the Harmsworths had scored an enormous hit amongst those poorer classes for whom a pound a week for life represented desirable security.[3] The attraction of such a simple concept has never dimmed. The 23 September 1988 issue of the *Daily Mirror* was to make a similar offer – 'Live free for a year on us'. For Alfred Harmsworth, and a large family recently made fatherless, this was a decisive turn of fortune's wheel. From now on they could look forward to wealth, power and the foundation of a family dynasty.

2
From Magazines to *The Times*

The suddenness of the change of situation for the Harmsworths, from a family of a boozy, failed barrister under threat from the bailiffs, to a family of energetic and successful publishers, whose brothers and sisters were headed by a journalist and a businessman of genius, was remarkable. They had the sense of adventure and of fun of youth. Alfred had only turned 24 the day before his father died. Harold, the more pessimistic but more orderly business-minded brother, was then only 21.

For their mother, who went down to stay with Alfred and Molly in a holiday cottage they had taken in Broadstairs the month after her husband's death, the turnabout seemed not quite credible. For her, seaside holidays had been beyond the bounds of financial possibility in recent years. The young Alfred, concerned that she should get on with his own still adored young wife, smothered her in dutiful affection. For the older Mrs Harmsworth the alteration in circumstances was hard to understand, and took some getting used to.

For the younger brothers and sisters, however, it was immediate, visible and, whatever their own interests or abilities, it swept them up. In the second half of 1889, as it was clear that *Answers* was getting established, more and more of them joined the firm. Dot (Geraldine), who had learnt to type in the office but had been making money giving music lessons, came down to the new Fleet Street office to cope with the 'pound-a-week' postcards. Leicester, who had been in a solid claims department job in the Inland Revenue, started out part-time but soon became a full-time *Answers* circulation rep in the provinces. Hildebrand did likewise. Cecil, who had won prizes at Trinity College, Dublin, joined on graduation.

The sense of exultation was nearly conveyed in a letter of congratulation sent to Cecil, who had passed his Dublin finals, by his 17-year-old brother Hildebrand. Posted from Plymouth in September 1889 it began:

Dearest Cecil, – Bravo!!! My heart throbbed with delight and I scarcely slept a wink last night. Bravo! Bravo! Bravo!!!

I can see that we shall be if not the first in the realm, certainly among the foremost families of the day. I, as you know, am going (no boasting, really) in for MPs and politics whenever my screw gets large enough and I propose that you and Leicester should rule the clergy and you be the Archbishop of Canterbury and Leicester Bishop of London, Alf at the top of the literary world, I to hold the reins of politics in the Conservative Government, Harold to be Chief Sec. of Ireland and the rest to hold minor posts.[4]

The attraction which was bringing members of the family flocking to join *Answers* and the company was having comparable effects on outsiders. H. G. Wells, then a young writer, was happy to earn shillings and guineas contributing to the magazine. Max Pemberton, Alfred's cycling friend of his teens who had been sold the first copy from Paternoster Row, became 'Mr Answers' – a journalistic touchstone for the growing readership of 'Answerites'. A youthful circulation man, Willie Scott, was a source of promotional gimmicks – turning up at an Olympia ball in special orange satin fancy dress, and riding along the Strand in the dark with the first electric lamp fitted to his bike. A clerk from the *Star* newspaper, with good shorthand, joined Alfred to look after his growing correspondence as personal secretary: his name was George Augustus Sutton, and he was nicknamed 'Satan' by the staff.

Family control over the firm was consolidated by Harold Harmsworth in his capacity as company secretary. It was he who controlled expenses, saving money on paper costs, introducing systems and fretting about unnecessary expenditures. In January 1890, Alfred told his readers that the editor of *Answers* was Alfred C. Harmsworth, who held half the shares in the company; the other shareholders were Edward Markwick, Captain Beaumont and Harold Harmsworth. But Dargaville Carr, whose unbusinesslike approach maddened Harold, returned to Dublin in that year and two years later Edward Markwick, who had not been getting on well with either the Beaumonts or the Harmsworths, transferred his 140 shares to them. (When Markwick, an older man, got married, Alfred Harmsworth gave him a gramophone as a present with a bust of himself on it: they never spoke after that.)

Meanwhile, relations with the Beaumonts were fairly sunny, even if the staff were not enamoured of Mrs Beaumont's lady bountiful habit of sending them inedible lunch baskets. Alfred and his wife spent a summer holiday with them in Viareggio, in 1890, after he had been seriously ill with flu, almost certainly exacerbated by long working hours and overstrain. Even on holiday Alfred could not relax. He was still sending articles and suggestions by every post.

For *Answers* his basic strategy was more of the same in 1890 – more of the same kind of journalism, more competitions and gimmicks, another Bank of England contest with £2 a week rather than £1 as a reward. In May, he promised a £50 note to any reader on 13 August if the sale had not reached 250,000 by that date. He did not make it, but the sale was rising all the same. The gimmicks included an *Answers* pipe, and an *Answers* waltz (composed by Captain Beaumont), *Answers* cigarettes and even a cure for toothache. The magazine offered free insurance to its readers (a ploy still being used after the launch of the *Today* newspaper in the 1980s) and sent 'Mr Answers' on a series of 'extraordinary adventures'. When, unexpectedly, the Treasury Solicitor threatened legal action against a £2 a week for life contest for guessing the reserves of the Bank of England, it was all more publicity. At all costs, Alfred liked his magazine talked about. Better still, by the second half of 1890 it was clearly profitable, even if the sale was still much less that that of *Tit-Bits*.

The security of success made Alfred expansive. *Answers* had been a dream, but it was not his only dream. He had once set out a 'schemo magnifico', the ambition of a media mogul, to create a whole series of publications which would help sustain each other. In 1890, he founded Pandora Publications, named after the north London road where he and his wife were now living, which rapidly launched *Comic Cuts* and *Illustrated Chips*. These publications were collections of jokes – 'smiles', 'jokes' and 'tiny chips' – sold at a halfpenny a week. They thereby undercut the penny dreadfuls which had hitherto dominated a large part of the youth market. They were totally undemanding, poorly produced, yet an immediate success. The first issue of *Comic Cuts* sold nearly 120,000 copies, in May 1890, and less than two years later it was making more money than *Answers* and was described by Harold as a milch cow of the business.

'Comic Cuts' entered the language and *Illustrated Chips*, shortened to *Chips*, gave birth to a cartoon character, 'Mr Chips'. Why were these papers, into which Alfred threw himself with his usual enthusiasm – he got *Comic Cuts* off the ground in only four days – so instantly appealing? They looked respectable. They made people laugh. (*Punch* did not like to see *Comic Cuts* described as the poor man's *Punch*, but there were a lot of poor men needing things to laugh at in late Victorian England.) And although their pitch was to boys and girls, an enormous public at a time of sharply rising population, the attraction went wider. It brought in partial literates of all ages, and was reaching out to what would be an important feature of twentieth-century newspapers, the adult audience for strip cartoons.

This period of expansiveness and flair for Alfred was typified by the purchase of a country house, Elmwood, near Broadstairs. He and his wife spotted it when they were driving in a dog-cart with their friend Max Pemberton, in 1890, and noticed it was for sale. It was two storeyed, made of brick and flint, with views down to the English Channel. It was not a grand house, like some of the places (for instance, Sutton Place near Guildford, subsequently owned by J. Paul Getty) which Alfred would own as his fame and fortune increased, but it was a homely, square, rambling sort of house, which looked Georgian although it contained a Tudor basis inside. By the second half of the twentieth century it had been split into two, and new houses had been built over its garden.

Elmwood was furnished by Liberty's, equipped with telephones in most of its rooms, and was set up to be a working base as much as a holiday cottage. Alfred, as the magazines took off, spent less time at his office and more time working from home with the faithful Sutton and other secretaries. At Elmwood he adapted a Canadian-style outhouse as a study for work and dictation. The three-acre garden included a large lake, containing a Florida alligator, melons, pigs and lilies of the valley (his wife's favourite flower since their wedding.) A lifeboat, from the expedition he sponsored to the Arctic in 1894, was a decoration.

The Harmsworths occupied Elmwood in April 1891. It had been bought with the aid of a loan from the Beaumonts, although Harold was for renting it and seemed rather hostile to the enterprise. People who visited them there remembered Alfred and Molly looking very young, playing on their bicycles and throwing tennis balls for the dogs. They became extremely attached to their home in the Isle of Thanet, a corner of England to one side of the main Channel ports which shares many of the characteristics of the east coast. It can be cold when the north-east wind blows, and in the nineteenth century its holiday resorts were already celebrated for their health-giving properties.

Alfred became a prominent local citizen in an area he also valued for its Dickensian associations. By 1897 he was financing the enlargement of a local school and, according to a local historian, may have designed the armorial bearings of Broadstairs.[5] He had a hand in a local tramway project and by 1898, when he bought the adjoining Joss Farm, he helped Father Dolling establish a boys' summer camp for children from the East End of London. By 1903, when his own money was flowing freely, he used some of this land to establish the North Foreland Golf Course at a personal cost of £50,000. Thanks to this he became a passable golfer and, as the club's first secretary, he remarked to an aide, 'Each new secretary spoils one hole, and when a course has had eighteen secretaries, it is ruined.'

Meanwhile, in the early 1890s, the magazine publisher became responsible for a magazine empire. He saw off the Beaumonts and failed to get elected for Parliament as a Conservative in Portsmouth. There was a velocity about the undertaking in the early 1890s which meant that new magazines were being launched at a rate of at least one every six months – youth papers, comic papers, Bible reading papers – and in one year, between June 1892 and June 1893, the combined sale of the Harmsworth publications rose by 40 per cent to 1.47 million. The avid demand for reading matter in Britain at the time meant that a market which Newnes had pioneered and Alfred and Harold had exploited was strong enough to carry new entrepreneurs: C. Arthur Pearson, a young man who had worked in the *Tit-Bits* office as a prize reward, launched *Pearson's Weekly*, which by 1892 was selling half a million copies on the back of competitions to fill in the missing words of sentences.

The issue on which the Harmsworths and the Beaumonts fell out was the launch of *Forget-me-Not*, described by Harold as 'a high class penny journal for ladies'. Basically, the row was about the price of a one-tenth share in the magazine which the Harmsworths first offered to Captain Beaumont at £1,000, then increased to £2,500. Harold explained to the captain that the concept for the magazine had changed. It was no longer to be 'a cheap novelette', but altogether a classier and more expensive product. Beaumont felt that the brothers had gone back on their word, and were no longer valuing him and his wife for the crucial role they had played in capitalising the business at the start.

It seems clear that Harold, the sharp financial operator who had turned the magazines into highly profitable properties as a result of a ruthless control of expenditure, was the brains behind the ousting of the Beaumonts. The captain resigned his directorships in December 1891, three months after Alfred had settled his debts for the purchase of Elmwood. It was not until August 1892 that a final financial agreement, which bought out the Beaumonts, was arrived at.

The strain of the quarrel with the Beaumonts showed through for Alfred, who then and later developed neurasthenic illnesses at periods of psychological pressure. It was also a touchstone in the relationship between the two brothers, Alfred and Harold. For Alfred the Beaumonts, with whom he had exchanged many friendly and chatty letters in the past, were part of his début in publishing and the launch of *Answers*. For Harold they were part of the disorganised history of the firm which had only become a financial success after his arrival. He was just as ready to 'knife' them, as to 'knife' unsuccessful magazines which showed a distressing dilatoriness in turning a profit. (Alfred, by contrast, preferred to alter and stimulate the journalistic mix when confronting magazines in difficulty.)

The arguments which Harold deployed with his brother were technical – that in a situation where the companies had not been paying much in dividends and Alfred had been underpaid for the journalistic and business leadership he had been providing, it was wrong that the Beaumonts stood to gain a large profit. In fact Harold was reckoning that the firm would earn a net profit of £50,000 in 1892, a very considerable sum. But the real message of the purge of the Beaumonts from their role as sleeping partners was that the Harmsworths, now they were successful, did not wish to share their triumphs. Furthermore, Harold, though deferring still to his elder brother, was now a powerful chieftain within the family firm.

In August 1894, a decisive change took place. Alfred became a newspaper proprietor. Admittedly, the paper in question was a loss-making Conservative evening paper in London, the *Evening News*, bought for £25,000 via an option held by two journalists on the rival *Sun*, Kennedy Jones and Louis Tracy. The paper was at the cheaper, halfpenny end of a market which was crowded with eight other evening papers for London. It had been subsidised for years by a Conservative MP who had just died. None the less, its sale was relatively healthy at around 100,000.

Newspaper ownership had not featured in the 'schemo magnifico'. At the time, when the purchase of the *Evening News* was achieved after covert negotiations, the Harmsworth brothers did not greet the diversi-fication as a cause for major rejoicing. It is possible that magazine and newspaper publishing may then have seemed less different than they subsequently became. Harold concluded that there was money to be made on the *News*. For Alfred there was the interest of a new challenge, which coincided with a growing temptation to become involved in Conservative politics.

Kennedy Jones was a tough Scots evening paper man who brought a news sense, an awareness of the selling power of crime – which in *Answers* Alfred had both disparaged and exploited – and a sense of having his feet on the ground. He rapidly became editor of the *News*, where he had 7½ per cent of the shares, and Alfred's editorial partner. The combination was extremely effective. Together they changed the type, got more items into the leader column, introduced a daily short story, banished turgid political commentaries, put in a woman's column and went hard on sport. Headlines became a little bigger, pages and stories were broken up to make them look more interesting. There were grisly stories about baby farming and burials alive in the *Answers* tradition. There were maps. There were contests to forecast football results – profitable to the proprietors since readers had to send in a penny stamp, but hardly approaching the sophistication of football pools.

Nevertheless, although Alfred was learning skills which would prove crucial when the *Daily Mail* was launched two years later, the journal-istic achievement – which reached a temporary but encouraging peak when 390,000 copies were sold on the last day of a murder trial on 15 November – almost paled into insignificance by comparison with the commercial turnabout. In the first week the Harmsworths owned it the *News*, which had been losing £100 a week, turned a profit of £7. By the third week it was making £50. A paper which had been losing £30,000 in the last year of the previous ownership made £14,000 in the first under the Harmsworths.

This, of course, was Harold's doing. He hoisted the price of advertis-ing. He knocked down the cost of newsprint: the previous management, because of its shaky position, had been held to ransom. He brought his concern to cut any unnecessary expense, honed by his experience at the weekly magazines, to bear on every item. The Harmsworths were not running their operations as a hobby, or for political reasons, but to make money. This was the approach they had developed in their magazines: it seemed brashly different from the norms then prevailing in newspapers.

The value-for-money element in Harmsworth publishing for readers has been repeated more recently in Britain by proprietors as diverse, and aiming at diverse markets, as Roy Thomson and Rupert Murdoch. In the late Victorian period, the sense of getting more for your penny or halfpenny was extremely important; lower middle-class people and artisans did not feel affluent, and needed to be persuaded to join the mass media adventure by clever mixtures of quantity, quality and conciseness at prices they could afford.

In other ways, too, Alfred's journalistic approach was in the spirit of the times. Though crime was an aid to sales, sex was out. Both in the public attitude of his press and in his more private views, he put women on their Victorian pedestal – modest, demure, non-swearing. Of course, Alfred and some of his brothers had affairs and mistresses, but he would have regarded titillation as a means of promoting circulation to be both wrong and vulgar. When later a sex film of an unpleasant nature was put on in London, Alfred gave orders to his journalists to kill it.

On the other hand, he had a good nose for what interested women. *Home Chat*, edited by his 25-year-old brother Leicester, was launched in March 1895. It was aimed at a Pearson publication, *Home Notes*, which Harold reckoned was making £12,000 a year. *Home Chat* had free paper patterns, a signed gossip column, and articles on careers for women. Although it had a bad patch about a year after the launch, when Harold became anxious about the number of unsold copies being returned by newsagents, it survived and thrived.

In the mid-1890s, Alfred was not doing anything that could be construed as investigative journalism: that would come later during the First World War. But he was early in grasping the fascination of royal stories (what the Queen ate, how she was addressed by her children, and – obviously – why the Prince of Wales was nicknamed 'Tum-tum'). All trivia was fascinating. Royal trivia was more fascinating than most. Victorian ethics would not allow of the modern soap opera treatment but the long reign of the Queen-Empress had seen great oscillations in her reputation, creating an appetite for tit bits of information.

Alfred, though he had a schizophrenic attitude to advertising – welcoming the income it brought, but resenting the space and attention it took from editorial – was also astute at recognising the overlap between salesmanship and journalism. He loved 'booming', the practice of using magazines and newspapers to talk up their sales and journalistic feats. Nothing the Harmsworths did could be accused of being under-publicised or sold short on its claims. Each of the magazines was used to boost the other. Repetition was the name of the game.

The same approach was applied to the practice of 'working up a story' in journalism. Alfred saw the value of building reader interest in a story or topic; he prided himself on his foresight and his empathy with public taste, and had the confidence to take risks. Soon after he bought the *News* he decided to go very strongly for coverage of a murder case, where a man named James Canham Read was accused of a woman's murder. Before taking a much-needed break in Paris, he and a sometime prison governor had an hour's talk with Read in his cell. It was coverage of this trial which temporarily quadrupled the sale of the *News*.

Religion was also in the spirit of the times and the Harmsworths joined in effectively. *The Sunday Companion*, a title which came to Alfred one day when he was fishing, was launched in 1894 as a non-sectarian Christian weekly. Alfred's non-sectarian approach – he himself always retained a soft spot for the Salvation Army – created the possibility of large sales, and when the *Companion* hit its stride after a couple of years it was backed up by other papers for this market.

Politics was a tricky area, at a time when Britain was sharply divided between Liberals and Conservatives, with a burgeoning Labour movement and cross-currents involving social reform, Ireland and protection. *Answers* had prided itself on being non-political, and Harold complained that a 'Britain for the Britons' agitation which it ran was getting dangerously political. In fact, in serials and articles, *Answers* was reflecting various political moods – pride in the Empire, and anxiety about the build-up of German military strength.

Even before the Harmsworths bought the *Evening News* Alfred, based in Thanet, had turned down an invitation to stand as a Conservative candidate in Folkestone. Private means was then an important qualification in the eyes of a constituency. The assumption that he was indeed sympathetic to the Conservatives and Unionists was strengthened when he bought a partisan evening paper. Yet its leader after the take-over indicated a certain eclecticism; while Conservative and imperial, it was also friendly to social reform and labour. Alfred's heroes now were Joseph Chamberlain and Cecil Rhodes.

In March 1895, Alfred agreed to stand as one of two Conservatives in the naval town of Portsmouth. He was not quite 30 and on the way to being a national figure, receiving thanks from Lord Salisbury for his efforts in reviving the *Evening News*. Proprietorship and parliamentary status went together more naturally at the turn of the century than later, but for Alfred it was not to be. After a stirring campaign, which had involved buying the local evening paper and running a scary serial entitled 'The Siege of Portsmouth', as well as having a patriotic song sung nightly at the Empire music hall, Harmsworth and his fellow Conservative were beaten by just under a thousand votes on 16 July.

Nationally the Conservatives won, and possibly the Harmsworth gusto, which signally failed to win over the dockyard workers, had proved counter-productive in Portsmouth. His campaigning wore him out, and Alfred found he did not much enjoy public speaking. He took defeat philosophically. 'At my age a defeat does one good. Too much success in life is bad for one. Besides, my place is in the House of Lords, where they don't fight elections,' he said. The experiment may have lent a subsequent disenchantment to his attitude towards politics and politicians, encouraging him to develop his more direct influences over the public mind.

As early as 1894, Alfred and Harold had been meditating on the launch of a morning daily paper. In 1895, they bought papers in Portsmouth and Glasgow. On 4 May 1896, Alfred published the first issue of the *Daily Mail*. It was very much his baby. Worried that Harold's habitual taste for economising would compromise his commitment to the best of journalism, on good quality white paper, he kept his brother out of most of the key decisions.

The new paper was carefully planned. Daily dummy issues, partly designed to test out new ideas and partly designed to fool any rivals who saw them, were produced from February onwards. They had news on the front page – something that the *Daily Mail* did not have when it got going – and a number of joke items. The dummy for 17 February included a front-page column labelled 'Some Interesting Items' in the *Answers* vein; one of them described 'the peculiar significance attached, among the humbler classes of the West Riding in Yorkshire, to the hanging up of a hat in the dwelling of a young woman for whom [a young man] has a fancy'.

Another little item, called 'What Governesses Must Be', stated that the onset of cheap education was undermining the demand for governesses, who must put up with snubs from their employers and be neither too beautiful nor too plain. Dummy headlines stated in capitals THE BOERS ARE BUILDING NEW PORTS AND GETTING NEW GUNS. A heading on 29 February told the trial readership, 'There will not be another 29th of February till 1904.' On 30 April, there was another cod headline, 'A £1000 Note would not purchase a copy of the *Daily Mail* today.'

When the first issue proper appeared on 4 May it had the secure air of a newspaper that has been around for years already, just like *The Independent* when it first appeared in 1986. The front page was filled with advertisements – in the first few weeks Alfred gave free ads to his rival George Newnes – and a distinguished gothic lettering was used for the *Daily Mail* title. Two slogans were adopted, 'A penny newspaper for a halfpenny' and 'The busy man's daily journal'. Inside there were sections on the law courts and the police courts, political gossip and 'In Society'. Page seven launched 'The Daily Magazine', what would now be seen as a combination of feature and women's pages, which included a romantic story.

Readers were constantly told that they were getting value for money. Items 'In Society' which were exclusive would be paid for at the same rate usual in the sixpenny society weeklies; the page seven magazine meant that a *Mail* reader did not now need to buy any other magazine; fewer advertisements meant that the new paper could give as much news as the old penny papers. A leader pointed out that forty years before a paper had appeared – in fact the *Daily Telegraph* – which offered for a penny as much as other papers were then providing for sixpence, fivepence, threepence and twopence. 'The project attracted about as much ridicule and opposition as the introduction of railways. The result has been seen.'

There was a certain amount of trumpeting about the mechanical typesetting and printing innovations which effected 'a saving of from 30 to 50 per cent' compared with rivals, and references to the handiness of the page size for commuters. The most audaciously Harmsworth sentiments were expressed as follows: 'But the note of the *Daily Mail* is not so much economy of price as conciseness and compactness. It is essentially the busy man's paper. The mere halfpenny saved each day is of no consequence to most of us. The economy of the reader's time effected by the absence of the usual puzzling maze of advertisements is, however, of the first importance.' When the whole selling pitch was that you were getting twice the value of any rival the suggestion that 'the mere halfpenny saved each day is of no consequence to most of us' was breathtaking flattery. The concept that an absence of advertisements led to an economy of the reader's time – though a marvellous justification for the inevitable shortage of ads in a new publication – also rings false to a modern ear.

Excitingly for Alfred Harmsworth, and the editorial and business members of the group whom he had inspired in the previous weeks, the *Daily Mail* was an immediate success. A total of 397,215 copies of the first issue were sold. On the first afternoon Kennedy Jones – generally known as KJ, who himself had the bravado to call his boss Alf – pushed through crowds outside the offices in Carmelite Street, waiting for further supplies. Some eight years after the launch of *Answers*, which had been a slow, hard struggle, the same rather wiser man – still only 30 – had achieved an instant hit in the competitive field of newspapers.

After an exhausting day following the launch Alfred Harmsworth had slept at the Salisbury Hotel. Over the next forty-eight hours congratulations came flooding in from friends, politicians and rivals. William Gladstone commented, 'The *Daily Mail* appears to be a most interesting experiment, to which I give my heartiest good wishes.' A generous telegram came from George Newnes, currently hitting severe problems with his new *Daily Courier* – 'a wonderful halfpennyworth'.

Even Sir Arthur Sullivan, composer of 'Onward Christian Soldiers' and fashionable comic operas, sent salutations: 'Wonderful and excellent publication. Wish you all success.'

The *Mail* triumphed not only because of its printing innovations and the relative cheapness of newsprint. Editorial factors were far more significant. The stress on a good news service, the gathering together of energetic and qualified journalists, and the change in content were factors which communicated themselves to readers. Long leaders and endless coverage of political speeches and events were out; brevity, variety, and an interest in topics likely to attract women were in.

New types of reader had been intuitively identified, for the *Mail* started long before the days of market research. These included the rail commuters, and working men and women who had never bought papers before. Just as *The Sun* uncovered new markets in the Britain of the 1970s, so did the *Mail* in the 1890s. But the latter was 'respectable', without the ancestors of Page Three girls, with dashes of snobbery and self-improvement.

Lord Salisbury, the Tory grandee, dismissively said that the *Mail* was produced by office-boys for office-boys. This may have had something to do with the fact that his secretary at Hatfield House complained that a *Mail* reporter was not properly dressed, a protest that led Harmsworth to put up a notice in the newsroom urging his staff to look smart. But the editor-proprietor was highly experienced in the social mores of his country: he laid down that the *Mail* was to read as if aimed at the 'thousand a year man', far above the readers attracted by the 'pound a week' contest in the early *Answers*. It was all flattery, of course. *Mail* readers were not that rich. But whereas Salisbury might disparage them, it was very much in Harmsworth's interest to boost their confidence.

On its second day, the *Mail* had a useful, exclusive story in reporting that Cecil Rhodes and Alfred Beit had offered to resign as directors of the British South African Company. Good journalists, such as G. W. Steevens who was an excellent reporter and feature writer, joined the paper. Max Beerbohm covered literature. Harmsworth surrounded himself with bright young men, many of them university educated. He was also quick to back new causes. In November, following the launch, he applauded editorially the first 'emancipation run' of automobiles from London to Brighton, now commemorated as a rally of ancient vehicles, which was designed to break the three mile an hour restriction on cars. A year later George Bernard Shaw, himself a journalist and critic, wrote to Alfred acknowledging clearly that the start of the *Mail* marked a break between the old journalism and the new.

Holidays, weather, the wisdom or otherwise of husbands and wives taking separate holidays were among the topics opened up in the early months. It might seem gossipy and trivial, but it was reflecting the ordinary lives and idle, occasional speculations of hundreds of thousands of ordinary British people. Alfred and his young men were doing their best to combat dullness at the breakfast table and on the early morning trains. Spoof letters and spoof ads could also be thrown into the brew if necessary. The paper was not only cool about politicians, and therefore not strongly political in tone, it was also unexcited by poverty and the more substantial social questions of late Victorian England. Readability was crucial.

The year 1896 was a kind of apogee for a young man who had worked extremely hard and was now tasting the fruits of success. At a company general meeting of Answers Publications Ltd in July, just after the appearance of the *Mail*, Alfred reported a record profit of £53,000 and a dividend of 22 per cent. The magazines were doing extremely well. Equally, the unexpected triumph of the *Mail* meant that he had spent only £12,500 of the £25,000 he had set aside for it.[6] He carefully kept the commercial arrangement of his newspapers aside from that of the magazines. By the end of the year all the magazine companies had been rolled up into the single Harmsworth Brothers Ltd.

Then, as happened periodically in his life, when faced with a psychological crisis or a long period of intense activity when he was living on his nerves, his body took its revenge. That autumn he was ill, under doctors' orders, suffering from nervous strain and being told to reduce his commitments. In December, he and his wife took a trip to India via Italy. He did not like being out of England at Christmas but dutifully saw the Taj Mahal by moonlight and rode on an elephant. Like most journalists he was bad at relaxing and was still writing letters to the office, and articles for the *Mail*.

Three years after the *Daily Mail* started, Britain was at war. The Boer War saw the Empire pitted against the farmers' republics of the Afrikaners in South Africa while the rest of Europe looked on. It was an imperialist war, designed to bring the gold, diamonds and natural resources of the region under the Union Jack. As an imperialist by sentiment, who was so friendly with Cecil Rhodes that outsiders had wondered whether Rhodes had put money into the *Mail*, Alfred had no doubt that it was his duty to cheer the British side on. Issues that were to cast dark shadows forward – such as the rights of the black tribes also living in southern Africa, or the concentration camps used to lock up the Boers' wives and families after the war degenerated into a guerrilla campaign – were of little concern.

None the less, the Boer War changed the *Mail* and changed Alfred Harmsworth, who was offered a knighthood while it was running and accepted a baronetcy shortly after its conclusion. First, the war was a great challenge to journalism, and to newsgathering at a distance. Harmsworth and Kennedy Jones spent unstintingly on war correspondents and cables, on maps and interpretation in London, in order to get the latest news and make it comprehensible. In September 1899, Alfred had telegraphed Winston Churchill to ask if he would act as a war correspondent, thus precipating the adventurous young politician into an advantageous deal with the *Morning Post* and capture by and escape from the Boers. G. W. Steevens, the *Mail*'s star reporter, died of enteric fever in Ladysmith, causing Harmsworth to reproach himself bitterly, to endow Steevens' widow generously, and to set up scholarships in his memory at the City of London School.

Interest in the war sent sales leaping, and *Daily Mail* war expresses – newspaper trains as they would subsequently be called – took early editions to the North of England from London, laying the foundations of separate printing in Manchester and giving the paper a truly national circulation. The war also altered the way in which the *Mail*, and therefore Harmsworth himself, were seen publicly: they became more respectable, for they had shown they could be serious and responsible in the face of setbacks and loss of life.

This empathy with the public was illustrated by the setting up of a *Daily Mail* fund to provide comforts for the troops. Harmsworth instructed the editor to request a poem from Rudyard Kipling. Several verses of sentimental doggerel entitled 'The Absent-minded Beggar' came in which reduced the office to despair and were printed as inconspicuously as possible. Simultaneously, Sir Arthur Sullivan had been asked to write some music to go with Kipling's words. He had been hoping for another 'Recessional' and got no inspiration. Fortunately, Kennedy Jones suggested that a tune on the lines of 'Soldiers of the Queen' might rescue the verses and the next day Sullivan obliged with a catchy setting. The song was an immediate hit and helped to raise around £100,000 for the soldiers' fund.

The Boer War straddled the opening of the twentieth century, itself a source of journalistic speculation. Queen Victoria died in January 1901 to be succeeded by a Francophile and less straitlaced monarch, Edward VII. In the Birthday Honours of June 1904, the newspaper and magazine proprietor became Sir Alfred Harmsworth Bart and joked that instead of being known as Mr 'Armsworth, he'd now become Sir Halfred. His wife sent him a poignant letter[7] of congratulation from their newly acquired stately home near Guildford, Sutton Place, from which she loved to entertain, and which he did not care for so much and rarely slept in:

My darling 'Sir Alfred', – I must be the first to tell you how glad and happy I am to know that you have gained recognition for all the hard work of years. No one, dear, deserves it more than you – but the happiest thought of all to me is that *we began* life together and have been together through all the years of work which have earned you distinction and fortune so young. My fond love and congratulation from
    Your loving
    Wife

The letter was poignant because although the couple would stay married until his death broke the relationship, something had come apart at its centre. Whether his wife Mary was physically incapable of conceiving a child, the fact was that they never produced offspring together. Each had affairs. Soon after the turn of the century, Sir Alfred had commenced a long-lasting liaison with an Irishwoman of mysterious origins who was known as Mrs Kathleen Wrohan. Together they had three children (Alfred in 1910, Geraldine in 1912 and Harold in 1914) who were brought up in some secrecy but were financially well endowed, until the affair petered out in the First World War.

Into the twentieth century the slim good-looking boy of the 1890s, accentuating his air of spotless destiny with light-coloured suits, had turned into a much heavier and jowlier figure. His amazing run of luck had made him supremely confident in his own opinions, larger than life, and sometimes autocratic towards his staff and ménage. He travelled a lot, somehow managing to take both his wife and Mrs Wroham around with him, though not exactly together. He worried incessantly about his health. He had become a public as well as a publishing personality, known to have enormous wealth. This meant that he was carrying on a large and wide-ranging correspondence with politicians, socialites who wanted money for good causes, and those with hard-luck stories. (Sometimes the hard-luck stories were from within his own staff: a Mrs Howard, wife to a printer who had been discharged by a *Mail* foreman with one week's notice, asked for her husband's job back because she had six children under 14 and he had since been unemployed for eleven weeks.[8])

Sir Alfred and Lady Harmsworth had a fine house in Berkeley Square and, though Lady Harmsworth had no shares in the companies, she had a huge allowance. (Kathleen Wrohan was also good at spending his money.) Sir Alfred still made a lot of use of Elmwood. When, less than two years after his baronetcy, he became a baron in the resignation honours of Arthur Balfour, he sought inspiration from a spot in Broadstairs known locally as the North Cliff and became Lord Northcliffe. The King nudged Balfour to elevate him; in addition to his successful pro-Tory London papers he had also run two loss-making papers which supported the party in Portsmouth and Manchester.

From now on he would be known as Northcliffe, sometimes signing himself just N as his obsession with Napoleon took off. In his offices he became the Chief, overlord of both journalism and business. In an age of imperialists he was running an empire. Amongst the arriviste new wealth of Edward VII he appeared both dynamic and outwardly conventional. But as Britain and Europe started the long downhill slippery slope towards the First World War – egged on by anti-German reports and comments in a *Mail* that worried increasingly about the threat from the Kaiser's militarist expansionism – a psychiatrist might have detected growing shadows and egomania.

Before he got his barony, though, he had a close run with disaster in the *Daily Mirror*. He had also launched an adventure in forestry and paper-making in Newfoundland with Harold. And he had unsuccessfully tried to buy *The Times*.

He had had some setbacks before, for instance when he had wanted to start a Sunday paper and had been bowled back by the weight of objection from readers of his religious papers. But the *Mirror*, whose story he subsequently described cheerfully as 'How I Dropped One Hundred Thousand Pounds on the *Mirror*', had come near to being a humiliation. It was launched at the start of November 1903 on the theory that women needed their own paper, which should be run and edited by women. Mary Howarth, who had been in charge of women's features at the *Mail* – one of its successes – was put in charge of 'a large staff of cultivated, able and experienced women'. The selling point was that gentlewomen could be persuaded to abandon their sixpenny weeklies for the joys of their own daily.

On this his insight into the public mind let him down badly. Women simply did not want their own daily – or at least the respectable, socially aspiring conservative women he sought did not. Furthermore, the elementary precautions he had taken at the start of the *Mail* – endless dummy issues and a heavy stress on journalistic competence – were thrown to the wind. Though the practice of 'booming' enabled the first issue to sell 276,000, the circulation rapidly fell to a nadir of under 25,000. Losses were rising, cultivated ladies found it difficult to stand the pace, and sexual innuendos were threatening to get into print.

Much earlier Alfred had boasted that failure was not in his vocabulary and he was reluctant to write off the *Mirror* if hard work and fresh thinking could save it. In January 1904, he relaunched it at half price (now a halfpenny) with a largely male staff and billed as 'a paper for men and women', but above all as the *Daily Illustrated Mirror*. Using half-tone blocks, developed by an employee called Arkas Sapt for fast press runs, he decided to go strongly for photographic illustrations. Under the shrewd editorship of Alexander Kenealy the paper became firmly established as a picture paper, the recognisable ancestor to the *Daily Mirror* which dominated tabloid journalism in Britain in the 1940s and 1950s.

There was a feeling that the Harmsworths created and bought newspapers and magazines much as other people collected stamps. Soon after the relaunch of the *Mirror* Sir William Ingram, head of the Illustrated London News and Sketch Ltd and Alfred's former employer, answered a worried shareholder who could see that a pictorial daily might be terminal for the old illustrated weeklies by acknowledging,

'The proprietors of the *Daily Mirror* are very clever and wonderful people.'

The magazines were still churning out sales and profits, the concept of the weekly-bought part-work had been profitably developed (first the *Harmsworth Encyclopaedia* then *Harmsworth Self-Educator*). The sense of exuberance and thinking big was conveyed by the purchase of large tracts of Newfoundland for paper-making in 1904, and the starting of a *Continental Daily Mail* the following year. The proprietor of *The Anglo-American Gazette* in Paris, who had lost three men and his manager to the *Continental Daily Mail*, complained later that the men had been bribed and the manager's wife had been got at. The same month that came out in Paris, May 1905, Alfred bought the loss-making but respected *Observer* – its sales as low as 2,000 – for around £5,000. But the challenge on which he had really set his sights was *The Times*.

The Times had emerged into the twentieth century as a British institution, but one in growing need of renovation. Journalistically its reputation was still high, yet it had a musty archaic air; whereas the telephone, the typewriter and the telegram had been basic tools from the inception of the *Mail*, at *The Times* all modern gadgetry was suspect. It seemed otherworldly. Its dividends and sales were falling and it was undercapitalised. It was also becoming the scene of a minor civil war among shareholders. Whereas the Walter family owned the printing business and premises the shareholders had been getting very little from the paper, and a few of them strongly disapproved of deals the paper had done to make money by selling the *Encyclopaedia Britannica* and creating a *Times* Book Club. On 31 July 1907, a court ordered a dissolution of *The Times* partnership. It was up for sale.

Northcliffe for years had advertised his interest in *The Times*. When Joseph Pulitzer had invited him to edit the first issue of his New York daily *World* in the twentieth century, he had admitted to Americans he met that he would like to own *The Times*. The previous year he had tried to use R. D. Blumenfeld of the *Daily Express* as an intermediary. He well knew that Arthur Walter would not approve of what he regarded as 'the yellow press' taking over. Subsequently, he was tipped off that Arthur Pearson planned to merge *The Times* with *The Standard* while attending a piano recital by Paderewski at a private house.

The negotiations by which Northcliffe came to be the chief proprietor of *The Times* in March 1908 were intricate and secret. For several weeks he himself was living in France in order to throw others off the scent. But essentially he gained control because Walter had sought to sell to Arthur Pearson without the knowledge or approval of Moberly Bell, the elderly but devoted general manager, or of G. F. Buckle, the editor. Bell then decided to deal with Northcliffe, on the basis that he would remain as manager for five years and Buckle and Valentine Chirol (the foreign editor) would stay in their posts. Bell kept Northcliffe's name a secret in the manoeuvring, and it was in Bell's name that the press lord deposited £320,000 in a Bank of England account. For about a year after Northcliffe owned the paper, he was still known as 'X', Bell's secret backer.

Northcliffe's attitude to *The Times* balanced reverence with frustration. He admired its status and news contacts. He criticised its lack of topicality, its narrow range of interests and, particularly in the early years, its unbelievably unbusinesslike management. He literally wore out Bell, who died at his desk just after his sixty-fourth birthday, with harassment. He died in April 1911 just after Northcliffe had started intervening significantly in the editorial approach of the paper. His more popular papers were campaigning against the Declaration of London which had been supported by the Liberal government, and which in Northcliffe's view would have made it harder for the Royal Navy to blockade a continental enemy in time of war. *The Times* had wanted to back the declaration: as a result of his influence it stayed neutral. Bell had, in February 1908, signed an undertaking to carry out his 'absolute instructions'.

In fact Northcliffe moved with some caution to stir up 'Ye Black Friars', as he satirised the inmates of Printing House Square. He sought to retain the interest and involvement of the founding family, the Walters, so that when his father died John Walter the fourth became chairman of the Times Publishing Company from 1910 until Northcliffe's own death in 1922. His first moves were managerial, rather than editorial, in that he brought in Reginald Nicholson to modernise the commercial side of the paper.

Although there was much struggle between Northcliffe and Bell over the slow progress of *The Times*, there had also been some humour. In a seasonal note to his proprietor at the start of the year in which he died, Bell suggested two New Year resolutions: 'For Lord N. To think twice before he telephones. For M. B. To think thrice before he writes letters.' But progress had been frustratingly slow for Northcliffe. In the first four years in which he actually owned the paper, the sales had risen by a mere 10,000 to just 47,400 and advertising revenue had actually fallen. It was still a loss-maker. The issue that was to haunt Lord Thomson and Rupert Murdoch in more recent times – how to make a national institution into a successful paying modern newspaper – was very far from being solved.

Northcliffe's determination that, in spite of his health problems and other interests, he wanted to get *The Times* right was probably one reason behind his sale of *The Observer* in 1911. He had put in a distinguished and independent-minded friend, J. L. Garvin, as editor at *The Observer*. The paper had done quite well. But the two friends disagreed politically about tariff reform and Garvin would have liked to have had more investment. For Northcliffe *The Observer* was a peripheral concern; for Garvin it was his life. The paper was sold to Waldorf Astor, the sale being an indication that Northcliffe was not the kind of proprietor whose sole desire was to amass more and more newspapers and periodicals.

At *The Times* he had resolved to sweep away the Old Gang and bring on thrusting younger journalists who would somehow embody the better traditions of the old paper, while adding to them a news sense and modernity of their own. In September 1912, he made a historic appointment of a young All Souls graduate who had been editor of the Johannesburg *Star*, and a protégé of Lord Milner in South Africa – Geoffrey Dawson. Dawson (who changed his name from Robinson for family reasons) was to edit the paper from 1912 to 1919 and again from 1922 to 1941. He was later strongly criticised as the editor responsible for *The Times*'s pro-appeasement policy under Baldwin and Neville Chamberlain.

In 1912, however, he seemed intelligent, Empire-minded and, above all, young. He represented a group of younger journalists on *The Times* who saw Northcliffe less as an ogre, come to destroy the paper's independence, but more as a beneficent and urgent force which would ginger up a sclerotic organisation. In a note to Dawson on becoming editor, his Chief wrote, 'Our task is great & worthy. If we get the barnacle-covered whale off the rocks & safely into deep water while we are comparatively young we may be able to keep it there until we discover others who can carry on the work.'

Northcliffe's power and reputation had increased as the twentieth century wore on. So had his belief in his own judgement and his desire for dominance over his undertakings in spite of erratic behaviour and problems of health, real and psychosomatic. In 1907, he had been out of Britain for much of the year, partly because his eyes needed rest, partly to avoid having writs for libel served on him. He had instigated a massive press campaign in the *Mail*, the *News* and the *Mirror* against the Lever Brothers' soap combine, on the grounds that the creation of a monopoly would put up the price of a public necessity. Levers' sales and share values crashed but they and other firms succeeded in winning over £150,000 in damages. Tom Marlowe, editor of the *Mail*, who had merely been doing his master's bidding, found his job on the line and Harold Harmsworth launched another drive on expenditure to try to make up the loss. (Marlowe retained his job, but thereafter insisted that news stories emanating from the Chief had to be carefully checked.)

In 1909–10, he had undergone some genuine illness which took much of the vitality out of him. At the end of January 1909 he talked of having 'ptomaine poisoning', and his wife, Lady Northcliffe, told Sutton that she dreaded that he might have a breakdown and should take a long holiday. (Significantly, she thought her husband would be more likely to listen to Sutton than to herself.) She persuaded him to go to Pau, where he met the Wright brothers and appreciated the potential of their aeroplane, and in all he was away from his offices – though not failing to bombard them with communiqués and advice – for seven months. A doctor said that Northcliffe had pancreatic trouble.

It was at this time the first rumours started circulating that he might have syphilis. The moral aura surrounding syphilis, as a sexually transmitted disease, was rather greater than the disapproval surrounding AIDS in some quarters today. In spite of Cecil King's statements,[9] in his own not entirely reliable memoirs, there is no proof that Northcliffe ever had a disease which at this period could lead to insanity and death. However, he had an active sex life and a ghoulish imagination and he may have thought that he had syphilis. By the end of 1909, Mrs Wrohan was pregnant with a child who would be born in August 1910, on precisely the day that Northcliffe and his wife and party docked in the *Mauretania* in New York.

His eccentricity, 'brainstorms' and periodic vindictiveness were remarked on. He even crossed his mother. He liked to use the telephone as an instrument of power – once calling up Lloyd George when he was a Cabinet minister and then slamming the phone down on him, firing editors ('Who is that?' 'Editor, *Weekly Dispatch*, Chief', 'You *were* the editor') and even conducting imaginary conversations in order to impress visitors. He could still charm with his blue-grey eyes, still make kindly gestures to dependants, but there seemed something abnormal about him.

In April 1910, he was down at St Raphael on the Riviera being told by his doctors to rest, and his visit to the United States and the paper operation in Newfoundland later in the year was also partly therapeutic. He did recover from the phase of illness in 1909–10 but he was never quite the same again. He resented the extent to which he was in the power of the machine he had created. Physically and mentally he was perhaps paying some price for the exertions he had made and success he had had in his twenties and thirties. From now on he worried more about his health and kept a doctor in his retinue.

He took to threatening to resign from the affairs of the Amalgamated Press, complaining about the vulgarity of some of its publications and personality conflicts among its editors and executives. In March 1912, this even produced friction with the faithful Sutton, who wrote to say that he felt he was being unfairly treated by Northcliffe and not paid enough. Northcliffe did not quite follow what Sutton was driving at but his more practical brother Harold interpreted for him. Sutton wanted to be vice-chairman of Amalgamated Press and a rise in salary. He got both. Later that year the Amalgamated Press moved into new quarters, Fleetway House. A souvenir publication for a banquet there that November stated that it now produced 8.5 million copies a week of nearly fifty journals.

In the years running up to the First World War, with the Northcliffe press pushing for armament against the German danger and simultaneously preparing to cover a civil war in Ireland, the proprietor's main journalistic and commercial concern following his recovery was to solve the problem of *The Times*. Differences of opinion over how to manage *The Times* led to a parting of the ways with Kennedy Jones, whom Northcliffe bought out on 1 January 1913. This left him even more dominant as a shareholder. His appointment of a first-class circulation manager in 1912, who had been able to do nothing with the sale, had demonstrated that there had to be changes to the nature and price of the product. He talked rather wildly about cutting the price from threepence to a penny, and turning *The Times* into a picture paper (at which the *Mirror* had become remarkably successful, outselling the *Daily Mail*). But in reality he moved cautiously. In the course of 1913 he reduced the price to twopence, at which it was still twice the cost of the *Daily Telegraph*, *Standard* and *Morning Post*. This added only just over 6,000 to the sale of 41,000 and did nothing for the advertising. Something more radical was needed.

With Dawson as a youthful and willing editor, Northcliffe strengthened the editorial team with Hugh Chisholm – a former editor of *St James's Gazette* – as day editor, Wickham Steed, an experienced foreign correspondent, brought back to be foreign editor, and George Beer, from the *Mail*, brought across to strengthen the news side. He decided that he had to broaden the appeal of *The Times* without losing its authority. He needed the editorials to retain their power of argument, the news to be more topical, the arrangement of the pages to be more reader-friendly (a contemporary compliment which Rupert Murdoch paid on seeing the first issue of *The Independent*) and the whole mix to be lighter and more digestible.

By December 1913 he was telling *Times* journalists in his daily communiqués that he was getting happier with the results of their efforts. In January 1914 from Paris, where he had gone to plan the finer points of a gamble on the price, he urged them to provide a light daily leader. On 16 March 1914, after the *Daily Chronicle* had leaked his plans three weeks before and he had ruled out a price cut to a mere penny halfpenny, *The Times* hit the news stands at one penny. It was a sensation.

The twenty-four-page paper included book reviews, articles on fashion and women's golf, a column of drama and feature items from Paris, and strong home and foreign reporting. It was recognisable to readers of the other penny quality papers but rather better value. Boosted by its own quality and the drumbeat of promotion from the other Northcliffe newspapers, it sold 150,000 copies. This was treble its recent sale, and more than half again the record number which had gone at the wedding of the Prince of Wales in March 1863. What was better, even after the initial excitement, its average sale was running at 145,000.

Of all his journalistic achievements – from the launches of *Answers* and the *Daily Mail*, to the rescue of the *Evening News* and the *Daily Mirror* – this was the most difficult and audacious because *The Times* was not like any other paper. It was a piece of living history and an article of national faith. It was hard to imagine that anyone else could have saved the barnacle-covered whale and yet have preserved so much of its essence. He had curbed his own impatience and endured hostility and losses for six years before he had got it right.

By 4 August 1914, at the outbreak of war, *The Times* sale climbed to nearly 280,000. But that was another story.

3

From 1914 to 1922

The Boer War had transformed the public's attitude to the *Daily Mail*. From being the butt of music hall jokes it had become valued for its unrivalled supply of news, and the patriotic music halls themselves swelled its 'Absent-minded Beggar' fund for the troops. The impact of the First World War, a much harder war for newspapers to cover because of the growth of censorship, transformed the reputation of Northcliffe himself. He was now seen as a political and national figure; not just a wealthy press proprietor, but a stalwart of the war effort and a maker and breaker of governments. Because he could also be unpredictable and megalomaniac, politicians and generals found him difficult to handle.

He seemed of central significance not only because he controlled several newspapers in an era before there were rival forms of instant communication, but the coming of the war itself, with the German Empire's attack on Belgium, appeared as a vindication of a press campaign of warnings and hostility in his papers which had run for a decade. Even during the Boer War he had been privately forecasting that there would be a war with Germany some day. The reporting in his papers had focused on German armament, Prussian efficiency, the aggressiveness of the Kaiser's empire, and – especially during the Dreadnought controversy – the threat to Britain's empire and naval supremacy implied by Germany's construction of a high seas battle fleet.

Sometimes, because of his German cousins, he claimed to have a better understanding of the German psyche than others. In 1909 he visited Berlin, where he told the citizens that they stared at visitors as if they were provincials, and Frankfurt, where an oculist examined his sight. He took the opportunity then to damp down scares in Britain about spying missions in airships over East Anglia. Later on, too, he played with ideas for increasing understanding between the two countries, like a Berlin edition of the *Mail* or the promotion of a book called *Our German Cousins*. But the more usual note was that Germany was sinister. Liberals like Hilaire Belloc accused the press proprietor of 'war scare' journalism. Northcliffe's anxiety about the new Germany was sincere and consistent: the press campaign was one ingredient in a mutual antipathy and a clash of interests which would ultimately lead to a bloody tragedy.

The war to end all wars, as it was dubbed by H. G. Wells, brought heartbreak to individual families and profound change to all the combatant nations. For a large family the Harmsworths suffered less than some others and the loss was heavily concentrated on just one of the brothers, Harold. Created Baron Rothermere of Hemsted in the county of Kent, in the New Year honours of 1914, he and his wife Lilian lost two of their three sons, Vere in 1916 and Vyvyan in 1918. It was a bitter blow for some one whose nature was anyway inclined to be pessimistic. His business skills, which he put at the disposal of the wartime government to organise army clothing supplies and then create an Air Ministry, were as irrelevant as his considerable wealth to a terrible private grief.

As a generalisation, the main reason why the family did not suffer more deaths was that the Northcliffe generation of brothers was too old to be called up, while most of their own children were too young. One of the two younger brothers who could have been involved, St John, – probably the most athletic of them all – had broken his spine in a motoring accident in 1906 and been severely paralysed. He had been driving back from his brother Harold's house in Norfolk, where it is suggested that he had been paying more than brotherly attentions to Harold's wife Lilian.

Up until the start of the war, St John's accident, which had brought out Northcliffe's own most caring side, and which had not stopped St John himself from developing the Perrier mineral water source in France into his own business, had been the biggest blow the Harmsworths had suffered since the relatively early death of their father. By the mid 1890s the fortune being created by Alfred's journalism and Harold's commercial sense was irrigating the lives of all members of the family. They were comfortably off and no longer had to work for an income unless they chose to.

In 1897, Alfred and Harold had bought a substantial mansion beyond north London for their mother. It was Poynters Hall at Totteridge, built in the Queen Anne style and overlooking a common. The house and its thirty-five acres had cost £9,000; she herself had an annual allowance of first £4,000, then £6,000. From then on Poynters became a family base to which married sons and daughters trekked for Sunday lunch in top hats and Sunday best. She became a stern matriarch, disapproving of alcohol and indelicate language, and was inclined to disapprove also of the husbands and wives her children married. She continued to practise thrift and her views were a mixture of religion and common sense.

In so far as the Harmsworths participated in the golden glow of Edwardian wealth, whose certainties were swept away by the First World War, their way of life was summed up not only by the rituals of

Poynters but by the more outgoing socialising of Sutton Place. It was here that Lady Mary Northcliffe ran large house parties and entertained on her husband's behalf. Famous golfers, musicians like Paderewski, politicians like Austen Chamberlain and Reginald McKenna were among those who came at weekends. The whole staff of the *Daily Mail* came on one occasion for a briefing by the Chief. His sense of Empire caused him to invite Mackenzie King, a young Canadian Cabinet minister who went on to be a very long-serving Canadian Prime Minister. Although Northcliffe did not like sleeping at Sutton Place, and acquired a bungalow on top of a down nearby where he did spend the night, it was a magnificent house for entertainment. It provided for shooting and golf and also simpler pleasures. Cecil, Alfred's brother, remembered getting up early to go bird-nesting. Alfred experimented on the estate by introducing American robins and grey squirrels into England.

The family was established, rich and diversified. Harold and his wife had an attractive house, La Dragonnière, above Monte Carlo which they and other members used, particularly in winter. While Northcliffe himself was known as a Tory, three of his brothers were active enough as Liberals to have run for election in autumn 1900 when Leicester squeaked in at Caithness by twenty-eight votes. Honours were beginning to accumulate; in 1912, Alfred had asked his younger brother Cecil, by then Liberal MP for Luton, whether he would like one but he declined for the moment. Inevitably, Alfred, as the best known in the family, but the rest to some degree became a target for those seeking favours or financial contributions.

The start of the war, in August 1914, straddled a Bank Holiday Monday (3 August) for which the *Mail* had made its usual journalistic preparations: it had its seaplane touring seaside resorts near Brighton, it was running a holiday story entitled 'The Marriage State' by Elizabeth York Miller, and it was maintaining a reader service for buying and selling shares (the Daily Mail Exchange) even though the Stock Exchange was closed. Six decks of headlines declared 'Great War Begun by Germany – France Attacked without a Declaration – War Declared Against Russia – INVASION OF LUXEMBOURG – VIOLATION OF TREATY – BRITISH WARNING TO GERMANY'.

The *Mail* editorial on 3 August was sombre:

The shadow of an immense catastrophe broods over Europe today. All hope of peace has disappeared with a crash. Germany has declared war upon Russia and has begun war without declaration upon France ... Europe might have been spared all this turmoil and anguish if Great Britain had only been armed and organised for war as the needs of our age demand. The precaution has not been taken, but in this solemn hour we shall utter no reproaches on that account. Our duty is to go forward into the valley of the shadow of death with courage and faith – with courage to suffer, with faith in God and our country.

The leader proposed a number of detailed measures: that £1 and ten shilling notes should be issued, to prevent a run on gold; that the state should promise to make good any losses at sea; that the Bank Holiday should be extended to the Wednesday; and, idealistically, that 'all should prepare to share food and resources with their poorer countrymen'.

The cataclysm, so long predicted in general terms, seemed to arrive suddenly and unexpectedly out of Balkan politics which were obscure to most of the British public. Initially, there was some neutralist feeling in Britain, particularly in Liberal and leftish circles, where a war that might aggrandise the reactionary regime of the Tsar seemed like one to be avoided. An awareness of these undercurrents as much as his own volatility may explain an odd battle inside the *Mail*, within the first couple of days of the war, where Northcliffe tried to run a leading article arguing that the British army should stay in Britain and not be sent to France. His headline would have been, 'Not One British Soldier to Leave England's Shores'. If this advice had been followed France would have been handed to the Kaiser and Britain would never have been forgiven. Tom Marlowe stood up to Northcliffe, however. As editor he refused to run his proprietor's editorial and succeeded in dissuading him.

The Times, supported by Northcliffe, advocated the immediate appointment of Lord Kitchener as Secretary for War; Asquith as Prime Minister did so. Within a fortnight of the outbreak of the war Colonel Repington, *The Times* defence correspondent, interviewed Kitchener who implied that the war might last three years. This was an unpopular and incredible idea to most of those who knew that the continental general staffs had planned for knock-out blows. But it was also shared by Northcliffe, who had always prided himself on his gifts of prevision and foresight.

The early weeks of the war saw the *Mail* reporting and encouraging spy fever in Britain, making much of German atrocities in Belgium – British and French propaganda greatly magnified the murder and rape of civilians – and castigating the Kaiser as mad and criminal. However, the difficulty for all British papers was that Kitchener and the generals were profoundly hostile to the notion of war correspondents. Information for the press was restricted to bland and inaccurate communiqués. Northcliffe, whose bias was to trust the generals, was not the ideal person to challenge this.

In consequence, the British public, like people in the Allied countries generally, were largely shielded from knowledge of the major defeats endured in the first month of war – notably the disastrous battle of the Lorraine frontiers where the French lost 300,000 troops, and the battle of Tannenberg where the Russians were defeated on the Eastern Front. The fact that journalists themselves had turned into censors was illustrated by Gerald Campbell of *The Times* who was in Lorraine during August. He never reported the French disaster either for the paper or in private messages to his editor.[10]

It was therefore a lucky fluke that enabled the Northcliffe press to break the news of the British army's retreat from Mons. The Press Bureau had covered up the fact that the British had been defeated and forced to retreat from the Belgian town. But two experienced correspondents – Arthur Moore of *The Times* and Hamilton Fyfe of the *Mail* – happened to be near enough to have learned what took place, and were sufficiently shocked to couch their reports in the form of a national warning.

Moore's copy reached *The Times* office on a Saturday afternoon, 29 August. It was strong stuff, comparing the prattle of the Paris papers with the reality of a serious allied defeat – 'bitter truths, but we can face them'. The French had broken and the British had fallen back, though maintaining their honour and discipline. 'Regiments were grievously injured, and the broken army fought its way desperately with many stands, forced backwards and ever backwards by the sheer unconquerable mass of numbers of an army prepared to throw away three or four men for the life of every British soldier.'

The Times, wary of the censorship, toned down this dispatch before sending it to the Press Bureau for clearance. The head of it then was F. E. Smith, later Earl of Birkenhead, an astute and self-confident barrister and politician. Far from trying to thwart publication Smith restored the editorial cuts, added a plea for immediate reinforcements ('The British Expeditionary Force has won indeed imperishable glory, but it needs men, men and yet more men') and clearly understood what he was doing. *The Times* brought out a Sunday edition, and printed beside Moore's piece a similar report from Hamilton Fyfe which appeared simultaneously in Northcliffe's *Weekly Dispatch*. The impact was enormous. Although Smith tried to backtrack on his responsibility and resigned soon after, and Asquith denounced the papers for alarmism and sensationalism, they had performed a real service in breaking out of the lies and complacency of the early weeks, and preparing the British for the German thrust on Paris.

Northcliffe's role in the first year of the war was as much propagandist as information supplier. His activity was unpredictable, in that he was hostile to the Asquith government as a basically peacetime government which was not full-blooded enough in its prosecution of the war. At the same time, he was trying to harness public opinion behind the national effort in the first total war. He used *The Times* as an agency to bring together the Red Cross and the Order of St John in a joint relief effort. He recognised that if the Germans invaded England he would be one of the first to hang. Sutton Place became a war hospital under Lady Northcliffe's direction. The *Mail* became 'the soldier's friend' – very much the position taken by the *Mirror* in the Second World War.

Against this background it was perhaps surprising that Northcliffe launched a major press campaign against Kitchener, hero of Omdurman and the Boer War, and now a symbol of British determination as War Secretary. But by May 1915 Northcliffe was convinced, as a result of contacts with Sir John French, the commander of the British Expeditionary Force, and with soldiers at the front, that there was a serious munitions scandal. The British army lacked sufficient shells of the weight available to the Germans. Kitchener was incompetent. Criticism of munitions workers for drunkenness was a diversion from maladministration at the highest level.

On 1 May, Northcliffe wrote to French saying that Asquith had been able to exploit official secrecy to assure the nation that no operation had been hampered by the want of ammunition. He added that 'a short and very vigorous statement from you to a private correspondent (the usual way of making things public in England) would, I believe, render the Government's position impossible'. French took the hint and told Repington, who reported in *The Times* a fortnight later that some British attacks had been frustrated because 'the want of an unlimited supply of high explosive was a fatal bar to our success'.

The first death in the family was reported to Northcliffe on the day Repington's article appeared; it was Lucas King – Geraldine's eldest son and elder brother to Cecil Harmsworth King who became the power at the *Mirror* – killed in action. The shells campaign moved from *The Times*, which was not prepared to go as far as Northcliffe wanted, to the *Mail*. On 21 May, the *Mail* ran a vitriolic leader, written by Northcliffe (with his mother's approval), blaming Kitchener for the shell fiasco. He knew that he would be making himself and his paper extremely unpopular but even so was unprepared for the reaction. Copies were burned on the London Stock Exchange and elsewhere, and individual readers posted charred remains to the proprietor. Sales of the *Mail* dropped by over a quarter of a million and *The Times*, although it had not shared in the campaign so strongly, suffered from its Northcliffe association.

Behind the scenes this agitation was paralleled by a crisis in Asquith's Liberal government. By the end of May it was reformed as a coalition. Though Kitchener was left in place as War Minister, the responsibility for munitions was passed to a new, separate ministry, headed by the fiery and energetic David Lloyd George. The public, and maybe Northcliffe himself, saw him as the man who had helped to break one government and replace it with another – even if Asquith was still Prime Minister.

Just after the change of government, in June 1915, Sir John French admitted war correspondents to his staff headquarters in France and

Northcliffe, who made periodic visits to the front, proposed that one of his own critics, Hilaire Belloc, should be attached as a British correspondent with the French armies. In July, the Chief celebrated his fiftieth birthday and was invited to lunch at the Ritz by his fellow directors and staff.

The year 1915 also saw the failed expedition to the Dardanelles. Northcliffe tended to be a 'Westerner' – one of those who thought that the war would be settled in France or at a stretch on the Russian Front, but not in Asia Minor. He was suspicious of Winston Churchill's enthusiasm for the Gallipoli campaign. Churchill had been one of the ministers most strongly hostile to *The Times* dispatch about the retreat from Mons, considering that 'such panic-stricken stuff' would damage Britain in neutral countries. He had tried to persuade Asquith to take over *The Times* as a national organ of government propaganda.

Northcliffe's shell campaign had been partly designed to help the exposed troops at Gallipoli, and more than once he went with H. W. Wilson of the *Mail* to London main line stations to see troop trains, bade farewell by weeping women, taking reinforcements for that expedition. In alliance with Keith Murdoch, an Australian journalist who had managed to get to Gallipoli on the justification of looking into postal services for the soldiers, Northcliffe tried to bring home to the Cabinet the nature of the disaster. Murdoch's report, describing the ineptitude of the generals which had led to such heavy casualties among his fellow countrymen, was passed on by Northcliffe and Lloyd George to senior ministers. It was the start of a continuing friendship between Northcliffe and Murdoch, whose son Rupert was to outstrip his father and Northcliffe himself as an international media tycoon.

The fierce passions aroused by Northcliffe's conduct, and his own contempt for the complacency of some politicians and of aspects of the war effort, boiled over in October 1915. Sir John Simon, the Home Secretary, seriously proposed to the Cabinet that the *Daily Mail* should be closed down. The ostensible reason was that it had printed a map entitled 'The Road to India' which was designed to explain to readers the issues at stake in the Balkans, Middle East and at Gallipoli. The Liberal press attacked Northcliffe bitterly. The map was accused of having brought Bulgaria into the war on the side of the Central Powers, and the Commons debated the issue. But the Cabinet was not persuaded by Simon and the *Mail* was not suppressed.

In spite of Northcliffe's criticism of Asquith, the government crisis which made Lloyd George Prime Minister did not occur until December 1916. The year was one of false hopes, symbolised by the summer battles of the Somme, in which relatively small advances were accompanied by horrendous casualties. Northcliffe, who was calling for conscription not only because it was a logical consequence of total war, but because in a voluntary system of recruiting the best men tended to be killed first, was deeply saddened by the death of another nephew in November. Vere, who as a boy had resembled the young St John, told Northcliffe before he died of wounds received in the battle of Cambrai, 'We don't mind being killed, but we do mind being butchered.'

At the beginning of the year both Lady Northcliffe and Dawson of *The Times* had been worrying about the Chief's mental balance – his rages and his habit of picking on dinner guests for expressing contrary opinions. But in February 1916, when he had visited the French defenders of Verdun with Wickham Steed of *The Times*, his companion had been struck by his toughness and stamina. Together they wrote a lengthy and influential article, arguing correctly that Verdun was unlikely to fall.

In fact 1916, which was a worrying year for a newspaper proprietor because newsprint prices were rising sharply, leading inexorably to newsprint rationing and a reduction in the size of newspapers, was an apogée of his own contribution as a reporter. He travelled extensively in France, Italy, neutral Switzerland and neutral Spain and the articles he wrote were collected in a book entitled *At the War*, published by Hodder & Stoughton, to raise funds for the joint committee of the British Red Cross and the Order of St John.

The articles, written in a homely and direct style, included portraits of the generals – Haig, Joffre, Cadorna, the Italian and Birdwood, the Australian. He criticised the lack of propaganda about the British contribution among the Italian allies and the neutrals. He denounced the cruelty of the enemy: 'Germans are naturally, so far as the Prussians and Bavarians are concerned, extremely cruel. German NCOs when taken prisoner with their men treat their private soldiers with a bullying savagery that is astonishing, and officer prisoners decline absolutely to pay any attention to their men, even though they have been wounded.'

His attitude to the British troops was a mixture of Rupert Brooke and *Boys Own Paper*. The opening chapter, datelined 'somewhere in France', conveyed this flavour well. 'I have not seen any description of the arrival of our dear soldier boys, many of whom have never before left England, in the country which is the destination, for good or ill, of the majority of those who leave England on the Great Adventure. Quite by chance I have on two occasions witnessed the landing abroad of a great number of them.'[11]

His insights into the effects of the war were far-sighted. The meetings at the front of men from different parts of Britain were creating a national awareness that would alter British politics. The Empire would benefit in a similar way. The significance of the aeroplane, which he had been among the first to divine when he remarked after meeting the Wright brothers before the war that Britain was no longer an island, was growing rapidly. 'Let it be realised that the practical aeroplane is not yet ten years old, that already our shores are within less than twenty minutes by air from the continent of Europe. Let it be realised that aeroplanes are very cheap to make and will become cheaper.'[12]

His sense of humour was still evident. He teased Sir Robert Hudson, a close friend of his wife's who had been chief agent of the Liberal Party and was now a key organiser for the Red Cross. 'Association with Sir Robert Hudson has taught me a great deal. For a number of years, in common with others of sound political views, I have been engaged in fighting the wicked machinations of the Radical Party in England. I surmise now that the reason for many of our failures was the presence of Sir Robert at Liberal headquarters. It is reassuring to know that he is a force with whom we shall not have to contend in the immediate future.'[13]

His common touch and humanity came over when he described his feelings on seeing a cannon fired in anger for the first time, the mummified corpse of a dead man on the calcified Italian plateau, or when he compared the winding Dover road with the straight, Napoleonic military roads of France. Where it was possible, which was not often, he shared a sense of beauty with readers. 'I came here to Pamplona because it is a convenient German centre [he was checking pro-German feeling in Spain] and because it is a pleasant place in a fair country. The days of early autumn in Northern Spain are crisp, yet warm, like the mimosa time in spring at Cannes. The Indian corn is now ripe; jasmine in great festoons and garlands, as we never see it in England, is everywhere, mixing its fragrance with that of the magnolia. The little, low-growing, purple wine-grapes in this, the famous Rioja district, are sweet enough to steal.'[14]

Such lyricism was a world away from the appalling carnage on the Western Front, where British casualty figures from July to November 1916 exceeded 400,000. Asquith's Cabinet, it was said, divided into Lloyd George's peace-through-victory faction, Lord Lansdowne's group for peace-by-negotiation, and the Prime Minister's cause for peace-by-muddling-through. Northcliffe's papers spearheaded the calls for a smaller war cabinet and a more vigorous prosecution of the war effort. It was a dark time for the Allies. Although *The Times* was on relatively good terms with Lloyd George, who was by now War Minister, there was a history of bad blood between Northcliffe and the *Daily Mail* and the energetic Welsh minister.

Northcliffe and the *Mail* had been bitter and contemptuous of Lloyd George's stance as a 'pro-Boer' during the Boer War, and had attacked what they saw as his appeals to class prejudice after 1906. Lloyd George represented that streak of radicialism which, according to hostile *Mail* editorials in the two elections of 1910, was virtually indistinguishable from socialism. As War Minister in 1916, Northcliffe told him to his face that he would break him if he continued to interfere in the strategy of the generals. Lloyd George reciprocated this distrust. He told Lord

Beaverbrook, the up-and-coming Canadian newspaper proprietor of the *Daily Express*, 'I would as soon go for a sunny evening stroll round Walton Heath with a grasshopper as try and work with Northcliffe.'

In fact both Lloyd George and Northcliffe were at one in their determination to win the war, and in their intuitive and practical understanding of what this required. Beaverbrook was not the only well-placed person to see that the mutual dislike of two tough-willed and patriotic men must somehow be bridged. At the end of November 1916, Lloyd George decided to push for a small directorate of three – the War Secretary, the First Lord of the Admiralty and a Minister without Portfolio – to run the war. On both 1 December and 2 December, Northcliffe saw him as the crisis within the Coalition boiled over. By 8 December, David Lloyd George moved into Downing Street as Prime Minister.

The Liberal *Daily News* stated that Asquith had been brought down by the hostility of the Northcliffe press and jokes started to circulate about the power of the press baron – 'Lord Northcliffe has called for the King.' In reality Northcliffe, unlike Beaverbrook, had not sought to manipulate the political crisis at close quarters. What he had done, when it seemed that Lloyd George might actually leave the government if his war directorate scheme was not accepted, was to arrange for a series of newspaper articles from him in that eventuality. Immediately after he became Prime Minister, and made a conciliatory phone call to Northcliffe, the press baron told him that he saw no purpose in them meeting again at that juncture.

For his part Lloyd George, though he understood the power which Northcliffe represented, saw him as capricious, unreliable and unstable. A memorandum during his Cabinet-making stated that neither of two termagents – Winston Churchill or Lord Northcliffe – would be offered ministries. He told a more friendly press proprietor, Lord Riddell, that if Northcliffe tried to wreck his government he would have to appeal to the Commons.

The scene had been set for the last phase of Northcliffe's life which almost exactly coincided with Lloyd George's prime minstership. The relationship between the brilliant and pugnacious Welshman and the country's leading pressman was one of wariness, mutual respect and periodic hostility. Lloyd George was determined not to let Northcliffe get him down. Northcliffe, who saw his newspaper ownership as a type of government in itself, and whose admirers saw him as the heart and soul of the war effort, did not wish to get entangled too far in the bureaucracy and responsibility of real government. There were also worrying signs, which would multiply over the last six years of Northcliffe's life, of his megalomania and uncertain mental state. Late in November, prior to the change of government, General Wilson had seen Northcliffe at his *Times* office and thought he was talking

nonsense. He contradicted himself and said that Germany was about
to collapse because there had been an unprecedented rise in the price
of eels.

Early in 1917 the war came to Northcliffe, when a German destroyer
fired a number of shells at night which burst close to Elmwood when he
was staying there. Local people were convinced that it was a serious
attempt to assassinate a man popularly seen as crucial to British morale.
A mother and baby were killed in Rose Cottage, a small house across
the road from Elmwood. Northcliffe refused to leave his bed and go
downstairs to the cellars. In his note to *The Times* the following day, 27
February, he commented, 'The authorities have no doubt that my house
was aimed at, and the shooting was by no means bad.' Another kind of
flattery from his enemies was the production of *The Great Anti-
Northcliffe Mail* via Zurich a couple of months later, German propaganda in a *Mail* format.

With the coming of the Lloyd George government the Harmsworth
brothers moved beyond newspapers in their efforts to help Britain win
the war. Early in 1917 Northcliffe himself agreed to chair an official
committee on the future of civil aviation. His brother Rothermere had
been put in charge of army clothing supplies and, in November, was
made Air Minister. Cecil, a Liberal MP, had been made an Under
Secretary at the Home Office in 1915 and in May 1917 joined Lloyd
George's private secretariat at 10 Downing Street, the legendary garden
suburb, so-called because it was lodged in an ugly, temporary building
in the Prime Minister's garden. Cecil was industrious and self-effacing.
Lloyd George valued him also because he gave an insight into his more
mercurial press-owning brothers.

It was against this background, and with the momentous change in
prospects for the war which took place when the United States entered
on the side of the Allies in April, that Northcliffe agreed to head a
British War Mission in America. The need for such a body, to
coordinate British purchases and to strengthen the Anglo-American
relationship, arose from a visit by A. J. Balfour, the Foreign Secretary.
Balfour had brought home to the Americans the desperate straits of the
Allies; Lloyd George, who asked Northcliffe twice before he agreed to
go, could see a series of advantages in getting a potential threat to
himself out of the country, and harnessing his undoubted drive and
patriotism. He stressed to Northcliffe the need for his business-like
qualities, in cutting through the muddles in purchasing supplies; he may
also have seen that his dynamism would get across to American
businessmen, and that his journalistic and public relations skills would
be invaluable in a country where there was still much pro-German and
anti-British sentiment.

Northcliffe had a strong premonition that he would not see England
again. The German submarine offensive was at its height and a US ship

in the convoy with the *St Paul*, on which he was travelling, was torpedoed. Before sailing from Liverpool he told Sir Robert Hudson, who may have been his wife's lover and was to marry her six months after his own death, to take special care of her if he did not return. He told Sutton that he wished him to inherit Elmwood in the same circumstances. He also informed Lloyd George as Prime Minister that his three chief henchmen – Sutton, the chairman of Amalgamated Press, Dawson the editor of *The Times* and Marlowe the editor of the *Mail* – were not to be called up.

On board ship he wrote to both his wife and his mother, to family members and old colleagues. He kept his watch on 'Totteridge time', so that he could imagine what his mother was doing. He wrote kindly about his wife: not many childless couples had lasted twenty-seven years of marriage as well as they had, and she had set an example to other rich women by her conduct during the war. He worried as to whether he was doing the right thing in taking on the War Mission, and at the scale of the begging operation on which he had embarked.

His arrival in New York was treated as a big story by the American press, which had a soft spot for a journalist who had scourged the old gang of British politicians. But he walked into a running battle with the British Ambassador, Sir Cecil Spring-Rice, who refused to have him greeted and regarded him as a threat and a menace. Northcliffe's newspapers had crossed swords in the past with a traditional diplomat – *The Times* had reported that Spring-Rice had been absent from his post and had travelled in German ships – and Lloyd George had first thought of replacing him as ambassador with Northcliffe. In circles close to President Wilson, Northcliffe may also have suffered from the eulogistic messages about him which arrived from the US Embassy in London, then occupied by a friend and admirer, Walter Hines Page.

Northcliffe was not in the United States for very long, from June to the end of October, and was required to play a role quite different from that of a newspaper magnate. He was enmeshed in government-to-government relations, coordinating a purchasing operation which was spending £2m a day (sufficient, for example, to force up the price of foodstuffs to American housewives), seeking to prop up a crucial British government loan of $400m, and conducting public relations for a war effort and Prime Minister of which he had often been violently critical.

He established himself in New York and took a house on Long Island Sound which he valued for its English atmosphere, close to a golf course. It was filled with pictures and books, with a garden filled with birds, honeysuckle and wild tiger lilies. He also gathered round himself various associates on whom he could rely; these ranged from an English butler and cook to Arthur Willert, *The Times* Washington correspondent whom he made his secretary, Hamilton Fyfe the veteran former editor of the *Mirror*, and Campbell Stuart, a young Canadian colonel who was his military secretary.

Stuart was a real find. He had managed to raise an Irish-Canadian mixed Protestant and Catholic regiment and was a good organiser, and Northcliffe quickly came to depend heavily on him in arranging his own programme and the administrative tasks of the mission. Stuart had been seconded to the war mission from the British Embassy. The connection made then was to last for the rest of Northcliffe's life.

Northcliffe in America had various qualities on his side. He had travelled to the United States and Canada many times before and liked Americans, and was clear in his own mind that the US could guarantee an Allied victory at a time when Russia was collapsing into revolution. He established a good rapport with President Wilson. His own grasp of facts commended him to American businessmen and his intuition was invaluable in the complex political situation: Where pro-German and isolationist sentiment persisted the European Allies were competing against each other for US support, and the presidential system meant that a vast range of decisions could only be finally settled in the White House. Even his Anglo-Irish connections turned out to be useful in a country where the Irish lobby was strong.

Northcliffe told friends in England that he had never worked so hard in his life, and this may well have been the truth. He had twenty-eight separate teams working under him and some of the negotiations – namely for oil for the Royal Navy, and for food for the British population at a time when stocks were running perilously short because of U-boat activity – were of a life or death nature. He found himself having to make speeches – he spoke to a crowd of 14,000 in Madison Square Gardens – and transacting much of the business over meals. Although the pressure was considerable he managed to maintain contact with his newspapers (and some politicans like Winston Churchill) in England.

In spite of his increasing tendency to bully the staffs of his own concerns, he was quite prepared to eat humble pie in the United States in the national interest. A case in point was his willingness to travel to Detroit to propitiate Henry Ford who had offered to give the British government 6,000 tractors at cost price. Ford himself had not had a good experience in Britain, where he had been criticised by Northcliffe's papers, and Northcliffe's official biographers have recorded that he may have been prejudiced against the Anglo-Irishman in the mistaken belief that he was Jewish.[15] Northcliffe succeeded in charming Ford, and getting the tractors.

His arrangement with Lloyd George and the Cabinet was to spend three months in the United States, though once there he said he was prepared to serve longer. Harold, his brother, told him he was prepared to come and take over; though Lloyd George would not have been able to tolerate the war mission becoming a family affair. However, the increasing significance of the financial relationship between Britain and the United States, where Northcliffe felt less confident in his prestige and skill, seems to have put an end to the exercise. At his request he was joined in September by a team of financial specialists led by Lord Reading and including Maynard Keynes. In the same month, he went up to Canada and in October followed this with a speaking tour in the Midwest where Britain's struggle was poorly understood.

At the start of November, after various precautions designed to put German spies off the scent, Northcliffe set sail again for Liverpool in the *St Paul*. He travelled back with Lord Reading and was in London again on 12 November. It had been an onerous but on the whole highly successful tour of duty. Lloyd George and Sir Robert Borden, the Prime Minister of Canada, sent him warm messages of thanks. Physically and psychologically, however, it may not have been so good for him. The flattery he received from Americans and his own perception of himself as a public man tended to strengthen his own vanity and depreciate British politicians in his own eyes. His own subsequent physical decline may also have been hastened by his exertions.

The sweet and sour situation in which he now found himself was illustrated on his return when he was given a viscountcy for his work in the war mission and had a public row with the Prime Minster over an offer, never specifically confirmed, to make him Air Minister. He snubbed Lloyd George by telling him that he did not feel loyal to the whole of his administration, and warned that the Americans would take over direction of the war effort if the European Allies were incompetent. His own contribution would be more effective if he remained an independent newspaper proprietor. On 15 November, his brother Cecil noted that the Prime Minister must be tired of the Harmsworth family. 'Alfred has declined the Air Ministry, Harold the First Commissionership and the Ministry of Food, and I the post of Chief Whip of the Coalition.' In fact Harold, who had a warmer relationship with Lloyd George, did agree to be Air Minister.

In London, there continued to be talk that Northcliffe wanted to be a minister or to go on playing an important public role. He hinted once that he might relish a role as confidential adviser to the Prime Minister, comparable to the position of Colonel House with President Wilson. At the end of 1917 and the beginning of 1918, he continued to be involved in the British end of the work being done by the war mission in the United States, and in assisting Colonel House in his mission to Europe. There was a possibility that Northcliffe might return to the United States, although he himself did not know what he wanted. In the meantime, his newspapers batted off suggestions for a negotiated peace, he campaigned for more effective naval action against the U-boats, and his loyal executive George Sutton paved the way for a baronetcy by

helping the Treasury to sell war bonds. Honours were also procured for
many who had worked in the war mission.

The feeling that his time in America had led to a change of gear for
Northcliffe, but an uncertainty as to which direction he was now
heading, was strengthened by changes in his personal and business life.
Whilst in the United States he had sold Sutton Place to the Duke and
Duchess of Sutherland; Lady Northcliffe was now running her hospital
for officers in Grosvenor Crescent, London. He wrote to his fellow
directors of Associated Newspapers on 1 January 1918 – the New Year
always had significance for him as a time for new directions and clearing
accounts – resigning as chairman. He proposed that the *Mail* editor,
Tom Marlowe should become chairman; the newly knighted Andrew
Caird was to be vice-chairman.

Much of 1918 was spent at Elmwood, where Northcliffe complained
of his ill health and a lump in his throat. Most of his impact was not in
person but by telephone, in daily memos and through a vast correspondence which he continued to maintain with both the prominent and the
obscure. At the start of the year Lloyd George, who had a high regard
for the value of propaganda and who also wanted to keep the press
lords out of mischief, invented posts for both Lord Beaverbrook and
Northcliffe. In deference to Northcliffe's desire not to compromise
himself – or particularly *The Times* – by taking a ministry, he was made
Director of Propaganda in Enemy Countries with access to the Prime
Minister. His appointment was announced in February. Beaverbrook,
who had been the go-between and had built up a solid reputation for
information work for the Canadian government, was created Britain's
first Minister of Information.

The negotiations surrounding these appointments were somewhat
comical, with the press lords offering to resign before they had even
been given their jobs, and the two of them carving up the world for their
exclusive activity like imperial powers. Inevitably, too, there was
political protest from both Liberal and Conservative wings of the
coalition, for neither of the proprietors could be described as sound
party men. Their actual qualifications for their tasks tended to be
ignored in the fear that they were getting a pay-off from Lloyd George,
or would be used to conduct domestic propaganda on his behalf. The
storm passed.

In the meantime, Northcliffe had established an office in Crewe
House, one of the great houses of Mayfair, from which he began a
propaganda assault against the Austro-Hungarian Empire. Advised by
Wickham Steed of *The Times* and R. W. Seton-Watson, he again
gathered a group of friends around him. Campbell Stuart was his
deputy, Hamilton Fyfe came too and H. G. Wells – whom he had first
met as a schoolmaster at Henley House School – also worked for Crewe
House until he resigned in protest at the contradiction between the

reasonableness of its anti-German propaganda and the 'hate-the-Hun' tirades of Northcliffe's popular press.

The decision to go first for the shaky Hapsburg Empire was shrewd. It was a multinational kingdom whose constituent nationalities had been encouraged by Woodrow Wilson's stress on self-determination. They wanted to be free. The tumultuous crash of the Tsars showed that even the toughest autocracy might collapse under the pressure of war. The German-speaking Austrians who ran the empire did not share the aggressive and militarist instincts of the Kaiser's Germany.

Crewe House organised the printing of leaflets, pictures with a religious or nationalist appeal designed to dishearten the Hapsburg troops, and a weekly newspaper in four languages. They were dropped by plane over the Austrian trenches on the Italian front and shot across no man's land in rockets. Patrols composed of deserters from the subject nationalities were sent out to pass on this literature. Northcliffe was particularly delighted by the Allied troops playing of Czech and Serbian national songs on records where the trenches were close together. He was annoyed that the Italians, perhaps because they coveted parts of German-speaking Tyrol, were not more appreciative of these tactics.

By April, Lloyd George was telling Northcliffe that classified information from the other side suggested that the propaganda offensive was having an effect. A month later he was appealing to Northcliffe to use the same approach on the Germans. With the withdrawal of Russia from the war the Germans had been free to unleash extra divisions on the Western Front; once again there were fears that Paris might fall (the *Continental Daily Mail* made contingency plans to withdraw to Nantes) and there was a mood of pessimism in London.

Tactics that would work against the Austro-Hungarian troops were not appropriate for the Western Front. Here Crewe House focused on the war weariness of the German soldiers. Leaflets emphasised the impossibility of defeating the Allies now that the United States had joined the war, the weight of German casualties, and the prospect for peace and security in future under a League of Nations. Balloons were used to send the pamphlets across enemy lines because of disputes over the use of airmen.

In an era before radio, this print propaganda certainly had impact. The German General von Hutier in an Army Order described Northcliffe as 'Minister for the Destruction of German Confidence – the most thorough-going rascal of the Entente'. On 15 August 1918, Crown Prince Ruprecht of Bavaria wrote to Prince Max of Baden that 'masses of propaganda leaflets have been thrown over to our troops by the enemy and are having a damaging effect on the morale of our exhausted soldiers'. The almost miraculous retreat of the German armies in the autumn of 1918, which was crowned by the armistice, was testimony to an erosion of will. The same sudden weakening led to the legend of a 'stab in the back' inside Germany which proved helpful to a demobilised Austrian-born corporal, Adolf Hitler; he concluded that he, too, would need an engine of propaganda.

Looking back later, Campbell Stuart thought that early 1918 had seen a beginning of the waning of Northcliffe's powers. In the early part of the year he suffered from bronchitis and flu. He worried about his mother, after being caught in an air raid with her at Totteridge, and personally warned the authorities of those he suspected to be German spies. He began eccentrically altering the by-lines of feature writers for the *Mail* – so that William Pollock was dubbed Pollock Pollock, for example – in the course of developing a new compressed feature page which was successful.

The end of the war brought an instant general election, in which Lloyd George's coalition had the support of most of the press. Northcliffe refused to give unqualified backing unless, he told Lloyd George's friend Lord Riddell, he knew definitely and in writing, and could conscientiously approve, the personal constitution of the government. Lloyd George dismissed the idea of a press lord's veto over his Cabinet with proper contempt. But from Northcliffe's standpoint, with his constant criticism of the old gang of politicians, it was unreasonable to sign a blank cheque. He wanted to safeguard his independence in order to be able to respond to public moods and his view of the public interest.

The *Mail*'s coverage of the election of December 1918 might have seemed strange to readers half a century later, but reflected various feelings that Northcliffe had picked up towards the end of the war. He recognised that women and the labour movement had acquired new standing and rights. Hence the *Mail*'s policy combined virulent hatred for the defeated Germany – the Kaiser should be tried, 'Huns' should be expelled from Britain, and a full indemnity paid – with social radicalism at home. The *Mail* wanted land for returning soldiers and sailors, new houses, financial support for ex-servicemen wanting to start new businesses, and better pensions. In addition it advocated nationalisation of coal mines and railways, and gave a daily column to the Labour Party leadership in which it could put its case. In general, it was kinder to Labour than to the Asquithian Liberals or to the reactionary wing of the Conservatives.

Lloyd George's victory at the election did not make his relations with the country's leading press proprietor any easier, though his apparent strength made him less willing to be pushed around by Northcliffe. At the end of the war Crewe House had prepared a summary of aims entitled 'From War to Peace' which went out over Northcliffe's signature and was reproduced in newspapers throughout the world. Lloyd George thought that Northcliffe wished to be a plenipotentiary in the peace negotiations at Versailles, and may have hinted that such a position was possible, but then stamped on it. Whatever the truth of this affair – and Northcliffe with a lump in his throat was not physically capable of such demanding public work – it further worsened the frictions between them.

The armistice had been celebrated by a fortnight's extra pay for all Northcliffe's employees, but the Chief's confidence in Geoffrey Dawson, editor of *The Times*, had dropped sharply. Northcliffe had harassed him with criticism, though the paper was doing well commercially, and Dawson had been indiscreet about his proprietor when dining out. In early 1919, *The Times* was too ready to see threats to the state and too unsympathetic to the legitimate grievances of labour in its reporting of stikes. In February, using Campbell Stuart as an intermediary and when he himself was in the south of France, Northcliffe replaced Geoffrey Dawson as editor by Wickham Steed who had been covering the peace negotiations. The change had to be endorsed by John Walter, as chairman of *The Times*; Stuart was put in as manager.

Wickham Steed's first day as editor, on 16 April, coincided with a tremendous onslaught against his proprietor in the House of Commons. It was as though the Prime Minister was taking revenge for all the jibes he had had to put up with over the years from the Northcliffe press. The occasion was a debate on the handling of the peace negotiations and the particular cause was a reference to a telegram he had received in Paris, titled 'Make the Huns Pay' and signed by 370 MPs. Responding to Kennedy Jones MP, Northcliffe's former colleague, Lloyd George said that he knew the source on which this was based but could not agree that it was reliable.

Making it clear that he believed the source was Northcliffe, he compared the limited peace terms published in 'From War to Peace' with what he described as hysterical demands for massive reparations and hanging everybody all round – 'especially members of the Government'. Northcliffe was totally inconsistent. 'Reliable! That is the last adjective I would use. It is here today, jumping there tomorrow, and there the next day, I would as soon reply upon a grasshopper.' He tapped his head, implying that Northcliffe was mad, and went on:

Still I am prepared to make some allowances – even great newspapers will forgive me for saying so – and when a man is labouring under a keen sense of disappointment, however unjustified and however ridiculous the expectations may have been, he is always apt to think the world is badly run. When a man has deluded himself, and all the people whom he ever permits to go near to him help him into the belief that he is the only man who can win the War, and he is waiting for the clamour of the multitude that is going to demand his presence there to direct the destinies of the world, and there is not a whisper, not a sound, it is rather disappointing; it is unnerving; it is upsetting. Then the War is won without him. There must be something wrong. Of course, it must be the Government! Then, at any rate, he is the only man to make peace. The only people who get near him tell him so, constantly tell him so. So he publishes the Peace Terms, and he waits for the 'call.' It does not come.[16]

This tirade was followed by a reference to *The Times* as 'merely a threepenny edition of the *Daily Mail*'. Many MPs loved the speech. Its main target took it calmly, assuring his *Times* staff that he had nothing personal against Lloyd George and would go on supporting or attacking him on the merits of his policies. In fact, in making Wickham Steed editor of *The Times* he had put an end to a situation in which that paper had been free to take a different line on major issues from the rest of Associated Newspapers. Wickham Steed accepted that this had become an embarrassment and was consoled by being trusted with policy guidance for the other papers.

In June 1919, Northcliffe was operated on for the thyroid growth in his throat which had given him discomfort for over a year and made it difficult for him to speak. Many people sent him their best wishes, including one coalition politician with whom he had crossed swords in the past, Winston Churchill. The growth had not been cancerous but the patient was warned to take things easy for three months.

Recuperation was slow and for the remaining three years of his life his restlessness and eccentricity would grow. By the end of 1919, he was seriously contemplating a risk of war between Britain and the United States. In the winter of 1920–1, he launched a campaign for the *Daily Mail* hat, an attempt to lighten the paper which became a bore to readers. He got embroiled in post-war labour problems – publishing a rejoinder to the father of the *Mail* machine managers who had complained about the paper's treatment of the railwaymen, threatening a lockout in 1920 if the printers went on strike, and backing his brother Harold in a long dispute at the Newfoundland paper mills where he was seeking to cut wages.

He inveighed against vulgar and overbearing advertisements, making fun of the *Evening News* advertising manager for adopting airs suitable to the peerage, and briefly appointed the *Mail* commissionaire, Robert Glover, as a 'censor of advertisements'. For those who had not worked closely with him in earlier days, or who did not hero-worship him, he seemed intimidating.

In July 1921, leaving Sutton with power of attorney, Northcliffe embarked on a world tour. It was partly supposed to be a health cure, though he was inundated with visitors and receptions wherever he went, and partly designed to satisfy his own curiosity about the Pacific and parts of the Empire he had never visited before, including Australia and New Zealand. The trip started badly, with an off-the-record talk by Wickham Steed, who had accompanied Northcliffe across the Atlantic, being attributed to Northcliffe and causing a brief sensation in Downing

Street and Buckingham Palace. Steed was talking about a conversation which was supposed to have taken place between King George V and Lloyd George in which the King was said to have told his Prime Minister that unless all the Irish were to be shot he would have to do a deal with them. There were denials all round. Lloyd George referred to Northcliffe's 'criminal malignity'. *The Times* rumbled on editorially about 'Some Misunderstandings' and Northcliffe resisted his brother Harold's recommendation to fire Steed.

The journey took him to the US and Canada, to Japan, China and Thailand, to Australia and New Zealand, to Java and Borneo, to Ceylon and India. It was only intermittently restful. He spent six or seven hours a day dictating – travelogues to his family and intimates, two letters a day to his mother, messages to his journalistic staff. He physically attacked his secretary Harold Snoad when he failed to find him a paper in the royal palace in Bangkok. He was suspicious of the Japanese and could not see the point in the British hanging on to India.

Wherever he went he was greeted as a celebrity. People he had known in his early days popped up to greet him. The mayor of Suva, in Fiji, wanted his boat to divert so that respects could be paid. He had three portraits of his wife in his cabin, yet Mrs Wrohan was expected to read the letters he circularised to describe his travels. He told his mother that he was reading a devotional work she had given him but could not escape her disapproval of what his papers were up to in his absence. When he was in Java she told him – apropos *The Times*'s less than hard-line stance on the Irish question – that she would not have Ulster coerced. Two *Times* men went out to Totteridge to receive a piece of her mind; on their return to London they took the advice of Cecil Harmsworth, then at the Foreign Office, not to ride roughshod over the objections of the protestant province. His mother cabled him on another occasion that both the *Mail* and *The Times* were equally vulgar that morning.

While he claimed that he had never felt better, there were ominous signs that he was losing his grip. A French newsreel film, taken of him meeting the French Governor General in Saigon, made him appear overindulged, irascible and fat. One day he started dictating a telegram to his aunt, Sarah Miller, who was dead. The death of his old colleague and partner Kennedy Jones, in October 1921, seemed hardly to move him when he heard of it. He suffered from memory loss and told his brother Leicester wearily, 'When a man is over 55 every extra job is a nuisance to him.'

Returning to Europe via the south of France in February 1922, where he was met by Lady Northcliffe, he lashed out at the managers and journalists on *The Times* where the paper was losing both sales and money. In Paris, he kicked a print leader at the *Continental Daily Mail* out of his office, calling him 'a damned ungrateful swine' for wanting a rise. A dismissive memo to the staff of the *Evening News*, telling them that it was never quoted at home or abroad and was not taken very seriously, caused so much ill-feeling that it was torn down, and W. J. Evans, the veteran editor-in-chief, told Northcliffe frankly that he had good men who would not stand abuse. His last visit to Carmelite House took place on 4 May, when he spoke at Evans' farewell lunch.

Northcliffe, who had been a hypochondriac for most of his life and who had suffered from several quite genuine illnesses, was now plainly becoming extremely sick. He looked haggard, his rages were worse; Wickham Steed of *The Times* believed he was moving into an advanced stage of syphilis. As spring became summer his moments of lucidity were increasingly concentrated on *The Times* where he cut the price dramatically to 1½d (following the *Daily Telegraph*) and authorised Sutton to buy out the Walter family interest.

In May and June, he was in France, Belgium and Germany travelling incognito as 'Mr Brown', becoming obsessed in Cologne by the engagement of a niece of his wife to a British officer, and writing to Sir Robert Hudson to ask a London doctor, Sir Frederick Treves, whether he was sane. From Boulogne at the start of June he tried to send a series of idiotic messages to persons on *The Times*, the editor of the *Continental Daily Mail* (who was told he would be punched for not promoting a pamphlet Northcliffe had written which criticised fellow newspaper proprietors) and even Sir Andrew Caird. He moved to Paris and then Evian, clearly out of mental control. Wickham Steed managed to get cartridges away from him when he was waving a pistol about, and cabled *The Times* to ignore all Northcliffe's messages, and to advise Carmelite House to do the same. His brother Leicester came over to take charge and on Saturday 17 June, in a coach provided by the French President, Poincaré, he was removed to Boulogne.

Northcliffe's last days were tragic. He was kept at his home at 1 Carlton Gardens under the twenty-four-hour attention of male nurses who were working under the direction of Sir Thomas, later Lord Horder. For most of the time he was delirious or under sedation, fasting or weeping. He tried to reassert control over his newspapers but his access to phones was cut off. His wife was not allowed to see him. Intrigues developed around his wills and particularly his ownership of *The Times* (where John Walter had seemingly just given up his option to regain control at Northcliffe's death). On 9 August, because Horder thought he needed more air, he was taken up on the roof of the house of his neighbour, the Duke of Devonshire. It was there, in a little hut on the morning of Monday 14 August 1922, that he died. His brothers Cecil and Vyvyan were with him.

What in fact killed him? In spite of the allegations by Wickham Steed and, later, Cecil King that he died from syphilis there seems little doubt now that the cause of death was, as stated at the time, bacterial endocarditis – an inflammation of the inner lining of the heart, and especially the valves. Horder's diagnosis was supported by that of an American specialist, Dr Emanuel Libman, and by a bacterial test carried out at St Bartholomew's Hospital. The *British Medical Journal*[17] suggested that Northcliffe may have had the infection for at least a year – it may have had something to do with a heart murmur of which he had complained – and the effects on his mind and body were what would be expected. Curiously enough, Leicester's third son, R. L. St John Harmsworth, had died two years before of the same disease and a medical research fund in his memory was set up in 1924 after the brothers decided that their mother would be embarrassed if Northcliffe's name was used.

Northcliffe's death was treated as that of a titan. Steed at *The Times* paid tribute to his genius and his greatness. The *Mail* honoured its founder. The funeral at Westminster Abbey attracted a large congregation, and ninety cars accompanied the body to North Finchley where he had asked to be buried. For the British press it was the end of an era. For the Harmsworth family it marked the first stage in the establishment of a dynasty.

4

Family, Personality, Impact

The Northcliffe who bestrode Fleet Street like a colossus, who tried on Napoleon's hat at Fontainebleau and found to his joy that it fitted, remained for all his life extremely conscious of his family. His almost neurotic attachment to his mother – his reference to himself as her first-born implied not only a claim on her restrained affections, but obligations to her and to his younger brothers and sisters – was only a part of this. Even in the ghastly final days he was anxious that, because he did not get on well with his brother-in-law Percy Burton, he had not been sufficiently generous to his sister Christabel in his will. On hearing that he was unlikely to recover, his brother St John wrote, 'He has been a great captain and has always done his duty, above all, to the family.'

In his attitudes and his career he epitomised much that was typical in middle-class Victorian families: the respect for the patriarch, transferred to a matriarch by his relatively early death; the utilisation of a large family for the creation of a family business (a feature still emulated by British families of Asian origin nearly a century later); social climbing, which meant that with Northcliffe's active support his generation bagged two viscountcies, an additional barony (for Cecil), two baronetcies (for Leicester and Hildebrand) and a knighthood (for Geraldine's husband, Lucas King); and an element of hypocrisy (for a shroud of secrecy surrounded Northcliffe's illegitimate children by Mrs Wrohan, and she was by no means his only mistress).

His sense of family was unaffected by his own inability to have legitimate children or by the fact that his brothers and sisters went their separate ways, differing from him in politics and, in the case of Harold, Leicester and St John, running their own businesses. His thinking was dynastic. As his official biographers put it, 'Like Bonaparte, but without the elements of farcical comedy, Alfred Harmsworth founded a dynasty. If he did not exalt his mother and the rest of his family to heights of splendour, he brought them wealth and position and made them immensely proud of the Harmsworth name.'[18]

When the third brother, Cecil, had a son, Alfred wrote to him, 'Despite our lack of fortune in these matters, the news will, I know, give my dear wife very great pleasure. I'm glad that it's another little son to head yet another branch of a family for which I am so ambitious.' When the little boy died after a few months he broke his holiday in France to come back to the funeral in Marylebone. The deaths of Harold's two sons, Vere and Vyvyan, in the First World War affected him, too, because they were in a sense his heirs; he gave discreet help to Harold's surviving son Esmond when he ran as a Conservative in a 1919 by-election for the Isle of Thanet, the Kent constituency which included Elmwood.

This consciousness had other aspects, too. While he could be daunting to adults, Northcliffe was good with children, getting down on the floor with them and giving them his whole attention. His sense of family was also part of his rapport with the public he knew: the smiles, riddles, bits of useless information and Christmas cracker repartee, which were so important to *Answers* and the early magazines, had their origin in the bursting Harmsworth household of north London. His hostility to sleaze and vulgarity matched prevailing values; late Victorian families disdained them as tasteless. His ambiguity where death, pain, cruelty and the ghoulish were concerned was a contemporary feature: families simultaneously condemned the penny dreadfuls while lapping them up.

Even though his real children could not take his surname, Northcliffe made sure that they had Harmsworth Christian names. He had two sons called Alfred (one by Louisa Smith, the second by Mrs Wrohan), and Mrs Wrohan's two other children were called Geraldine and Harold. When they were little he saw something of the Wrohan children at Elmwood but when his affair with their mother came to an end at the start of the First World War, he inevitably saw less of them. They were well looked after financially – Northcliffe's dealings with Mrs Wrohan involved his solicitor, chauffeur and a handful of trusties – and there was a story of him coming incognito to watch one of his sons playing games at school. Wisely, Mrs Wrohan refused to send her Alfred to meet him at Boulogne in 1922, when Northcliffe was suffering from his fatal illness.

His relations with his brothers and sisters were very much those of a big brother and a financial provider. The elder brothers, who had worked with him in the business in the early years and had there formed the basis of their own considerable fortunes remained the closest to him. His habit of providing financial allowances for his sisters and other relations (and indeed to large numbers outside the family) started early on. On 15 January 1892, when he only had four papers and his sister Geraldine produced her first baby daughter, he wrote to her from *Answers*:[19]

My dearest sister – When I got home to Maida Vale last night I found the joyful news of the safe arrival of a little niece. Terrific excitement among the tribe immediately ensued and everyone is in the full dignity of Aunt and Uncle, not to forget Grandmama. Boo's [Vyvyan's] remark was: 'If I am uncle, what's Leicester and Hilder?' He is sorely puzzled over the problem ... I am seeing my solicitor just now with a view to settling £50 on my niece and godchild, who will not be forgotten in my will, also being made today.

Later on, he would be making the same sister Geraldine, Lady King (known as Dot in the family) an annual subsidy of £1,400 a year. She had married Lucas White King, one of a well-off family of Dublin protestants, who took her off with him to India where he worked in the Indian Civil Service. Later still, Northcliffe cut her subsidy because he was angry that he could never see his mother except in her presence; he restored the allowance to the original figure just before his death. His greatest munificence was given to his mother and to his injured brother St John, for whom no efforts of nursing care, therapy and transport were spared.

As was not unusual at the time, the early death of his father turned Northcliffe into something of a father-substitute to the younger brothers and sisters. Even as his businesses multiplied he found time to maintain correspondence with them, and interested himself in their education. He paid for St John and Hildebrand to go to Oxford. He and Harold supported the backward brother Charles, who lived in his mother's house in Sussex and took no part in the affairs of the family, and he took him abroad on some of his trips. But from around 1900 onwards, fortified by financial independence, the brothers and sisters were increasingly going their separate ways; the Northcliffe who was unchallenged in his newspapers and a force in public life could no longer dominate an individualistic family.

The person who did, by sheer force of character, was his mother. In some ways, by reason of her sex and her own quite comfortable family background in Ireland, her own attitudes were not greatly affected by the wealth and servants that her sons put at her disposal. She travelled to North America with Northcliffe in 1908; she worried about his health; she bossed her maids at Poynters; and her son Harold thought she was a tougher and more combative personality than most of the Cabinet in the First World War.

Strong men quailed before Mrs Harmsworth and she could be quite sure of what was best for her daughters and granddaughters. For example, her granddaughter Enid King, who was one of her favourites, was offered a gardener's cottage at Poynters after she got married; Enid's husband was simultaneously offered a job in the paper business in Newfoundland. The young couple would have been split in a transparent attempt by Mrs Harmsworth to retain the services of Enid as a companion, and the deal was rejected. On another occasion, she caused some ill-feeling between Geraldine's family and Leicester's by ordering Geraldine to go round and tick off Leicester and his wife Annie; she was worried that the couple had lost children in infancy and accused them of neglect.

Northcliffe's own remarkable deference to her strengthened her authority over the rest of the family. Long after he was married he stayed with her regularly, and it was notable that he tended to retreat to her for moral support during major crises of his journalistic and private life. Disagreements or jealousy over her could bring him into conflict with his brothers and sisters, as for instance with Geraldine, or when he found that Leicester had given her a house in Campden Hill, furnished with antiques. His anxieties over her, after the bombing at Totteridge which led to the purchase of a summer house near Hassocks, or when she had a serious illness at Broadstairs in September 1920, he communicated to his brothers and sisters.

If their mother was their conscience, Northcliffe's brother Harold – subject of the next section of this book – was the leading businessman and worrier. The third brother, Cecil, was different in that he was less ambitious. He married Emily, a first cousin on the Maffett side, was good looking and pursued a low-key career in Liberal politics. He was sympathetic, emollient and later on wrote up his memories of Northcliffe and St John for circulation in the family. His son and heir, Desmond, was to become a serious painter for whom a peerage was no real advantage; the barony of Harmsworth of Egham was obtained for Cecil by Rothermere in 1939, long after he had retired from politics and the year before Rothermere died.

The next brother, Leicester, went round the world with Cecil in 1894 and set up *Home Chat*, the Harmsworth's first domestic magazine for women, a year later. He married the daughter of a colleague he had worked with at Somerset House before Alfred struck it rich with *Answers* and, though gloomy and with a strong religious streak, he became an independent and interesting figure. Elected a Liberal MP for Caithness in 1900, Leicester succeeded in representing his constituents for over twenty years while virtually never making a speech. He was, however, an entrepreneur, bibliophile and collector.

He bought a golf magazine of his own before the turn of the century which required him to sell back some *Answers* shares to Alfred, and in 1906, the year of the Liberals' sweeping election victory, he disentangled himself from the boardroom and shareholding of the Harmsworth magazines. There seem to have been a mixture of reasons; Leicester was wanting to build his own business career, he was cross that Harold had killed a magazine whose launch he had encouraged, and it may have been embarrassing for a Liberal MP to be closely associated with a firm whose head was now, through the *Daily Mail*, so usually Tory.

Leicester sold his shares to Sir John Ellerman, the shipowner, over Alfred's objections and subsequently made money from oil investments and the import of the Darracq motor car into Britain. He stayed on reasonable terms with Northcliffe, who visited his first son in France, in 1916, after he was seriously wounded in the Somme battles. In the early 1920s, he brought the *Western Morning News* as an investment. His houses – one of which in Campden Hill was eventually demolished to make way for Holland Park School – were intensely gloomy and he had various phobias. His children were not allowed to go on the beach at Bexhill for fear of catching cold; they were not allowed to go on a swing, after his daughter Rosemary fell off a pony in Rotten Row. Although he was a noted and imaginative art collector, he and his wife were cruel to their aesthetic son Geoffrey, who was beaten at one stage if he was found with a paintbrush in his hand.

As a young man, Leicester had been debonair. His wife Annie had been pregnant when they married and their first son Alfred laughed in later years at the thought of old Mrs Harmsworth dandling a strapping 2½-month-old baby on her knee which was supposed to be new-born. There was always a secretive side to Leicester. At some stage, he was bigamously married to a woman he had met in South America. After his death his widow Annie claimed to have known about various girlfriends.

Hildebrand, the next brother, was also a Liberal and had a reputation as the family joker. He had had fun with *Comic Cuts* but by 1900 was helping Cecil start a political magazine, the *New Liberal Review*. His brother Alfred thought he needed to work harder, but he resisted the opportunity to run *Vanity Fair* and in 1905 he left the Amalgamated Press. Three years later he bought the London evening paper, *The Globe*. But although for Alfred and Harold the purchase of the *Evening News* had been a profitable introduction to newspapers, for Hildebrand *The Globe* was a serious loss-maker. None the less, in spite of parting with £80,000 before selling *The Globe* in 1911, Hildebrand built a respectable fortune on the basis of his Amalgamated Press and *Mail* shareholdings. (Hildebrand and Leicester had each a sixth of the magazine profits over £150,000; in 1898, Hildebrand had 5 per cent of the shares in the company which published the *Mail*.) As he grew older, Hildebrand retired to the country life of Sussex.

St John, who had been slight and nervous as a small boy, grew up handsome and athletic and somewhat like Northcliffe in appearance. Although briefly a director of one of the Harmsworth companies, he never had time to get seriously involved because one of Northcliffe's plans rebounded in an unexpected way. The elder brother insisted that he learn French. It was when the *entente cordiale* was in the air – the *Continental Daily Mail* was launched in Paris in 1905 – and in 1902 St John was sent to France to learn the language. On holiday later that year in Provence with his tutor, M. Methol, he was introduced to a gassy spring of natural water at Vergèze where a M. Perrier ran a medicinal bathing establishment.

Almost at once St John decided to buy the source and build up a mineral water business. What now seems a stroke of incredible foresight was at the time greeted with horror in the Harmsworth family; early in 1903 he disposed of what shares he had to buy the spring, and only Molly, Alfred's wife, gave him much support. It was several years before he showed a modest profit on the investment, and this he ploughed back. In the meantime, of course, he had had his car accident which paralysed him from the waist down. (The motor cyclist who found him by the side of the road in Hertfordshire had been an advertising salesman; St John rewarded him with £52 a year – the pound a week of the *Answers* contest – for the next twenty-seven years.)

Thereafter, St John ran his business from a wheelchair. He took most of the decisions – the shape of the Perrier bottle was inspired by his Indian exercise clubs; he did deals with Wagons Lits to get his mineral water on to the continental trains, and exploited a Harmsworth family friendship with Sir Thomas Lipton, the developer of a grocery chain, to make inroads in Britain. It is said that Mussolini was one of the workmen to be employed in building the factory at Vergèze, where St John spent much time. He had a thoroughly Harmsworth ambition for his business, but his operations, poor health and maybe a lack of financial acumen meant that it was never a great money-spinner in his lifetime. After the First World War Northcliffe was guaranteeing a Perrier overdraft of £40,000.

The accident meant that he never married, though he was briefly engaged to the daughter of Alfred's friend, Herbert Ward. But he remained close to the family, establishing ties with his nephews and nieces; he had a particularly close relationship with Vere, Harold's second son, who seems to have found it easier to get on with him than with his own father. Northcliffe and the rest remained extremely fond of St John, who decided early on that his sisters were to inherit the Perrier business.

St John's special kingfisher blue Rolls-Royce, modified so that the wheelchair could be got in and out, was just one small symbol of the financial impact of the Harmsworth fortune, established by the end of the nineteenth century. Northcliffe himself was comfortably a millionaire by the early 1900s. In 1904–5, for instance, he was reporting a net income of £115,000 and stock worth £300,000 outside the family businesses. In five years' time, his income was running at £200,000 a year, a fabulous sum in the money values of the early twentieth century, and more than sufficient to sustain a viscountcy. Only with wartime taxation did the Inland Revenue begin to make a dent on an income of this scale – Northcliffe took no salary for the US War Mission – and after 1918, in the uncertainties of the post-war world, he complained more about his overpaid directors and the innumerable suppliants to his purse. But by then he had taken various steps, through allowances and share allocations, to ensure that his family were well provided for. (Furthermore, trusts were settled on the Wrohan children.)

The impact of Northcliffe and the media revolution he spearheaded was diverse because of his own energy, his interest in fact, people and the everyday; it dovetailed with other changes that it hastened – values of compression and speed, and the dawning of a more democratic order. This symbiosis between a more popular press and other developments of the twentieth century was shown by his lifelong interest in modern transport. He had started journalism with bicycling. He saw the point of the motor car, campaigning to end speed restrictions and to introduce a rear mirror for safety; he sponsored air races and saw at once the significance of aeroplanes in ending Britian's island status for defence purposes. (In 1906, after Santos Dumont recorded the first flight in Europe, Northcliffe offered a £10,000 prize for the first flight from London to Manchester; he launched a model aeroplane competition that was won by A. V. Roe, whose company built the Avro Lancaster bomber in the Second World War.) When others scoffed, Northcliffe was prepared to trust his imagination.

Another area he changed enormously was the relationship between politicians and their public. He added a new dimension to what had been a limited number of contacts – the restricted readerships of the pre-*Mail* daily newspapers, and the audiences who could get to public meetings – by building circulations among the lower middle class and the skilled artisans. He was helping to enfranchise a wider group of voters (during the First World War he overtly encouraged the leaders of the women's suffrage movement) by giving a platform for their concerns. He had also subtly changed the rules between politicians and the press: politicians were not reported automatically because that could be boring and harked back to the subsidised party press; they were only reported for their public or entertainment interest.

Many of the rows between Northcliffe and the politicians prefigured those that would take place later when other types of communication became dominant, between politicians and BBC radio, and politicians and television broadcasters. Fundamentally, these were quarrels about power and representation: a journalist-proprietor, reporting events and public needs, was claiming to be more representative and caring for the public mood than the MPs and governments returned by the electors. Before opinion polls inserted a more accurate and regular test, this could often be true. This knowledge meant that politicians like Lloyd George and Churchill alternated between resenting Northcliffe's power and turning to him for support. In the 1918 election, the press was one of the main pillars behind the return of Lloyd George's coalition.

Northcliffe's own maverick qualities, and his talk of the independence of the press, made him an uncomfortable and unreliable ally. Although generally supportive of the Conservatives and Unionists he was hardly in their pocket and was often critical of the crustier and more reactionary type of Tory. He held the national interest as more important than party or government interest – which was why he was prepared to take considerable risks in his anti-German campaign before 1914, or in his exposure of the shell scandal. The adversarial element in his relationship with government was strengthened by the fact that from 1906 to his death there were Liberal or Liberal coalition governments. But on the underlying constitutional question – who governs Britain, the elected government or the press? – Lloyd George as Prime Minister gave an unflinching answer. This was an important test of parliamentary government when the perceived power of the popular press was at its apogee.

Northcliffe's influence on the development of the popular press was, of course, manifold. His special love was always the *Daily Mail* and it, rather than *The Times* or *Mirror, The Observer* or *Weekly Dispatch*, most faithfully expressed his own ideas and approach. It had several qualities that seemed fresh: it was unashamed in blending fact with comment; it sought to brighten up people's lives; it went in for stunts – hilarious ones like the *Mail* hat, or more serious ones like the pre-war campaign for wholemeal 'standard bread'; it saw reportable copy in the mundane features of daily life (what people do on bank holidays, the weather, the progress of newfangled inventions like the telephone or typewriter); it was seriously interested in what appealed to women; it was concerned about the price and value of things (quite late in life, after the First World War, Northcliffe was campaigning against government waste); it also valued fine writing by journalists.

He loved the immediacy of news but he was also against vulgarity – which included vulgarly large advertisements and words of which he disapproved. He would have been aghast at much of British tabloid journalism in the 1970s and 1980s with its intrusions into privacy, its fetishes for sex, and its obsessions with showbiz and sporting personalities. He never exploited Lloyd George's colourful private life in his bouts of opposition to him, and from time to time he kept material out of his newspapers on grounds of taste. He was also never reconciled to aspects of his own success: for instance that the more popular press, because it could deliver large numbers of readers, became a stimulus to advertising and then economically dependent on it; or that the press had become an industry which had its own labour problems with print and journalists, and where he would be seen increasingly as an employer rather than as editor-in-chief.

Yet in fact it was his own industry's interest as much as the public interest which led Northcliffe into one of his most famous and expensive campaigns: the bitter attack in all his papers against Lever Brothers' proposed soap trust in late 1906. The trust would have reduced Northcliffe's advertising income, and Lever's tried to cut off an ounce from the standard 16 ounce bar of soap. A lot of Northcliffe's phobias came together in this vitriolic battle: his anxiety that American-style trusts should not get a grip in Britain (although Associated Newspapers was on its way to exerting a major if not monopolistic power in the British press); his concern about value for money and everyday necessities. There was an extremism about the reporting which, while it caused a collapse in Lever's market and in its share price, also laid open the *Mail, Mirror* and *Evening News* to enormous libel damages. In the course of 1907, Northcliffe had to pay the best part of £200,000, much of it from his own pocket, and the affair adversely affected his relations with senior staff who were on profit-sharing arrangements, and with his loyal editor Tom Marlowe, whom he thought of sacking and who never trusted his Chief's news judgement to the same extent again.

In his social attitudes he was of his time, and yet because of his skill in guessing what the readers might think and then playing it back to them with the authority of the *Mail,* he reinforced them. Attitudes and prejudices became the *Mail's* opinion, which became public opinion. Support for the British Empire, British values and the British race underlay not only the justice of the British case in the Boer War, but also the rivalry with imperial Germany which led up to the First World War. The late twentieth century would see some of this as unattractively racist: it was an era of Anglo-Saxon clubs (Lady Randolph Churchill, Winston's American mother, was planning a magazine round the turn of the century to be called *The Anglo-Saxon* with the motto, 'Blood is thicker than water'.) The Northcliffe who sterotyped 'the Hun' in the First World War could also make prejudiced comments about Jews and Scotsmen while employing and working closely with both.

He also had blind spots. He was not closely interested in the Irish question, even though as an act of family piety he bought the house outside Dublin where he had been born, and the Irish Free State came into existence in the year he died. Just before the outbreak of the First World War, when it looked as if a civil war was round the corner in Ireland, he took over large and expensive journalistic teams to be prepared: but this was for a story and not for any personal crusade.

Similarly, he was not often interested in social questions in England, even though issues of poverty, poor housing and unemployment were giving a fillip to the trade union and labour movements in the years before 1914. His own background and stance made him more concerned with flattering his readers that they could be 'thousand a year men'. This outlook changed somewhat towards the end of his life. The First World War and the Bolshevik revolution in Russia were searing experiences and he was concerned to see justice for the fighting soldiers on their return home, and to make sure that social improvements rendered Communism unnecessary. Hence the radical tone of the *Mail* in the 1918 election; his platform for Labour in that election was also a sly dig at the Lloyd George coalition, which the paper endorsed without enthusiasm. In 1921, he toured the coalfields in Yorkshire, Lancashire and Lanarkshire in his Rolls-Royce, admiring the fortitude of miners who had gone on strike after a wage cut: 'their only desire seems to be that their children shall get enough to eat', he told Rothermere.[20] He was appalled by the single room hovels in which whole families were living. But though he could respond to the suffering it was all rather baffling: the whole question was damnably complex, he told his brother.

His genuine curiosity, and his appetite for facts and things rather than theories, gave an unpredictability and a freshness to the *Mail* which he never injected into the establishment-minded *Times*. In spite of his considerable efforts and mordant criticism of the staff, *The Times* remained driven by editorial policy, some of it very long-standing, rather than by the drama of daily news. He enjoyed the prestige of being proprietor of *The Times*, but as with his other papers he could find it difficult to disabuse critics from the idea that he had written every word that was published.

Plainly he was a man who enjoyed power. Although he talked about the virtues of fairness in his press he could be immensely one-sided, as in the war with Levers, in his criticism of Churchill over the Dardanelles, or in the edict by which Edward Marshall Hall the barrister appeared only rarely in the *Mail* and then as Mr M. Hall, after he had unnecessarily referred to Mrs Alfred Harmsworth in a libel action. He could humiliate brutally, as well as be surprisingly generous to the members of his staff. The power of a more popular press became the intuitive, unforecastable power of one man, which could be frightening. Northcliffe's 'brainstorms' could cause reverberations throughout the country. And yet in some ways a man whose megalomaniac tendencies made it difficult to tell at what point physical or mental illness had taken over was ready to offset his own power: he sponsored the growth of the National Union of Journalists, and had little love for the combinations of press proprietors.

Underpinning his immense self-confidence and his sense of the responsibility of the press was awareness of his own good fortune. From a hand-to-mouth freelance he had made himself a successful publisher by the age of 30. Given his rocky home background of shabby gentility and too many mouths to feed, this amazing leap remained a source of wonder to him: he prized his luck, though he was not overmodest about the sustained hard work. Nor really is it right to see his publishing career as a sequence of effortless success. He had to struggle to make *Answers* work, to struggle with the *Mirror*, and to struggle with *The Times*. He also had failures: a Sunday paper was short-lived due to sabbatarian opposition, and his provincial papers in Portsmouth and Manchester were a write-off.

His mental restlessness was also a physical restlessness. He was always travelling – in France, across the Atlantic, between his various houses in Britain. Like many journalists since, he was bad at taking holidays, in that he could not stop working or sending comments and suggestions to his editors and managers. He did play golf, he enjoyed fishing for trout or tarpon, and from an early age he had a gift for playing tunes on the piano by ear. Yet he was also a man without convincing relaxations, prone to hypochondria, and whose health was as much a worry to his mother as his mother was to him.

In considering his impact there is a danger in rationalising Northcliffe's achievement so that it appears more consistent than it was: Lloyd George's 'grasshopper' gibe struck home because contemporaries saw him as erratic. Yet while details of tariff reform might bore him, he had powerful insights. One of these was into the inevitablility of a clash between imperial Germany, economically expansionist and building a powerful navy, and Britain and its empire. Northcliffe publicised the irreconcilable difference of values and interests between the two. At the same time, he foresaw the critical, growing importance of the United States (and to a lesser extent of Canada – in 1906 he told his mother that it had no poor people and could provide homes for millions of British immigrants). His work, not only in the War Mission, helped to lay the basis of a 'special relationship' between the two English-speaking countries which would be of significance for much of the twentieth century. He also, as an enthusiast for the Wright brothers, helped to spread the impression in Britain that technological and other novelties tended to originate in the United States.

Northcliffe was seen as a titan, which was why he founded no ordinary family business and no ordinary dynasty. Unlike more modern press proprietors he was not hungry for personal publicity in his own papers – though in a lucid moment towards the end he did ask that the best person on the night should be put in charge of an obituary tribute at *The Times*. He also tried to keep on terms with public figures with whom he differed on political or editorial grounds. This was shown in his relationship with Churchill whom he congratulated warmly on his marriage, but who returned a white china bust of Napoleon in 1916 when he was out of government after the Dardanelles, thinking that Northcliffe had insulted him. Apologising for a joke which Churchill had taken to heart, Northcliffe wrote, 'The attitude of my public newspaper towards public men has nothing to do with my private disposition towards individuals.' A year later Northcliffe was thinking that Churchill, as half American himself, could be suitable to run the War Mission.

Churchill, whose natural spirit was magnanimous, wrote to his own wife from France on 9 August 1922, in the last days of Northcliffe's life, after seeing Beaverbrook at Deauville:

Max gave me a most sombre account of Northcliffe's closing scenes. Violent resistances to treatment, two male nurses, great constitutional strength fighting with a foul poison, few friends, no children, mania, depression, frenzies. Lady Northcliffe receiving the doctor always in the presence of Sir Robert Hudson. Rothermere extremely interested in every turn of the case. Poor wretch – his worst enemies could not but grieve for him. Max professed great sympathy and sorrow and generally maintained a most correct attitude about the fate of his formidable rival. It cannot be long now.[21]

PART II

Harold Rothermere
The Brother

5

The Founder of the
Sunday Pictorial

Harold's career has often been treated, particularly by journalists with an admiration for his brother, as an uninteresting, sinister or comic addendum. Less well documented – he is said to have disposed of many of his own papers[1] – he has therefore been judged rather more on the public record of his newspapers, which gives an erratic picture. But his own personality was fully formed long before his brother's death: he had won recognition as a businessman and financier, he was running his own chain of newspapers, and had suffered grief in his private life.

In the impecunious north London homes of Alfred Harmsworth senior, Harold, as the second son, had no special privileges. He was not sent to a boarding school like Alfred who went to Stamford. Instead he was sent to the Philological School in Marylebone Road, later the Marylebone Grammar School, where an early report described him as particularly good at arithmetic. (Years later, right at the end of his life, he resigned as a governor of Marylebone Grammar School, in April 1938, in protest that the London County Council would not permit any of its schools to establish cadet corps.)

He left school early, and through the influence of his father's friend, Fred Wood – whom the family kept up with for years – he got a clerical job in a Tower Hill office of the Board of Trade. The most exciting thing that happened to him there was that a rat ran up his trouser leg, but in reality he was acquiring a grounding in office administration. Given his shyer more nervous disposition than Alfred, the civil service life, with its regularity and security, might well have suited him.

Still only 20, Harold had been working in the evenings at 26 Paternoster Square, helping with the *Answers* competitions and the inadequacies of the bookkeeping. It was at his suggestion that the magazine was extracted from Carr & Co. by the new company known as Answers Company Ltd, and in consequence he was offered the post of company secretary. Whether or not to accept was not an easy choice for him. It was not only that he was being asked to take a gamble, he was also being asked to give up an independent career and put himself at the command of a volatile and demanding elder brother.

The strong sense of family bore down on him, and the pill was sugared by an offer of a higher wage than he was already earning. On 10 May 1889, he wrote to the secretary of the local Marine Board at St Katherine Dock House on Tower Hill:[2]

> Sir – Having accepted an appointment in a publisher's office, I beg most respectfully to place in your hands my resignation of the post I now hold in this office. With your kind permission, I will leave on the 1st prox.
>
> I would take advantage of this opportunity to ask you to convey to the Local Marine Board my thanks for the great kindness which has been shown me during my period of service here. With yourself, Captain Watson, and the other gentlemen with whom I have served, my relations have been equally happy, and if for this reason alone, it is with great reluctance that I sever my connection with an office where I have spent so many pleasant days.
>
> I am, Sir,
>
>> Your most obedient servant,
>> Harold Harmsworth

For his next brother down, Cecil, this resignation letter was the most important single document in the history of the family. For those who lived through the tribulations of the early days, two facts stood out. One was that without the inspiration of Alfred there would have been no *Answers*, no other magazines. The second was that without the active participation of Harold, cutting costs, introducing systems and poring over ledgers, Alfred would probably have gone bankrupt. The margin between triumph and affluence on the one side, and calamity and Carey Street on the other, seemed narrow at the time.

Whereas Alfred demonstrated an editorial flair that was ruthless – his pound a week for life contest was a jugular blow to the greed of a certain section of the late Victorian public – Harold's ruthlessness was of a different kind. He had no sentimental attachment to the Beaumonts who had helped to stake Carr & Co. He knew that *Answers* and the other 'rags', as he would sometimes dismissively call them, were cheaply printed on poor paper so that someone like himself with weak eyesight could scarcely read any small type. He did not share Alfred's affection for journalists, asking once why his brother went on seeing his old friend Max Pemberton socially, now that he had become an employee.

In the Harmsworth offices Harold brought a dash of cold water and pessimism. A house magazine poem about billiards summed up the way he was seen:[3]

> There was a young cueist named Harold
> A fluker of shots, double-barrelled.

'How much? More expense?
Frightful rush – loss immense!'
You know him; you've heard it; that's Harold.

As the architect of the business success of the group, making the magazines profitable and turning round the loss-making *Evening News* almost instantly, it would be unfair to see Harold as merely a Scrooge. He was quick to see the growing circulations as market-places, opportunities to sell an *Answers* pen or an *Answers* watch to add to the revenue from the magazine itself. Whereas Alfred saw the growth of advertising as a mixed blessing, Harold seized it as valuable income. Harold, as the magazines multiplied and the brothers moved into newspapers, was also the driving force behind a major development for the newspaper industry – the introduction of certified net sales. Throughout most of the nineteenth century, newspapers and magazines had lied shamelessly about their sales which was all of a piece with small circulations, political subsidies and restricted literacy. But in the media revolution which the Harmsworths were promoting the stakes were different. Real net sales, achieved after the newsagents' returns had been deducted from copies distributed, were a badge of achievement and influence. They made possible a rate card for advertisers which told them reliably how many readers they would reach for a given expenditure. Certified net sales – certified by chartered accountants – took circulations out of the realms of propaganda and into a world of accurate comparison.

Substantial and genuine circulations could also enrich proprietors in another way, opening up a market for the publishers' shares. Here Alfred's skill in identifying with readers and getting them to identify with a perishable paper product – first as *Answerites*, later as *Mail* readers – was complemented by Harold's commercial acumen. By 1893, the year he got married, Harold was pushing hard for a public flotation of Answers Ltd. He estimated that the successful flotation of George Newnes Ltd had netted Newnes £600–700,000. In fact in that year the brothers only offered 50,000 ordinary £1 shares and 125,000 7 per cent preference shares to the public. They took care to encourage newsagents in particular to buy them.

Harold displayed creativity of a different kind a decade later in starting a vast timber and pulp business in Newfoundland. The idea was Alfred's. He had heard that the only paper to continue publishing during the French Revolution was one which owned its supplies of newsprint. One evening over dinner at Elmwood in 1902, reflecting on the inflation of newsprint prices during the Boer War and his fear that an Anglo-German war could cut off supplies from Scandinavia, he asked Harold what would happen to their publications if a European war broke out. Harold remarked that it would be very serious. Alfred then told his brother and Mayson Beeton, a *Mail* journalist who specialised in economic geography, to hurry to Newfoundland and buy tracts of timber. Within a week they were on board ship. Over the following three years Harold masterminded the purchase of 3,100 square miles and the establishment of a diversified Anglo-Newfound-land Development Company. Although its prime object was to produce pulp and paper, it became involved in housing, railways and shipping. It was the brothers' major investment outside newspapers and magazines. Harold subsequently argued for investment in Newfoundland at the expense of the British media, and thereafter he was chary of putting all his eggs in one basket.

According to Leicester, however, real divergences between the elder brothers began in the early 1890s. They were partly a matter of temperament and partly the product of specific business and editorial decisions, but did not damage the strong mutual affection which united them with the rest of the family. Nor did they put an end to a business collaboration which lasted to a significant degree until Northcliffe's death. However, they prefigured Harold's independent fortune, built up in the early years of the new century on the basis of the dividends and fees from the combined publishing ventures, and his separate newspaper interests in the *Daily Mirror* and *Sunday Pictorial*.

As a generalisation Alfred tended to be more optimistic and to think more of the long-term future. He was also quite sentimental about people, newspapers and periodicals. Harold, by contrast, prided himself on his unsentimentality; tended to fear that things would turn out wrong; and believed in taking what was going while you could.

With the magazines in the 1890s, Harold's passion for economy had led to friction when he successfully opposed the purchase of a periodical called *Black & White*, whose prospects he thought poor. He was also prepared to 'knife' magazines which were losing money or only marginally profitable: his advice was not taken in the early stages of the *Sunday Companion*, the Harmsworth religious weekly which he wanted to kill. The friction with Alfred on issues like this was also complicated because he sought to instill office discipline into the younger members of the family working in the firm. As has been seen, Alfred kept him out of the planning of the *Daily Mail* and when Leicester left the board of the magazine company in 1906, it was partly because Harold had killed a periodical in which he was interested.

On the other hand, one should not overdo the differences between two people with masterful personalities. Although Harold was kept out of some of the planning of the *Mail*, for instance, it was largely his money which had bought the Glasgow *Daily Record* in 1895, which in typographical and other ways was used as a test-bed for the *Mail*'s launch a year later. Similarly, Harold's skills came in handy when the *Mail* needed to cut costs after loss of the Lever soap libel cases; he advised Alfred on the private financial arrangements he needed to make to buy *The Times*; and crucially, he was as much in the confidence of George Sutton, the man who was effectively running the Amalgamated Press magazines at the start of the twentieth century, as Alfred himself. Indeed it was Harold at Cap Martin, in 1912, who proposed that Sutton should be made vice-chairman of the company and given a large salary increase when Alfred had failed to realise that Sutton was being unfairly treated.

Harold's affection for his older brother was whole-hearted. At a time when Alfred was suffering from one of his periodic bouts of ill-health, Harold wrote to him in November 1910 from Carmelite House; 'I do wish you would do as little work as possible. All your strength should be reserved for the purposes of recuperation. Business does not matter a rap when your own health is concerned. Even if anything did go wrong, what does it matter if the dividends of The Amalgamated Press are 25% instead of 40%, when the dividends are 25% you are in good health, and when they are 40% you are in bad health?' If the sentence was convoluted – and Harold had never been a journalist – the sense was clear.

An element of hero worship continued in Harold's attitude towards his older brother in spite of the divergences, which were also political at a time when Harold was basically Liberal and Alfred basically Conservative. Alfred respected him, even when he did not agree with him. Responding to a complaint from A. J. Balfour about some coverage in the Glasgow *Daily Record*, by 1910 fully under the control of Harold, Alfred wrote: 'My brother and I are great personal friends, but I have nothing to do with his political career and I never see his beastly paper. He and my brothers Leicester and Cecil have Radical bees in their bonnets. Harold is a particularly obstinate and determined man.'

Harold had married in 1893. Although shy and heavily built, he was good looking with a moustache which was popular among the Harmsworth men and their close associates. He was around 25, the magazine business was firmly established, and he was ready to move away from home. The girl he married was a pretty, blonde 18 year old named Lilian Share. She came from Forest Hill in south London, off the familiar Harmsworth territory. Her father, George Wade Share, was an unsuccessful City hardware merchant who subsequently went bankrupt. Her mother came from a strict Baptist background. It was a rather lower middle-class match.

Lilian was a bright girl and, it is said, had always wanted to marry money. Harold tended to be attracted to slim, good-looking women but his habits were unromantic: on honeymoon in Scotland he dictated business letters to a secretary at breakfast. She learnt quickly that in her husband's world, though money might be plentiful – and he was generous to those he loved – business came first. Following their honeymoon they went to live in North End House, Hampstead. Later they bought a country house for weekend use in Norfolk, Horsey Hall.

For a while they seem to have been reasonably happy together. Three sons arrived over four years – Vyvyan in 1894, Vere in 1895 and Esmond in 1898. They were duly destined for Eton. Their grandmother, old Mrs Harmsworth, would have taken the same interest in them that she did in all aspects of her expanding matriarchy. But although Harold and Lilian had increasing quantities of money, and all the domestic and nannying staff they could want, their actual relationship seems to have foundered in the early years of the twentieth century.

It is tempting to see their ample resources and the social influences of the Edwardian era as undermining the marriages of Alfred, Harold and Leicester. Fast money and fast women were in; dreary Victorian puritanism was out. But the truth is more complicated, more individual and in the case of the collapse of Harold's marriage, difficult to establish. Before his crippling car crash St John was carrying on a discreet affair with Lilian, and she helped to nurse him afterwards much to Harold's irritation. Nevertheless Harold and Lilian stayed together up to the end of the 1900s, by which time they had established a family base at La Dragonnière, near Monte Carlo, which was much used in the winter. Northcliffe, Churchill and many others were to stay there, and it would provide happy memories for Harold's grandchildren many decades later.

La Dragonnière seems to have established a taste for France in Lilian, and when she separated from Harold she stayed in that country. She was well provided for and, though Harold at least once seriously considered marrying again – to Rita Redhead – his anxiety that his mother would disapprove of a divorce stayed his hand.[4] It may have been through St John, however, that Lilian first got to know a group of French writers for whom she became a friend and patron. André Gide's mother owned a house by his Perrier source at Vergèze, which Harold had helped to buy for St John before his accident. Through Gide, Lilian, after she was living on her own, got to know T. S. Eliot and many others. But she is remembered as rather cold, cutting off contact with her own children, and arbitrarily switching her favour from writers she had taken up and who had come to depend on her subsidies. She never attended the wedding of her one surviving son, Esmond, and her grandchildren could only remember her visiting their house twice. Harold, however, retained some feeling for her until her death, in Switzerland from cancer, in 1937. He continued to wear a medallion of her and visited her when she was dying. Although her home was filled with valuable first editions and literary mementoes, Esmond sold the lot without compunction.

The disappearance of Lilian inaugurated a much more unstable phase in the life of Harold, who had been made a baronet in 1910 and sold his

Daily Mail shares at about the same time. Just as Northcliffe had adopted a restless pattern of perpetual movement from place to place, so did Harold. He wandered between the south of France, Dornoch in Scotland, Norfolk and Hemsted in Kent where he bought an estate of 10,000 acres, largely because his eldest son Vyvyan loathed London. In London, he lived in hotels, occupying suites in the Ritz and elsewhere. It was a rackety kind of existence, not ideal for the teenage boys for whom he was now responsible. He had his girlfriends. His business came to him wherever he was. Over everything there hung shadows of international upheaval: a potential civil war in Ireland and an arms race with the Kaiser's Germany.

Of his sons he got on best with Vyvyan, much less well with Vere and Esmond. Vere, thought to look like St John, related more easily with St John and Northcliffe. The memory of the two who were killed is inevitably overlaid by a sense of gallant youth snuffed out, of loss that was cruelly commonplace in a generation largely wiped out in the combatant nations. Vyvyan and Vere responded to the Rupert Brooke moment in British history, strongly urged not only in their uncle's newspapers but also in their father's *Daily Mirror* – bought by Harold in 1914 and carrying columns of stirring patriotic propaganda by Horatio Bottomley, editor of *John Bull* and later convicted of swindles in Victory Bonds.

The younger boy, Vere, was killed first. He had been wounded at Gallipoli, came back to Britain, and then as a lieutenant was killed in the battle of the Ancre, in France, on 13 November 1916. He was leading his company in an attack. An account by his commanding officer, published in the *Daily Mail*, stated:

> In going across No Man's Land he was wounded in the throat. In spite of this he rallied a party of another battalion and such of his own battalion as were in the immediate neighbourhood and led the attack on the first German trenches. He saw that these were cleared of the Germans and advanced with a number of men on the second line. In or near this line he was again wounded, this time in the right shoulder. He sat down and lit a cigarette. Almost immediately he got up and collected such men as were near him and led the attack on the third line. On or just before reaching it he was hit by a shell and instantly killed.

It was Vere, who had been at Osborne and Dartmouth, who had written the letter to his uncle St John a month before which had so moved Northcliffe and other members of the family. He had dwelt on his attachment to his fellow soldiers, on the impossibility of imagining that he might grow old, on his fear that he would be no good in business. He also set down frankly his feelings about his father:

> He has been so good to me, and he has built up such a position for his three sons that it will be heartrending for him to have part of his life's work wasted

... It is curious how reserved he is with me and I with him. The feeling – awfully strong – is there on both sides, but what is bred in the bone of every Englishman stops it coming out. If I fall, do not mourn, but be glad and proud. It is not a life wasted but gloriously fulfilled.

Both Vere and Vyvyan received and resigned staff posts, so that they could be in the front line. Both left nearly all their money to their regiments. Of the two Vyvyan, who died in 1918 after winning a Military Cross, had made the biggest impact in his brief life. Handsome, he had won prizes and recognition at Eton. Years later Lord Alexander of Tunis told a niece that he had been one of the most remarkable young officers in the Irish Guards. Like his brother he had a strong attachment to his regimental comrades, worrying about going to a music hall on leave and amusing himself while his friends were suffering.

Vyvyan was first wounded in Flanders, then receiving mortal wounds at the battle of Cambrai, but actually dying in Lady Northcliffe's nursing home in London in early 1918. He had won the MC by putting two machine guns out of action. Before he returned to France for the last time his father told him that there was no need for him to go back: he would not hear of it. His father had invited the young Peggy Redhead – who subsequently married Vyvyan's brother Esmond – with her sister to stay at the Ritz the night before Vyvyan returned to France. Peggy was more than a little in love with him at the time.

Much later she recalled how she had seen Vyvyan off at the station after they had gone to the theatre together the previous evening. They sat together on a bench and, to pass the time, she said, 'I like your boots.' He replied that no one had said such a nice thing to him before.[5]

Dying in London, Vyvyan was buried in Highgate Cemetery, better known for the memorial to his father's nightmare, Karl Marx. His younger brother Esmond, when Lord Rothermere, would be sending a poppy wreath from Carmelite House to his grave on Armistice Day, long after the Second World War. For their father the premature death of his two eldest sons was a blow from which he never really recovered. He endowed a professorial chair in naval history after Vere at Cambridge University, and another in American history after Vyvyan at Oxford.[6] He made sure that his third son, Esmond, would not serve overseas. And towards the end of his life, at Stody House in Melton Constable, his bed faced a wall hung with de Laszlo portraits of his mother and the two dead sons.

Meanwhile, Sir Harold Harmsworth, Baronet had become Baron Rothermere of Hemsted,[7] a newspaper proprietor in his own right, and had made his own contribution to the war effort. The barony may have been partly for services to the Liberal government in hushing up the Marconi affair. His mother saw him introduced into the House of Lords in 1914, which was also the year in which he bought the *Daily Mirror*

7. Northcliffe (*left*) with his brother Harold, 1st Viscount Rothermere (*right*) and Harold's son, Esmond Harmsworth, MP (*centre*).

8. Northcliffe leaving the White House in Washington with T. Wickham Steed, Editor of *The Times*, in August 1921

9. Lilian Harmsworth and her three sons, Vyvyan, Vere and Esmond.

10. Harold and his wife Lilian at Ascot in 1911.

11. A view of the paper mills at Grand Falls, Newfoundland.

12. Sir Harold Harmsworth in 1912.

13. Nikitina the dancer by the Hungarian sculptor, Strobl.

SUNDAY PICTORIAL, Sunday, March 14, 1915.

PAGES AND PAGES OF PICTURES :: ALL THE NEWS

SUNDAY · PICTORIAL

24 PAGES. THE GREAT SUNDAY PICTURE NEWSPAPER. **24 PAGES.**

No. 1. SUNDAY, MARCH 14, 1915. One Penny.

THE TASK OF THE RED CROSS

Carrying a soldier to the base hospital.

This is a case of frost-bite, and it will be seen that both the patients' feet are bandaged. This was the work of the Red Cross man who is now carrying him to hospital for treatment.

EARL'S SISTER SENTENCED.

Oliver Herbert, acquitted. Lady Ida Sitwell. Julian Field, guilty.

The trial of Lady Ida Sitwell, Lord Londesborough's sister, for conspiracy to defraud was concluded yesterday, when she was found guilty and sentenced to three months in the second division. In the circles are the co-defendants, Julian Field and Oliver Herbert. The Old Bailey was crowded with well-dressed people who came to hear the concluding stage of this strange case.

ALL THAT WAS LEFT OF A BIG GUN.

Gun destroyed by heavy shell fire.

This picture gives an idea of the damage done when an official report baldly states that " we destroyed an enemy battery." The gun has been reduced to scrap iron, but no gunner will leave his post while the weapon can be worked.

14. The first issue of the *Sunday Pictorial*, 14 March 1915.

from his brother for £100,000. It was a shrewd buy. While Northcliffe never greatly cared for the *Mirror* – once he had defied the fates by turning it from a failure into a success – Rothermere took it over at exactly the right time.

The outbreak of war created an instant demand for pictures. No special journalistic wizardry was needed. A picture paper specialising in photographs, drawings and cartoons was simply carried upward by the demand for war news amongst those with modest reading abilities. It is difficult to appreciate, from the perspective of the late twentieth century, how valuable a poorly reproduced picture newspaper might seem in a period before radio, let alone television. Rothermere's sharp eye on costs maximised the profits; Northcliffe, much to his annoyance, saw the *Mirror* outsell the *Mail*. From 1914 to 1922 the *Mirror* supported the Liberals.

Within six months of the start of the war, Rothermere decided to capitalise on his success by launching a Sunday version of the *Mirror*. It was launched at very short notice, two weeks ahead of a Sunday edition of the *Daily Sketch*. Called the *Sunday Pictorial*, and appearing for the first time on 14 March 1915, it was a phenomenon. On its first three successive Sundays it sold 1,033,203 copies, 1,554,276 copies and 1,840,722 copies. It was fabulous – four times the initial sale of the *Daily Mail* by its third issue.

Priced at a penny for twenty-four pages, it mixed patriotic commentary pieces and light gossip with pictures on the front and back, a two page picture spread in the centre, and two other picture pages. The cartoons included German and American ones. Artists' drawings were obtained from other sources, such as the *Sphere* and *Illustrated London News*. Page three, the *Sun*'s girlie page sixty years later, was the main news page.

Looking at the first issue one can see its appeal. There were drawings of two soldiers who had won VCs, Michael O'Leary and Sergeant Hogan, and photos of 'The Brides in the Bath', the four women involved in a sensational murder case. A tough leader demanded better treatment for British prisoners of war in Germany, suggesting that German POWs should not be treated so well. A page of gossip by 'Mr Mayfair' was called 'Nuts and Wine – Gossip for the After-Dinner Hour' and a strip cartoon described the adventures of Mr Jerry of Jerrybuilt Villa, Suburbia. There were Christmas cracker puns in the style of the old Harmsworth magazines, a word-changing competition to be accompanied by a sixpenny postal order, a page for 'little people', a romantic serial, sport and a football competition. Feature writers in the early days included Horatio Bottomley (referring to 'Germhuns' and 'Germhuny'), Arnold Bennett and Austin Harrison, who edited the *English Review*.

Some items were amusingly written. An article in the first issue on night clubs showed how the *Sunday Pictorial* tried to lighten the drama of war.

> The new order prohibiting military officers in uniform from entering London night clubs came into force on Friday night. It has led to an amusing situation, for the order does not apply to naval officers or private soldiers in uniform. The military, it was stated by one of the authorities, had no power over naval officers. It did not appear necessary to extend the order to affect private soldiers as well as officers.
>
> Large numbers of young officers in mufti may be found at most of the night clubs every night, paying almost as much for cider-cup as in the old days they used to pay for champagne. The night club is a comparatively harmless institution. It certainly induces young men to pay ridiculous prices for food and drink and it keeps them up when they ought to be in bed, but the police supervision is very strict, and there is nothing about the modern night club to move the moralist to tears.

The first issue also included a message from Northcliffe in the list of those sending good wishes, as well as a Harmsworth in-joke headed 'Sir Thomas Lipton's Peril'. Lipton, friend of old Mrs Harmsworth and promoter of St John's Perrier through his grocery chain, had written to Sir Robert Hudson, later to marry Lady Northcliffe and at that time head of the British Red Cross, to say that he was 'very nearly finished off' by an Austrian shell in Belgrade. It was like a private postcard to all the Harmsworths who would be reading Rothermere's first Sunday number.

The successful launch of the *Sunday Pictorial* was the one genuine journalistic triumph in Rothermere's life. Compared with the difficulties which Lord Beaverbrook encountered in getting the *Sunday Express* established after 1918,[8] or the problems Rothermere's grandson faced with the *Mail on Sunday* in the 1980s, he scored a quick bull's eye. Starting Sunday papers presents particular hazards, compared with daily papers, because it can take longer to imprint the paper's character on readers. Without the confidence of having his own Canadian newsprint supplies he might never have launched such a venture in wartime.

With two national papers and a significant Glasgow regional paper under his control by 1915, Rothermere was no longer just Northcliffe's younger brother but a significant public figure in his own right. Just when he was launching the *Sunday Pictorial* he was trying to buy *The Observer*. His skill at investment had made him rich. It was not surprising that Lloyd George, possibly egged on a little by Northcliffe, wanted to make use of him.

His first job was to sort out the army clothing department where the huge wartime demand had shown up incompetence and profiteering. Meeting him in the Ritz his brother Cecil, who was later remembered as extremely anti-Semitic himself, found him alleging that the supplies were endangered because East End Jewish tailors had been running away from the Zeppelins. Whether because he was reckoned to have done well with army clothing, or simply on the principle that it was better to keep the Harmsworths occupied, Lloyd George in November 1917 made him Air Minister. (Beaverbrook claimed to have suggested this as a way of weakening Northcliffe's criticism.) He was the first holder of the office, and his task was to merge the Army's Royal Flying Corps with the Navy's air section.

Rothermere's time at the Air Ministry was unhappy and punctuated by rows, but not totally unsuccessful. The two services did merge on 1 April 1918, Rothermere having gained royal approval for the blue colour to be worn by the Royal Air Force. But he himself resigned just over three weeks later, pleading ill-health. In fact Northcliffe told his friend Evelyn Wrench that he and their mother had feared Rothermere was on the verge of a complete breakdown.

The trouble was that he had been pitched into an extremely tricky situation, where the Harmsworth reputation for fair-mindedness and his business ability were insufficient, at a time of personal crisis. It was simply not possible to transfer the authority of a businessman or press lord into a new ministry being welded together in wartime, where servicemen and civil servants had to collaborate, and the army was resisting the loss of its air arm. His shyness, lack of diplomacy and weakness at intrigue all told against him.

The appointment started out well, in that Rothermere took on the post after it was known that his brother had publicly refused it. But disasters began when he summoned the strong-minded Sir Hugh Trenchard to see him in his suite at the Ritz, in December. In Northcliffe's presence he offered him the position of Chief of the Air Staff. But the brothers also said that they were about to launch a press campaign against the generals, Haig and Robertson, and it would be good for them to have his assistance.

Trenchard turned down the offer at once, and an angry argument followed which lasted $12\frac{1}{2}$ hours. Eventually he agreed to take it, on condition that he consulted Haig first, in the clear realization that he would have to fight Rothermere and Northcliffe for the duration. The mutual dislike between Rothermere and Trenchard, shown on issues great and small, wore out both men. Trenchard went first, on 12 April, in effect fired. Rothermere who had received violent memoranda from Trenchard, then circulated round the Cabinet a hostile memorandum describing his opponent as 'perfectly impossible ... entirely without imagination ... a square peg in a round hole'. Bonar Law, the Conservative Leader who was deputy prime minister, was shocked at the personal vitriol: he rang Rothermere and told him he ought to resign, and should get Beaverbrook to help him draft an appropriate letter. When he left on 25 April Air Force officers and civil servants at the Hotel Cecil, the Air Ministry building in the Strand, cheered and waved newspapers. One told the passers-by, 'A victory at home. Lord Rothermere has gone.'

It was a very low point in Rothermere's career. The difficulties of his unfamiliar job had been compounded by seeing the slow death of his son and heir Vyvyan, who finally died on 12 February 1918 from the wounds he had received the previous autumn at the battle of Cambrai. Vyvyan, described by Northcliffe as 'a very able young man', had joined the Irish Guards within days of the outbreak of war, and was at the front by the end of 1914. He had been wounded twice before, each time returning to the battlefield. He was the most gifted of the boys and the one his father could relate to.

Although his time at the Air Ministry was brief, the episode had a considerable impact on the rest of Rothermere's life. It immediately entitled him to a rise in the aristocratic world – a viscountcy which the baron acquired in 1919. His experience of the civil service also fuelled his first post-war campaign, against waste and 'squandermania', in which Northcliffe's papers also joined. It gave him considerable insight into the needs of the air force, and its potential in modern war, which became important in the 1930s. And it also drew him closer to two significant personalities – Lloyd George and Beaverbrook.

While no doubt aware that his time in the ministry had been less than triumphant, Lloyd George wrote generously at his departure: 'It is no small thing to have taken over the conduct of an entirely new arm of the Services ... and bestowed on its administration an initiative which has given the new force a real supremacy at the front.' Rothermere swung his papers behind the re-election of Lloyd George and the coalition in 1918. While not close to Lloyd George, he remained on generally friendly terms with him throughout the 1920s as his own concerns became more coloured by anti-socialism, and his antagonism to Stanley Baldwin soured his rapprochement with the Conservative Party.

The connection with Beaverbrook, who was eleven years younger, was to be significant for both men right up to Rothermere's death when he was carrying out a task rather thoughtfully conceived for him in 1940 by the then Minister for Aircraft Production. It was a commercial and a political relationship, and also a warm personal friendship. It was sometimes difficult to fathom for journalists on two papers which were deadly rivals in the 1920s and 1930s, the *Mail* and the *Express*. Though the facts of what happened in 1918 after Rothermere had been forced to go from the Air Ministry cannot easily be established, both the Harmsworth and Aitken families are agreed that Beaverbrook took Rothermere in hand and nursed him back to self-respect.[9] Beaverbrook sought to conceal the extent to which Rothermere had left under duress, and had him to stay at Cherkley, his home at Leatherhead in Surrey.

From Rothermere's point of view, Beaverbrook had many pleasing qualities: he was a self-made millionaire, he was a Canadian, he was exuberant, he was a good host, and he had come into politics and then newspapers via his money and unabashed imperial sentiments. He had guile and a remarkable talent for helping people, particularly those who had had their troubles. From Beaverbrook's side, at a stage when he thought of himself chiefly as a businessman and financier, Rothermere was the Harmsworth with whom he could get on most easily.

As Max Aitken he had only come to Britain in 1910 and had had a whirlwind career. In 1910–11, he had been Unionist MP for Ashton-under-Lyne. He led a consortium of Conservatives and Unionists which had bought *The Globe* evening paper from Hildebrand Harmsworth, and his skills as a go-between in the fields of business and politics really took off when his friend and fellow Canadian, Bonar Law, became leader of the Consevatives in 1911. After making a loan to R. D. Blumenfeld, American editor of the *Daily Express* in the same year, he acquired the controlling shares in that paper five years later. He had been knighted in 1911, made a baronet in 1916 just prior to the toppling of Asquith in which he played a vigorous part, and was made a baron in December of the same year, over the doubts of King George V. When he entered the House of Lords the following year, Rothermere was one of his two sponsors.

Because of what the Harmsworths had achieved, and Rothermere's business genius – he had for instance advised Reginald McKenna on the liquidation of British investments in the United States to help the war effort – there was a sense in which Beaverbrook looked up to him. But at the end of the 1914–18 war, when Beaverbrook and Northcliffe were dividing up the propaganda territory between them on behalf of the Lloyd George coalition, Beaverbrook may also have seen him as the more malleable of the brothers. There is some evidence, too, that when Rothermere was recuperating from his near breakdown, the intimacy between them gave Beaverbrook some knowledge and information which he could have used against him.

Between the end of the war and Northcliffe's death in 1922 Rothermere tried to get his own life together again after the traumas he had been through. He worried about Northcliffe's increasingly doubtful health – his brother was staying at La Dragonnière in early 1919 – kept in touch with their mother, was pleased that his son Esmond had become MP for the Isle of Thanet, and interested himself in his anti-squandermania campaign. The idea that Esmond should become MP for Thanet – the constituency which included Elmwood and which half a century later was to be represented in parliament by Jonathan Aitken, a scion of the house of Beaverbrook – was apparently put together by Northcliffe and Rothermere one day at Elmwood when they realised there was a vacancy. This was a period when the support of a

Conservative association could be gained for a subscription of £1,000 a year; the Harmsworths were a prominent family in the district; and Esmond actually wanted to try a career in politics.

When elected he was the youngest MP in the Commons and was immediately taken abroad as Lloyd George's ADC – and also a two-way contact with the press proprietors – at the Versailles peace negotiations. Esmond made a few anti-waste speeches while his father, to show his small regard for party affiliations, used the *Daily Mirror* to get an Anti-Waste candidate elected in the next door seat of Dover in 1921. In fact Rothermere's campaign for national frugality had satirical aspects: he took to having austerity lunches, at which no wine was served, and moved out of his hotel suites into a small flat.

His business interests seem to have flourished despite the post-war difficulties. In 1919 he had thought of selling his provincial papers, but nothing came of it. By 1922, before Northcliffe's death, the *Mirror* had achieved the world's greatest sale, in excess of 3 million copies.

In spite of post-war unemployment the heartbreak of the war years was giving way to the roaring 'twenties and Rothermere himself was not left untouched. His son Esmond had married Margaret Hunam Redhead in 1920. She was a fun-loving Roman Catholic girl who had already eloped to Ireland with someone else;[10] she had got to know Esmond after Rothermere had met her mother. It was through Esmond's wife, known as Peggy, that Rothermere came to know her cousin Rita: his affair with Rita Redhead became probably the most serious of his liasions after his wife left him. He seriously thought of marrying her, a prospect which filled Esmond and Peggy with anxiety.

He also found a job in the firm for her half-brother, Robert, who eventually became managing director of Associated Newspapers. Robert Redhead's memory of his hiring throws an amusing light on the Rothermere of those years. He had been invited by Esmond and Peggy, in 1921, to join them on holiday in the South of France. Rothermere arrived unexpectedly. Redhead was having a late breakfast on the terrace when Rothermere suddenly appeared and barked, 'What are you doing here?' He explained. 'Do you want a job?' asked Rothermere. Nothing at the time was further from Redhead's mind – he was part way through an undergraduate course at Cambridge – but on the spur of the moment he said, 'Yes.'

Rothermere then told him he must travel to London at once and hand a letter, which he then promptly wrote, to Andrew Caird, a senior manager. Caird then sent him to start on the *Leeds Mercury*. In a space of forty-eight hours, therefore, Redhead had lost his holiday and Cambridge place, but gained a job and a career. (On another occasion, after someone had told Rothermere that Redhead, known as Bobby, was going to be 21, Rothermere asked him round to his Savoy suite on his birthday. When he arrived, Rothermere asked why he had come.

Reminded that he had invited him on his birthday, he shouted out to his secretary to give young Redhead a cheque for £100. No wonder Redhead concluded that his gruff and aggressive manner was rather misleading.)

The fleets of Rolls-Royces, including Rothermere, still called regularly on old Mrs Harmsworth at Poynters where the frock-coated men with top hats who were her sons came to call on her; and she, wheeled down in a chair to feed her ducks, would make sure that the weaker ones got their fair shares.

Around the Harmsworths themselves, other dynasties of friends and dependants had begun to flourish, in spite of Northcliffe's campaign against nepotism at the *Mail*. One of the more interesting involved the Bartholomews. Ivy Bartholomew was Lilian Rothermere's sister; her relative was Harry Guy Bartholomew who had joined the *Mirror* almost at birth. 'Bart's' origins were obscure – one senior Associated Newspapers executive firmly believed that he was an illegitimate son of Northcliffe – but he worked his way up the *Mirror* until as editor in the 1930s, supported by Rothermere's nephew Cecil King, he turned it into a downmarket crusading paper of the left.

At Northcliffe's death in 1922, therefore, Rothermere was already a rich man with a distinct character of his own. He did not really need the Northcliffe inheritance. The energy and ingenuity which he put into untangling the complex legacies of his brother owed much to the strong family sentiment which had bound them all together, in spite of their differences. He probably did not feel the world took him as seriously as it should, or as it had taken his brother. Behind the political campaigning that lay ahead, which on the whole was not to the commercial advantage of his newspapers, lay an elusive quest for the recognition to which his millions of readers and wealth might have entitled him.

6
From 1922 to 1929

Northcliffe's death brought out Rothermere's insight into finance and his skill as a negotiator. Because of his brother's delight in mystification and complicated private life, there was the potential for immense litigation and family scandal as Mrs Wrohan and other girlfriends staked claims or baulked others. Furthermore, the future of *The Times* was at stake: while Northcliffe's 1919 will had given John Walter and his family the option to buy back the paper, Walter had actually sold his remaining shares just before Northcliffe's death, and a doubtful will drawn up within weeks of that event had made Lady Northcliffe sole executrix and no mention of the Walter option. There were various groups keen to get their hands on *The Times*, not least one composed of the friends of Lloyd George who planned to install him as editor.

The March 1919 will, whose executors were Henry Arnholz and Sir George Sutton, was extremely comprehensive and showed Northcliffe trying to remember everyone for whom he had had affection. He confirmed the settlements he had made for his illegitimate children long before; he left his Carlton Gardens home to his wife, until whenever she might marry again; Elmwood was left to St John, on condition that he used it for at least two months a year and let those who had traditionally stayed there go on borrowing it. St John's nurse was left £500, the printer of *The Times* £100; every father of a print chapel received £50 and every director got £1,000.

The Sylvan Debating Club 'founded by my revered Father' was left £100 a year, but was required to appoint his private secretary Francis Humphrey Davy as its secretary. Codicils required Rothermere to sell the companies only to a British-born person, or predominantly British organisation, and ensured that if either Tom Marlowe or Sir Andrew Caird were dismissed following a sale of Associated Newspapers, then each of them would receive £25,000.

The main body of the will, however, concerned the division of his income into hundredths and its careful allocation to his widow, relations, and friends. For instance, Lady Northcliffe would have 25 per cent of the income, cut to 10 per cent if she married again. His mother would receive 8 per cent. His sisters Violet, Christabel and Geraldine got 2 per cent each, St John 3 per cent, Vyvyan 1 per cent and Charles 0.5 per cent. His former mistress and secretary, Louise Owen, was left 2 per cent. Sutton and Arnholz, the trustees, got 7 and 3 per cent respectively. Tom Marlowe had to make do with 0.25 per cent. In a catch-all clause he asked his trustees to go on making payments to those to whom he had been giving periodical subsidies.

Although he was not an executor, Rothermere worked closely with Sutton and Arnholz to sort out the Northcliffe legacy. There were three issues which were interrelated: dealing with Lady Northcliffe's claim to supersede the 1919 will, buying or selling *The Times*, and reconstructing his own newspaper business so that it could take on board the *Mail, Sunday Dispatch* and *Evening News* at a fair price to the Northcliffe estate.

Sutton, as the leading executor, now demonstrated the confidence which Northcliffe and Rothermere had placed in him for years. He moved at once to have the 1919 will recognised as definitive. This caused Lady Northcliffe, who was well advised legally, to threaten action to have 'her' 1922 will asserted instead. This was probably bluff, since the 1922 will had been signed 'Harmsworth' and showed other indications that it was made when Northcliffe was of unsound mind. But it opened the way to a settlement between the executors and Lady Northcliffe, under which she received a larger immediate payment of £225,000. This was a better deal for her because the 1919 will contained the stipulation that her income would be cut drastically on remarriage, when she would also lose Carlton Gardens. It was an open secret that she and Sir Robert Hudson were wanting to marry – Northcliffe himself had anticipated this – and they did so less than a year after his death.

The possibility that Lady Northcliffe might be in a position to dictate the future of *The Times* had drawn her into the intrigues surrounding the future of her husband's press properties. Indeed the pressures on Sutton were immense. The Lloyd George coalition was cracking up. The line to be taken by *The Times* in particular was seen as of political importance. Its reputation for authoritative independence, totally compromised if it fell under Lloyd George's direct control, might be affected to some degree by any other formula. And in all this Rothermere himself was an interested party. Within weeks of his brother's death he had bought his shares in the *Mail*, and he was acting as though he would like *The Times* as well.

Sutton, as executor, had another problem; the Northcliffe estate was liable to very considerable estate duty. By 8 September 1922 he had to pay £850,000 to the Inland Revenue – which he borrowed from Coutts Bank – and he estimated that he would need to find a further £1.8m within six months. Fortunately for the estate, however, the political situation meant that *Times* shares could command fancy prices.

The upshot was that John Walter's option to buy back *The Times*, which had apparently died in the summer of 1922, was resuscitated without opposition from Lady Northcliffe and Walter secured financial backing from J. J. Astor, whose father W. W. Astor had bought *The Observer* in 1911. The Astors were an American family with plenty of money. Even so the courts ruled that the estate had to get the 'best price' for *The Times*, and Rothermere believed that by offering £1.35m for Northcliffe's shares it would be hard to equal him. However, Astor, who had to produce £1.58m to buy out the Northcliffe estate and Sir John Ellerman, was able to do just that. The new proprietors took over on 23 October 1922, the day Bonar Law formally accepted the task of forming a new Conservative government.

There has been some speculation that Rothermere was not totally committed to his own bid – that he was upping the stakes for the benefit of his brother's estate and all the members of the family and old retainers who stood to benefit. Indeed in those terms he was remarkably successful. *Times* shares which Walter had sold to Northcliffe for £1 each as recently as June were required to change hands at 52 shillings and sixpence (£2.62½p) only four months later.

However, the evidence is strong that Rothermere was completely serious in his attempt to buy *The Times*, and upset when it slipped away from Harmsworth control. A letter he wrote to Sir George Sutton on 12 October stated that 'the sum I am prepared to bid is probably higher than would be offered by any other possible purchaser', but he was not prepared to bid just to fix a price at which the shares could be offered to the Walter family. In reality, this was what happened; given that the courts had accepted the Walter option as valid, it was probably inevitable.

Rothermere had also taken steps to arrange finance to buy *The Times*, as part of an operation in which debentures were being issued to pay for his purchase of the *Mail*, and there was talk, too, of Esmond being installed in *The Times* offices as a manager. Certainly, more recent Harmsworths have felt that the family was outwitted in its attempt to hang on to its most prestigious paper, as a result of collusion and disloyalty. Lady Northcliffe, who made retention of the Walter option possible and at whose remarriage no Harmsworths turned out, was regarded with distrust. So, too, was Sir Campbell Stuart, Northcliffe's confidant, who was managing director of *The Times* and helped put together the Astor package. (J. J. Astor then added insult to injury by being elected a Conservative for Dover in the general election of November 1922, the seat where Rothermere's Anti-Waste candidate had triumphed.)

Behind the opposition to Rothermere buying *The Times* was not only the Walter family's keenness to regain a portion of its inheritance, and some antipathy to the way in which Northcliffe had intervened there, but also suspicion of Rothermere himself. He was undoubtedly seen as someone who would intervene in the editorial policy of the paper, though in unpredictable ways: a maverick, with vaguely coalitionist sentiments and a personal regard for Lloyd George, he was not loved either politically or personally by solid, respectable Conservatives.

At the height of this drama over *The Times* the Walter family had been told – but refused to believe – a report that Rothermere had been to see Bonar Law to offer his support in the political crisis and impending election in return for an earldom for himself and a ministry for his son. Both J. C. C. Davidson, private secretary to Law, and Law's son have testified to the truth of this: Lloyd George's trading in honours and attempts to influence the press were precisely what Law and the anti-coalition Conservatives wanted to have done with.[11]

The death of Northcliffe also precipitated a reconstruction of Rothermere's own newspaper interests and the papers he bought from the estate. On 27 September 1922, the Daily Mail Trust was registered. This was to become the master company of the Harmsworths' press and other interests up to the present day. It was capitalised at £1.6m, divided into £1 ordinary shares and its directors were: Lord Rothermere of Hemsted, Benenden, Kent (he was just about to sell this estate, and the house would be incorporated into Benenden School, the new boarding public school for girls); Leicester Harmsworth, MP; S. H. Lever (an accountant who became a director of the Bank of Montreal); Frederick Szarvasy (Hungarian-born chairman of the British Foreign and Colonial Corporation, who was a close financial associate of Rothermere's and may have encouraged him in his Hungarian adventure five years later); and Sir Mayson Beeton.

Rothermere produced £1.6m in cash to buy Northcliffe's newspaper shares from his estate, was given shares in the trust in exchange, and then brought together the *Mirror* and *Sunday Pictorial* with the Northcliffe concerns in a new firm he controlled through the trust. The accompanying statement showed how tightly he had held the purse-strings of his own two national papers: he had owned almost half the ordinary shares in the *Mirror,* and 700,000 out of 750,000 ordinary shares in his own creation, the *Sunday Pictorial.*

Although from Rothermere's viewpoint the creation of this trust – subsequently known as the Daily Mail and General Trust – may have seemed a run-of-the-mill financial initiative, it was to be of enormous importance to his family, and to the newspaper group which he and his brother had created. Although shares might be sold to outsiders, it was to remain family controlled. It was also to prove a remarkable instrument for continuity, a major advantage which family companies can have over others and which can offset such disadvantages as caution and lack of incentive to perform.

From the first the trust's articles were widely set, entitling it to invest wherever it saw fit and reflecting Rothermere's philosophy of eggs-in-many-baskets. Its role in continuity was apparent in that, twenty-five years after it was formed, it still had three of the same directors (Sir Samuel Lever, F. A. Szarvasy and Sir Mayson Beeton); two other directors, Sir George Sutton and Lt-Col Wilfrid Wild (husband of Northcliffe's sister Violet), who had roots in the origin of the business, were still serving as late as 1947.

One sadness, for both Rothermere and Sutton, was that the need to pay death duties on Northcliffe's estate led to the sale of the Amalgamated Press. These were the original Harmsworth Brothers magazines – the ones which Rothermere had not knifed – which had proved the golden nest egg which had made possible the *Daily Mail*, the *Sunday Pictorial* and the great enterprise in Newfoundland. Rothermere had always had a soft spot for the magazines. In the post-war years they had been paying Sutton the stupendous sum of £30,000 a year as managing director. The Amalgamated Press was sold to the Berry brothers, Gomer and William, who already owned the *Sunday Times* and were building up a formidable provincial chain. Sutton switched to the *Mail* newspaper group.

It is possible that frustration over the loss of *The Times*, plus the fact that he had set aside funds which now needed another home, launched Rothermere on a newspaper alliance with Beaverbrook. Although this might seem confusing to journalists on the *Mail* and *Express*, who increasingly saw each other as deadly rivals, it was the product of almost a decade of friendship and business cooperation between the two men. As early as May 1913, less than two years after he came to Britain, Aitken had invited Rothermere to join him on a trip to the west of Canada to prospect for investment opportunities. They had worked together on press campaigns and in expunging unflattering comment about each other's friends. Significantly, in January 1914, Rothermere had suggested to Blumenfeld after talking with Aitken, that if he and his friends could buy the *Express* 'I think I could show you how a large profit could be earned by interworking with the *Mirror* ... I might or might not put up a lot of money.'[12] In 1917 and 1918, they were collaborating over investments in the Bank of British North America and British Columbia electricity.

At a personal level, too, their friendship had been ripening. During the war, as a Canadian eye-witness in France, Beaverbrook told Rothermere that he had looked up Vyvyan. Rothermere used Beaverbrook to assist in obtaining a knighthood for his brother-in-law, Lucas White King. As has been seen, Beaverbrook was attentive to Rothermere in 1918–19 when he had been severely depressed. And the business collaboration continued: in May 1919 they agreed that the *Mirror* would produce the *Express* in case of fire or breakdown; a year later Rothermere invested in Pathé Freres' film business at his friend's suggestion; and Rothermere encouraged him to keep plugging away at the *Sunday Express* when the going was tough.

Eventually this led up to a full-blown partnership. In November 1922, Rothermere wrote, 'How would you like me to purchase an interest in your newspapers?' Beaverbrook agreed. They first bought out minority shareholders in the *Daily Express*; then the Daily Mail Trust bought 49 per cent of Beaverbrook's holding in the *Express* group, paying him £200,000 and 80,000 of the profitable Daily Mail Trust shares. A year later the two of them pulled off a famous coup. A combination of Beaverbrook's speed in negotiation and Rothermere's money enabled them to buy out Sir Edward Hulton's largely Manchester-based press empire; Beverbrook passed all of it on to Rothermere within a week – hanging on only to the *Evening Standard*. Briefly, Rothermere was said to be the largest owner of newspapers in Britain before he sold the bulk of the Hulton interests on to the Berrys. It was a deal in which everyone seemed to make money, and a reminder that, however great their interest in politics, Rothermere and Beaverbrook were businessmen first.

The 1920s were good times for Rothermere as businessman, with the Daily Mail Trust paying 40 per cent dividends on its shares and many other opportunities. But post-war unemployment, the German inflation and his own pessimistic nature meant that his money-making was shot through with anxiety. In a gloomy letter to Beaverbrook in late 1921, for instance, he wrote:[13] 'My own opinion is that we are only on the threshold of the world slump. In its momentous consequences it is I am sure going to dwarf even the Great War. In the economic collapse of Russia, Austria, Hungary, the Balkan States, Turkey, Europe and Asia – and the approaching collapse of Germany, we see steadily being unfolded before our eyes a drama fraught with more perilous consequences to the human race than anything recorded in history.' Cheekily he offered Beaverbrook six articles on this theme, price £250 each.

Rothermere's insecurity where his wealth was concerned was illustrated by his habit of ringing up Sir George Sutton in the middle of the night to ask what he was worth. A fall in stock prices or some international alarm triggered his anxiety. This happened so often that Sutton developed a technique for calming his employer. He would flannel about movements in values until Rothermere asked him for a rough figure. Sutton said it would take time for him to work it out. He then asked the telephone operator for an alarm call and went back to sleep. When he was woken up he would ring Rothermere and give him a figure plucked out of the air. This seemed to satisfy him: it was never as bad as he thought.

In the newspaper world Rothermere was as masterful as his brother had been before him, though it is said that he only once visited the *Mail* office after he bought it, to be present when the Prince of Wales opened new buildings. His control was exercised by telephone and telegram, and by summoning underlings to see him. Senior executives knew that he disapproved of holidays, and that he was likely to require their presence after they had been away for only a couple of days.

He cannot have been an easy man to work with. In 1926, two of Northcliffe's most loyal assistants resigned – Tom Marlowe, editor of the *Mail* and Sir Andrew Caird, regarded as the outstanding newspaper manager of his generation. The main issue seems to have been political. Marlowe, who had edited the *Mail* for thirty years since its launch, could not accept that Rothermere wanted to back Lloyd George rather than Baldwin and the Conservatives, and that he seemed to be so much under the thumb of Beaverbrook in day-to-day manoeuvring. The departure of these two was a bad loss: the *Mail* group seemed to lack punch journalistically thereafter, and the *Express*, where Beaverbrook was not looking for profits, remorselessly caught up in sales.

Rothermere's main newspaper initative was in the late 1920s when he sought to build up a provincial chain to rival the Berrys. It may have been caused by pique because the Berrys were claiming an enormous empire; it may have been an offshoot of his political battle with Stanley Baldwin; or it may just have been a desire to invest in what he saw as a growing market. But in 1928 he formed Northcliffe Newspapers to create and acquire provincial evening papers.

It was all very exciting, as Rothermere launched opposition papers in Manchester, Sheffield, Cardiff, Bristol and Newcastle. Altogether William McWhirter, the Scottish former editor of the *Sunday Pictorial* found himself setting up eleven papers. The Rothermere journals were called *Worlds* and the struggle of the *Evening World* in Newcastle was especially hard fought. In both Derby and Aberdeen, where evening papers came on the market, the Conservative Party machine intrigued with the Berry brothers to prevent Rothermere from getting them.

The conventional view at the time was that Rothermere's provincial campaign had been an expensive and resounding flop. By 1932, when his son Esmond who had been a Conservative MP was beginning to play some part in the business, a general composition was agreed with the Berrys under which the Newcastle *World* was one that died. But in a longer perspective the foothold established by Rothermere was important. Although the provincial interests were not great for the next forty years, and concentrated on Humberside and the West Country, by the 1970s, with cheaper printing, they were making an important contribution to the profits of the whole *Mail* group. It was one piece of the diversification which protected the Harmsworth family from the fate which forced the Aitkens out of newspapers.

Rothermere as a businessman was never afraid to sell. When the Wall Street crash, which he had so long predicted in his bleaker moments, actually occurred in 1929, he had liquidated most of his investments there.[14] Unlike his friend Winston Churchill or his own son Esmond – both of whom lost money in the crash – he was said to have made £3m by manipulating the bear market. Curiously enough, Beaverbrook, whose Daily Mail Trust shares Rothermere had tried to buy out in 1927, had sold his ordinary shares, his cinema and Canadian cement interests at a good price just prior to the crash.

In politics Rothermere was masterly at giving inconsistent signals. Although the *Daily Mail* was seen as the backbone of middle-class Conservatism he was in an almost perpetual state of war with Stanley Baldwin, who took over from Bonar Law as Conservative leader in 1923. The things he was fervent about in the 1920s were his hatred of bureaucracy and 'waste', his increasingly bitter anti-Communism (spasmodically transferred into hostility to the unrevolutionary British Labour Party), and his enthusiasm for the Empire. He was one of a generation, including Churchill as well, which in the 1920s was swinging from the Liberals to the Conservatives. Others, too, thought Baldwin a lightweight, but the vehemence of the attacks on him in the Rothermere press may actually have strengthened his position. Rothermere's nostalgia for Loyd George and his undoubted gifts overlooked the reality that his party was split and in terminal decline, and no one trusted him any more.

His erratic views of Bonar Law, Beaverbrook's hero, gave a foretaste of the unpredictability he brought to the Mail group. On 24 October 1922, he wrote to Beaverbrook,[15] 'What a hash Bonar Law has made. I always knew he was no good.' But by April the following year, writing from the Hotel Claridge, Paris, he told Beaverbrook, 'Sometime early in June I propose that you, Bonar and myself have a discussion as to how his administration can be made one of the most successful of modern times ... If Bonar places himself in my hands I will hand him down to posterity at the end of 3 years as one of the most successful Prime Ministers in history.'

The arrogance of his belief that he could make (and therefore unmake) prime ministers was only offset by periodic bouts of weariness and his willingness to defer to Beaverbrook's political judgement. Long before, when urging Northcliffe to rest, he had implied that neither of them could expect to live long. Writing to Beaverbrook from La Dragonnière in May 1923 he said,[16]

I don't think those who were really hard hit during the war have any real zest for affairs. I know I haven't and if I received from my doctor or other source a peremptory order to get out I should really welcome it. For some weeks I have been cudgelling my brains to devise a scheme by which you could be associated in the political direction of my papers. It must be managed somehow because I am tired of being a galley slave. Moreover my ambition is a life largely of solitude and obscurity. I am now 55 and a poor life at that.

In the general election of November 1922 the *Mail* had avoided endorsing any party. Its position was summed up on 15 November by the advice, 'Vote for the Bonar Law Party [the probable victors] or the Lloyd George Party, or the Asquith–Grey Party, if you will, but DON'T VOTE SOCIALIST!' The propaganda against Labour was virulent: the *Mail* warned that the Labour party would raise taxes on beer and 'close up the village alehouses', that the party would abolish private ownership, and that even women's gold wedding rings might be seized.

The *Mail*'s advice was not entirely followed, for the socialists, as the paper insisted on describing Labour, strengthened their position and were able to form a minority government under Ramsay MacDonald. By the 1924 election, which followed the collapse of this government on the issues of a loan to the Soviet Union and the failure to prosecute J. R. Campbell for inciting servicemen to mutiny, the *Mail* was going full bloodedly for the Conservatives. It painted Labour as having Communist sympathies, MacDonald as the British Kerensky, and socialism as a 'doctrine borrowed from a bilious Prussian, Karl Marx, who hated cheerfulness and hopefulness and was the undisguised and bitter enemy of the British people'.

It was in this climate that a bogus letter from Zinoviev, head of the Comintern, was leaked to the *Mail* which passed it on to the rest of the press. It instructed the British Communist Party on how to prepare insurrection in Britain, was taken as genuine by the Foreign Office which protested at it, and became an instant sensation. For the *Mail*, which suddenly seemed to be making the election news, it was manna from heaven. The Conservatives were returned with a big majority under Baldwin. Rothermere wrote to Beaverbrook that the letter had 'altered the situation to the extent of something like 100 seats. It was the culminating blow'.

Rothermere's suspicion of Baldwin was balanced to some degree by the fact that his friend Winston Churchill was now Chancellor of the Exchequer. On the eve of Churchill's 1925 Budget, he told the Chancellor that he would back him whatever he did: if he reduced taxes, well and good, if not he would applaud the courage of stern finance. This friendship was important the following year during the general strike when a precipitating fact was the unwillingness of the *Mail* printers to bring out the paper because they disliked the editorial. Esmond Harmsworth and Sir Andrew Caird met Churchill and other newspaper proprietors on 3 May 1926 to discuss publishing the *British Gazette*, Churchill's pro-government paper. Alfred Hawkins, chief stereotyper on the *Mail*, was one of the key men who helped to bring out the *Gazette* on *Morning Post* presses.

The general strike, comfortably defeated by Baldwin's government, was as near as Britain came to justifying Rothermere's anxiety over British bolshevism. His own thinking was swaying around again, becoming more critical of the political parties, more tempted by anti-democratic solutions. Just before the general strike both the *Mail* and *Sunday Pictorial* had carried an article over his name asking 'Do we need a Mussolini?' Though the answer was no, he thought that national finance should be taken out of parliamentary control and given to three wise men. By the following year, when Churchill was telling Baldwin that Rothermere 'will crab anything your Administration proposes', he was trying to persuade Lloyd George to advocate 'a very modified political dictatorship' backed by the inner core of the Conservative Party! Baldwin was anathematised for giving votes to women, and much else.

Baldwin, though he disliked the press lords, was not much afraid of them. When in 1928 Rothermere used his son Esmond to get a message to Churchill to discourage him from introducing a profits tax, Baldwin told his Chancellor, 'And don't worry about Rothermere . . . I think you are a little disposed to overrate his influence in the country. It is suburban mainly, in a wide sense, but the provincial press is very strong and it is working well for us.' The general strike had indirectly proved a milestone in the loss of press power: the role of John Reith's BBC had demonstrated the power of radio as an alternative medium of communication.

The 1929 election, which produced MacDonald's second Labour government, was a curious affair for Rothermere and his papers. Strange noises from the South of France suggested that his lordship was seriously thinking of endorsing Labour, the hated socialists of the last election, and only a Conservative mention of the injustices suffered by Hungary – Rothermere's new interest – might avoid this eventuality. In fact the *Mail*'s coverage was much less partisan than before and, though the election day issue urged readers to 'keep out the socialists' an eve-of-poll message from Lord Rothermere, entitled 'I am an anti-Socialist', said that he was neither a Conservative nor Liberal. It was perhaps the dying kick of the coalition Liberal he had once been: it was certainly not a clarion call for the Conservatives, the only party which could actually defeat Labour by then.

Rothermere's extraordinary crusade for Hungary erupted out of a motorcade visit to Budapest in June 1927, and for a while it dominated his life and that of his papers. The British Foreign Office thought he had been got at. The revisionist movement within Hungary went so far as to offer him St Stephen's crown, which he was wise enough to refuse. (This was a period when C. B. Fry, the cricketer and scholar, was also touted for the throne of Albania.) Why he took up what some British readers felt was a ruritanian cause is still mysterious.

The campaign began with an article by the proprietor, datelined 11 June 1927 from Budapest, entitled 'Hungary's Place in the Sun'. He argued that of the three treaties which had reorganised central Europe after the war the Treaty of Trianon was by far the most unfair and ill advised: 600,000 Hungarians had been transferred to Romania, 1 million to Czechoslovakia and 400,000 to Yugoslavia. This was a recipe for instability in the Balkans which contradicted the principles of self-determination enunciated at Versailles. In articles over the next year Rothermere, and journalists acting on his behalf, criticised the Czechs (whose campaign for their own state had been supported by Northcliffe) for oppressing their Hungarian minority. The whole treatment of Hungary as a defeated enemy was questioned, given that the Hungarians had been dragged unwillingly into the 1914–18 war behind the Viennese government.

The booming power of the Rothermere press may not have done much for sales in Britain but it won enthusiastic responses in Hungary. The very unexpectedness of such loud support from someone who was regarded as an English aristocrat produced a huge effect. One group of twenty senior officers asked him to take over the government; his family was showered with gifts and toys; 1.2 million signed a petition of support (still sitting in bound volumes in his grandson's office sixty years later); and when his son Esmond visited the country in 1928 he was treated like royalty.

Rothermere's contact point with Hungary's Revisionist League was via the *Pesti Hirlap*, a liberal Budapest paper run by the Legrady brothers, whose leading columnist Jena Rakosi broke a vow in order to travel to London to see him. He also took on the London correspondent of the *Pesti Hirlap*, a bright young man who went on to have a distinguished journalistic career in Britain, as his 'Hungarian secretary': he was Lajos Lederer, later East European correspondent for *The Observer*, who rescued paintings he lent to Hungary in cloak-and-dagger circumstances at the end of the Second World War.

Rakosi discussed with Mussolini – another who was supporting Hungary's claims – the possibility that Rothermere might become king. Mussolini did not object. But some Hungarian conservatives resisted the idea of a king coming from outside the traditional line, and Rothermere poured cold water on the plan, saying later that 'nothing is more uncongenial to my temperament than to be the object of ceremonial attentions'.[17]

It has been suggested that it was Lederer, knowing Rothermere's fickle passions, who stimulated the royal initiative as a way of retaining his employer's interest in Hungary. There is no doubt that Rothermere, frustrated at his limited political influence nearer home, was genuinely flattered to be recognised as a sage and champion in central Europe. Although the steam had gone out of the campaign within a couple of years, the Hungarian issue remained a thread of interest for the *Mail* throughout the 1930s. Rothermere visited the country again in 1928, by which time Hungary had regained its

Czech lands and people as a by-product of Munich and Hitler's spreading hegemony.

Two aspects of the Hungarian agitation were remarkable in a longer perspective. The first – given that one of Rothermere's most incautious campaigns only a few years later was to back Mosley's Blackshirts – was that a number of the people who encouraged his Hungarian interest were Jewish. This was true of Lajos Lederer, whose home town was in one of the areas excised from Hungary, and of Princess Stefanie Hohenlohe-Waldenburg, the divorced wife of a Hungarian nobleman who is thought to have elicited his concern. There was also some Jewish influence in the *Pesti Hirlap*.

The second aspect was the insight the Hungarian affair provided into Rothermere's own character: it showed not only his common-sense qualities, of which he was proud, but also his fervent romantic side which caused him to go over the top. The idea that he was 'nobbled' before or during his 1927 visit to Budapest does less than justice to his own skill at appreciating the obvious – that a nation which had lost a high proportion of its own citizens had a sense of injustice and was a factor for instability. Few others outside Hungary had spotted this. In the 1980s, when a freer Hungary was able to complain about Romania's treatment of her Hungarian minority, Hungarians recalled Rothermere for his far-sightedness.

He was also a man who responded to the fervour of others and who tended to use his newspapers as a battering-ram, cutting out letters or articles which took a different line. One or two articles on the Hungarian issue would have diverted *Mail* readers: the heavy barrage actually laid down might cause them to reach for the *Express* instead. Hungary was after all next door to a country which Neville Chamberlain, over a decade later, would dismiss as 'far away', whose fate was of no intrinsic British interest.

In another sense, it showed Rothermere reacting against the First World War. The shot that started it was fired at Sarajevo: seemingly obscure Balkan events could land Britain and France in the horrors of renewed bloodshed. His Hungarian extravaganza was consistent with other attitudes he would express over the next few years – his support for the appeasement of Germany, or the youthful virtues he extolled among Blackshirts and Nazis – as part of a psychological hangover. After 1918 he always carried mental scars from the war to end all wars.

His personal life in the 1920s was a mixture of travel, girlfriends, family concerns and almost excessive generosity. He listed one of his recreations as motoring, and when he travelled he went in style, accompanied by journalists like George Ward-Price of the *Mail*, a doctor, a masseur, friends and flunkeys. (At least some of the articles which appeared over his name were drafted by trusted journalists like Ward-Price for his approval.) His habits were those of a rich bachelor and could seem eccentric to a child: his granddaughter Esme recalled later that it looked odd at Dornoch in Scotland when he took long walks before breakfast, and then had breakfast in bed.

Much of the winter he spent at La Dragonnière on Cap Martin, between Menton and Monte Carlo. (Beaverbrook was to buy a house at Cap d'Ail, on the west side of Monte Carlo in the late 1930s.) There Rothermere was in touch with the fashionable Riviera society immortalised by F. Scott Fitzgerald. It was a time when Diaghilev's Russian Ballet was based in Monte Carlo. Rothermere put money into the ballet and became friendly with a number of the dancers. As a big, heavy man he admired the slim, athletic girls of the world famous ballet.

One of his dancer girlfriends was Alice Nikitina, of whom he arranged a sculpture by the Hungarian artist S. Strobl. In November 1927, Ernest Outhwaite, a director and factotum of Rothermere, wrote to Lajos Lederer from the Savoy Hotel: 'Lord Rothermere would be personally obliged to you if you would tell your Editor that Mlle Alysia Nikitina, one of the most brilliant ballerinas of the Russian Ballet, will arrive in Budapest on Monday from Paris and Lord Rothermere would be glad if your paper would give her *good* notices in its columns. Of course the paper should not mention Lord Rothermere's name in this connection.'[18] There were more advantages to his lordship's favour than the jewels and monetary gifts he spread in profusion.

Rothermere's newspapering nephew Cecil King – whose memoirs were not entirely accurate and caused bitter anger in the wider Harmsworth family – alleged that his uncle once told him that old mistresses were much more expensive than Old Masters, and he had plenty of experience of both. According to King one of his uncle's mistresses, who used to clatter away at a typewriter with an enormous diamond ring, became such a nuisance that he offered his brother Leicester's homosexual son Geoffrey £10,000 a year to marry her. The offer was not accepted.[19]

Certainly, Rothermere was quite aware of the usefulness of a marriage of convenience. His serious affair with Rita Redhead, his daughter-in-law's cousin had begun when he had met her at the christening of his eldest grandchild, Lorna. Rita, though half the old man's age, was quite shrewd at handling him: she refused one of his early gifts, of a mirror surrounded by diamonds. Although the idea of marriage had been put on one side their affair bubbled on for a few years until Rothermere started to lose interest. His presents became less valuable and he asked friends to look out for a suitable husband for Rita.

After a possible match fell through with a penniless duke with a castle on the Loire, the lot fell to another Frenchman with an aristocratic name, d'Estainville. He had done well in the First World War. The wedding reception was held in the Ritz Hotel, Paris, and the happy couple received a telegram from the Pope. Rothermere, the fairy godfather, hummed a tune happily at the reception: he helped them financially and gave Rita his house at Cap Martin. Instead he bought the Villa Rocque Fleury in Monte Carlo which was set amongst pine trees and had its garden on the roof. Although it only had four bedrooms, it was filled with valuable French furniture and Chinese porcelain and became a joy to his son Esmond and his family after Rothermere's death.

Although he seemed shy and hated making speeches, Rothermere came across in the family as devoted and humorous. Nothing could staunch the cornucopia of his giving, some of which showed considerable personal care and imagination. He had given his wife Lilian some of Marie Antoinette's jewels and his daughter-in-law a string of pearls which a Czar had bought for a leading ballerina in the Bolshoi. One Christmas he gave his sisters Rolls-Royces. He gave his sister Geraldine – in danger of becoming one of the 'poor Harmsworths' through marrying a civil servant – £100,000 in 1926. In the same year, following his mother's death, he bought the site of the Bethlem Hospital and presented it to London County Council as a park to commemorate her.

He gave more money to charities than they asked for and could be an embarrassment to beggars. Walking one day in Hyde Park with McWhirter he was propositioned by a beggar for the price of a cup of tea. Rothermere said, 'Well Mac, give him something.' The only money McWhirter had on him was a white five pound note. The man was spellbound and asked if he could change it. 'If I try and change it I'd get nicked,' he said. Rothermere was the sort of person who was always giving large tips, weekend prizes for putting and bagatelle scores, and would toss coins for his grandchildren to chase. In the early 1920s he said that he was giving away £30,000 a year to nephews and nieces, and women were costing him up to £20,000.

Though prickly and difficult he was loyal to people who served him well. He liked to know what was going on in the world of public affairs. 'What's fresh, Fish?' he would say with predictable regularity to Walter Fish who succeeded Marlowe as editor of the *Mail*. 'What are they saying?' he would ask Outhwaite. He could also be occasionally nervous of his own family, particularly his petrifying sisters. He asked an associate to accompany him one day when he had promised to call on Geraldine, Lady King, in St John's Wood. He knew she wanted money and was rather afraid of the meeting. When he came out he remarked, 'I got away very cheaply.' His colleague asked, 'How much?' He replied, '£30,000.'

The truth was that Rothermere was a very rich man, with the facility for almost effortless accumulation that goes with a good financial brain which has an already considerable fortune to play with. By 1926 he was said to be worth £26m: he did not take up an offer by Beaverbrook to buy the Beaverbrook newspaper interests just prior to the Wall Street crash. His joke about Old Masters was well made; his purchases of pictures by Botticelli, Rembrandt, Rubens, Holbein and Cranach were good investments, as were his furniture and porcelain. His political interventions might seem jejune, but where finance and acquisition were concerned his touch was generally sure.

7
From 1929 to 1940

The Labour Party's victory in the elections of May 1929 and the Wall Street crash brought Rothermere's quarrel with Baldwin to a new pitch. The world in which he believed seemed to be tottering. The Conservatives were ineffectual. Within a couple of months of the election Beaverbrook had launched a new campaign, for Empire Free Trade, which drew in Rothermere, too, but the motives of the two press proprietors were different. At a time when autarchy seemed a path to economic salvation Beaverbrook envisaged a sharing of markets between industrialised Britain and the agricultural producers of the Empire: he recognised that this would involve food taxes in Britain. For Rothermere, who like his brother Northcliffe and his old Liberal compatriots had no fondness for food taxes, the motivation was much more political. He wanted to put some stuffing into the Empire, to assert Britain's great power role, to bring the independence movement in India to heel, and to use the Empire campaign as a new front against Baldwin. Significantly, in November 1929, Rothermere ran an article in the *Mail* by Churchill, who was not seduced by the Empire Free Trade agitation, which attacked MacDonald's government for offering Dominion status to India.

The Empire crusade lasted until 1931. It involved the creation of a party, the United Empire Party, which put up by-election candidates, and stung Baldwin into a series of rejoinders against irresponsible attempts to dictate to politicians, which brought the bulk of the Conservative Party behind him. It also marked the end of the constitutional threat which had first appeared during the First World War, under which press magnates might with their own whims usurp the role of MPs and voters in the political process. Although it was a muddled period, with Beaverbrook oscillating between negotiation with Baldwin and confrontation, with Baldwin only an opposition leader, and with Rothermere standing slightly in the background, it was of great significance. Just as the general strike had been seen on the Conservative side as a potentially revolutionary movement, and the Conservative press in the 1945 election criticised Harold Laski and Labour's national executive for attempting to dictate Attlee's Cabinet, so there had been a serious risk that Conservative papers – that is their proprietors – could have ended up running the Conservative Party.

Rothermere did not much care to be a front man in a political movement, with the speeches, diplomacy and organisational worries such a position entailed. He was also a friend and admirer of Beaverbrook, even though they had business and political differences. He endorsed a proposal, originally floated by Ward-Price in the *Sunday Pictorial* and taken up by the *Mail*, that Beaverbrook should succeed Baldwin as Conservative leader. (In a flowery response Beaverbrook referred in public to Rothermere as 'the greatest trustee of public opinion we have seen in the history of journalism'.) When the crusade became a party – operated almost single-handed by Beaverbrook – the *Mail* made it the main front page news for twelve days in succession, and its owner put in some money to assist candidates who would take a hard line on India.

The imperial agitation made a lot of noise and, though it did not capture the Conservative Party for Beaverbrook's pet cause, it may have helped to put back the prospects for Indian self-rule and stimulate the movement for imperial tariffs; the Statute of Westminster of 1931, sometimes regarded as the birth of the Commonwealth,[20] also put the relationship between the white dominions on a more adult basis.

However, the campaign in the *Mail* group illustrated the heavy-handedness of Rothermere's approach. After twelve days of non-stop propaganda in the *Mail*, for instance, there was a sudden silence over the United Empire Party. In early 1931, Churchill, who was a die-hard over India, complained that Rothermere's *Mail* was giving too little coverage to his speeches. Rothermere, holidaying in San Remo in February, telegraphed to Churchill, 'You have a superb chance. Be untiring and unfaltering. Chuck holidays and live laborious days.'[21] (It was perhaps unfair of a proprietor with unorthodox work habits to chide the politician for lack of industry.) Within a fortnight of his complaint, Churchill was telling his wife that there was a serious danger that the Rothermere press was overdoing its support. Such zig-zags could irritate readers, and embarrassed the more feline Beaverbrook. He likened Rothermere to an elephant, trampling over his precious crusade.

In British domestic politics the whole episode, which was a kind of response to the slump which could only have been refracted through Beaverbrook's personality and Canadian background, died almost without trace. Its most memorable legacy was the series of speeches, often directed more against Rothermere than Beaverbrook, by which Baldwin put down the challenge. At Caxton Hall, in June 1930, he said, 'There is nothing more curious in modern evolution than the effect of an enormous fortune rapidly made, and the control of newspapers of your own ... It goes to the head like wine, and you find in all these cases attempts have been made outside the province of journalism to dictate, to domineer, to blackmail.' Unless he made peace 'with these noblemen' he was warned that they would run candidates all over the country: 'The Lloyd George candidates at the last election smelt; these will stink.'

Baldwin said that a representative of Beaverbrook had said that his lordship would want to be consulted on certain offices in the government if they were to become allies. He also read out a letter which Rothermere had sent to a Conservative in which he laid down conditions for supporting Baldwin: he would need to know his policy, to have guarantees that such policy would be carried out, and to get the names of at least eight to ten of his most prominent colleagues in the next government. 'A more preposterous and insolent demand was never made on the leader of any political party. I repudiate it with contempt, and I will fight that attempt at domination to the end.'

The sight of the unemotional Baldwin fighting back was electrifying: the press lords had overreached themselves in the eyes of respectable opinion. Indeed the references to 'noblemen' – when everyone knew Rothermere and Beaverbrook were first generation peers who might indeed have bought their peerages – and to Lloyd George – which to a Conservative audience was a code word for political immorality – showed that Baldwin was at least as good at propaganda as his opponents.

He went one better on 18 March 1931 at an eve-of-poll meeting in Westminster when Rothermere and Beaverbrook were running a candidate against him in the St George's by-election. He attacked the editor of the *Mail* who had stated in the paper that Baldwin had lost a fortune he had inherited from his father and was therefore unlikely to restore the nation's fortunes. This was a lie. The editor was a cad. A high legal authority had advised that he could sue for libel. 'I shall not move in this matter, and for this reason: I should get an apology and heavy damages. The first is of no value, and the second I would not touch with a barge-pole.'

Borrowing a phrase from his cousin Rudyard Kipling, who had written 'The Absent-minded Beggar' for Northcliffe in the Boer War and was godfather to Beaverbrook's son Peter, Baldwin produced his most cutting sentence. 'What the proprietorship of these papers is aiming at is power, and power without responsibility – the prerogative of the harlot throughout the ages.' It was magnificent, and it was decisive. Although press campaigns might subsequently influence the policies of parties and governments there could never again be a successful attempt by newspaper proprietors as such to dictate a leadership or to a government. Northcliffe's idea of the press as an alternative government, which Rothermere had crudely and naively sought to exploit, had broken on an immovable obstacle.

Frustrated by the custodians of parliamentary democracy in Britain, and worried by developments in Europe and the world economy,

Rothermere's authoritarian instincts came to the fore. His capacity for gloom and doom – what Northcliffe had once described as his tendency to panic – was working overtime. In a long letter to Beaverbrook in November 1930, from the Hotel Splendide in Piccadilly, he had argued that the significance of a wheat price fall in Winnipeg was 'almost too grave to think about'; troubles in Fleet Street were only just beginning; 'personally I don't see daylight anywhere'. He had the air of one almost relishing woe. Writing to Beaverbrook just over a year later, in December 1931, he said that 1931 had been worse than 1930 and 'I think 1932 is going to be an exceptionally bad year'.

The only beacon of hope, for a man now in his sixties, was the rise of the National Socialists in Germany. They were anti-Communist. They were out to revive their nation and represented the ardent spirit of post-war youth. That they also practised thuggery, anti-Semitism of a potentially genocidal kind, were hostile to British and French interests and would march Europe inexorably to war was perhaps not so obvious in September 1930 when Rothermere wrote his first laudatory article. But he was not looking to criticise. He was looking for a hero. What was more, following the return of the National government with a massive majority in the 1931 elections and the collapse of his imperial agitation with Beaverbrook, he was looking to someone in Britain who could offer the nostrums of Hitler and Mussolini. By December 1931 he was pressing Oswald Mosley to lead fascism in Britain, and offering the support of his papers.

In a formal sense Rothermere's backing for the Blackshirts, as the British Union of Fascists were popularly known, lasted for only six months, from January to June 1934. It was briefer than his campaigns against squandermania or for Empire free trade – but it cast very long shadows. Along with his sympathy for appeasement in the rest of the 1930s it tended to devalue his pleas for rearmament in the air. As late as the 1960s the memory of his flirtation with Mosley was held to have discouraged *News Chronicle* readers from switching to the *Mail* after the merger, and to have undermined the credibility of Mike Randall's attempt to liberalise the *Mail*'s leader line.

Mosley, the son of a baronet and grandson of the enthusiast for stone-ground bread who had been taken up by Northcliffe, had started his political career as the object of *Mail* abuse. Running as a Labour candidate in the Smethwick by-election of 1926 the *Mail* made fun of him and his wife – he for being born with a silver spoon in his mouth, she for her clothes. (Half a century later another socialist born to a title, Tony Benn, would meet similar treatment.) But Mosley won, was rapidly seen as a coming man in the Labour Party, but then veered off into the woolly socialism of the New Party which was wiped out at the 1931 election.

Rothermere, who realised that both Mussolini and Hitler had

emerged from a socialist background, was initially held at bay by Mosley. Possibly Mosley did not at first see his movement as the sort of super right-wing Conservatism which an alliance with the *Mail* group would tend to make it. But by 1934, with the BUF up and running, they were, politically, both outsiders; nor perhaps was it easy to keep Rothermere out once he had decided you were a good thing.

His clarion call on the *Mail*'s leader page on 15 January 1934 – 'Hurrah for the Blackshirts' – showed the proprietor rewriting British fascism to suit himself. It was 'the Party of Youth'. Blackshirts proclaimed that the new age required new methods and new men. Italy and Germany were 'beyond all doubt the best-governed nations in Europe today ... We must keep up with the spirit of the age. That spirit is one of national discipline and organisation.' The replacement of party government by a National government in Britain demonstrated that the old parties had failed. Britain's survival as a great power depended on the existence of a well-organised party of the right. A footnote to his article suggested that young men could join the BUF at the HQ, King's Road, Chelsea.

In the paean to youth it is hard not to see Rothermere's continuing remorse for the lost generation of the First World War. In his distrust of the conventional parties there was not only a proprietor who had exhausted those he could support, helping to invent a new one. He was also continuing to rail against the duds of the 'Old Gang' which he and his brother had denounced in 1916. But he tried to sanitise the Blackshirts and to mask the uglier aspects of their Nazi model.

Writing in the *Sunday Pictorial* on 21 January he argued that the German public believed that atrocities were committed in the concentration camps of the Boer War, and that Socialists were being equally credulous in accepting stories of Nazi brutality. 'That isolated outrages may have occurred in Germany is possible. But in comparison with other revolutions far smaller in scope the Germans have set the world a model of moderation,' he declared.

In the same article he said that the British Blackshirt Movement (in capitals) was 'one hundred per cent constitutional and national. Persuasion, not violence will be its path to power ... Nor is there the slightest ground for believing that the Blackshirts are, or ever will be, antagonistic to such bodies as the Jews, the Trade Unions or the Freemasons'. There was, of course, willing self-delusion in all this. The Rothermere press was not investigating hard to see whether the stories of Nazi brutality were true; it needed little research to show that anti-Semitism and anti-unionism were powerful motivations for the Blackshirts.

As with other Rothermere campaigns the readers were knocked over the head with repetitive publicity and few hostile letters were printed. But it was not good for sales and not good for advertising. Jewish

companies and readers were not the only ones offended; a plan by
which Rothermere and the Fascists intended to go into a joint business
to sell cigarettes had to be abandoned. The respectable *Mail* readers and
the street fighters in black shirts did not go together, and Mosley was
really happier marching up the cul-de-sac of his fascist revolution than
dancing to a press lord's tune. For Rothermere, the whole thing had
become an embarrassment. He wrote to Eric Wollheim, who was
Jewish, authorising him to tell his friends his 'true feelings in regard to
the anti-Semitic question'.[22] By May he was even having to apologise to
Beaverbrook: 'I intend to tell Mosley that if he attacks you I shall drop
his Blackshirts. You are my greatest friend and this is the least I can
do.'[23]

Rothermere pulled out of the Blackshirts with an exchange of letters
with Mosley, and a clarification that he was in favour of democracy and
against fascism and anti-Semitism. It marked the end of his erratic
attempts to reconstruct party politics. His judgement had been warped
by his hostility to revolutionary socialism, by his vulnerability to
fervour in others, especially when coated with a pretence of youth, and
possibly by his own implicit anti-Semitism. There was quite a lot of
anti-Jewish prejudice amongst the insecure London middle classes at the
end of the nineteenth century and beginning of the twentieth. The
Harmsworths were certainly not immune. Cecil, who believed that
Jewish diamond merchants were responsible for the Boer War, was
perhaps the most extreme: he used to say that Jews were either on your
back or under your feet. Northcliffe, though he was ready with what
would nowadays be described as ethnic stereotyping, was not really
anti-Jewish. Rothermere, who too easily swallowed the Nazi lie that
Jews were playing a malevolent role in Germany, came somewhere in
between.

It may have been coincidence, or it may have been due to Rothermere,
but in 1934 the BUF started to form flying clubs. Mosley was an old
Royal Flying Corps man and the appeal of individual daring and
technology meant that a number of flying enthusiasts, such as A. V.
Roe, were drawn towards fascism. The following year, after he had
dropped fascism but was beating the drum for a bigger air force,
Rothermere paid for a prototype aircraft which would show the Air
Ministry how to improve performance. He dubbed it 'Britain First' –
one of the BUF slogans – and it played a significant part for the RAF in
the Second World War as the Blenheim light bomber.[24]

The Blackshirt diversion was a brief sideline in the unhappy saga of
the 1930s, when Rothermere simultaneously advocated appeasement of
the dictators and rearmament. His enthusiasm for Hitler, as representing a new anti-Communist force, blinded him to the corruption and
cruelty of the Nazis: it made appeasement seem perfectly natural. But
whereas appeasement was a popular policy in Britain until late in 1938,

his enthusiasm for rearmament and a strong air force put him well in advance of the public; indeed he was accused of speculating in aircraft shares. But he firmly and, as the Battle of Britain would show, rightly believed that the next war would be settled in the air.

It was as if two tendencies in his personality were in conflict – the panicker who wanted no more war, who found qualities to admire in the dictators and grievances that were justified against the Versailles treaties, and the common-sense believer in *realpolitik*, who could see that the dictators were a threat to British interests which only armed might would repel.

Rothermere recalled later that on 31 January 1933, when Hitler became Chancellor, he told George Ward-Price that 'this will prove to be one of the most historic days, if not *the* most historic day, in the latter day history of Europe'. Six months later, writing from 'Somewhere in Nazidom', he urged British young men and women to study the progress of the Nazis, dismissed atrocities as a few isolated acts of violence, and alleged that Germany had been 'rapidly falling under the control of its alien elements'.

He constantly derided the idea that Hitler was a Charlie Chaplin figure, not to be taken seriously, met him and other Nazi leaders – he spent Christmas with them in 1934 – and maintained a regular corres-pondence with Hitler throughout the 1930s. Even Hitler tried to discourage him from offering to return Germany's mandated colonies, and he adopted a fawning tone which he later explained was normal and necessary when dealing with dictators. His brother Leicester worried that 'Hitlerism worship' would rebound unfavourably on the *Daily Mail*, whose older readers had been brought up on a diet of Germanophobia. And he carried his admiration into his private life, telling his niece's German husband, Peter Bielenberg, at dinner that he would not take a drink himself because 'The Fuhrer neither drinks nor smokes.'

Although politicians and other newspapers were pro-appeasement, it was the enthusiasm which Rothermere showed which seemed objection-able later. It also caused strains with his friend Winston Churchill, who could not understand how Rothermere and his associates had shaken hands with 'those murderous Nazis'. In April 1935, just after the British government had admitted that the Luftwaffe was bigger than the Royal Air Force, Churchill wrote to his wife: 'Rothermere rings me up every day. His anxiety is pitiful. He thinks the Germans are all powerful and that the French are corrupt and useless, and the English hopeless and doomed. He proposes to meet this situation by grovelling to Germany. "Do Germany, do destroy us last!" I endeavour to inculcate a more robust attitude.'[25]

The following month, after Hitler had written to him suggesting an Anglo-German condominium in Europe, Rothermere wrote to Churchill saying that he did not trust Hitler as a statesman; he was sure that he and the other Nazi leaders harboured the most ambitious designs. The following year, however, he was one of Churchill's friends who was trying to persuade him to tone down his criticism of Nazi Germany, and in early 1937, following a stay with Hitler at Berchtesgaden, he was telling Churchill from the South of France that the Nazis were professing complete assurance that England and France would be vassal states by the end of the decade.

Against these anxious zig-zags Rothermere's pursuit of rearmament in the air seemed a model of far-sightedness and consistency. On 7 November 1933, after Hitler had come to power, he published an article in the *Mail* headlined, 'We Need 5,000 War-'planes!' By 14 May 1935, a *Mail* editorial he inspired urged that 10,000 planes were required. He subsidised a National League of Airmen. Along the way he had pleaded for an 'air dictator' to cut through Whitehall incompetence and interservice wrangling in the way Lloyd George, as Minister for Munitions, had done during the First World War. Presciently his plea was answered in 1940 when Churchill made Beaverbrook the Minister for Aircraft Production.

In some ways, the air campaign showed Rothermere at his best. There was nothing in it for him or his newspapers commercially – indeed the *Mail*'s unpopular stress on rearmament, which was not echoed in the *Express*, was thought to be one reason why the *Express* pulled ahead in sales from 1933 onwards. At the same time, Rothermere was able to draw on his personal experience in the First World War and the family commitment to air transport development. He was conscious that air power now was as important as the need for naval strength in the run-up to 1914.

However, the uneasy balance between appeasement in Europe and rearmament at home – for if the Hitler regime was not dangerous and Britain could have a pacific relationship with it why waste money on planes and guns? – was not the only doubt overhanging this crusade. It also lent itself to alarmism and, in Churchill's view, exaggeration. An article by Rothermere in November 1933 predicted that as soon as war was declared 'the Commander in Chief of the enemy nation will press a button and 20,000 – perhaps 50,000 – aeroplanes, laden with bombs and gas, will rise into the air and set off at more than 200 miles an hour to rain destruction on this country'.

This nightmare vision of immediate aerial attack, not dissimilar to the fears of nuclear war in the 1950s and 1960s, took a powerful grip on the British imagination in the 1930s. It was not helpful to prudent and intelligent defence planning. During 1935 Churchill was worried that by overstating his case – for Rothermere was arguing that Germany would have an air force of 20,000 by the end of the year – the press proprietor might really be persuading weaker brethren that Britain's task in catching up was hopeless.

In spite of their political differences, though, the friendship between Rothermere and Churchill remained strong in the 1930s. For Rothermere, Churchill was a fascinating contemporary, sharing the same views on India and defence, and sharing much common history; even in the political wilderness Churchill belonged to the world of public events, public platforms and public influence about which Rothermere loved to gossip. And for Churchill, worried about his financial situation and his journalistic access to the public, the press lord offered the generosity and hospitality of wealth, and a daily requirement of column inches to be filled.

The belief is strong in the Harmsworth family that, one way or another, Rothermere helped Churchill to finance the purchase of his Chartwell home. Certainly, his kindness to Churchill and his family went far beyond merely paying him for the articles he wrote for his newspapers. He was part of the famous twenty-first birthday party at Claridge's for Churchill's talented but irascible son Randolph which brought together famous fathers and sons in 1932; it included Rothermere and Esmond, and Hailsham and his son Quintin. Rothermere gave Randolph his first job – as a reporter on the *Sunday Graphic*, sent to cover the German elections in July 1932 – which did not stop Randolph from rounding on the second Lord Rothermere for publishing pornography in the *Sunday Dispatch* some twenty-one years later. When Randolph was planning to stand as a Conservative candidate opposed to the India Bill at a Wavertree by-election, Winston had no doubt that Rothermere would pay his share of the election expenses.

The Churchills and Rothermere stayed together quite regularly, at La Dragonnière and elsewhere. At Christmas in 1935, for instance, Churchill and Rothermere and Ward-Price met up at Tangier, and then went on to see Lloyd George who was holidaying in Marrakesh. Rothermere, who loved wagers as much as his brother Hildebrand, bet Churchill £2,000 if he went teetotal in 1936. Winston calculated that, allowing for tax and the saving on liquor, this fine offer was worth £4,000 but 'life would not be worth living'. However, he did take a second bet, worth £600, not to drink any brandy or undiluted spirits in 1936.

Rothermere, who was 60 in 1928, agreed that Esmond should not run for re-election in Thanet in the 1929 general election and that it was time for him to join the business. The political world saw this as part of Rothermere's wobble on the eve of the elections, but Esmond's wife had been pressing for him to become more fully involved in the management of the *Mail* group. The next eight years saw a steady divestment by Rothermere of control of his business empire. At the same time, on an even more dramatic scale, he was giving away his fortune. In addition to good causes and friends, he was settling money on his son, his other relations and in trust for his grandchildren. Of all his acts of generosity this give-away in the last part of his life was the most remarkable: between 1926, when he was said to be worth £26m, and 1940, when he died with a British estate proved at £281,000 which after death duties was insufficient to pay all the legacies, he dispersed his wealth with as much vigour as he had created it.

In the late 1920s and early 1930s, the cross-holdings between the *Mail* group and the *Express* group were gradually liquidated, not without fierce bargaining between Rothermere and Beaverbrook of which Beaverbrook on the whole came off the better. For instance, in 1933, when the Daily Mail Trust wanted £324,405 for its 49 per cent stake in Beaverbrook's *Evening Standard*, Beaverbrook managed to get it for £275,483 – less than his first offer. Rothermere was irritated that his philosophy of owning papers to make money from them was being exploited to his disadvantage. Whereas Beaverbrook was earning good dividends on his *Mail* shares, which he ploughed into the improvement of his papers, Rothermere was getting very little from his *Express* and *Standard* shares, because Beaverbrook was running his group for fun and propaganda.

While Rothermere was travelling, and occupying himself with the fate of Europe, his son Esmond was gradually gaining authority over the business side of the group. He had been a director of Associated Newspapers in the 1920s when he was an MP. By 1931, Arthur Christiansen, the up and coming star of the *Express* whom Sir George Sutton, managing director of Associated Newspapers was trying to lure over to edit the *Sunday Dispatch*, believed that Esmond's approval of the appointment was necessary. By 1932 Esmond was chairman of Associated Newspapers and in 1937 he became chairman of the Daily Mail and General Trust. In that year the trust's return of directors firmly listed Rothermere as 'retired'.

Nevertheless, so powerful was Rothermere's personality that this gradual transfer of responsibility was masked. At the *Mirror* and *Sunday Pictorial* he put John Cowley in charge in 1931. Cowley had been a young accounts clerk who joined the Harmsworths when they took over the *Evening News*, but even though Rothermere told him that he and his fellow directors were in charge, and he began dispersing shares, Cowley continued to act as Rothermere's nominee until 1935.

The problem was that in the early 1930s the Rothermere papers were not doing well. There were many reasons and the proprietorial campaigns had not helped. In a competitive business the vitality of papers as diverse as the *Express* and the *Herald*, and the war of gifts to readers, were gnawing away at the markets of the *Mail* and *Mirror*. The sale of the *Mail* had peaked at 1,954,635 in 1929 and thereafter was in gentle decline. The situation of the *Mirror* was more serious: its sale was going down by 70,000 a year in the early 1930s, and had dropped below 800,000 in 1933.

Rothermere's disinterest in journalistic matters and his preference for the commercial managers over the editors were becoming more harmful with the passage of time. By virtue of age, personality and his substantial periods abroad he was becoming increasingly out of touch. The moment of succession is always awkward in a family business and the hiatus of transfer, when Rothermere was still perceived as the boss and Esmond's authority was incomplete, was dangerously long drawn out.

In a dynastic sense, two critical decisions were taken at this fluid time. The first was that preference was given to the *Mail* group, the Northcliffe inheritance, rather than the separate *Mirror* group which Rothermere himself had built up. Esmond was put in to manage the *Mail* papers, as if they were the cornerstone of his heritage. And far from merging the two businesses completely, in 1935 Rothermere and the Daily Mail Trust sold a large quantity of their shares in the *Mirror* group, effectively forfeiting control.

Rothermere had been worried about the decline of the *Mirror*, and in 1930–2 a Canadian pulp and paper subsidiary had got into financial trouble in developing interests on the north shore of the St Lawrence river. According to Hugh Cudlipp, Rothermere thought the *Mirror* group was about to go bankrupt when he sold. However, in a fine irony, Guy Bartholomew, Hugh Cudlipp and Rothermere's nephew Cecil King rebuilt the group in the late 1930s as campaigning, working-class tabloids. In addition to a brash kind of journalism, they took advantage of the new science of market research. The trick which Rupert Murdoch was to play on the *Mirror* group over thirty years' later, when he bought the ailing *Sun* for a song after King's overthrow and then pushed it in front of the *Mirror*, was pioneered by the *Mirror* itself. (The *Mirror* at this point passed out of the control of any proprietorial group, being owned by a multitude of shareholders; rather to his embarrassment the second Lord Rothermere found he was the largest individual shareholder in 1944–5 when Randolph Churchill maliciously suggested that the famous slogan 'Forward with the People' should become 'Backward with the Press Lords'.)

Apart from his pleasure in travelling, and buying and selling or giving away his houses, Rothermere was not a man with a large number of recreations. George Ward-Price, who knew him better than most, wrote at his death that he was a good though unorthodox golfer, and enjoyed playing tennis. He was not a great socialite, though he liked dining in the Middle Temple. (He had made benefactions out of respect for his father, and was an honorary bencher at this inn of court from 1928).

Moreover, although he seemed prickly at times he evoked considerable loyalty in others, and was loyal to them in his turn. A good example was the dancer Nikitina, of whom he had been passionately fond in the late 1920s. At Christmas 1929, for instance, he had given her a present of a million francs and told her, among other things, to use some of the money to buy a car. The steam went out of the relationship in the 1930s but a lot of mutual affection remained. In 1938, for example, when she was training to become a singer in Milan, he visited her frequently and she accompanied him as far as the German frontier when he was invited to see Hitler at Berchtesgaden. For Nikitina he always seemed well mannered, humorous, forceful yet kind. He made a similarly favourable impression on his daughter-in-law, even though her marriage to his son had hit the rocks.

He was a loving grandfather and, in the wake of his sons' deaths and the sinking of a favourite King nephew in the *Leinster*,[26] he liked to have younger people around him. At an early stage in getting to know her he had suggested to Nikitina that he might adopt her. He frequently travelled with his brother Hildebrand's eldest son, also a Hildebrand, who was known as Sonny rather like Northcliffe as a child. His role was to act as entertainer to his uncle.

In the 1930s also he virtually adopted the family of his first cousin once removed, Judith Wilson, who lived in Dublin. He brought them all to London, flirted with Judith and she and her mother Adelaide lived with him for a while at his house in Virginia Water, acting as hostesses.

He signed letters to his grandchildren 'your devoted grandfather', which made it seem that he almost loved them more than his son who signed his letters to them more plainly, 'Love, Daddy'. One year in the early 1930s, when his two granddaughters were around 11 and 8, he said they could choose anything the length of Bond Street. Lorna, the elder, made straight to Cartier the jeweller and bought a brooch. Esme, the younger, bought a spaniel in a pet shop. Later she felt he did not really approve of her choice, whereas he thought Lorna had been sensible.

Rothermere's strong political views occasionally cut across his equally strong feeling for the family. He helped his sister Christabel, who was running a campaign for school meals, by providing a canteen at Coram's Fields in central London. But he was appalled to discover that Christabel's son, John Burton, had joined the Communist Party when he was at Cambridge. He found out one day when his Rolls-Royce was stuck in traffic caused by a Communist-backed march in Oxford Street and he looked up to see a nephew. There was a stupendous row and he cut off allowances and monies from his sister and her family. Her husband, Percy Burton, although rather conservative himself, reacted strongly. He had already survived the wrath of the Harmsworths himself when Northcliffe had ordered his minions to give no business to Burton's advertising agency after he thought Burton had slighted him.

The actual outbreak of the Second World War, in September 1939, seems to have provoked mixed feelings in a man who was now old and tired. On 11 September, he sent a telegram from Dornoch to Beaverbrook to say, 'No one should be gloomy because we are sure to win the war. As you know I know a great deal about Germany and I make this prediction with complete confidence.'[27] It is possible that Beaverbrook, whose *Express* had been proclaiming that Britain would not be involved in a European war up to thirty days before war was declared, had rather lost the taste for prediction. But seeing his nephew Cecil King at the Savoy Rothermere said he did not see how Britain could win: the war would peter out after four years and the country would be financially exhausted.

His sadness at the collapse of appeasement must have been slightly mollified in May 1940 when Churchill became Prime Minister and his other friend, Beaverbrook, came into the government as the aircraft dictator he had called for. He was in France only a few weeks before the German breakthrough and offered to help Beaverbrook in gingering up aircraft production on the other side of the Atlantic. His health was already deteriorating because he was anticipating going into a clinic in Arizona.

It is possible that Beaverbrook's acceptance of Rothermere's offer was in part an act of kindness, for giving him something to do in Canada and the United States was in the Northcliffe tradition, while it meant removing him from a perilous Britain which could be embarrassing for former appeasers. Two of his grandchildren, Esme and Vere, were also being evacuated to Canada. Much to their disappointment their grandfather travelled separately, because his bitter memories of the torpedoing of the *Leinster* in the Irish Sea in the first war – when Bobby (Alfred) King was killed – persuaded him that it would be unwise for all three to take the same boat.

Esme, now Countess of Cromer, recalls joining up with her grandfather in a big hotel in Quebec. He was silent and depressed, and felt that Britain did not have a hope. At a fashion show to raise money in the hotel she was asked to dress as a Canadian Red Cross nurse and was the last to walk down the catwalk. She remembers the band playing 'There'll Always Be an England' as she came. Looking across at her grandfather she saw tears streaming down his face.

While Vere was sent to Kent School, Connecticut, Esme was staying with a financial contact of her grandfather's, Frank Humphrey, outside New York. Humphrey was a partner of the stockbroking firm, Kidder, Peabody on Wall Street, became chairman of the Anglo-Newfoundland Development Co, and was a key figure in the operation of Rothermere's US-based trusts. However, Esme found him somewhat anti-British, a pious dictator in the home, and hostile to her personally. It was with some relief that she found war work in an organisation called Bundles for Britain where, not quite knowing what was going to happen, she saved her lunch money to make a small nest egg.

Rothermere, who was sorry to find her in a difficult situation and worried that she was on her own in New York, became seriously ill there in late 1940. With his 18-year-old granddaughter, a valet called

Morrison and a masseur – by his standard a rather small entourage – he sailed on a Grace Line ship to St George's Bermuda to recuperate. He reached Hamilton on 3 November where he had a relapse and was taken into the King Edward VII Memorial Hospital.

Most of the big hotels had been commandeered but Esme stayed in Horizons and cycled over daily to be with him. He had never been one for small talk and spent much of the time gazing at her. He remarked to her once, 'I like looking at you because you look just like my mother.' It was an odd comment to make to an 18 year old, but a testimony to the immense influence that tough old Mrs Harmsworth had had on all her children right to the end. He finally died on 26 November. He had been diabetic; but dropsy was diagnosed as the cause of death. Mr Butterfield of Butterfield's Bank in Burmuda arranged for his funeral and gave £200 without question to Esme, who was hard up. Morrison was inconsolable and got severely drunk on the boat to Lisbon with Esme and the masseur after the funeral.

In spite of his own anxiety about the war, Rothermere felt that his own campaign for rearmament had been vindicated. He published a collection of his articles entitled *My Fight to Rearm Britain* three months after war broke out. In August 1940, when they were both on the other side of the Atlantic, he gave his granddaughter an inscribed copy. On the flyleaf he wrote,

> My darling Esme,
> Here is a copy of my last book. It was published after the war had been going for three months. Although it makes no claim it does largely tell the reader what would happen. From the outset I knew a war between England and Germany would be decided almost entirely in the air. The English people did not believe a war was inevitable and therefore took no steps to prepare for the decisive encounter.
> Your devoted Grandpa

8

Dynasty and Impact

If Northcliffe, driven by demons though he might have been always seemed one of nature's gentlemen, his brother Rothermere appeared both more ordinary and more obviously a self-made man. He liked showy things and he worried about his wealth. They shared, however, a tremendous confidence in their own judgement, even while reserving the right to change their minds. They shared, too, a belief that the Harmsworth family and its business was bigger than any of them. After his brother's death, Rothermere faced the challenge of consolidating a family business against burgeoning competition, the toll of death duties, and with commercial rather than journalistic gifts to guide him. He had also inherited from his brother, and the special circumstances of the press in the First World War, a public role which was difficult for him to fulfil and liable to rebound against him.

During the eighteen years which elapsed between Northcliffe's death and his own, an already large, extended family became a great deal bigger – so big in fact that it was becoming hard for any member to keep in touch with all the rest. One way or another, as a result of the detailed bequests in Northcliffe's will and Rothermere's own gifts and settlements, most of them continued to have a financial interest in the success of the group. But it was not, after the first generation, seen as a source of employment. Family members who went in to any part of the business were few: Esmond Harmsworth and Cecil King stayed in newspapers, but Desmond, Cecil Harmsworth's son, resigned after three years on the *Continental Daily Mail* in 1929 to become a painter.

It was therefore during the first Lord Rothermere's time that the *Mail* group took on an unusual characteristic, that it was a family business in which virtually nobody from the proprietorial family except the chairman took part. There were other reasons for this apart from Northcliffe's campaign against nepotism, and the undeniable fact that it was more attractive to draw dividends than to wrestle with the tough and grinding world of newspapers, paper and allied interests. It reflected the individualism of a family which had differed politically and gone its separate ways in commerce. It may also have reflected a family perception that Harold Rothermere's charm concealed an autocrat of decided views with whom even his son found it hard to get on.

Of his brothers he outlived Hildebrand, who died in 1929, St John, who died in 1933, and Leicester, who died in 1937, as well as Alfred. St John, frustrated in his wheelchair but with a charming French nurse and girlfriend, lived on the Isle of Wight when he was not at the Perrier source. He would dive fearlessly off cliffs into the sea. He undertook various cures without success and was liked by the younger generation, and had been the only Harmsworth brother to turn up to Esmond's wedding. Although the Perrier business made progress it was not a great money-spinner in his lifetime. The sisters he had left it to did not really want it – it is said that Violet's husband Wilfred Wild was against making the investment it needed – and eventually it passed into the hands of the French state. (At the end of the Second World War, however, Neill Cooper-Key, the second Lord Rothermere's brother-in-law, was offered the chance of running it, but preferred to become a Conservative MP.)

Hildebrand, who died of cirrhosis at the age of 57, had carried the family delight in jokes and wagers through to the end; he used to embarrass his sons at Eton by affecting a cockney accent. Leicester, by contrast, had an appearance of the most gloomy piety. Old Mrs Harmsworth used to joke about his 'four little undertakers' for he and his wife Annie dressed their sons in black to visit her at Poynters.

Leicester was perhaps the most underrated Harmsworth of his generation, for in some ways he united the journalistic skills of North-cliffe with the business insight of Rothermere. Born late enough to benefit from his eldest brother's largesse, he had been educated at Westminster School and Christ Church College, Oxford. It was while he was still a Liberal MP for Caithness, in 1920, that he bought the *Western Morning News* in Plymouth, a Conservative paper, and shortly after merged it with the ailing Liberal *Western Daily Mercury*. Local Conservatives, including Lord Astor, were worried that he would change the political line of the paper. He did not intervene politically but he made a considerable impact on the paper and in the West Country.

He used his wealth to become an expert bibliophile and collector, and made many benefactions to museums and art galleries in Plymouth, Exeter, Truro and to Exeter Cathedral. He bought the chapel near Honiton which was the burial place of General Simcoe, the first governor of Upper Canada, and gave many volumes of manuscripts which had belonged to General Wolfe to Canada. He gave material on Captain Scott's expedition to the Antarctic to the National Library of Australia, on Nelson to *HMS Victory*, and books to the British Museum, the Bodleian in Oxford and to help rebuild a library in Louvain destroyed in the 1914–18 war. A significant part of the Folger

Library in Washington DC was based on books originally collected by him.

Other members of the family regarded him as eccentric. His nature was melancholy. He had his 'secret' family in Caithness – a boy with a strong resemblance once came in and said 'Hello, brother' to his son Geoffrey – and his collecting was extremely catholic. A rare book dealer, valuing part of his collection in 1934, noted items ranging from early printed bibles to books by C. L. Dodgson (Lewis Carroll) and P. G. Wodehouse, from John Bunyan to Wordsworth and Coleridge. He kept many of his books in old barns.

He seems to have had a Harmsworth knack of money-making. His West Country purchases – he also bought *The Field* magazine – seem partly to have been opportunistic, and partly to provide occupation and income for his sons Harold and Geoffrey. His eldest son Alfred, who had been badly wounded in the First World War, became a recluse and took no part in the papers. Harold, who also went to Westminster and Christ Church, was a lieutenant in the Royal Marine Artillery from 1915 to 1919. On coming out of the forces he went into journalism on the *Northern Ensign* at Wick, in his father's constituency, and gradually took over the West Country interests as Leicester succumbed to heart trouble. With Alfred due to inherit Leicester's baronetcy, Leicester managed to get Harold a knighthood in 1935.

Rothermere's brother Cecil had pulled out of public life long before his death, establishing himself at Egham and in a fine house in Hyde Park Gardens which became a centre for family parties. Thought to be the best looking of the brothers, he was gentle, spoke beautifully, wrote careful memoirs of the family which presented them in the best possible light, was prejudiced in matters of race and religion but not, as his nephew Cecil King inaccurately wrote, an alcoholic.

If Cecil, who became Lord Harmsworth of Egham, was someone who had been in public life but abandoned it, Charles the backward brother was protected from the public to a considerable extent, and Vyvyan ('Boo' as a child) preferred to live quietly as a farmer. Modern Harmsworths believe that, now that so much more is known about mental handicap, Charles could have lived a much freer life; indeed, he may only have appeared retarded by comparison with the pushful brothers and sisters round him, and his mother, who had a strong protective instict beneath her flinty exterior, assumed more was wrong than it was.

Of Harold Rothermere's formidable sisters all – Lady Geraldine King, Violet Wild and Christabel Burton – had married and produced children long before Northcliffe's death. Geraldine, who had lost two sons in the First World War, was the most difficult personality. She had been part of the explosive success of *Answers* before going to India with her husband. She had also been close to their mother. But she was nothing like as well off as the brothers who were close to her in age and she nursed a bitterness which helped to poison her relationship with her surviving son Cecil, giving him complexes in his turn.

Cecil Harmsworth King, one of the most interesting of the next generation, launched his career thanks to his Rothermere uncle. Educated at Winchester and New College, Oxford – and therefore inclined to regard himself as more intelligent than his cousins – he spent nine months as a trainee in 1922–3 on the *Glasgow Record*. Then he spent three years on the *Mail* where he was made assistant advertising manager. In 1929, he became advertising director of the *Mirror*. In the mid-1930s, he came to have a dominant position in the *Mirror* group as circulation built up in the Bartholomew revolution. He had an intellectual grasp, contacts and the Harmsworth confidence. But by then his position rested not on ownership but on merit.

One person who knew the first Lord Rothermere well believed that he did not have a high regard for Cecil King's talent. Certainly, by the late 1930s there was considerable family criticism for what was seen as the vulgarity and radicalism of the *Mirror* and *Sunday Pictorial*, and a cooling off between Cecil King and his cousins and uncles. (The others later nicknamed Cecil 'Cesspit', and Lord Harmsworth of Egham, after whom he had been named, refused to propose his godson for membership of the Reform Club.)

As a young left-winger it must have been galling to have climbed a long way up the ladder thanks to nepotism. Cecil King shared some of the characteristics of his uncles – arrogance with pessimism, and a certain shyness with a desire to use newspapers to make very public explosions. He also, like his cousin Esmond and so many others after the First World War, could not quite throw off the guilt of the survivor. By what chance and for what purpose had he been spared when two of his brothers had died? With all his quirks, Cecil King was the Rothermere nephew who most consciously reached for the mantle of Northcliffe, at a time when Esmond Harmsworth might well have preferred to stay a backbench MP. And in retrospect the political line of the *Mirror* group on the European dictators in the late 1930s looked a good deal more robust than that of the *Daily Mail*.

Of course, Northcliffe had been unusual in his generation in being a Conservative supporter from his youth. His youngest sister Christabel, named after Christabel Pankhurst because old Alfred Harmsworth believed in women's suffrage, remained a genuine radical until she died in the 1960s. She campaigned for free school milk and meals in state schools, reprimanded relations who complained of paying supertax that they must be very rich to have to pay, and refused to invest in armament or alcohol shares. She had a particular aversion to investing in companies whose boards of directors were headed with peers of the realm or retired generals. As a left-wing liberal she travelled to the Soviet Union in the 1930s to see what it was like, and presided over a family which her husband described as 'a cockeyed League of Nations'. Her eldest son married first a Russian, then a French girl. Her daughter Christabel – whom the first Lord Rothermere said looked like his dead son Vere – married Peter Bielenberg, an anti-Nazi German lawyer who was put in a concentration camp after the failure of the bomb plot against Hitler. Her other daughter married an Australian, who at one time worked as a *Daily Mail* aerial photographer. Her youngest son married an Italian.

Christabel had an authentic Harmsworth confidence and the financial skill which was common to her brothers and sisters. Quite late in life she remonstrated with a clergyman who wanted her to donate money to mission work overseas, remarking, 'I've never believed in trying to turn good Muslims into bad Christians.' On one occasion when her stockbroker was trying to persuade her to buy some shares, her daughter Christabel remembers her telling him to sell everything and put her money in a building society: shortly afterwards there was a collapse of share values on the Stock Exchange.

Living in a big Elizabethan manor house near Hatfield, where things periodically went wrong and needed mending, her children were amazed by the alacrity with which she would say, 'I must telephone Mr Laing', when a tap leaked or a slate fell off the roof. By then John Laing was already running one of Britain's largest building firms. Nevertheless, within an hour or so, a team had turned up to put things right. Sometimes they were accompanied by Mr Laing himself. When one of her children asked him why such a busy and important person could be bothered to attend to Christabel's needs, he replied that there was nothing that could kill a small businessman more quickly than unpaid bills that were owing to him. 'When I was starting up in Whetstone, large or small, your mother always paid me immediately and I am only too happy to get the chance to thank her,' he said. It was an echo of the small business world of north London from which the Harmsworths themselves had sprung. When Christabel died in 1967, at the age of 87, she was buried at Totteridge.

The Victorian sense of family was demonstrated in another way, in the recycling of first generation names in the second generation. An imperfect count would reveal at least seven Alfreds, four Harolds, Cecils and St Johns, three Geraldines, Hildebrands and Vyvyans, and a couple of Leicesters. Confusion was avoided by the free use of nicknames, but even so the number of titles meant that the grander shops could be baffled by the proliferation of Lady Harmsworths.

Although Harold Rothermere could be undiplomatic and brusque, his employment of Sir George Sutton and Major Wilfred Wild as directors of the Daily Mail and General Trust showed that he wanted to preserve the concept of a family enterprise embodied in the original Harmsworth Brothers. Sutton, who never lost his London accent was the soul of fidelity, integrity and discretion. He knew who was who, and indeed was responsible for some of the payments to Northcliffe's illegitimate children. Wild, Violet's husband, also had a role as a kind of trustee for other members of the family. With Rothermere giving away so much money towards the end of his life, it was important that the children and grandchildren should have additional indirect representatives on the board.

In assessing Rothermere's impact it is necessary always to remember that he was a businessman. If he had not sorted out the accounts at *Answers* and worried about the profits of the comics, boys' and ladies' magazines, the publishing group associated with his brother's name might never have got established, or put on a firm footing. Furthermore, if he had not created an independent fortune in the twentieth century, it is hard to imagine that the *Mail* group would have survived as a family-controlled entity after Northcliffe's death. No other brother had the means, skill and inclination to step in. Even so *The Times* and Amalgamated Press had to be sold.

The boy who was good at mental arithmetic and had learned basic accounting routines in an offshoot of the civil service never lost his commercial attributes. From purging the costs at the London *Evening News* to establishing the timber and pulp business in Newfoundland he moved more widely: interested in investment opportunities in western Canada before the First World War he was, in the 1920s, speculating on Wall Street, owning the Bowater paper business in Britain, buying property in Budapest during his Hungarian phase. By the 1930s he was involved in British Movietone News, which provided newsreels for cinemas, and the diversification he set on foot led to ownership of the London General Cab Co., West End theatres and much more.

Some millionaires go to great lengths to conceal their wealth. Rothermere was one of the Edwardian rich who went out of their way to be seen to be well off: wintering in the South of France, living in majestic hotel suites, buying and selling imposing houses (one of Rothermere's houses, in Regent Park, became the official residence of the US Ambassador), travelling with a party in Rolls Royces. The appearances mattered so much that, it is said, he subscribed extra funds to St John shortly before the latter's death so that his estate, proved at £55,000, should not let the family down.

It was Rothermere's misfortune not only to be measured against Northcliffe as a public personality, but to be a press magnate in a period when the press was losing ground, and his newspapers in particular were in decline. By the time he died it was radio, with the nightly battles between Lord Haw-Haw in Berlin and the measured standard English voices of the BBC from London, which had become the dominant news medium. A hint of competition from another quarter had been dropped when the BBC started small-scale TV broadcasts from Alexandra Palace.

The advance of technology was not something he could have resisted. But the reputation of the press with the public, and the situation of his own newspapers, could have been different. The press in the 1920s and 1930s had overreached itself, not only by its propagandising and inconsistencies but also by its canvassing and free gifts. The attempt by Rothermere and Beaverbrook to take on the Conservative leadership was only a high point of folly by proprietors who confused influence with power, using readership as if it was a card vote in the pocket of a union boss. The rather puritanical calm and even-handedness of John Reith's BBC exposed the erratic and one-sided news management of the press.

It was odd that a paper owned by someone with the loosest of political affiliations, which came over as the super-Conservative paper of the middle classes, should be engaged in a constant feud with Baldwin. It was confusing for the staff of the *Mail* and confusing for the readers. With the departure of Marlowe and Caird some of the punch went out of the paper, and journalistic talent began to spread rather thinly. (At one point McWhirter was editing both the *Mail* and the *Sunday Dispatch*.) Rothermere, like Rupert Murdoch, had little regard for journalists on the whole, and it showed. The fact that he let go of the *Daily Mirror*, which had been highly successful during the First World War, was entirely because poor journalism was leading to a commercial rundown.

It was difficult perhaps, for someone who had been so closely involved in the popular press revolution which brought the *Mail* and *Mirror* into being, to be self-critical when papers like the *Express* and *Herald* were snapping at their heels. In newspapers, as in other areas of life, the radicals of one generation became an establishment for others to take pot-shots at in the next. Imposing his own campaigns on his papers became an additional cross for them to bear: against socialism, against Baldwin, nostalgic for Lloyd George and the Liberal coalition, for Empire Free Trade, for Blackshirts, for rearmament, for appeasement – there was a kind of jerkiness about the papers' line which did not communicate confidence.

When in the throes of a campaign his papers published almost no deviant reports or letters. Indeed Communists, wanting to get free tickets to the Fascist meeting at Olympia to try and disrupt it, exploited this weakness by writing pro-Blackshirt letters to the *Evening News*. At the same time, he used the power of suppression as well as of 'booming'. Just prior to the Abdication, Rothermere and Esmond were part of the cabal with Beaverbrook and Churchill which was plotting to keep Edward VIII as King, and actively suppressed material about his relationship with Wallis Simpson.

The friendship with Beaverbrook could be important not only for public campaigning but for discreet suppression. On one occasion H. G.

Wells, a great womaniser and a friend of Northcliffe, Rothermere and Beaverbrook, suffered a domestic contretemps when a girlfriend arrived on his doorstep clad only in a fur coat and stockings. On being let in she cut her wrists in an attempt at suicide. Wells rang Beaverbrook to ask him to keep it out of the papers. Beaverbrook rang Rothermere. Beaverbrook told his employees on the *Express* that nothing about Mr H. G. Wells should appear for the next three weeks.

In terms of press history it is clear that Rothermere, with his big signed articles and obvious influence over his newspapers, actually contributed to the decay of the idea that a press proprietor could be a major political force in Britain. Baldwin and the Conservative Party saw him off. More recent press controllers in this country, though they have relished the insight and occasional influence they have acquired, have stayed in the background and concentrated more on newspapering as a business, sometimes subordinate to other businesses.

On the other hand, it would be wrong to suppose that Rothermere's campaigns had no effect in the convoluted politics of the inter-war period, or were all ill-judged in themselves. He contributed to the overthrow of the first minority Labour government and to the consensus support for appeasement in the 1930s. History has vindicated his sustained call for aerial rearmament, some of his criticism of Baldwin, and his recognition that Hungarians had been badly treated after the First World War. His adventure with the Blackshirts, and the unattractive mixture of fear and admiration with which he regarded the Nazis, were part of a broader canvas.

His personality was as complex as Northcliffe's. For left-wingers in the 1920s and 1930s he appeared the arch-reactionary, and in some Conservative circles he was distrusted for disloyalty to the party and its leadership; some of his business dealings – particularly the boosting of shares in which he was interested – and aspects of his private life attracted disapproval. But the closer people got to him, the more on the whole they liked him. Though some of his donations might seem excessive, it was also hard actively to hate a man who managed to give away nearly all of arguably Britain's third largest private fortune.

His air of shyness and authoritarianism could be off-putting, but he mixed it in with charm and humour. His anxieties went along with obstinacy and ruthlessness. As with Northcliffe he had an air of unpredictability, and a self-made man's feeling that anything was possible: he could establish a massive development in Newfoundland, start new papers, make peace with dictators, launch a new political party. Projects which would have covered lesser mortals with tergiversation and worry were not only manageable to him but often done at short notice.

He could also be extremely considerate of individuals, inside and outside the family. A case in point was Mrs Redhead, mother of

Margaret Hunam Redhead who was to marry his son Esmond. He and his family had first met the Redheads on holiday in Switzerland. He was in Vancouver on business when Mrs Redhead married again, to Sir Edmund Lacon, a major in the lancers. Rothermere acted as best man at the wedding and later offered to accompany her by train across Canada, since she was returning to England to have a baby. On the train journey Rothermere learned that her new husband had died, tragically and unexpectedly, and decided to keep the news from her. Back in Britain he kept a friendly and supportive eye on her and her children.

His worries about bolshevism were real to him, and communicated to others. He used to encourage his son and family to come down from London to Benenden because it was 'safer' – there was less danger of street riots. When Esmond first married he bought a house in Grosvenor Street, Mayfair, but Rothermere persuaded him to move to Campden Hill, as they were less likely to be at risk from demonstrations or civil disturbances. When his grandchildren Lorna and Vere visited the United States in 1937, he insisted that they should have a bodyguard because he had been alarmed by the Lindbergh kidnapping case.

His charm was powerful. In 1926, when he met the young Russian dancer Alice Nikitina, who was one of the stars in Diaghilev's Ballet which he financed, he made an immediate impact on her. Recalling it later in her autobiography, she wrote:

> Lord R was at that time 58 years old, but looked much younger. His superlative manners, his youthful humour, that came straight from the heart, made me feel very soon at my ease, as with a friend of old standing, when we went to have supper together. In spite of his dazzling personality he knew how to raise you on to a pedestal and make you feel superior to himself. He questioned me on my life, my childhood, and admired my love and devotion to the dance.[28]

Diaghilev, who was sometimes irritated when Rothermere tried to intervene to promote individual dancers, told his troupe that the English peer could 'conjure up or stop wars'. Around him, after Northcliffe's death, there clung an aura of power, even though in reality his only completely effective power was over the newspapers and business he controlled.

By the mid 1930s he had passed over much of that, so much of his appeasement and rearmament campaigning could be regarded as the interest of a retired businessman. Although he was not a journalist on a par with Northcliffe, and at least some of his articles were drafted for him, he had a gift for a forceful phrase. Writing in the *Mail* in 1933 to dismiss useless gestures by pacifists he said, 'they might just as sensibly try to pacify a Bengal tiger by blowing kisses at it.' Writing to his friend Churchill in July 1939 he said, 'I think Hitler has been badly handled.

Instead of the language of reproach and rebuke constantly applied to him, I should have tried out the language of butter.'[29]

Like Northcliffe he tended to worry about his health and would take a doctor in his entourage. He got pleasure from walking, from his fruit farm in Kent, his pictures and furniture, from motoring, from his grandchildren, but above all he got joy from giving presents. He was a most generous friend. When Churchill was staying with him on the Riviera in January 1939, for instance, he provided him with money to play with on the Casino tables at Monte Carlo. Forecasting in July of that year that a great responsibility would be placed on Churchill before long, he offered him a further £600 if he would abstain again from drinking brandy for a year.

Dying abroad, after the great calamity which he had foreseen and tried to avert had come to pass, meant that Britain in November 1940 had too many other things to think about. The decease of the 1st Viscount Rothermere, when bombs were falling nightly and an invasion scare was fresh in readers' minds, gave a quality of remoteness, the sense of a vanished era, to the obituaries and Ward-Price's appreciation in the *Mail*.

Yet one of his friends, whom he had succoured when he was in the political wilderness, was Britain's Prime Minister. Another was playing the role of air dictator, almost exactly as he had recommended. The exploits of the Spitfire and Hurricane pilots in the Battle of Britain were making invasion impossible, just as he had been saying for seven years. At the same time, a family estate, which frankly might have collapsed when his elder brother died, was still in being and substantial. Even after his mistakes were taken into account, he had handed on a solid heritage of achievement.

PART III

Esmond Rothermere

The Son

9
From 1898 to 1937

Although his family was famous and affluent, there were various unhappinesses in Esmond's childhood. In later life he did not talk much about it to friends. But it is likely that, as the youngest brother, he suffered most from the breakdown of his parents' marriage which happened in his early teens. He was 16 and at Eton in the year the First World War started, which overshadowed the rest of his studies. His experience of schooling was not that these were the most marvellous days of his life: he was bullied, was severely ill with mastoiditis, had the disadvantage at Eton of following an eldest brother who was a star at everything, and was recalled afterwards as something of a martinet. There may also have been a down side to bearing the Harmsworth name, with a father who was ostentatious about his wealth and an uncle who was tending to irritate the establishment by his attacks on various aspects of the war effort. Above all, with his mother vanishing, there was little to protect him from a father who, though devoted, was extremely overbearing.

Growing up during the war, when his brothers were already fighting and the casualty lists were lengthening, must have made for a pressurised adolescence. A university education, which might have been automatic in peacetime, was out of the question. Instead, in 1917, he was commissioned in the Royal Marine Artillery. By that stage his brother Vere, who had been to Osborne, was dead; before the end of the year his brother Vyvyan would be severely wounded again, leading to his death in London. It was understandable that their father would not wish to put his last son at risk and prevented him from going overseas.

None the less, the war had a huge impact on Esmond's life, catapulting him unexpectedly into a position where he was heir to both Northcliffe and his own father. It was a daunting responsibility, and the qualities of remoteness and suspicion that people sometimes noted in him later may have originated as a protective camouflage: to be associated with a man popularly seen as the most powerful Englishman outside the government, and an Air Minister who was one of the richest millionaires, could expose a young man to envy, hostility and the unwelcome attention of gold-diggers. The sudden burden also had another effect; when the war was over he sought release in practical jokes, pillow fights, and water fights with his family and friends. The fact that he had not served in the trenches or won gallantry medals was also embarrassing. During the 1920s his wife would sometimes go alone to court balls where medals would be worn, and he would send apologies.

With the end of the war Esmond became part of the great game which the Harmsworth brothers were playing with the Lloyd George coalition and the dictation of the peace terms. There was little chance of him being demobilised to go to university or to learn the newspaper business from the bottom up. It was Northcliffe's will that he should be elected Conservative and Unionist MP for the Isle of Thanet, that is, not a coalition Liberal like his own father and uncle Cecil, but a Conservative.

Whether Northcliffe was looking ahead, anxious that his beloved *Daily Mail* should not fall into the hands of a young man who, if precautions were not taken, might share the radical bees in Harold's bonnet, is hard to tell; he may also have been looking back to his own campaign as a young man in Portsmouth. But at a council of war at Elmwood, he, Harold and Esmond agreed that his nephew should run for Parliament. He was boosted in the family papers as an Anti-Waste candidate. Horatio Bottomley came down for the eve-of-poll meeting for Esmond and drew a large crowd. Esmond was duly elected and, in 1919, was the youngest MP in the Commons at the age of 21.

After all the fulminations from Northcliffe about the peace terms, and his anxiety to play some part at Versailles, there was then a curious sequel. Lloyd George appointed Esmond as his ADC in the peace negotiations. There was no way that a man of Esmond's age, just embarking on a political career, could be said to have won this privilege on his own merits. He got it because of who he was and the name he bore. Rather like Lloyd George's use of his father and his uncle Cecil, he was part of the Welsh wizard's contact system with the press in an age of active proprietorship, before government public relations had been institutionalised. For Esmond, of course, though a relatively humble onlooker, it was a marvellous opportunity – the equivalent of a graduate course in politics and international relations.

For a decade Esmond was a backbench Conservative MP and by all accounts he was happy in an undemanding and gentlemanly role. Although he was a director of Associated Newspapers, and had an office in the newspaper building, he was perceived more as an MP than as a press proprietor in waiting. He and his family spent summer holidays in Ramsgate, in the constituency, and his wife developed a sure touch with local people. 'Are you feeling better now?' she would ask of those she did not know well in a sympathetic way. Since the Isle of Thanet was filled with aches and pains which were crying out to be comforted, this was a winning formula.

Tall at 6 feet 4 inches and good looking, Esmond was well endowed with the Harmsworth charm and could make a good speech. But although he enjoyed the Commons he did not shine there and his children, when young, were hardly aware that he was an MP. His reputation suffered from the feeling among other MPs that he was just a megaphone for his father. But there were certain things that he personally cared about. Although he did not much like flying, for example, he flew back from Italy to be able to vote to preserve the Book of Common Prayer. He was not terribly religious, though he usually took his children to church on Sundays, but he was fond of the sixteenth-century language of the Anglican prayer book. He also voted against the partition of Ireland.

On arrival he was the third Harmsworth in the Commons, joining Cecil and Sir Leicester. Cecil, with his melodious voice, played an active part in defending the coalition government's foreign policy. Sir Leicester, who did not stir much beyond specialised questions relating to his constituency in the North of Scotland, would have been a less prominent example. By 1923 Esmond was the only Harmsworth MP.

Esmond was more active than many MPs in asking questions, and in taking up constituency issues, including specific injustices affecting ex-servicemen in Thanet. His Anti-Waste views broadened out into a dislike of public expenditure which sixty years later could be described as 'dry' or 'Thatcherite'; at a time of post-war depression and unemployment he saw taxation and public expenditure as a waste of money which prevented private enterprise from prospering, and providing jobs.

For instance, on 21 July 1921, he wanted to know what steps the President of the Board of Education (the historian H. A. L. Fisher) had taken to reduce expenditure by 20 per cent as part of the government economy measures. 'Does not the right honourable gentleman think that it is the enormous cost to the country of the present education schemes that is causing unemployment and high taxation?' he asked. This led to some heckling from a Labour MP, Mr J. Jones, who commented, 'The biggest waste of all is the money they spent on your education.'

Probably echoing a niggle of his father's, he took a particular dislike to a public relations and publishing section set up by the RAF, and asked several questions about the cost and usefulness of the RAF's Central Editing Section which was run by an Air Vice Marshal. Addressing the House, in November 1922, in the debate on the King's Speech after the general election, he criticised a British loan to Austria (which he described as 'a tinpot state'), called for British evacuation from Iraq and Palestine to save expense, and uged the government to cut taxation.

By 1924, with a minority Labour government in power, he was busy asking questions on a host of matters, some of them relating to East Kent, others possibly inspired by his connection with the *Mail* group and his father. In July of that year he initiated a Supply debate on claims for compensation due to enemy action during the war. Although six years had gone by those whose homes had been hit, or whose fishing boats had suffered from shelling or bombing, had not had any reparation. Obviously, the numbers of people who had suffered in that way were quite small – although Elmwood was not the only part of East Kent to suffer from German gunnery – but the fact that the issue had to be raised was itself a comment on the effectiveness of the 1918–19 campaign in the *Daily Mail* to make Germany pay. The post-war world had proved frustratingly recalcitrant to the slogans with which the war had been won.

Sometimes his views on economy and public spending could make him appear hard-nosed. By 1926, when Baldwin's Conservative government had defeated the general strike and the miners had been forced back to work, he got figures published in *Hansard* which demonstrated that several Boards of Guardians in mining areas were technically insolvent. They had been raising loans without authority in order to pay relief to miners' families. The poor law system, always shabby and mean, was simply overwhelmed by mass unemployment and the effects of strikes and lock-outs. Boards of Guardians had been doing what they could to stem hunger and destitution; but this meant that the Bedwellty board, for instance, was in debt to the extent of £779,905 in its part of Wales.

His father was against 'the flapper vote' – the final extension of the suffrage to all women which Harold Rothermere blamed for Labour's success in the 1929 election – and Esmond argued against it in a Commons speech on 29 March 1928. He made an epigrammatic comment. 'It [the Bill] is to the Socialists, I firmly believe, a stunt, to the Liberals, I think, a very doubtful point but probably a conundrum, and I certainly say that to the Conservatives it is a snare.' While he admitted that it might seem illogical to stand against votes for women he said that the whole British constitution was built on illogicality. He believed, for example, that the dominance of one House of Parliament, the Commons, was an even greater defect.

Esmond did not run for Parliament again in the 1929 elections and went into the business instead, which he had to learn from the top down. By that stage his marriage was becoming unsteady and a whole phase of his life – when he seemed young, rich, with a boisterous family, and was shielded from newspaper responsibilities by activity which revolved round politics – was coming to an end.

There had been more than a hint of family disapproval of his marriage, on 12 January 1920 at St John's Church, Bromley to Margaret Redhead, usually known as Peggy. Peggy was a Roman Catholic, educated at the Sacred Heart Convent, Roehampton, whose father William Redhead had died when she was only 10. He had had various business interests – in Barnsley coal and a South African emeralds mine – but at his death, even though six bags of gold nuggets were discovered, his widow was not well off. She married again, to Sir Robert Lacon.

Peggy was stunningly beautiful, fair and with a lovely bone structure. She had known all the Harmsworth boys after her mother had been befriended by old Lord Rothermere, and she might well have married Vyvyan had he lived. She was full of life and charm. However, she was a year older than Esmond, she had been brought up a Catholic whereas he, like most of the Harmsworths, was Church of England, and she may already have been through a form of marriage to a soldier which was either invalid or annulled. Although Harold Rothermere quickly made it up with her – he commissioned an artist to paint a picture of them on their honeymoon – he may also have hoped that his son might have made a more ambitious match. As it was, the wedding was conducted by Canon Buchanan-Barker, a cousin of the bride's father, and St John (Uncle Bonch) was the only senior Harmsworth present. An Etonian friend of Esmond's, Leo d'Erlanger, was his best man.

Their children came quickly and were all born at home. Lorna Peggy appeared on 24 October 1920, actually at her grandfather's house at Hemsted, Benenden. Esme Mary Gabrielle was born on 6 July 1922 at Hill Lodge, Campden Hill, Kensington. And Vere Harold Esmond was born on 27 August 1925 at Warwick House, St James's during a dinner party: two of the guests, Harold Rothermere and Winston Churchill, were taken upstairs to be introduced to the new scion of the house.

Looking back there is an idyllic quality about Esmond's family life in the 1920s, of fun and high spirits. They knew plenty of 'roarers' – the youngsters with money and without inhibitions who were letting off steam in reaction to the Great War and in hopes of a new age dawning. It was a foretaste of the swinging 'sixties, but restricted to a narrower segment of society, which was enjoying itself publicly when millions of Europeans were feeling very far from prosperous.

Esmond and his young wife and children holidayed on a farm at Fairlight, near Hastings and at Malta Cottage, Yarmouth, Isle of Wight where they had a boat. Their children recalled the Yarmouth cottage as a time when they were a real family, and old home movies show Esmond firing water from a hosepipe at children and guests, and even getting his mother-in-law sucked into the games. He and Peggy often had friends staying, sometimes Esmond's cronies whose role was not only to be companions but to assist him in the sports of a gentleman.

Being good at sport, like being an Old Etonian, formed part of the transition to second generation security and respectability at which Esmond worked hard. He was a member of the All England Club at Wimbledon and played tennis in doubles tournaments there and in

Monte Carlo. He was a good cricketer, helped by an old professional named Bligh who joined his retinue. He rode to hounds with the West Kent hunt, later on taking his daughters with them and sitting down afterwards in front of a roaring fire to sausages and mash. He loved swimming, insisting when he was in his sixties that his guests at Daylesford should swim in his pool, more or less whether they liked it or not.

In the 1920s the cronies included Charles Kingsley, England's number one tennis player in the Davis Cup for many years, who was known as 'Mickey' to the Harmsworths because they thought he looked like Mickey Mouse. Another was 'Cammy' – Ewan Cameron – who was the manager at the Mereworth estate in Kent which Esmond bought in 1927. 'Cammy' was the butt of many jokes. Indeed, Esmond is recalled as having a child-like sense of humour, reminiscent of the previous generation, but with an occasionally hard or cruel edge. While the fun and games might be a release from the awesome responsibilities he would inherit there remained a ruthless aspect to him, and it was difficult for him and for others to establish an easy equality of friendship.

By the mid-1920s Esmond and Peggy had acquired two attractive and desirable homes: Warwick House in St James's, opposite Lancaster House which was not very far from the house in Carlton Gardens where Northcliffe had died; and Mereworth Castle in Kent, a house with two wings which had been built in imitation of Palladio's villa at Vicenza in Italy, which carried with it a substantial estate on which both Esmond and Peggy kept their own strings of horses.

Warwick House, originally built by Henry Errington, was one of the finest of London private houses, although rambling and not easy to manage later with a reducing number of servants. It was furnished with crimson velvet curtains made out of a Delhi Durbar tent. The cooks' and servants' quarters were in the basement and when there was a soufflé for dinner they had to run a relay race to get it to the table before it collapsed.

The house was Esmond's home for half a century and both Vere and his young stepbrother, little Esmond, were born there. Piquantly, it was also a semi-detached neighbour to Stornoway House which belonged to Lord Beaverbrook, Harold Rothermere's friend and popularly supposed to be a deadly rival to Esmond when he took command of the *Mail* group.

In fact, though Warwick House was the scene of much entertaining, there was surprisingly little traffic between the two press barons as neighbours. Beaverbrook was guest of honour at a dinner in Warwick House in 1962, shortly before his death, yet the two Harmsworth girls grew up hardly aware of the existence of the two Aitken boys, Max and Peter, next door.

Both Warwick House and Mereworth were very grand, with butlers and footmen in uniform, and a great deal easier to run in the 1920s and 1930s when household and garden staff were plentiful and cheap to hire. At Mereworth, for instance, there were twenty gardeners before the Second World War. The children had a posse of nannies and under-nannies. Mereworth, where county cricket was played, was particularly difficult and costly to manage as a house because of its wings. During an economy drive instigated by Harold Rothermere after the Wall Street crash, Esmond and his family withdrew into just one of the wings. The buildings were taken over by the Royal Air Force, whose West Malling fighter base was nearby, during the Second World War and Esmond sold the house and estate after the war.

Whereas both Northcliffe and Harold Rothermere came to see themselves as movers and shakers, people who made things happen in the world of public affairs, Esmond in the 1920s was much more an apprentice and a witness. In addition to knowing the friends of his father's generation, like Winston Churchill (and long after the Second World War he was a regular at Churchill's private dining club, the Other Club), he made his own friends among the younger Tory MPs. He must have had a ringside view, for instance, of the 1926 general strike. But he was not an actor on the stage, influencing events.

The one point at which he was propelled into the foreground was when his father's Hungarian agitation sent him to Hungary in 1928. He accepted an honorary degree at Szeged University, commented with a double meaning that the iron crown of St Stephen was too heavy to wear, and was applauded when he visited the Parliament. It was an exciting, high-profile time which offered few chances to relax. When he and his party wanted to go to a night-club in the evening in Budapest, for example, their pleasure was somewhat interrupted when all present got up to sing the national anthem. Esmond was also reminded of the risks of Balkan politics when an assassination threat from conservative monarchists hastened their withdrawal over the border.

None the less, with his tact and political nous, as well as his still youthful appearance, Esmond represented his father in Hungary with considerable skill. When, sixty-one years later, in different circumstance, his son Vere visited Hungary as a guest of a liberalising Communist government, he retraced some of his father's footsteps and found the family name still held in esteem. Esmond had made his own contribution which consolidated his father's newspaper campaign.

Although editors might later feel that Esmond treated them in a cavalier fashion he was capable of great loyalty, a trait which he first demonstrated in the 1920s. For instance, from 1922 to 1929 he employed Gerald Sanger as his private secretary. Sanger, a Surrey man, was of his own age. He had first met him in the Royal Marine Artillery. It was a firm rule of Northcliffe that you should have a male secretary – 'a good top hat man' – and Sanger, who was interested in Conservative politics, intelligent and good looking, served Esmond as a colleague and periodic confidant for the rest of his career.

From 1929 to the 1950s Sanger was editor of British Movietone News, the cinema newsreel service where Esmond owned nearly half the shares, and he finished as a *Mail* group director. He kept a diary for many of those years which showed Esmond close to, in all his moods. Sanger regarded him as his benefactor, and as a big man. But he also felt that he could be pompous and ridiculous, and that he needed standing up to if he was tempted by a course of action which could be damaging to the papers or group. This was a process which Esmond, who had been brought up in the belief that newspaper proprietors were usually overbearing and got their way, did not much like.

But the overlap between a working and social relationship was also considerable. On one occasion Sanger was asked to take some medical supplies to Esmond in the South of France, and was then kept three weeks to play tennis. On another, Sanger's wife, who was Canadian, was asked to bring a favourite hat of Peggy's down to Southampton before she sailed, being put up at a Southampton hotel at Esmond's expense for her pains.

Esmond treated Sanger loyally, not only rewarding him with a lifetime's career in the group. By 1947, for example, it was clear that Sanger had been enabled to invest in Associated Newspapers and five other companies which were either subsidiaries or closely connected with the group. In the 1960s, Esmond paid for one of his sons to attend Harvard Business School. There were others like Sanger who served him with discretion and with whom he could relax. His children felt that 'Cammy', the Mereworth estate manager who was much teased, was also a great consolation to Esmond.

From 1929 to 1937 Esmond was working full time for the business, although the habits originated by Northcliffe and his father did not mean that he had to spend every day from nine to five in the office. In fact he spent time in the South of France and at Mereworth, conducting business as they had done by telephone and telegram. However, he had a room next door to Sir George Sutton in Carmelite House which he used regularly.

This must have been a difficult time for Esmond who had no grassroots experience of journalism or newspapers as a business, and who was permitted to gain authority only gradually. His father was a looming presence, with views on everything from Mosley to Baldwin and appeasement, which were not only published in columns over his own name but which ordained the news and editorial coverage of the papers. Old Lord Rothermere, though he was divesting himself of control of the *Mirror* and was happy for his son to take on day-to-day responsibility for the detailed operation of the *Mail* group, did not find it easy to give up his power.

Esmond was not only in tutelage to his father, liable to be treated as a factotum, but he was surrounded by tradition. Sutton, regarded by the younger journalists as the link with the old man, was there all the time and sat in on most of Esmond's meetings. Then and later Esmond found it difficult to make up his mind: his father, Sutton and many others were only too happy to try and do so for him.

Esmond was made chairman of Associated Newspapers in 1932 and, in the first five years of his chairmanship, he had a good introduction to the difficulties of his inheritance. Although the *Evening News* was still selling nearly 2 million copies and was highly profitable, and the *Sunday Dispatch* was in the secure hands of Harry Lane as editor, the flagship *Daily Mail* was hitting problems. The *Express* overtook it in sales, spurred on by Beaverbrook's journalistic enthusiasm and his willingness to spend money. The zig-zags of Harold Rothermere's political campaigning damaged the *Mail*'s credibility, and his Blackshirt period had affronted an important section of advertisers. The response of Esmond and his father was drastic and ineffectual: to keep on changing the editor of the *Mail*. In the first half of the 1930s the editor was changing almost annually, and not always for the best journalistically. In his autobiography, *Leap Before You Look*, Aidan Crawley records that one untalented editor was thought to have got the job largely because he had found the girlfriends old Lord Rothermere liked in Paris.[1]

While Esmond was interested in the political coverage of the *Mail*, which had a good political correspondent at this time in 'Jack' Broadbent, there is no evidence that he quarrelled with the direction laid down by his father. On the other hand, there is reliable testimony that he disagreed with him about business matters.[2] In particular he objected to false economies which he saw his father trying to impose on the papers, for publicity and other purposes, which Esmond saw as necessary in the competitive climate of the 1930s. It was partly the old man's tendency to panic coming through again. Also, times had changed. Whereas it was possible in the 1920s to treat the papers as milch cows, Esmond, as a younger man, could see that with the growing success of the *Express* newspapers, the *Mail* and its sister papers were going to have to fight hard to hold their corner. (By the 1930s the *Sunday* as well as the *Daily Express* was becoming a serious force.)

A sense that new men were needed for the new conditions facing the press meant that Esmond encouraged a number of people of his own generation in the firm. Coming up on the management side were Robert Redhead and Stuart McClean (known as Donald), who was a bright young man, a nephew of Percy Burton whose education had been paid for by Christabel, and who in his turn had been able to pay for much of a younger brother's education through the scholarships he had won. One of Esmond's protégés on the journalistic side was Aidan Crawley.

Aidan Crawley was one of three talented sons of an archdeacon. He had played county cricket for Kent while still an undergraduate at Oxford. A mutual friend, who worked for the wine firm of Justerini and Brooks, told Esmond that he was just the sort of young man whom he should recruit. A letter from Esmond and an interview followed and in October 1930 Crawley joined the *Mail* as a young reporter. The day he arrived the R101 airship had crashed, and he was sent round six addresses the paper had for the mistress of its designer.

Looking back over fifty years later, Crawley thinks that Esmond had marked him out soon for a senior job either in journalism or newspaper management.[3] He was given a very privileged apprenticeship, invited down to Mereworth for tennis, sent on a tour of six of the Northcliffe provincial papers in 1932, and to cover the New Deal for the *Sunday Dispatch* a year later. The same year, 1933, he was invited to be Esmond's companion on a round-the-world tour. His task would be to write articles for the *Mail* and *Sunday Dispatch* as the trip proceeded.

The idea for the tour was Harold Rothermere's, who wanted a sea cruise in the Mediterranean. It was from his home in Monte Carlo that the expedition began, when the party drove to Genoa to pick up an Italian liner, the *Vittorio*. In addition to father and son and Crawley, the group included the inevitable Ward-Price, and Sir Perceval Phillips, a Foreign Editor who somewhat resented being part of a rich man's junket. Ward-Price and old Lord Rothermere played shuffle-board, Ward-Price being sent at intervals to buy and sell enormous quantities of currency via the ship's radio operator. Crawley played deck tennis with Esmond.

Lord Rothermere had planned to leave the young men at either Alexandria or Port Said, but in fact got off at Haifa. From then on they were on their own with their retinue. In India, Esmond arranged for a private train with four coaches and the Maharajah of Bhopal laid on a tiger shoot in Esmond's honour. In Delhi, they were ticked off by Lady Willingdon, the Viceroy's wife, for sending a telegram to say that they would be twenty-four hours late. This was not the way a Viceroy should be treated. They apologised humbly; Crawley was blamed for letting Esmond commit such a social error. It was almost as though the son of Viscount Rothermere was the heir to an Indian principality who could never by convention make a mistake, but could only be badly advised. (In England, the well-mannered Esmond once let Queen Mary be greeted at Mereworth by a butler.)

For Crawley it was all entertaining, a mixture of work and holiday. Everywhere they went the party was treated with deference, much as Northcliffe himself had been on his world tour. But Esmond got bored and he and Sir Perceval left Crawley at Singapore to go home. He did not want Crawley to cut short the trip, and indeed Crawley had a fascinating time crossing a China dominated by warlords, and visiting a Hollywood where he had introductions to all the studio bosses and was surprised to find that guests were invited to sample the charms of any of the female stars under contract.

Conscious that such a mark of proprietorial favour was bound to evoke jealousy among other journalists, Esmond showed some sensitivity about Crawley's return. 'I think I'd keep out of the office for a while,' he told him, and for a year he became the *Mail*'s hunting correspondent. This involved him in hunting with sixty-six packs one season and writing consumer reports in a light vein; he also took eight or nine days riding over the downs from Oxford to Exeter in an experiment to see whether it was still possible, in 'thirties England, to find inns which could accommodate two riders and two horses.

The political controversies of the later 1930s inevitably had an impact inside the offices of the *Mail* group. The policy line of the papers was criticised both from the left, where a more vigorous anti-fascist stance was demanded and the group's sympathy for Franco in the Spanish Civil War seemed abhorrent, and on the right, where followers of Churchill were denouncing appeasement of the dictators. The tradition of proprietorial dominance in matters of editorial policy meant that there was nothing much anyone who disagreed could do except leave.

In 1936–7, there was a trickle of such departures. Crawley himself, then being attracted into the Labour Party, found a verbal instruction passed round the office that nothing unfavourable should be written about Hitler, Mussolini or the Emperor of Japan to be the last straw. George Ward-Price had just been sent to interview each of them in a sympathetic light. At the same time, an Old Etonian sub-editor left for political reasons and Randolph Churchill, who had been given great encouragement by Harold Rothermere, ceased writing for the group.

Crawley, who had seemed destined for high things, was impressed by the generosity with which Esmond reacted to the news that he was leaving. Although he said that he wanted to run for Parliament as a Labour candidate, Esmond implied that to be an MP was what was important, it did not matter much which party you were in. He also made clear that Crawley's decision would in no way affect their friendship, and he would always be a welcome guest.

In fact Esmond was as good as his word, and Crawley has paid tribute to Esmond's qualities of personal loyalty. When Crawley was hard up he became a deputy presenter to Leslie Mitchell on British Movietone News. When he married the American journalist Virginia Cowles four days after being elected Labour MP for Buckingham in the Labour landslide of 1945, Esmond gave them both a wedding lunch. And when, at Esmond's dinner table, some other friends including Anthony Head and Leo d'Erlanger were being critical of Crawley's then Labour views, Esmond told them sharply that he would never hear anything spoken against Crawley in his house.

By 1937, when Esmond became chairman of the Daily Mail and

General Trust, he was 39 and his father was a wearying 69. For as long as his father was alive there would always be a slight doubt as to whether he was complete master of the firm, but by the outward signs of company title and responsibility he had now entered his inheritance. He had had a long apprenticeship and his transition from agent to independent authority had been slow.

Although in the 1930s and 1940s he was more interested in journalistic content and quality than he became later, his period of preparation had stressed political and business concerns rather than journalism. These were what his father had worried about for most of his life. Esmond, seeing *Mail* editors come and go in the 1930s, inevitably regarded journalists as dispensable. What is different about newspapers compared with other commodities, what makes them more than a loudspeaker for political views or a report in a balance sheet, is that they have souls, quirks and the affection of their readers. Northcliffe had understood this well, the area in which the magic of journalism has free play.

For Esmond, however, this was a weakness. His education in newspapers had not developed his confidence and judgement in analysing reporting, subediting and that way of mixing material which makes all the difference between a lively and a dreary newspaper. This defect was compounded by the fact that his own mind was reactive rather than innovative: he was surrounded by advice and trained to respond to it, sometimes finding it hard to make up his mind. And in the outside world the Rothermere press was living in a more competitive industry. Beaverbrook, originally a financier, had discovered that he was an editor-in-chief of genius. Down-market of the *Mail* the *Daily Herald* had achieved a fancy circulation with its offers and promotions, and the *Mirror* had begun a steady rise based on a new kind of popular, tabloid, left-wing journalism.

The eight-year period of induction, from 1929 to 1937, had coincided with a change in Esmond's personal life. After two or three years teetering on the brink, he and his first wife split up in 1930, although nearly eight years went by before they were finally divorced. The marriage breakdown seems to have involved a fair amount of bitterness, though at times his wife Peggy hoped that a reconciliation might be possible.

For about seven years the two had been relatively happy. As always on these occasions there was a variety of causes which contributed to the final result. There were general causes which affected a whole generation. The 1920s were not good for marriages. The spirit of release in the jazz age, the shortage of men who had survived the war, the greater opportunities for those who were good looking and wealthy – such things were hazards for others too.

There were also particular causes affecting them alone. Temperamentally they had diverged. They had been young when they married and as time passed such divergences showed through. Esmond, though he had enjoyed fun and games with the family, was fundamentally a serious person. Peggy was more light-hearted. Parliament and newspapers meant that Esmond was committed to spending time in London. Peggy preferred the country. The personal chemistry which had kept them together had lost its force.

For Esmond the example of his father – pursuing pleasure with the opposite sex with such system that a servant sent to accompany a mistress departing from a Paris main line station was instructed to collect an arrival, too – was bound to be unsettling. In France, where the couple had bought a house at Cannes, they had mixed with the fast Riviera set. Esmond in particular became friendly with the Prince of Wales and his group. Were he not married already, Esmond would have been the supremely eligible bachelor. And he had opportunities, when Parliament was sitting but his wife was in the country, to meet people on his own. Peggy, for her part, was not only pretty but could be flirtatious.

The collapse of the marriage was accompanied with various bits of untruth and unpleasantness. On one occasion, Esmond met his wife off a train and warned her that he had a girl staying with him; he said she had been taken ill at a party and had stayed on, and his wife must not make a scene. When they met the girl she had on a new ruby bracelet and flew at Peggy for daring to be married to Esmond. In the South of France, in that Scott Fitzgerald milieu where chambermaids could pass themselves off as princesses, friends would push girls in Esmond's direction.

The children were still quite young when, at the height of the marital crisis, their mother took them from Warwick House and moved into Claridge's Hotel. A much-loved nanny was sacked and the children had no outings for a while. With Lorna 10, Esme and Vere around 8 and 5, respectively, it was an unsettling time; Vere as the youngest, who had been specially fond of the nanny, was perhaps the most affected. The long period in which their parents were separated but not actually divorced may also have been tense at times.

It was during this period that Esmond gained the custody of his children who normally stayed with him for most of the school holidays. When a settlement was finally reached with his ex-wife, it was on the basis that he had custody and she had the children with her for two months a year. She received a handsome allowance and was bought Athelhampton Hall in Dorset as a home. In the meantime, Lorna had inherited her mother's rooms at Warwick House, and she and her sister had also inherited their mother's chauffeur as a driver and chaperone.

Such were the different mores of the 1930s, and so considerable was the power of a press baron that the separation and divorce were kept out of the press. Yet for several years when Esmond was still technically

married he was acting as though he was a bachelor. When there was
county cricket at Mereworth, for instance, part of the fun was a house
party to which chorus girls from a London show would be invited; old
Lord Rothermere would be seated with one on each arm. As for
Esmond's first wife, who went on like him to marry twice more, she had
a lengthy affair with Prince Aly Khan with whom she shared an interest
in racing. In fact he used to study the racing form book at breakfast.

When the divorce finally came to the courts Peggy cited a number of
co-respondents. Jokingly, one of them is alleged to have said at the time,
'I didn't mind being cited – but I was cited as one of twenty-eight!' As
for their children, when the divorce was finalised, it was as though the
teenage girls were older and their father was younger – a situation in
which they could become closer friends, but where the teenage
daughters could occasionally exploit a doting father's feeling of
affection and guilt. He naturally felt more responsible for his children in
the new circumstances, and in fact did not marry for a second time
himself until both his daughters were married themselves.[4]

Esmond was extremely fond of his children. His daughters remember
him as being good fun, playing games with them and their friends. They
in turn could run rings round him when they wanted to, asking to
switch schools, for example, for little better reason than that their
friends had done so. But there was a more serious side to the relationship, too. He would take the children to see any Shakespeare plays on in
London during the holidays. They remember him too, uncommunica-
tively, pacing round and round a room at Warwick House as they
watched, as if the cares of the world were on his shoulders.

His attempted round-the-world tour and his immersion in the
newspaper business in the 1930s took place against the background of a
private life in England which was financially comfortable but
emotionally in disarray. From Mereworth he would dictate editorials
for the *Mail*, and he carried out much of his management of the group
over the telephone from whichever house he was in. For much of his life
he had a routine phone call at 5.30 pm from the editor of the *Mail* to
discuss the news of the day and the leader the paper would carry.
Throughout that time, too, he took pains to keep himself fit, occasionally going to a sanatorium for a cure – the equivalent of the health
farm cure which became fashionable in the 1960s.

By the time he became chairman of the Daily Mail and General Trust
in 1937 he was a man of considerable experience, even if this was much
less dramatic than the learning curve of his father's generation. To
people who knew them both it was clear that the son was quite different
from Harold Rothermere: more liberal and gentlemanly in his attitudes,
less likely to dash off at tangents, more cautious about using newspapers as engines of propaganda, but also perhaps less self-confident,
less willing to take a gamble. It was inconceivable that he would try to

remake British party politics, or carry out a vendetta against the leader of the Conservative Party.

Esmond never had stand-up rows with his father, but they disagreed about some aspects of the business and they do not ever seem to have been close. In the 1920s, on one occasion, he had pretended to be ill to put off seeing his father; on another, when he was so worried about some bill that needed paying that he had actually made himself ill, his father sent a cheque round and he recovered at once. Generally speaking, his father was always encouraging Esmond to spend money, to maintain the image of family wealth.

Unquestionably, Esmond took over the *Mail* group in a less flourishing state, especially journalistically, than his father had inherited from Northcliffe. The *Mail* itself, a broadsheet paper with a respectable layout not dissimilar from that of the *Daily Telegraph* in the 1960s and 1970s, had lost fire and credibility. The political stance stamped on it in the 1930s by Harold Rothermere, so different from the anti-German warnings which Northcliffe had carried for a decade before the First World War, meant that the *Mail* and its sister papers were ill-prepared as, relentlessly, the prospect of a war between the British Empire and Nazi Germany increased.

By the later 1930s papers like the *Mirror* and *Sunday Pictorial* were becoming fervently anti-Nazi, which helped them to build new circulations. But amongst the British middle classes, where the *Mail* was psychologically at home, there was a strong current of opinion which believed that Nazism and Fascism were much less obnoxious than Bolshevism. The expropriation of private wealth in the Soviet Union, the hard-luck stories of White Russians, the collectivisation of the peasantry and grim rumours of terror added up to a widespread fear and loathing.

The anxiety about another war and the general support for appeasement in Britain was arguably better reflected in the *Express* group – whose line was that the country ought not to worry too much about what was going on in Europe and could bask in imperial isolation – than in the *Mail* group. *Mail* circulation reps felt that their paper's advocacy of rearmament, especially in the air, was damaging in the battle with the *Daily Express*; Harold Rothermere himself had to deny that he was trying to make money in aircraft and armament shares.

The cruel march of events, and especially Hitler's cynical invasion of the remains of Czechoslovakia after Munich, meant that British middle-class opinion and the *Mail* group, too, awoke to the realities of Nazism in 1938–9. Esmond's own antennae among Conservative MPs, and the family friendship with Churchill, may well have made it easier for the new proprietor to change the editorial course. (After Churchill became Prime Minister in 1940 there is family evidence that he supported Beaverbrook in encouraging Harold Rothermere to cross the Atlantic on his aircraft mission; whatever Britain's fate might turn out to be in that dangerous year, old Lord Rothermere's presence could have been an embarrassment.)

Esmond's succession to command of the family newspapers was not a sudden affair, as happened when Northcliffe died and his father bought the *Mail*. It was so gradual that some of the staff found it hard afterwards to recollect exactly when the first Lord Rothermere had bowed out. What was not in doubt was that he was taking over in circumstances far more testing than 1922. Britain, which had looked forward to an unbreakable era of peace in 1922, was in sight of another struggle for survival fifteen years later. And, whereas Northcliffe had left the *Mail* at a peak of prestige, it was Esmond's destiny to have to fight to hang on to readers and advertisers in a much tougher Fleet Street.

10

From 1937 to the 1950s

The outbreak of war, in September 1939, caused a sharp rupture with the *Mail* attitudes of the early 1930s. An editorial, under the heading WAR, declared on 4 September, 'We now fight against the blackest tyranny that has ever held men in bondage ... Let us face the truth. This war was inevitable whether it began with Austria, Sudetenland, Bohemia or Danzig ... It became inevitable from the day HITLER seized power in Germany and began his criminal career by enslaving his own people. For his one aim since then has been gradually to enslave all others by the methods of brute force.'

It was not just the leader column which epitomised the change. The *Mail*, restricted to twelve pages, put news on its front page for the first time in history, 'to enable its readers to see the news of the war immediately they picked up their newspaper'. In fact as late as 1 September, when the *Mail* had been reporting the evacuation of London children for fear of instant air raids, the paper had argued that war was no more inevitable then than it had been a week or a month ago. But the spirit was different. On 1 September, the editorial had said that it was certain that if Poland were attacked, the Western democracies would march immediately.

POY, a favourite cartoonist in the First World War, returned to the *Mail*.[5] A special 'exciting animal story' was carried, for children to read on their evacuation trains. Herbert Morrison, Labour leader of the London County Council, sent a message to the children: 'London children are cheerful and friendly. I want you to be cheerful and friendly on this journey and when you get to the other end.' The *Mail* also reported that Morrison was telling others to 'Keep calm. Keep a cheerful British smile on your face.' If London's Labour leader was now getting more favourable publicity, the paper also noted with satisfaction that the Amalgamated Engineering Union had agreed to the dilution of labour in the interests of war work.

Unpleasant though the outbreak of war was, and understandable the fear of instant aerial attack, there was a clear feeling in those September days that the *Mail* was casting off its recent history, supported by a much more robust and youthful proprietor. An editorial on 2 September, following publication of the British white paper on German claims to Danzig and Poland, poured scorn on Hitler for his empty promise to 'accept' the British Empire and 'pledge himself personally for its continued existence'. Future historians, the *Mail* said, would read this with incredulous amazement.

The same leader released a flood of pent-up hostility against a man whom the first Lord Rothermere had been wont to praise, whose word he had trusted, and whom he had addressed in the language of butter.

So comes the climax in the career of a man for whom the words honour, humanity and truth have no meaning. His perjured record is written in the history of the last six years. His first act now is a murderous assault upon Poland and the bombing of women and children without warning and without mercy ... Now he has made his big mistake. It is a mistake that will bring him, and his region, down in ruins. He has persisted in the belief, up to the very last moment, that Britain and France would not act against him. It is a common fallacy among liars that others will not keep their word ...

World dominion – that is the heart and centre of the Nazi philosophy. But the British Empire stands in the way, with its ideals of reason and tolerance, sanity and goodwill. These things the despot cannot understand, and in his malice he strikes at them. The British people will never become slaves of the Swastika. They will never allow other free and independent nations to fall by force beneath the sway of that dark terror. So once again this country resumes her historic role of the defender of freedom and of individual liberty.

It might be thought that the *Mail* also was resuming its historic role of patriotic defender in this positively Northcliffian philippic. Attentive readers, however, would note that not all the star writers would find it so easy to change gear. Harold Cardozo, who had reported the Spanish Civil War from the Franco side, went up to the Maginot Line on the day war was declared and completely misread the morale of the French troops: 'France has now the soul and the determination of St Joan, and that soul and that determination can never know defeat.'

More sinisterly, G. Ward-Price was still in October refighting the battles of the inter-war years. 'In the present war we have three adversaries – the Germans, the Bolsheviks and the bureaucrats. The Germans threaten us with conquest; the Bolsheviks with contagion; the bureaucrats with control.' He also, in an article with heavy anti-Semitic overtones, criticised enemy aliens and Jewish refugees for living too well in Britain and concealing enemy agents in their midst.

Many of these alien immigrants are Jews. They should be careful not to arouse the same resentment here as they have stored up in so many countries. I dislike as much as anyone the Nazi persecution of that race, but it is a fact that the Jews were getting a stranglehold on German life out of all proportion to their avowed numbers. Many of the German Jews, often themselves recent immigrants from Eastern Europe, were the worst of their kind. In this country the national character is strong enough to absorb the better Hebraic type; in Germany, the Jewish aliens found a class-conscious, self-interested community, and the misdeeds of some brought down reprisals on the rest.

Compared with the spy fever of 1914 the British public in 1939 was rather less excitable, but articles of this sort underpinned the mass internment of enemy aliens.[6] They also obscured the extent to which refugees from Hitler, especially when they were Jewish, would want to contribute to Britain's war effort.

The phoney war, which had so falsified fears of instant aerial attack on the declaration of war, petered out in 1940 when the Germans attacked Scandinavia. Esmond's *Mail*, like other British newspapers, did not immediately appreciate that the Norway campaign would lead to the overthrow of Neville Chamberlain as Prime Minister. On 3 May 1940, after the loss of Norway but before the Commons debate, Wilson ('Jack') Broadbent, *Mail* Political Correspondent, reported that 'Although unrest among members continues and may increase there seems little likelihood of an immediate political crisis.' In the same article, however, he noted that there were secret meetings of Conservative MPs and approaches to Labour (no longer the Socialists) taking place.

By 6 May, however, Broadbent was writing that the Prime Minister faced the most critical week of his career. The *Mail* published a front-page letter from an anonymous British politician suggesting an all-party government with Lord Halifax as Prime Minister; its editorial on the same day called for a change of government. But it was clear that the paper was not sure who should succeed Chamberlain. The next day a possible alternative government, with Winston Churchill as Prime Minister, was listed on the front page as the proposal of Robert Carey, Unionist MP for Eccles in Lancashire. But on 9 May, after Chamberlain's majority in the Commons had been catastrophically cut from 213 to 81 at the end of the Norway debate, the *Mail* in a front-page editorial was calling for a victory Cabinet led by Lloyd George with Churchill as vice premier in 'complete control of the Empire's grand strategy'.

As late as 10 May, when the leader said that the *Mail* could no longer support Chamberlain, whose government had completely lost the confidence of the nation, the paper was running a feature by Emrys Jones asking whether Lloyd George was too old to be Prime Minister at the age of 77. The answer was no. On 11 May, its coverage of the formation of Churchill's government was not the main lead story of the day. This was that the British Expeditionary Force had raced north across the Belgian border in response to the German blitzkrieg attack.

For Britain the real war, with all its unpleasant surprises yet to come, had started with a vengeance.

The beginning of the war, and the government changes which took place eight months later, were the first major tests of how Esmond planned to direct his inheritance. He was almost certainly as well informed as his own political staff in the May crisis which felled the Chamberlain government. In retrospect it seems odd that his paper was so reluctant to press the claims of Winston Churchill, but the political drama blew up very suddenly. Churchill was still perceived as a maverick who might find it hard to win the support of Conservative MPs and the country at large which had been supporting appeasement until so recently. The 'booming' of Lloyd George, which could have been assisted by Harold Rothermere but which also represented a current of Commons opinion, responded to the need for a national figure associated with victory.

For Esmond the war had two main consequences for his business. The first was that it gave him a special role in the heart of the establishment, where the newspaper proprietors dealt with the government over censorship, newsprint supplies and all matters of common interest. The second effect was that the war between the newspapers took second place to the real war, and with reduced paging and pegged circulations those papers which had not been doing so well in the circulation battle up until 1939 were thereafter protected. The act of producing a paper at all was a struggle, with staff called up and heavy bombing in the Fleet Street area and disruption to the rail network; but the *Mail* at least never missed an issue.

Esmond had been made chairman of the Newspaper Proprietors' Association as long ago as 1934. His special role in the press establishment had been illustrated in the abdication crisis of 1936 when he, Beaverbrook and Churchill were counselling Edward VIII and trying to find ways by which he could continue to be king without giving up the woman he loved. He had been at Fort Belvedere, Edward's home, on the night of the abdication and had witnessed the tension between Edward and the younger brother who succeeded him as George VI.

It was not surprising, therefore, that Esmond was made a member of the Advisory Council for the Ministry of Information when that was set up. His significance increased after the government changes of May 1940 brought Churchill to power. He knew Churchill well, Beaverbrook was also in the government, and another press crony of Churchill's – Brendan Bracken, the mysterious red-haired Irishman who would be associated with the growth of the *Financial Times* – was another friend who became Minister of Information.

However, Esmond, unlike his father or uncle Alfred, never allowed himself to be coopted into the wartime government. The nearest he got was to be chairman of the Newsprint Supply Company, from 1940 to

1959, which allocated newsprint rations to the press. Although he was personally loyal to Churchill, Churchill's attitude to the press was bound to make for difficulties for editors and proprietors. He was inclined to interpret any criticism of the war effort as criticism of himself and the government, possibly of a subversive kind. Earlier in his career Churchill had taken a 'Square it or squash it' view of the press, whose power he had always rated highly and which he had enjoyed controlling when he ran the *British Gazette* during the general strike.

Ironically, some of the most sensitive fence-mending which Esmond had to do on behalf of the press related to the perceived sins of the *Daily Mirror*, now largely run by his cousin Cecil King. The month after Churchill became Prime Minister Esmond called on King at the *Mirror* offices with a message from the Premier, asking him to end the attacks on the remaining Chamberlain supporters in the government as they could bring the whole government down. Esmond told King, who then went to see Churchill himself, that Churchill himself was partly to blame for the government's lethargy. In the disastrous Norway campaign, Churchill had wrongly assumed that the Germans could easily have been pushed out. Esmond remarked that Churchill had told him once before that he had never resigned in his political career, and never would.

That particular contretemps was settled but twice, in October 1940 and March 1942, Churchill and his government's anger with the *Mirror* and *Sunday Pictorial* came close to introducing a general censorship of the press. There were particular reasons why attacks from this quarter, on incompetent ministers or muddles in the war effort, were so resented. The first was that the *Mirror* stable presented itself as more Churchillian than Churchill. The Prime Minister had not only written for these papers in the days when they were firmly under the thumb of the first Lord Rothermere, but had continued to write for them in the late 1930s when he had been a lonely voice and they had adopted a strongly anti-Nazi campaigning flavour.

Secondly, there was a strong anti-establishment spirit about these papers, zestfully promoted by the young Hugh Cudlipp with King's strategic support. They attacked 'brasshats' and 'dope survivors' – incompetent and big-headed officers and civilians in positions of responsibility who were preventing ordinary soldiers and factory workers from fighting the war successfully. Although he, too, had been a rebel and a radical in his time, Churchill saw all this as a threat to confidence in the war effort. Yet it was popular with the troops who felt these were papers which understood their own frustrations. In consequence, the *Mirror* became the soldiers' paper in the Second World War, just as Northcliffe's *Mail* had been in the first.

The first row, in October 1940, was caused by Cudlipp writing in the *Sunday Pictorial* that Churchill himself had warned – in his book *The*

World Crisis – that wartime decisions had to be clear and ruthless. Clement Attlee, deputy prime minister and leader of the Labour Party, asked Esmond to bring a deputation from the Newspaper Proprietors' Association to discuss the government's complaints. Esmond, Lord Camrose of the *Daily Telegraph* and Lord Southwood of the *Daily Herald* met Attlee and Beaverbrook. Attlee said that the Cabinet had considered the conduct of the *Mirror* and *Pictorial* at a recent meeting, and that if the irresponsible criticism continued the government would introduce censorship. The NPA delegation replied stoutly that censorship would wreck the government and damage the country's morale. King and Bart then had their own meeting with Attlee, cooled off their editorial criticisms for a while, and the row blew over.[7]

The second quarrel, in March 1942, was more serious. By then the government had actually closed the *Daily Worker*, the Communist Party paper. A cartoon by Philip Zec, the *Mirror*'s cartoonist, showed a sailor drifting on a raft with the caption, 'The price of petrol has been increased by one penny.' Like many cartoons it was capable of different interpretations according to the outlook of the reader. Zec had wanted to illustrate the courage of the sailors, and the fact that every drop of petrol which had to be brought in the Atlantic convoys was precious. But Churchill, and Labour ministers like Ernest Bevin and Herbert Morrison, saw it differently. The war had been going badly and now the *Mirror* was implying that sailors' lives were being sacrificed for oil companies and garage owners. Bevin even thought the cartoon could affect recruitment into the merchant navy.[8]

Beaverbrook managed to persuade the government that a warning would be wiser than immediate closure of the *Mirror*, but when Morrison as Home Secretary saw Bart he told him that he was ready to shut down the paper without further warning; he told the House of Commons that he was prepared to use one of the Defence Regulations, 2 D, as his authority. At this point, not only the NPA but MPs and others drew back, exerting pressure on both the government and *Mirror* to cool off. It was, of course, nonsense to accuse the paper of subversion. It was also arguable that the criticisms of the war management by King's young turks were less insurrectionary or to the point than Northcliffe's campaign against Kitchener and the shell shortage, which had never closed the *Mail*.

In the Second World War, the *Mail*, though it played a significant role in forming opinion and an honourable role in reporting, was of immeasurably less importance than it had been in 1914–18. Shortly after the Zec cartoon appeared Cecil King wrote dismissively of his cousin to Lady Cripps, 'The policy of the *Daily Mail* group depends entirely on Esmond Rothermere. He finds it difficult to keep interested in any subject for long, so the papers he manages tend to pursue a rather erratic course.'[9] He added that the *Mail* circulation, by now subject to newsprint rationing like the rest, was 1.45m; this compared with 2.7m for the *Express*, 1.9m for the *Mirror*, 1.6m for the *Herald*, and 1.2m for the *News Chronicle*.

King's poor opinion of Esmond was reciprocated by other members of the Harmsworth family with regard to himself, for King appeared shy and conceited, and was linked to papers which were not thought respectable. Endowed with the sense of intellectual superiority of a Winchester and Oxford education he had been made a director of Empire Paper Mills, then owned by Harold Rothermere, when he was 26; and his uncle made him a director of the *Mirror* for which he was sent off to the United States to examine new techniques in tabloid journalism, when he was still under 30. Although the power at the *Mirror* from the late 1930s, King was formally only one of the directors; during the war Bart became chairman in place of John Cowley, a nonentity appointed by the first Lord Rothermere, and it was not until 1951 that King organised a palace coup against the by now alcoholic Bart by which he became chairman.

Behind the edgy relationship between Esmond and his cousin there lay not only a jostling for reputation and political and temperamental differences, but a subdued power struggle. This was played out in the 1940s and resulted from a mixture of circumstances, some of which are still obscure. But essentially the death of Harold Rothermere in 1940 left his estate in debt, and Esmond was not in total financial control of the *Mail* group for a few years afterwards. At the same time, the cross-holdings between the *Mirror* group and the *Mail* group, established by Harold at Northcliffe's death had survived in some form in spite of the flotation of the *Mirror* shares in the early 1930s. The result was that in the middle of the war the *Mail* group was thought to be the largest single shareholder in the *Mirror*, and this situation was not resolved until 1947 when Esmond, who had been buying more *Mirror* shares in order to exert pressure, sold them and managed to buy out the *Mirror* shares in the *Mail* simultaneously with the aid of Bart and against King's opposition. Until then each cousin, even if unlikely to mount a take-over bid, was in a position to tweak the other's nose.

Esmond in fact had had to overcome a serious financial crisis following his father's death, which must have added considerably to his wartime anxieties. He told Aidan Crawley at the end of the war that he had had to find as much as £36m to meet losses on his father's estate, an enormous sum for the period. Even if this figure was exaggerated there is no doubt that, when he died, a man rated as one of Britian's best financial brains had left his affairs in an appalling mess. His estate was unable to pay a modest legacy of £10,000 to his brother Cecil, for example.

Quite how Harold Rothermere had run through a substantial fortune in the last decade of his life is still a matter for speculation. Much he gave away to his family, good causes, and old girlfriends. He also gambled heavily at the casino – in Monte Carlo girls would hover near him until he gave them chips and milles plaques to play with – and in buying and selling currencies, and on the Stock Exchange. He also belonged to a generation of self-made millionaires who believed in spending money and acting rich: he always stayed at the best hotels, and told Esmond to buy a new car each year. In spite of his notorious panics it is quite possible that in the last years of his life he went on behaving as though he was one of the country's wealthiest men when this was no longer the case, and it did not occur to anyone, least of all himself, to challenge this assumption.

For Esmond, discovering the liabilities at his father's death must have been a searing experience, and may well have reinforced his own cautious instincts in business. He had other problems in the United States and Canada, where his father had left excessive power in the hands of Frank Humphrey, partner of a Wall Street stockbroking firm, Kidder, Peabody and chairman of Anglo-Newfoundland Development Co. and Anglo-Canadian Pulp and Paper. He also ran a number of investment trusts set up by Harold Rothermere, dealing for them through his stockbroking firm. Although the British Finance Act of 1936 was supposed to circumscribe the operation of overseas trusts by British supertax payers, Harold was allergic to paying tax unnecessarily.

The result was that Humphrey had come to run a largely independent empire during the war years, in which he had been able to use the Harmsworth trust investments to advance his own position in firms like McGrory Stores and Lone Star Gas where he became effectively managing director. When Esmond visited the United States in 1946 Humphrey tried extremely hard to get his son also made a trustee – something which Harold had promised in writing just before his death – and refused to sign a new trust deed until after Esmond had sailed back to England.

Esmond's personal life was transformed by the war. His two principal homes were commandeered – Mereworth by the Royal Air Force whose West Malling fighter base was at the end of the drive, and Warwick House by the Red Cross. His two daughters married. And he himself married for a second time to Ann, née Charteris, the widow of Lord O'Neill, a brilliant, witty person who had already fallen in love with the man who was to be her third husband, Ian Fleming, and of whom it was said that something always seemed to go wrong in the taxi coming back from a registry office. Ann herself said that she had first fallen for Esmond in 1936 and Fleming and Ann were actually staying with him, in October 1944, when Ann received the telegram informing her that O'Neill had been killed.[10]

During the war Esmond divided his time between a smallish house at Lovel Dene, on the edge of Windsor Great Park, a house near Swinley golf course, and the Dorchester Hotel in Park Lane which attracted a stylish clientele of Londoners who had lost the use of their own houses. In addition to the facilities of a top hotel, and their own company, refugees in the Dorchester revelled in its reputation for bomb-proof solidity. It was in these surrounding that he got to know Ann O'Neill better.

Both Esmond's daughters, good-looking girls, made wartime marriages first. Lorna had been an early water skier, giving demonstrations in Monte Carlo in the last year of peace. Ann O'Neill organised her coming out and Lady Hudson, Northcliffe's widow, her presentation at court. She then became a Red Cross nurse and married Neill Cooper-Key who was an officer in the Irish Guards; after the war, when he went into politics, he was given a directorship in the *Mail* group and ran one of the subsidiaries, the London General Cab Co. Esme, who never felt that the Harmsworths, for all their titles, were real aristocrats married one for herself in Roland Errington, another Guards officer, in line to become the 3rd Earl of Cromer. She had had an adventurous return to England via Portugal, after her grandfather's death in Bermuda, and as a St John Ambulance nurse had found herself working in a ward at St Bartholomew's Hospital next door to a family-endowed Harmsworth ward. An ancestor of Roland Errington, Henry Errington, had built Warwick House and his family combined traditions of imperial service (Cromer of Egypt) with merchant banking (Barings).

Lorna married in January 1941 and Esme almost exactly a year later. Vere was still at school in the United States. Esmond may well have thought that he had sufficiently fulfilled his paternal responsibilities to think seriously about marriage again. In Ann O'Neill he found someone intelligent, vivacious, interested in power. She could flirt, she had a gift for repartee, and she could be malicious. She thought Esmond's existing children dull, called the Cooper-Keys the 'Cooper-Cows' and nicknamed his much-loved Warwick House 'Warwick Hut'. The night before she married Esmond, in 1945, she dined with Fleming and agonised as to whether she was doing the right thing; walking round with him in the park, on the evening of 27 June, she felt she would have married Ian Fleming if he had asked her.

Esmond's seven-year childless marriage to Ann was a glittering affair which ended in bitterness. At Warwick House, she was a society hostess who invited celebrities and the intelligentsia to her dinner table; only Lady Pamela Berry, wife of Lord Camrose's son, was a newspaper hostess to match her. She was actively interested in newspapers, particularly the *Mail*, encouraging certain writers and sometimes getting on with and sometimes getting in the way of Frank Owen, a fiery Welshman who was editor immediately after the war. It was a period when Esmond seemingly was at the top of his career, assisted by her to a new peak of recognition in a London society which was striving to offset the austerity and socialism of post-war Britain. But there was a canker in the marriage: she never entirely relinquished her relationship with Ian Fleming, called 'Lady Rothermere's fan' by those in the know, whose own prospects at the *Sunday Times* were baulked by Lord Kemsley's profound disapproval of an affair with another proprietor's wife.

There was an age difference of some sixteen years between Ann and Esmond. Even when still married to Shane, 3rd Baron O'Neill, she had been simultaneously encouraging the interest of Fleming and Esmond as well. Hard and brilliant as she was, in matters of the heart she had genuine difficulty in sticking to one man at a time. Aidan Crawley, whose wife Virginia Cowles, the US journalist, had shared a wartime house in Bryanston Square with Ann, considered that underneath the surface glamour the marriage of Esmond and Ann was never a success. Peter Quennell the writer, brought on to the *Mail* as a books reviewer with Ann's encouragement, noted that when the fun at Ann Rothermere's dinner table became too uproarious Esmond would slip away with a detective novel.

In the whole history of the Harmsworth dynasty there has not been another case of a proprietor's wife taking such a part in the editorial workings of the business. Many of the people she spotted or pushed were genuinely talented. She persuaded Stanley Morison, *The Times* designer, to redesign the *Mail*'s front page. She helped to bring in Frank Owen, editor from 1947 to 1950, Alastair Forbes, the political commentator for the *Sunday Dispatch*, and she gave a hand to Noel Barber, a rising star who ran the *Continental Daily Mail* until it closed before becoming the *Mail*'s chief foreign correspondent.

Inevitably, Ann's activity created jealousy amongst journalists and managers. In mid-1950, when Owen was fired and close observers believed that her influence was waning, *Time* magazine took a crack at her 'petticoat control' in its inimitable style:[11]

Esmond Cecil Harmsworth, 52, 2nd Viscount Rothermere, owns London's stoutly Tory *Daily Mail* (circulation 2,280,000) and for three years fiery, loquacious Frank Owen, 44, has been the editor. But it has long been common knowledge in Fleet Street that the real boss wears a petticoat. For several years, pretty, vivacious Lady Ann Rothermere, 36, has tried to run the *Mail* from Warwick House. Without consulting Editor Owen, she often summoned staffers to her home to assign stories or suggest new features.

The arrival of a strong-minded woman gave an extra dimension to the friction between proprietor and managers which dated back to Northcliffe. McWhirter, managing director of Associated Newspapers until he was pushed out shortly after Owen's departure from the *Mail*, told Sanger in 1947 that he had to stand up to both Esmond and Ann.[12] 'I've had to say to him, "If you do this, you'll ruin the paper; and while

I'm here, I won't let you ruin the paper." When it comes to that point, he gives way, but he doesn't like it. And of course Ann doesn't like it.' But Sanger felt that Ann was a constructive influence on Esmond, determined that he should be a success and making him more persistent.

In fact Esmond seemed for a long time to have been unaware that Ann and Ian Fleming were continuing their affair. Although this may seem strange, with separate phone lines to big houses, staff who were famously discreet, and a lively social life which included Ian Fleming among many who came and went to Warwick House, it was perhaps not so remarkable. To begin with, Esmond had been passionate about Ann. He was, for at least a couple of years, blind to the possibility that she could be in love with someone else.

The moment of truth came in 1948. In September of that year Ann, who was expecting a baby which Esmond thought was his but which in reality was Fleming's, accompanied Esmond and her sister Laura, Duchess of Westminster, on holiday to Perthshire. While there, there was a crisis in the pregnancy. Ann was rushed to hospital in Edinburgh and delivered of a baby daughter, born two months early by caesarian section. Beside himself with anxiety, Fleming kept in touch as well as he could by letter and telephone. The premature baby died after twenty-four hours and Esmond was profoundly distressed.

Esmond, who took Ann to Paris and Portofino to recover, then discovered that the baby was not his. He gave her the first of several ineffectual ultimata that she should give up Fleming. Increasing numbers of people came to know of the affair. In Paris, for instance, where Ann was made a director of the *Continental Daily Mail*, she and Fleming used to stay at the Hotel de St Pierre. They would ask Noel Barber to borrow the firm's car and chauffeur, and the chauffeur would remark, 'Madame la Comtesse is here with her lover.'

In May 1949, a director of Associated Newspapers, Blos Lewis, told Sanger that Frank Owen had seen Ann, who told him that Esmond had sent a reporter to meet her at Southampton with an ultimatum in a sealed letter. Either she would never see Fleming again or he would divorce her. Lewis and Sanger agreed that confiding in Owen was like broadcasting the news all round Fleet Street. She said to Owen that she had not decided what to do, but that Esmond was being perfectly absurd. 'He knows Ian Fleming has been my lover for the past fourteen years,' Lewis reported her as saying.[13]

The dénouement could not be long delayed and was brought on by Ann rather than Esmond. In late 1951, just before Christmas, Ann left Warwick House and joined Fleming in Jamaica. As her published letters show, their affair had survived the setback of the baby's death and become fiercer then ever. In Jamaica, with Noel Coward as best man, Ann and Fleming got married. One of the first results was that he wrote the first of the James Bond novels, *Casino Royale*, at top speed.

For Esmond, a shy man with a prominent position, the whole business was a source of prolonged anguish. He suffered from loss and humiliation, retired into fourteen years of bachelorhood, and afterwards wrote to his daughter Esme to say that he realised that he was not a good judge of women, and that if he ever threatened to marry again she was to give him her advice. The *Mail* group did not review the James Bond novels, even as they climbed up the bestseller lists.

The dissolution of his second marriage had other consequences also. He had always been more interested in the business rather than in the journalistic aspects of newspapers. Stimulated by Ann's fascination for the journalistic side he was probably more alert to editorial factors than he had ever been before; after his marriage broke up he lost appetite for them. At the same time, he found a new, non-human object for his affections – Daylesford in Gloucestershire, a stately home built for Warren Hastings in the Cotswolds.

He had minded very much the break-up of his marriage to Ann, living for a couple of months with his daughter Esme and her husband at French Street, just by Churchill's Chartwell estate in Kent. He had come out with a nervous rash at the time. He had also sold Mereworth and bought Daylesford, which was in a very poor condition. His family felt that his dedication to restoring Daylesford – which was not easy because of post-war shortages – had an element of revenge; Ann would have very much liked Daylesford.

For three or four years he immersed himself in the history of Daylesford and Warren Hastings, collecting Hastings memorabilia, restoring the lake as well as the house, and getting John Fowler, a well-known interior decorator, to attend to the furnishings. He put in a swimming pool. One of the most exciting moments, for someone who had become almost obsessive in his desire to collect all the pictures that Hastings had originally hung in the house, was when a servant came to tell him that he had found six rolled-up canvases, covered in dung, in the corner of the stable. On examination they turned out to be scenes of India, painted by William Hodges RA, and commissioned by Hastings himself.

The responsibilities of running a newspaper group in the 1940s, and his own somewhat brittle personal life, did not prevent Esmond from showing acts of thoughtfulness to those of whom he was fond. Early in the war the young Noel Barber, who had just joined the *Mail* as a journalist from the *Express*, asked to see Esmond to discuss going into the RAF. His easy good manners and qualities as a tennis player and sportsman attracted Esmond to him. Esmond told him that he should come and have tea with him every Thursday, and that it was a good idea that he should go into the RAF. But he made Barber promise that he would not become a rear-gunner in a plane, because he thought the gunners were the first to be shot down.

After the war Barber had a meteoric ascent in the group. In February 1948, at a time when he was talking of getting divorced and marrying a sister of Ann Rothermere's, George Ward-Price told Gerald Sanger that Barber had told him in Paris that he had stayed in a hotel in Nassau at a cost of £12 a day. The bill had been paid for by Esmond. Ward-Price's comment was, 'Whoever heard of Esmond paying a £12-a-day hotel bill for anyone?' He did not doubt Barber's statement, but concluded that he must be a very strong favourite, and possibly a potential director of Associated Newspapers.[14]

Esmond also remembered his cousin Christabel Bielenberg and the pictures his father had lent to Hungary, in the chaotic days after the collapse of Hitler's Reich. Christabel, who subsequently wrote a brilliant autobiography, *The Past is Myself*, about her experiences in Nazi Germany, had braved the Gestapo in the difficult period after the 1944 plot against Hitler when her husband Peter was arrested and sent to a concentration camp. At the end of the war she and her children were living at Rohrbach, a village in the Black Forest. Her relations in the Burton and Harmsworth families in England had no idea what had become of her, but Esmond managed to establish contact via General Morgan of the UN relief organisation, UNRRA.

The story of the Rothermere pictures was even more unlikely. Harold Rothermere, after he visited Hungary in 1938, had loaned the national gallery there almost all his collection of Old Masters. There were twenty of them, and they were extremely valuable. Among them was a portrait of the artist by Rembrandt, a Virgin and Child by Rubens, and a portrait of a woman by Holbein. All these hung in the Budapest Gallery of Fine Arts. In view of the problems over Lord Rothermere's estate, the recovery of these pictures was of considerable importance.

However, with the collapse of the Nazis and the Russians becoming the dominant force in Eastern Europe this was hardly a straightforward task for British executors. Esmond, and the trustee department of Coutts Bank, turned once more to Lajos Lederer, Harold Rothermere's 'Hungarian secretary'. Lederer, initially interned but released at the intercession of Randolph Churchill among others,[15] had monitored broadcasts from occupied Europe for the Rothermere group during the war years. He was now given a generous amount of money, accredited as a correspondent to *The Observer* – the start of a long journalistic career for that paper – and arrived in Budapest in October 1945.

He found that the head of the Gallery of Fine Arts, Dr Istvan Genthon, was an old acquaintance who agreed that the Rothermere paintings should now go back to Britain. But the pictures themselves had disappeared. Along with the Crown of St Stephen and many other national treasures they had been removed by Hungarian Young Nazis on a 'gold train', a few days before the Red Army arrived in Budapest in April. No one knew what had become of them. Although the guards had been instructed to steam west and meet the advancing US armies in Austria, they had in fact disappeared with their loot when they crossed the Austrian border.

Lederer now used all his contacts and guile. The current Hungarian Prime Minister, before the Russian takeover was complete, was Zoltan Tildy; like Lederer he had been a writer for the *Pesti Hirlap*, and his Smallholders Party was the one for which Lederer had stood as a candidate. Tildy appointed him to the Hungarian Commission of National Property Abroad, and gave him a letter of authority to negotiate with responsible authorities in Austria and elsewhere.

Through Hungarian refugees in Vienna he got a lead to Denes Csanky, now living in a remote village in Bavaria, who had catalogued the Rothermere paintings in 1938 and was suspected of having directed the removal of art works on the 'gold train'. After Lederer called on him the first time, when he was deeply suspicious, he disappeared. However, Lederer tracked him down again, gave him 3,000 dollars and a jeep-load of food, and assured him that he was not going to be arrested. He then gave a list of fourteen villages where the pictures might be found and Lederer persuaded the American Third Army headquarters in Munich to help in the search. A great quantity of material was recovered.

Nevertheless, much to Lederer's chagrin, the US Army returned eight of the most valuable Rothermere paintings to Budapest where Russian control was getting steadily tighter. With the support of the two senior British figures on the Allied Control Commission in Budapest, and the active help of Dr Genthon, Lederer arranged for the pictures to be taken from the gallery after dark and put on a British military plane which landed in a field outside the city. They were then flown out to Vienna where they were handed over to a grateful Humphrey Brooke, then a lieutenant-colonel in charge of the monuments and fine arts branch of the British section of the Allied Commission for Austria, and subsequently secretary of the Royal Academy. The Rothermere collection was later auctioned, to raise money for the estate.

In politics Esmond kept his papers, and especially the *Mail*, supremely loyal to Churchill and the Conservatives in the post-war years. Although he admired and was a friend of Churchill he was not uncritical. Meeting his cousin Cecil King in 1942, for instance, he described Churchill as 'a muddler' and given to dramatic ups and downs of mood; when in a depression he relied on Beaverbrook to cheer him up. Lunching with King again, in December 1944, Esmond commented that many of Churchill's political views were based on personal prejudice. He was in favour of King George of Greece because he had known him for years; he favoured Tito for some reason while King Peter of Jugoslavia did not interest him; he had disliked General de Gaulle, and made jokes about him, until they had gone to Paris together after the city was liberated and Churchill had been moved by the popular reception.

The *Mail* played a vigorous part in the elections of 1945, 1950 and 1951. In 1945, it concentrated hard on the authority of Churchill as a national war leader, in contrast to the team approach being projected by Labour. The election, coming so soon after the collapse of Nazi Germany but whilst the war against Japan was still in progress, was a difficult one in which to inject rabid partisanship. None the less, perhaps sensing that the result was not going to be a pushover for the Conservatives, the *Mail* warned from the start that if Labour won 'the State would become the arch-employer, arch-planner, arch-administrator and arch-caucus and boss'. State socialism would require a form of 'Gestapo' police to carry out its designs.

Two other lines taken up by the paper were that if Labour won there would be 'no road back', and that a Labour government would be controlled by factions, the trade unions, or Harold Laski's national executive committee. A dispute between Laski and Attlee, as to whether Attlee should attend three-power talks in Berlin as a member of Churchill's delegation, was seized on by the *Mail* with joy. On 20 June, it quoted a provincial paper which alleged that Laski, speaking at a public meeting, had said that he was prepared to use violence to achieve his socialist aims.

Echoing campaigns of the 1920s and 1930s the *Mail* was all set to make much of this, until Attlee and Laski filed libel writs and drove the whole affair *sub judice*. None the less, possibly tapping some residual anti-Semitism, it continued to harp on about Laski, accusing him on 23 June of being either a 'sinister revolutionary' or a 'figure of fun'. There was an element of hyperbole in some of the attacks on Labour, which could have been self-defeating, for instance that 'there would be no Parliament as we know it, and no law which did not favour the State'.

Although its editorial campaigning was not well attuned to a nation that had just emerged from a war for survival which had been fought in a bipartisan spirit, the *Mail* clearly had some inkling of the changes in public opinion. It warned Conservatives against complacency, pointed out to confused voters that if they voted Labour it would mean saying goodbye to Churchill, and on the eve of the poll it promised that if Labour won it would give them a fair chance and avoid 'malignant comment'. None the less, when the size of the Labour victory was realised, it confessed on 27 July that it was staggering, and like 1931 in reverse. It had difficulty in coming to terms with the change in public opinion, blaming poor advice to Churchill and weak Conservative party organisation.

Nearly five years later, after the Attlee government had established a national health service, nationalised coal and the railways, and had spent much of its radical vigour on the recalcitrant problems of the Cold

War and reconstruction, the *Mail* fought a much more skilful battle in the inconclusive election of 1950. Again it lavished praise on Churchill. It mocked Labour's class war rhetoric and attacks on the Conservatives built on past grievances. For example, it pointed out that Hartley Shawcross, the Labour Attorney General who was earning over £10,000 a year, was far too rich to understand the problems of the middle class. And in a humorous leader on 17 February headlined 'Wot about Wat Tyler', attacking an election broadcast by Ernest Bevin the night before, the *Mail* lampooned him for following a familiar Socialist road and stomping back into the past. Why did Labour stop at Tonypandy – a historic event when a much younger Churchill had used force against trade unionists – why not go back to the Luddites, the Ironsides or even Wat Tyler?

The *Mail*'s line in 1950 was much closer to the public mood, when the electorate was getting fed up with restrictions and shortages, and aspiring to an end to austerity. It supported the Conservative manifesto as a 'policy of freedom and adventure', offering tax cuts and a reduction in waste, public spending and the number of civil servants. It rubbished Labour's management of the economy, and pointed out that while the British were still enduring wartime levels of rationing the French and Austrians were ending rationing, and even Germany was about to abolish petrol rationing. 'We have spent £200 million on the Germans – and now they can fill their bellies with meat, work 60 hours a week, and beat us hollow in the coming trade war,' it commented astutely on 21 January.

The one danger foreseen by the paper was that the large number of Liberal candidates standing might deny the Conservatives their comeback. The *Mail* therefore tended to stress the common elements in the Conservative and Liberal cases. While certain lines in the *Mail*'s coverage were traditional – for example its references to the authoritarian or subversive elements tugging at the arms of the mild Clement Attlee – much of it seemed fresh and relevant. It offered its columns to politicians from all parties, and in the week before polling its editorials were written on two days running from Manchester.

By October 1951, the Labour government re-elected with a tiny majority in February 1950 was going to the polls again. Nye Bevan, John Freeman and Harold Wilson had resigned when rearmament added £500 millions to the defence budget and charges for false teeth and spectacles were introduced in the 'free' national health service. The *Mail*, which had viewed the government as drifting and divided, was relieved that the prospect of one more heave would remove it from office.

In fact the 1951 election was much calmer than the two previous ones, and fought very largely on the issue of foreign policy where Churchill's reputation still stood high. In Iran, then known as Persia, Dr Mossadeq had taken over the assets of the Anglo-Persian oil company – ancestor of British Petroleum – at Abadan. The crisis was a difficult one for Labour to handle because it was arguable that Mossadeq's nationalisation was not so different in kind from Labour's nationalisations in Britain, while it reflected an anti-colonial feeling to which Labour had already responded by withdrawing from the Indian subcontinent and Palestine. The Conservatives had a field day. So did the *Mail*, which on 28 September headlined its comment on the occupation of Abadan by Iranian soldiers as 'Black Day for Britain'; the editorial memory could recall 'few such humiliating disasters'. By 3 October it had decided that the loss of Abadan was a 'Munich', and the following day it was the biggest blow to Britain, great wars apart, since the loss of America in 1783.

Out of the turbulence in the Middle East, where Mossadeq's action was followed by an attempt by Iraq to revise the 1930 treaty under which Britain could station troops on its territory, and by the Egyptian government abrogating the 1936 Suez Canal treaty, emerged the biggest talking-point of the campaign. This was Labour's allegation, taken up by Emanuel Shinwell and the *Daily Mirror*, that Churchill was a 'warmonger' because he favoured a tougher military response.

The *Mail* naturally rejected this attack. Interestingly, in view of its own history, it stated that 'appeasement and weakness led to the last war'; ironically it asked editorially whether, if Anthony Eden succeeded to the prime ministership, the result would be bloodshed and destruction. (In fact it is arguable that the line of the Conservative Party and press at this time, protesting at the financial risks and indignities associated with imperial withdrawal, was sowing the seeds for the Suez adventure five years later.)

On the home front, the *Mail* belaboured the divisions between Gaitskellites and Bevanites, the high cost of living, Labour's negativism, and the economic risks facing the country as US Marshall Aid was about to come to an end. It thought that the surface calm of the campaign meant that electors were pondering deeply. And in fact, when the polls closed, a record number had voted. The Conservatives had won, by a small but still larger margin than that enjoyed by the outgoing Attlee administration, and the paper welcomed the 'salvation of our country'.

For Esmond the year of 1951, which had brought his marriage to the brink of collapse, had therefore offered one major consolation. There was a Conservative government again, bringing with it the prospect of lower taxation and a more sympathetic environment for private enterprise. And it was headed by an old friend of the family and a man he greatly admired, Winston Churchill.

The early post-war years were, in retrospect, quite successful for Esmond as a newspaper proprietor. Fears that a Labour government might attack the concentration of press ownership – which was much less than it became subsequently – or the predominantly Conservative sympathies of the owners were not realised, in spite of the setting up of a royal commission. Newsprint restrictions were lifted in September 1946 and sales of the group's papers rose gently from their pegged wartime levels. The *Mail*, though now selling roughly a million a day less than the *Express*, saw its sales go up to 2.08m in 1947. The *Sunday Dispatch*, following a path rather downmarket of the *Sunday Express* with a dash of scurrility under the editorship of Charles Eade, added 500,000 to its sale by serialising the novel *Forever Amber*.

Esmond had also used the interlocking shareholdings between the *Mail* and *Mirror* groups, and the problems over his father's estate, to good advantage. As a result he had consolidated his own control over the *Mail* group. He had formed a trust, the One Eighty Nine trust, to buy extra *Mirror* shares. On 1 March 1947, he achieved the composition he desired with Bart under which he bought from the *Daily Mirror* and *Sunday Pictorial* their holdings in the Daily Mail Trust and in Associated Newspapers Ltd. Bart saw the One Eighty Nine shares go into friendly hands and Esmond's Daily Mail and General Trust ended up with 50 per cent of the deferred shares and thereby absolute control of Associated Newspapers. It was a deal of which the first Lord Rothermere would have been proud.

But Esmond shared one pessimistic trait with his father, even though he was regarded as good in a crisis, and unlikely to panic. This was his fear that disasters might lurk round the corner. Lunching with Cecil King in July 1942, for instance, he had foreseen a big political crash a couple of months later when he thought Russia would be collapsing, and the British public would realise with a shock that there would be no second front against the Germans.

Roughly seven years later, in July 1949, he told Gerald Sanger that Britain was destined for a tremendous economic crash. He thought people had fooled themselves that they had found the secret of everlasting boom conditions – this was in an era of faith in Keynesian economic management – but this was an illusion. He said that the British had been living in a boom ever since the war ended, and now they were in for a slump. The slump would be that much worse because Britain's was a closed economy.

Russia did not collapse in 1942, and there was no repetition of the slump that was triggered by the 1929 Wall Street crash in the late 1940s. The fact that the second Lord Rothermere believed quite vehemently at the time that such disasters were about to befall were more than a clue to his own character. They also gave a defensive quality to his management of the group and sent a signal to his journalists which contrasted with Lord Beaverbrook's sunny optimism, which radiated with mischief and political propaganda through the pages of the *Daily Express*.

11

From Coronation Year to 1978

For many people of a conservative disposition 1953 was a quite special year. It was the year of the coronation of Queen Elizabeth II, the first queen to reign since Victoria and a symbol of youth and renewal. Commentators wrote articles about the 'new Elizabethans', as though out of the chrysalis of war and austerity a new renaissance of British enterprise, valour and the arts was about to be conjured. The crowds who lined the coronation route were touched by the contrasts: a beautiful young queen, an aged Prime Minister in Winston Churchill, the representatives of an Empire turning into a Commonwealth, from Pandit Nehru to the large, popular and exotic Queen Salote of Tonga. At home, millions more watched the ceremony on television for the first time; it was the year in which the rental and sale of sets really took off, part of a spread of items ranging from telephones, cars, fridges and foreign holidays which led to the era of Conservative government from 1951 to 1964 being described as the age of affluence. And just before the day of the coronation the news came through of a British and Commonwealth climbing feat which seemed to give substance to the Elizabethan nostalgia. Edmund Hillary, a New Zealander, and Sherpa Tenzing, a Nepalese from the people who had manned the Gurkha regiments, had accomplished the first ascent of Mount Everest in a British-organised expedition. Covering the coronation the *Daily Express* managed to weave the two events together in a front page headline of triumph and joy, 'All this and Everest too.'

But for Esmond Rothermere, whose papers participated in the excitement with the enthusiasm their readers expected, coronation year had one ugly and embarrassing aspect. It had been used as an excuse by Randloph Churchill, the Prime Minister's hot-tempered and volatile son, for a major attack on the 'pornography', as he saw it, of two of the Rothermere papers, the *Sunday Dispatch* and the *Daily Sketch*. Under Charles Eade the sex and crime quotient in the *Sunday Dispatch*, which in Northcliffe's day had been an exact Sunday companion of the *Mail*, had risen sharply. Esmond had just bought what was then known as the *Daily Graphic* from Lord Kemsley and renamed it the *Daily Sketch*. He and his managers faced a problem, not resolved until Rupert Murdoch revived the *Sun* in the 1970s, of how to give identity to a popular Conservative tabloid in a market which then was totally dominated by the *Mirror*.

Randolph Churchill, who had the difficult task of being only son to the most famous Englishman in the world, had been a journalist for most of his life, though he had been a wartime MP and fought several celebrated election campaigns both before the war and after in Plymouth against Michael Foot, the Labour MP. Because of his background he had never been frightened of quarrelling with press proprietors. On one occasion, complaining about gossip published about one of his sisters, he threatened the proprietor concerned with unwelcome publicity about his own private life.

In September 1953, chairing a Foyle's literary lunch at the Dorchester Hotel in honour of Hugh Cudlipp, who had just written *Publish and Be Damned*, the story of the *Daily Mirror*, Randolph Churchill suddenly let fly.[16] He said that in coronation year it would be right to appoint a Pornographer Royal and Criminologist Extraordinary. Cudlipp and the *Mirror* would not even get onto the shortlist.

> By far and away the strongest candidate for the new office, indeed the People's Choice, was, in the early spring, Lord Rothermere's editor of the *Sunday Dispatch* Mr Charles Eade. If the new post had been filled in the spring then I think the choice must have fallen unanimously on him. But since then Lord Rothermere has gone into business with the *News of the World*, has acquired the *Daily Graphic* from Lord Kemsley and has changed its name to the *Daily Sketch* ...
>
> A Mr Clapp, the editor of the *Daily Sketch*, entering new into the race, has set so fast a pace that old hacks like Mr Eade have now seriously to look to their laurels. It was, I understand, the rise of Mr Clapp which robbed his stable companion, Mr Eade, of the coveted and envied position of Pornographer Royal and Criminologist Extraordinary. It was thought to be a dead-heat for Lord Rothermere's two horses.

He went on to add that the newspaper proprietors would not allow anyone to read about his attack, because they had the power not only of the press but of the *sup*press. Then, referring to his status as Chancellor of a Canadian University and the fact that as Chairman of the Newspaper Proprietors Association Esmond should be setting a better example, he moved beyond satire to make some personal remarks.

It was, Randolph Churchill added,

> a little disquieting when you find a man like Lord Rothermere, who inherited three or four million pounds from his father, romping around in the gutter with those whose economic fetters still deny them an escape into a more honourable and salubrious profession ... I have known Lord Rothermere all my life, but I can only confess myself as utterly baffled that so rich

and cultivated a man should hire people to prostitute his papers in this way. It must be a case of pornography for pornography's sake. He has no need to do it to earn a living like some others.

This was strong stuff for 1953, an era before the sexual permissiveness of the 1960s, or the *Sun*'s photographs of large breasts and pouting nipples in the 1970s, and the frank fabrications of the *Sunday Sport* in the 1980s. Randolph Churchill's campaign, which he followed up with speeches in Manchester and to the Fleet Street Forum, caught Esmond on a sore point. And, although the Rothermere press published nothing about it, the campaign was not ignored elsewhere; the *Manchester Guardian* quoted substantially from the Foyle's speech which became a talking point among journalists, and a subject for comment in the weekly press. The impact rumbled on for another three years, for it led to a libel action by Randolph against Harry Ainsworth, editor of *The People*; this, which allowed the plaintiff to repeat his original allegations, was not settled until October 1956 when Randolph won £5,000 damages.

The assault was wounding for a variety of reasons. Esmond was the epitome of the newspaper establishment and a viscount. Neither his father nor uncle had permitted 'sleaze' in their papers – though they had done quite well out of reporting crime since the days of *Answers* and the first purchase of the *Evening News*. In addition, Esmond himself had been going through a bad patch in his personal life, while Randolph was the son of a hero, and someone he and his father had helped in his youth. As a businessman Esmond faced the task of reviving the tabloid *Daily Sketch* and the attack on 'pornography' – however unjustified the charge by later standards – cut off the possibility of using sex and violence as circulation-builders. When the Australian outsider Rupert Murdoch wanted to build up the *Sun* in the 1970s they were, of course, crucial ingredients, and he succeeded in creating the first best-selling, working-class Conservative daily newspaper. (It should be added that when Lord Stevens' *Star* tried to repeat the experiment in the 1980s by going into partnership with the more outrageous *Sunday Sport*, it was a boycott by advertisers, worried about their public image, which brought it to an end.)

Winston Churchill told his wife on 21 September 1953 that he had seen Esmond for lunch the previous day and that he was very friendly, and not at all vexed by his son's performance. But inside the Rothermere group the campaign paid off. Herbert Gunn, father of the poet Thom Gunn, was installed as editor of the *Daily Sketch* with instructions to make it more respectable; indeed in a joke parodying Goering it was said of Esmond at the time, 'When I hear the word culture, I reach for my Gunn.' But although moralists might approve it left the *Sketch* with a me-too relationship *vis-à-vis* the *Mirror*, as a second paper for middle-class households rather than a mass-market success.

The 1950s were a decade in which the *Sketch* made deceptive progress and the *Sunday Dispatch* was faltering, the Conservative Party had to come to terms with the end of empire and much enhanced competition in world markets, and Associated Newspapers sold out of commercial television just before it started to make enormous sums of money. And in 1956, the year of Suez, when the prices of the *Express* and *Mail* went up from 1½d to 2d, the foundation of the Harmsworth fortunes, *Answers*, published its final issue.

Far and away the most important development for Esmond's business was the arrival of commercial television. This was as significant as the coming of radio or the talkies, for the timid BBC television monopoly was revolutionised by the competition of an advertising-based service open to fresh ideas and clamorous for ratings. And here Associated Newspapers was in on the ground floor, with 50 per cent of the potentially lucrative London weekday TV franchise.

Going into TV was arguably Esmond's best business decision, just as pulling out of the London franchise was his worst. The Churchill government put a Television Act on to the statute book on 30 July 1954; this brought commercial television to Britain and set up the Independent Television Authority to regulate it. But earlier in the year a crucial lunch meeting had taken place, on 21 April, between Esmond and John Spencer Wills, the entrepreneurial chairman of Rediffusion, when they agreed that if either company applied for a licence they would do so jointly with the other. Broadcast Relay Services, a subsidiary of British Electric Traction, had experience in running broadcasting stations in Canada and in British colonies overseas.

By 26 October 1954, the Authority gave the London weekend franchise to BRS (the BET/Rediffusion company) and to Associated Newspapers. It was an amazing coup for Esmond and, more particularly, for his strong and brilliant managing director at the time, Stuart McClean. McClean was a half-relation of Esmond's through his Burton cousins. In a firm that was oriented towards management rather than editorial, he had probably more power than any other executive Esmond ever had. He was a friend of Wills, and he could see the potential of commercial television. Even Cecil King, not a great admirer of Esmond's acumen, paid tribute in public to Esmond's success. A new joint company was formed, Associated Rediffusion, with Wills as chairman and McClean as deputy chairman; by November 1954 50 per cent of the shares were held by Associated and 25 per cent each by BET and Rediffusion. A former naval officer, Captain Tom Brownrigg, was their general manager.

Gaining the contract gave rise to controversy, with attacks ranging from *The Times* to the Labour Party. The fact that Lord Kemsley had

an interest in the Midlands consortium, and that none of the Liberal or
left-wing press had shown much desire to come in – Cecil King at the
Mirror believed that considerable sums might be lost before they would
be recouped – made it seem as though the ITA had been handing round
franchises to the government's Conservative friends. There was a strong
possibility that, if the Labour Party had won the 1955 election,
commercial television would have been stopped in its tracks.

As it was, however, ITV was launched in London on 22 September
1955 with appropriate razzmatazz. Peter Black, the *Mail* TV critic, had
written nine days before that AR had achieved four different miracles
and was responsible for 'the most sustained process of hustling ever
undertaken by a commercial undertaking in Britain'. Nevertheless, on
the day of the launch only 188,000 of the 4 million sets licenced for TV
in the country had been converted to take ITV.

There were indeed considerable risks attached to investment in ITV,
even after the Conservatives under Anthony Eden had handsomely won
the 1955 election. Labour problems surfaced early, with a strike at
Shepperton Studios in April when AR was filming a TV play in
advance; this brought the Association of Cinematograph and Allied
Technicians (shortly to be ACTT, with television in their title) into
ITV. Early in 1956 there was an advertising recession; by March,
Independent Television News – owned jointly by the commercial
companies – was facing a financial crisis; in May, the ITA reduced the
rental it was charging by 40 per cent for the first half of the financial
year, in recognition of the losses being carried by the London and
Midlands companies. The companies at the same time were campaigning for the ITA or government to subsidise the public service
element in their output, which was required to provide the 'balance'
insisted on in the Television Act.

By July 1956 AR's accumulated losses amounted to £2.7m and there
were estimates that the company might lose as much as £4m in its first
twelve months of transmissions; furthermore, it had unsecured
advances of £4.75m from the banks. At the annual general meeting of
Associated Newspapers, on 6 July, Esmond told shareholders that the
growth in the number of adapted TV sets, and the results attained by
advertisers in the new medium 'encourage us to view the future with
confidence'. Behind the scenes, however, Esmond was beginning to get
extremely anxious.

His worry was that the losses on AR, if they continued for much
longer, could cause Associated Newspapers and the Daily Mail and
General Trust to pass up the dividends on which so many family
members depended; the losses could, in certain extreme circumstances,
even bring down the newspaper business. Significantly, his daughter
Esme was advising him to sell the AR shares – though her husband Lord
Errington said he could raise a loan through Barings at the favourable

rate of 3¼ per cent which would enable Esmond to hang on to the AR holding – and it was Neill Cooper-Key, his other son-in-law, who opened negotiations with Wills for the sale. Wills said that AR would earn profits from January 1957, but that if Associated really wanted to sell he would buy out its holding at a discount of 25 per cent.

In retrospect, the misjudgement that led to the sale of the AR shares was so colossal that several explanations have been advanced: that the Associated directors were being fed inaccurate figures for the conversion of sets to take ITV, which made it appear as though it would take longer to create a viable advertising market; and that Stuart McClean was already suffering from the thyroid cancer – diagnosed when his custom-tailored shirts no longer fitted round the neck – which eventually killed him. Both Wills, and Harley Drayton, the financier who was chairman of BET, did all they could to discourage Esmond from selling. (It is said that Drayton told Esmond to walk twice round the garden before he would take his offer.)

Certainly, both McClean and Frank Coven, an Associated director on the AR board, argued vehemently against the sale which realised £1.65m for four-fifths of the Associated holding. Only three months before Esmond sold, his cousin Cecil King had bought into the Midlands contractor, ATV, and the sequels were dramatic. Within a month or so of the Associated sale, well before the end of 1956, AR was making money. By early 1958, Associated had another chance to get into commercial television. It became a shareholder, with Rank and Lord Camrose's Amalgamated Press group, in Southern Television. At that point the ITA forced it to divest its remaining 10 per cent of AR which Esmond did extremely reluctantly: although the 10 per cent produced more than the 40 per cent had two years ago, Associated received only £4 a share when the open market value would have been £30.

In the City, this sudden liquidation of most of the AR holding, when shrewd brains were scenting big profits to be made from commercial TV, was summed up as 'to do a Rothers'. It was an episode which seemed to show that the head of the family firm was definitely not a risk-taker in the league of the previous generation. The truth may have been that it was family considerations which were decisive and that the newspaper business itself was not strong enough to bear the haemorrhage of large and possibly continuing losses in another field. Lord Kemsley had pulled out of the ATV consortium at an even earlier stage.

The AR investment was a big 'if only' in Esmond's career. Roy Thomson's investment in Scottish Television, a much smaller franchise than the London weekday contract, financed his purchases of the Kemsley Press and *The Times*. There is little doubt that if Esmond had hung on and reaped the reward, TV revenues could have catapulted the *Mail* group into a major multimedia conglomerate in the 1960s –

exactly on a par with the Thomson Organisation and King's International Publishing Corporation. Along the way there would have been more money to invest in the newspapers themselves, and there would have been no pressure to merge with the *Express* group on unfavourable terms at the start of the 1970s.

The gloom which led Esmond to sell when he did, or possibly the rather swift realisation of his error, may have coloured his response to the Eden government's Suez adventure that autumn. Conservative loyalist though he was, he did not get carried away with jingoistic fervour against President Nasser, or the government line that standing up to Nasser was somehow equivalent to standing up to Hitler and Mussolini. Journalists on the *Mail* recall him coming into the news room, on one of the critical nights for British military intervention, and saying, 'This is a catastrophe for the Tory Party.'

In this he was out of step with the then editor of the *Mail*, the gentlemanly Arthur Wareham, who had become friendly with Eden and gave him uncompromising support over Suez. The idea that the editor of the *Mail*, might take a different line from the proprietor on an issue which was dividing the nation would never have occurred to either Lord Northcliffe or the first Lord Rothermere. In the case of the second Lord Rothermere, it just led to rather frosty relations; Wareham, who had first distinguished himself as a night editor in 1950 when Esmond had dramatically sacked most of the senior editorial executives round him, was duly sacked in his turn in 1959 to make way for William Hardcastle.

The essentially defensive management style of Esmond was illustrated again in 1960 with the controversial purchase of the *News Chronicle* and its stablemate, the London evening paper, *The Star*. The take-over caused an enormous storm which broke mainly over the heads of the Cadbury family who were the vendors. This was partly because of the suddenness of the merger – journalists on the *Chronicle* had virtually no warning, the readers woke up one morning to find a copy of the *Mail* stuffed through their letter-boxes – and partly because of the political differences between the two groups. The *Mail*, quintessentially Tory, had been slugging it out for most of the century with the Liberal *News Chronicle* and its various predecessors (for the *News Chron* was described as a 'veritable alligator' among newspapers).

The end of the *News Chronicle* was announced on 17 October 1960. It put 3,500 people out of a job and the whole group, including titles, sites, printing plant and a wharf were bought out by Associated Newspapers for only £1.5m. There was bitterness over the size of compensation for employees – described as 'the cocoa handshake' – cynicism that the Cadbury family hung on to their holding in Tyne Tees Television, and a sense of betrayal in the Liberal Party and amongst those who purchased the *News Chron* every day, who still numbered over a million.

The precipitating factor in the sale was not the predatory ambition of Esmond Rothermere but rather the weariness of Laurence Cadbury, chairman of the *Chronicle* group, who was elderly, no longer prepared to nurse losses, and who had become more anti-socialist as he had grown older and drifted out of sympathy with the Liberal Party. In fact the *News Chronicle*, although it still possessed some fine journalists, had become rather disoriented in its latter years, veering in typography and content between the *Daily Express* and the old *Daily News* tradition which went back to Charles Dickens. However, the Liberal Party, although a small political constituency compared with the 1920s, had just been going through a minor revival: in the wake of Suez and disillusion with Conservative governments, it had won a dramatic by-election victory at Torrington in 1958 and performed creditably in the 1959 general election.

In the 1950s, Laurence Cadbury had turned down an offer from Lord Beverbrook to buy his papers, on a basis which would have kept both of them going, and in 1955 the *News Chronicle* actually bought the Manchester-based *Daily Dispatch*. In the run-up to the sale to the *Mail* group Cadbury rejected a better offer from Sir Frank Packer, father of Kerry Packer, whose Australian Consolidated Press saw this as an opportunity to establish a foothold in Britain which could have interestingly predated Rupert Murdoch's purchase of the *News of the World*. Instead, in great secrecy, Cadbury opened negotiations with Esmond.

For Esmond, and most of those around him, it seemed like a good deal. At £1.5m the properties were grossly undervalued. He undoubtedly thought he was protecting the position of both the *Daily Mail* and the *Evening News* by buying circulation. A year earlier he had had to close the *Sunday Dispatch* because of circulation losses, merging it into the *Sunday Express*. Put broadly, the circulation of the *Mail* had been relatively static in the 1940s and 1950s but no one knew what the effect of burgeoning commercial television might be; he had no great confidence that journalistic endeavour alone would restore the *Mail* to the pre-eminence it had enjoyed thirty years before.

The political difference between the two groups was either underestimated or seen as an advantage of the merger. Esmond, by temperament a fairly liberal Conservative, was ready to accommodate a more liberal editorial line; his son Vere, who favoured the merger, was going through a pro-Liberal phase. But his daughter Esme and son-in-law Lord Errington saw real problems in trying to mix a Conservative with a Liberal newspaper.

In the *Mail* office, on the evening of the merger, the news was kept from most of the journalists. Keith McDowell, an industrial correspondent, was rung up by Peter Paterson from the *Daily Telegraph* and told the rumour. He went to see William Hardcastle who closed the door and said, 'Keith, the *Daily Mail* is safe in your and my lifetime. Tonight we are going to print 3.6m copies. Go and throw dust in their eyes.' With that he rang back the *Telegraph* to say that there was no truth in the story.

The upshot of the take-over was probably harmful to the Rothermere group in everything except balance-sheet terms. The crucial factor was the loyalty of the *News Chronicle* readers to their own paper. They never took to the *Mail*, which gained almost nothing in sale after the first few months, and which hired few of the *News Chronicle* writers (exceptions included Roy Nash, James Cameron and William Forrest, a former Spanish Civil War veteran). The affair demonstrated forcibly that a newspaper is not like any other product; it is a friend who comes daily to your house, providing not only information and entertainment, but a part of your identity. An ill-assorted merger is like following murder by insult, and for many *News Chronicle* households the *Daily Mail* was still the paper of those two demons, Alfred Northcliffe and Harold Rothermere.

Worse still than the absence of permanent circulation gain in what looked like declining markets for newspapers was the destabilising effect on both the *Mail* and the *Evening News*. As a *Mail* journalist at that time put it later, 'Were we a Tory paper or not?' George Murray, the leader-writer and columnist who had written speeches for Churchill – he was nicknamed 'Gunboat' Murray for his robust line – was confident that the basic Conservatism of the paper would win out.

But this was far from obvious for some years. Harold Macmillan, when Prime Minister, met William Hardcastle at a party at the Conservative conference and said, 'It's nice to meet the editor of an opposition newspaper.' The feeling that the paper was moving further from its Conservative moorings was more palpable when Esmond said he would try a thin editor after a fat one, and appointed the more radical Mike Randall in Hardcastle's place. Randall used Bernard Levin as a columnist and Gerald Scarfe as a cartoonist: both were highly talented, neither were then particularly sympathetic to the Conservatives.

The era of satire and the swinging 'sixties had dawned, and it was not clear how far the *Mail* was celebrating or opposing the social and political changes. Esmond seemed to veer about and Randall, editing the paper and making the regular 5.30 pm phone call to his proprietor, felt there was no consistency there. Bernard Levin was a particular bone of contention. When he was still working as a theatre critic, and Hardcastle was editor, he reviewed a play whose subject was premature ejaculation which he described in specific detail. The night editor ran the review uncut, but was carpeted the next day by Hardcastle who had been given a rocket by Esmond. In the 1964 election campaign, when Levin told his readers to vote Labour, Esmond was apoplectic. He told Bob Hammond, then managing director, to dismiss everyone involved.

In fact Hammond who supported Randall persuaded Esmond to handle the problem his way. Levin did not leave the paper until later; Randall was sacked in 1966.[17]

More subtle damage to the group was done by the take-over of *The Star* by the *Evening News*. Though not glamorous the *Evening News*, which had produced one editor for the *Mail* in the early 1950s in Guy Schofield, had been a financial sheet anchor for the whole group. A broadsheet paper, when both *The Star* and *Evening Standard* were tabloid size, its strengths were in news, crime and sports reporting; in spirit it was a lower middle-class and working-class London paper but it was actually circulating as far as the Midlands and West Country.

Merger with *The Star* created identity problems for the *News* which was also facing other commercial and journalistic difficulties. The growth of TV squeezed all evening paper circulations, and there was a steady retreat by the *News* to the metropolitan area and in sales in the 1960s. The more up-market and featurish *Standard* was a dangerous competitor with the death of *The Star*, and the balance of commercial advantage moved to the *Standard* in the late 1960s when Jocelyn Stevens carried out a successful and lasting raid on the *News's* valuable pool of classified advertising. The paper which had provided the Harmsworth brothers with their first foothold in Fleet Street, and had been an unsung hero of the balance sheet for eighty years, was moving towards loss by the end of the decade. A system of production which required edition changes every hour by a grossly expensive print and journalistic labour force, using antiquated machinery, had economics stacked against it. By 1970 the problems of the *News*, entwined with those of the *Mail* and *Sketch*, were to bring the whole group to the edge of disaster.

For the fourteen years between the dissolution of his second marriage to Ann, and his third marriage to Mary Ohrstrom in 1966, Esmond's own life had a certain regularity. It was largely divided between Warwick House, Monte Carlo in the winter, and his much loved Daylesford. Everywhere he was most hospitable, though his hospitality could be somewhat frightening for employees who were a little uncertain of their social eitquette. When he invited Jeffrey Blyth, who had got an exclusive interview with Prince Rainier on the eve of his wedding to Grace Kelly, to stay with him in Monte Carlo, he asked, 'Tell me, Mr Blyth, whose money do you use when you go gambling at the casino?' 'Yours, Lord Rothermere.' 'And what do you do with the money when you win?' 'I keep it, Lord Rothermere.'

Many stories were told by visitors to Daylesford, where Esmond regularly had a dozen to twenty people to stay with him at the weekend. He used different rooms for morning drinks and evening drinks. Fine paintings hung in the lavatories where leaves of toilet paper were set out on Dresden china. Visitors were provided with swimming costumes and expected to make use of the pool. Dinner was always a formal affair, requiring dinner jackets, and the maids served early morning tea on trays which had covers matching the curtains in the guests' bedrooms. When asked once how many bedrooms there actually were Esmond replied laconically, 'Enough.'

Bob Hammond, one of his managing directors, was a frequent guest at one stage. Marmaduke Hussey, who was another, was said to have found the sleeping arrangements socially intimidating when he and his wife, a lady-in-waiting to the Queen, were given separate bedrooms. Esmond's granddaughter, Lady Lorna Baring, sometimes acted as hostess for him and two Christmases running he had large family parties which included his first wife, Lady Harmsworth Blunt. The US Ambassador, politicians like Edward Heath and women friends like Iris Ashley, a *Mail* fashion writer, were amongst a great variety of people who passed through his Cotswold home.

Esmond was extremely popular there with his staff and the villagers, giving a Christmas party and with a word for the gardeners and the men on the combines. He used to spend a long weekend, from Friday to Sunday, and had a considerable staff: three or four daily helps coming in every day, a butler and two footmen living in, seven or eight gardeners, a cook and a kitchen maid living in, and three housemaids living in also. But he preferred simple cooking: steak and kidney pies and apple puddings were among his favourites.

This bachelor phase of his life came to a dramatic end in 1966 when, in his late sixties, he married for a third time. His bride was an American, Mrs Mary Ohrstrom who was the wife of a businessman in Virginia, and the eldest daughter of Kenneth Murchison of Dallas, a member of a wealthy Texan family. He first saw her when he was on holiday at the Round Hill Hotel in Jamaica and was struck by the character of a youngish not very tall woman who went down to the beach, blew a whistle, and got six little boys running out of the sea to meet her. She was vivacious, sporting – like Esmond she was keen on tennis – and she had push. She pursued the good-looking viscount who was nearly twice her age and, when she and her husband came to London, he offered them lunch.

To marry Esmond she not only had to divorce Richard Ohrstrom but had to move to Europe and drastically reduce her contacts with her six sons. She was a determined Texan lady. For Esmond, who liked women's company, a third marriage when he was not far short of 70 must have seemed like a grace note. But he gave his daughters little notice of his intentions, perhaps because they might have discouraged him.

It is possible that there may also have been an element of calculation in this late romance. Esmond had become increasingly depressed that his son Vere, who had married as long ago as 1957 had so far only produced two daughters. There seemed a real possibility that the direct

Rothermere male line would die out in the third generation. In spite of his age a third marriage – especially to someone who had successfully mothered six boys already – just might ward off that danger.

He was therefore overjoyed when, in June 1967, just after his sixty-ninth birthday, his wife Mary gave him a second son. The boy was named Esmond Vyvyan, and nicknamed 'Little Es'. The baby consolidated a marriage which, because of the disparity in ages and backgrounds, always had some handicaps to overcome and which had been heading for breakdown, according to some.

Mary set about livening up her husband. His daughters and grandchildren came to stay more rarely at Daylesford while his wife encouraged new and younger friends to visit. She also revolutionised his working habits. For many years he had hardly called in at the Fleet Street offices of the group; indeed in the early 1960s one of his editors had occupied his room. This now changed. It was as though, after the honeymoon was over, his American wife had said, 'Now dear, what time do you like to go to the office?'

The result was that a chairman who had seemed rather distant to journalists and even to the more trusted managers suddenly became a presence. He was in his room almost every day, calling executives in to report to him. This marked a breach with the practices not only of much of his own life, but of his father and uncle before him. It was also hard for the staff to adjust to.

The last editor who served him on the *Daily Mail*, Arthur Brittenden, did not always find it easy to make conversation when he made the regular phone call to his proprietor at 5.30 pm. Usually he could get a response when he talked about the weather: Esmond, who had taken to heart one of Northcliffe's dicta that the weather was always a serious subject for the British, deserving proper coverage in the popular press, was fascinated by the subject. One day, however, Brittenden could not get a reaction. There was a long silence, then, 'Why are you telling me that? I'm sitting in my office across the road from you, looking at exactly the same weather as you are.'

Continuity of the Rothermere male line had been doubly guaranteed in 1967 when, to the delight of their friends, Vere and his wife Patricia produced their first son on 3 December. He was given names which included three forebears – Harold, Jonathan, Esmond, Vere – but he was called by his second name, Jonathan. Esmond, who had made provision for his earlier children and grandchildren already, drew up a will in the late 1960s under which he left all his remaining wealth to his third wife and new son.

Regular attendance at Carmelite House, plus a sharper concern with the future of the family business now that he had a new young heir, brought home to Esmond the grave position of the group. Sales of the *Daily Mail* were slipping from 2.65m in 1961 to 1.9m in 1970, the paper was losing money and there was no real budget for promotion. The

Sketch, where a lively former *Express* journalist named David English who had worked for Rothermere in the late 1950s was putting up a good fight with miniscule resources, seemed hopeless as a commercial prospect. The signals were turning red for the just profitable *Evening News*. All that was keeping the group going was the profit from Northcliffe Newspapers, the provincial subsidiary, and the various investments ranging from Southern TV to National Opinion Polls, from London taxis to the pulp and paper interests in Canada.

Journalists working for the group felt it was heading for some kind of crisis, and the chairman himself was not immune from responsibility. The *Daily Mail*, which had rerun the London to Paris air race first, and then a London to New York air race in 1969, had little success when it serialised Henri Charriere's bestseller about Devil's Island in French Guiana, *Papillon*. Esmond said afterwards that the *Mail* should never have run it, he always knew it would do no good; when this was reported back to his editor, Arthur Brittenden marvelled at the proprietor's powers of amnesia or self-deception, for it had been Esmond who had pushed him to take the book.

A management error was committed when Lord Barnetson's United Newspapers group ambushed Associated into the hasty purchase of a south London printer, Samuel Stephens, which specialised in preprint colour. Barnetson said that it was the most advanced plant in the country, and he would either sell to the *Standard* or to Associated for the *Evening News*. Quite soon it was apparent that a mistake had been made and Esmond called in an executive, Michael Mander, to organise a sale over the head of the director, Frank Ellis, who had been charged with running the print firm.

Mander found a potential buyer in Garrod and Lofthouse and reported to Esmond that he would have to show Norman Garrod over the works. 'Absolutely out of the question.' 'But I can't sell it if I can't show him over, Lord Rothermere.' 'Out of the question. You may ask why. Furthermore I will tell you. It's Ellis. He doesn't know the firm is for sale. I said to Ellis a few weeks ago, "This is a pig in a poke." But he's fallen in love with the pig.' In consequence, the group never could sell the print firm, which it had to close down at considerable expense.

It was in this climate that Esmond authorised his managing director, Marmaduke Hussey – later of Times Newspapers and chairman of governors of the BBC – to begin serious talks with the *Express* group for mutual cooperation. These ran on in secrecy during 1970 in working parties of the two managements. On the *Express* side the managing director, John Coote, wanted to raise funds by capitalising on his modern print plant to publish a merged *Standard/News* and potentially, though the operation would move in stages and Associated wanted to see how a *Mail/Sketch* merger would work out first, a merged *Express/Mail*. Because the *Sunday Express* was to be kept out of the equation, and Sir Max Aitken was to be chairman in the first year of the joint company which would hold all the titles, it was generally felt that the *Express* group would be getting the upper hand in the deal.

Given Esmond's advancing years – he was 72 in 1970 – this probably seemed a sensible way of securing the future, even if job losses for printers and journalists appeared inevitable. The effect would probably have been to make the Daily Mail and General Trust rather more of an investment holding company, rather less of a newspaper-based concern.[18] So far as he could he had continued his father's policy of diversification and, through a brother-in-law of his third wife's – Fred Hamilton of Hamilton Brothers in the United States – he was putting Associated in the way of participating in the exciting new world of North Sea oil exploration.

Esmond was a businessman first and a newspaperman second. His journalists might get their adrenalin from the daily battle with the *Express* or *Standard* but he was old enough to remember the cross-holdings between the *Mail* group and the *Express*, and times when his father had owned half the shares in the *Standard* and he himself had been the biggest single shareholder in the *Mirror*. In that perspective there could be little objection to a joint holding company with the *Express* in a world where print and paper costs had risen astronomically, and the market for middle-brow papers was uncertain.

The deal got very close to agreement. Indeed at an evening meeting at Warwick House in January 1971, when Esmond was accompanied by his son Vere, and Sir Max Aitken and John Coote were accompanied by Lord Goodman as their legal adviser, it is said that verbal agreement was reached. But two factors baulked a legally watertight treaty. On the Associated side, Esmond's son Vere made a successful bid for his newspaper inheritance. On the Beaverbrook side, Jocelyn Stevens, from the Hulton family which had originally sold the *Evening Standard* to Lord Beaverbrook in the 1920s, was strongly opposed to merging the *Standard* with the *News*.

According to the Associated version it was in fact Sir Max who reneged on the deal first; this would not be the last time that the issue of the *Standard*, for which Jocelyn Stevens had just made a £1.5m profit, was to derail collaboration between the two groups. But Vere's attitude was to have a far more remarkable impact. Esmond's son had been vice chairman of the group since 1963, but his duties were not well understood in a group which was run in a quirky and autocratic fashion by his father, and he was greatly underrated by most of the senior managers. Editors were aware that he was quick to spot if they had been beaten on some story by the *Express* group, and that his wife was interested in the fashion and social pages. But they had no reason to suppose that he harboured journalistic powers or ambitions.

The talks between the two groups had been running for quite a while. Vere was fully aware of them, and had not voiced an opinion either way

15. Esmond Harmsworth as a young MP.

16. Warwick House, Edmond's London home.

17. Esmond in his robes as Chancellor of the Memorial University, Newfoundland.

18. Esmond Rothermere dressed in his viscount's robes for the Coronation of 1953.

19. Esmond hosting the Prince of Wales and his friends: (*Back row*) Ewen Cameron ('Cammy'); Esmond, 2nd Viscount Rothermere; Victor Cazalet. (*Front row*) Helen Wills Moody; Lady Cunard; Mrs Helen Fitzgerald; Mrs Simpson; and the Prince of Wales on the far right.

20. Vere Harmsworth as a child holding a bird, photographed by Madame Yevonde.

21. Esme, Vere and Lorna as children.

22. Vere aged about 23.

23. Vere, the morning after becoming chairman of Associated Newspapers, in January 1980.

24. Patricia, Lady Rothermere, in July 1980.

25. Lord Northcliffe's room in Fleetway House.

26. Vere Rothermere in Northcliffe's room which was formerly at the *Daily Mail* in Carmelite House, now moved to the new building at Northcliffe House.

27. Vere, the third Lord Rothermere, in the foyer of Northcliffe House, June 1990.

28. Lord Rothermere with the journalists of the *Evening Standard*.

to the executives doing the negotiating. However, senior managers noticed signs of animosity between Vere and Duke Hussey, the chief protagonist of a deal with the *Express*, and in retrospect many felt that he must have been hostile all along to what must have felt like an attempt to sell his birthright.

Dramatically, following the collapse of the deal, Esmond called a board meeting of Associated in January 1971 and announced that he was resigning as chairman, and that his son Vere was taking over. Some present felt that the commendation of his successor was slightly equivocal. Esmond slipped away without fuss to spend a lengthy holiday in South Africa. On his last day, at what must have been an emotional time, his secretary asked the editor of the *Mail* to come up for a farewell drink. Brittenden hung around for half an hour and was then sent away, as father and son stayed closeted together.

Had there been an argument between the two or did Esmond retire voluntarily? There was speculation both inside the firm and amongst competitors. Vere's recollection is that, following the breakdown of the *Express* deal, his father asked what he thought they should do next. Vere replied that he would like the chance to run the group as an independent entity. His father, who had already agreed in principle to step aside to let Sir Max Aitken chair the proposed holding company, said that he would be happy to let Vere take over, and that he would support him in whatever needed to be done.

In reality, Vere had a clear idea of what he wanted to do and the courage to handle the redundancies and heartache which were foreseeable. He planned to merge the *Sketch* and *Mail* and create a new brand of middle-market tabloid, attractive to women, the aspiring middle class, and chic. He had discussed his ideas with Howard French, a former editor of the *Sketch* and long-time Rothermere employee who had been forever embarrassed by a photograph of himself in a Blackshirt uniform. And he was ready to gather a small team, headed by David English on the editorial side and Mick Shields in management, to see the project through. How he succeeded will be recounted in the last section of this book.

Esmond was not entirely spared from the torments of the merger, as long-established *Mail* journalists were sacked and printworkers whose families had worked for his family suddenly lost their jobs. Esmond in fact had always got on rather well with his printers and the *Daily Mail*, unusually among morning papers, went on carrying advertisements for posts in the print. Jeffrey Blyth, the sacked New York correspondent for the *Mail* who had enjoyed his proprietor's hospitality in happier times, wrote to Esmond to say that it was the saddest moment of his career. The recently retired chairman must have had many such letters.

Holidaying in South Africa for three months, immediately after the handover, he was looked after by Peter Younghusband, the *Mail's*

Africa correspondent. Younghusband thought he was at times dis-
tracted by recent events and that his wife was taking particular care of
him, but that his spirits revived as time went by. He talked of visiting
East Africa, but never did so, and Younghusband arranged a meeting
for him with John Vorster, then the National Party Prime Minister of
South Africa. Younghusband himself was laid off as a result of the
merger but Esmond, who had never been told, believed he was still
employed by the paper and frequently asked him to send messages to the
editor and other executives. He assured him of a bright future on the
new *Mail* and, when an *Express* journalist tracked him down and asked
for Lord Rothermere's comments, Younghusband relayed his answers
back over the phone.

In his retirement Esmond remained chairman of the Daily Mail and
General Trust and kept an office, coming in regularly on a Tuesday and
going home on a Thursday. Although some who knew him felt there
had been signs of hardening arteries even before he passed on the
chairmanship of Associated Newspapers to Vere, his secretary felt he
stayed remarkably young until around 1976. He was, however, rather
sensitive about his deafness.

Although he had the pleasure of seeing little Esmond growing up,
Vere's triumph with the relaunch of the *Daily Mail* and the flow of oil
revenues from the Argyll field – there would also be an Esmond gas field
– his last few years had a darker side, too. The great inflation in Britain
from 1973 to 1975 left him worrying about money, and feeling that he
could no longer afford his expensive houses. His wife Mary would
possibly have preferred him to move to the United States, where they
bought a home in Palm Beach, but his life and most of his family were
centred on Britain.

The first home to go was the villa in Monte Carlo, an emotional loss
as it was a legacy from his father. Then he gave up Warwick House, his
London base for over fifty years, and moved into what had been the
chauffeurs' accommodation round the back in Stable Yard. From there
he moved into a house in South Audley Street. Finally, the last
Christmas of his life, he spent on his own with a nurse, surrounded by
packing cases at Daylesford. The house and estate was being sold to
Baron von Thyssen; many of the valuable pictures had been packed up
and transported to the United States. He finally died in July 1978,
shortly after his eightieth birthday.

The loss of these homes, and all they had meant to him, upset him
deeply and probably contributed to a sharp decline in the last couple of
years of his life. He was possibly suffering from Alzheimer's disease, and
failed to recognise old friends such as Thelma Cazalet. An odd incident
occurred when he went missing at Monte Carlo airport. Mary, his wife,
had left him sitting in a seat when he disappeared. He was subsequently
found lying by a roadside and someone who had seen him and found

out his identity from his papers rang London. He was unharmed, and it seemed that he had taken a cab by himself and then forgotten where he was. His daughter Lorna and son Vere flew out to be with him, and his ex-wife Ann Fleming remarked bitchily that at least *she* had never mislaid Esmond at an airport.

After his death a memorial service was held at the Daylesford church which went with the estate. Esmond had chosen where his grave would be and it was inscribed with some lines from Rupert Brooke:[19]

> And think the thoughts by England given
> Her sights and sounds, dreams happy as her day
> And laughter learned of friends
> And gentleness, in hearts at peace
> Under an English heaven.

The stress on Englishness harked back to the values of his father's and uncles' generation; the quotation from Brooke's elegy was peculiarly apt for a man who had lost two brothers in the First World War and whose whole formation had been dominated by that war and its aftermath. At the memorial service in Daylesford, estate workers rubbed shoulders with grandees and newspaper folk. One of the hymns chosen was 'All Things Bright and Beautiful'. Whoever chose the order of service, no doubt seeking to be tactful, arranged for the omission of the verse which starts, 'The rich man in his castle, the poor man at his gate ...'

About three weeks later Mick Shields was with Vere and brought up the subject of the service, and the fact that this verse had been left out. 'I can't think why they did it. It's the best bloody verse in the hymn,' the third Lord Rothermere was reported to have said.

12
Family, Impact, Personality

Esmond Rothermere's sense of family was at least as strong as it had been in his father's generation. He is alleged to have told his daughter-in-law that she ought to realise that she would be marrying into a dynasty, and during his period at the helm the Daily Mail Ideal Home Exhibition family lunches every January – often the only occasion that Harmsworths would see each other from one year to the next – became an institution. The Earl's Court exhibition centre, of course, was itself a group subsidiary. Esmond was a favourite nephew of Christabel Burton, who outlived all her brothers and sisters. In 1967, the year she died, when she was already in her late eighties, he invited her to be guest of honour at the Ideal Home lunch. 'Dearest aunt, do come – you'll be the belle of the ball,' he wrote. Sadly she was not well enough to attend.

There were three distinct layers of family with which he was concerned: his wives, children and grandchildren; the relatives and associates of his wives who came to play some part in the group, giving what some executives felt was a 'courtier' feel to the inner workings of the company; and the rest, some of whom like Cecil King or Bart might play a part in his professional life. (Complaining that the trade paper, *World's Press News* was not properly reporting his campaign against Esmond's 'pornography', Randolph Churchill told the Fleet Street Forum in 1953 that 'it may, perhaps, be of some significance that the proprietor of *World's Press News*, Mr Basil Burton, is a first cousin of Lord Rothermere'.)

Obviously, his chequered marital history made for some difficulties but he was close to and much loved by his children and grandchildren. Vere came into the firm and gained experience in paper, advertising and management; his two sons-in-law, Neill Cooper-Key and Lord Errington (who succeeded as Earl of Cromer in 1953) were directors of the Daily Mail and General Trust. He saw a lot of his daughters, particularly when he was between marriages. Both his daughters had tragedies in their own families: Lorna Cooper-Key's son Adrian was killed in a car crash near Malaga, and Lady Cromer's epileptic daughter Lorna died in her twenties. Understandably, Esmond doted on his belated son, little Esmond (one of the Cooper-Key boys was also called

Esmond); those who saw father and son playing together thought it was poignant to watch how the little boy, throwing a ball for a father in his seventies to catch, threw it directly at him so he hardly had to move.

For his business each of his marriages had certain consequences. As a result of his first the group acquired the services of Robert 'Bobby' Redhead, who had given away his first wife at their wedding in Bromley. There was some speculation after the marriage to Ann O'Neill that Redhead's career in management might suffer, but Esmond was far too loyal to individuals to let that affect him, and he became a managing director in the late 1950s.

Other executives thought Redhead should never have had the job, and that that was a bad example of a family oligarchy in control of a major business. But Redhead had considerable charm and in addition to his relationship to Esmond he struck up a good working friendship with Bob Hammond, a former printer, of a quite different background, who had climbed the management tree. He was fond of motor cars, once buying a Thunderbird when he was in New York, and like Esmond he married more than once. Near the end of his career he described his style of management to colleagues at a meeting in the United States. 'Behind each of your chairs there is someone standing ready to take over,' he is remembered as saying. 'And who's standing behind yours?', someone asked cheekily. When Redhead returned to Britain he lost his job.

A bigger wave, mostly associated with journalism, came in after Esmond's marriage to Ann. One of her connections was the Earl of Arran, nicknamed 'Boofy', who had a role in management as well as writing a zany right-wing column for the *Evening News* (he once famously dismissed the Swiss as having invented nothing but the cuckoo clock). He was visibly terrified of Stuart McClean, the Burton relation who was so powerful in the 1950s, calling him 'Sir'. However, he also tried to stand up to McClean, once telling Esmond that he would have to fire him because he had humiliated his son Vere.

The impact of his third marriage was not that it brought a new wave of recruits into the *Mail* group; Mary Rothermere took a while to find her feet in Britain, and Esmond himself was nearing the end of his career. Her arrival divided his friends – one move that made her unpopular with some was when she had warning notices fixed to the cars of friends who parked by Warwick House when on their way to White's Club. But the marriage had a powerful effect on the group none the less: it indirectly precipitated Vere's succession, with his go-it-alone philosophy for the newspapers; and, because the Hamilton brothers needed a British partner for their North Sea oil exploration, it helped to provide the financial ballast for Vere's reconstruction of the 1970s.

Further out from the family that was still closely connected with the firm there were of course the multiplying cousins and relations, many of whom still had a dividend relationship with the group as a result of the ingenuity of Northcliffe's will and the first Lord Rothermere's benefactions. It seems indeed to have been part of the object of the first generation founders that by giving the family an ongoing financial interest, via trust holdings, the cousins and siblings could be kept out of the actual management.

Far and away the biggest figure on the wider family scene was Cecil King. His shyness, difficulty to talk to, and illusion that he could enter and leave a room without being noticed – although he was well over six feet – were traits he shared with Esmond. But in the foundations of their personality they were very different. King was an empire-builder in publishing, and keen to use his power to intervene in British politics. Esmond, by contrast, was more concerned to preserve the empire he had inherited and, whether because he was reacting against the ways of his father and uncle or because he had actually been a backbench MP, he had neither the desire nor the talent to use his press for all-out political propaganda.

Esmond's relationship with King seems for the most part to have been courteous but uneasy, with always a competitive edge. From 1951 when he ousted Esmond's connection on his mother's side, Bart, to 1968, when King was dismissed in a boardroom coup after writing a front-page article in the *Mirror* telling Harold Wilson to resign as Prime Minister, King was totally dominant in the *Mirror* group. With Hugh Cudlipp to provide the journalistic zest and himself offering the cerebral strategy, nothing seemed to go wrong. Sales of the *Mirror*, whose shares Harold Rothermere had sold in the 1930s when he thought it was getting too left-wing, hit a peak of 5 million at one point. The revenues allowed King to buy Amalgamated Press, the old Harmsworth magazine business which now included the Iliffe technical press for which Alfred had once worked and, after meeting the chairman of Odhams at one of Esmond's Christmas parties, he bought Odhams with its dowry of magazines and the *Daily Herald*.

However, King was neither such a good manager nor so far-sighted as he supposed. Furthermore, in the 1960s he succumbed to the megalomania and superiority complex which had afflicted his uncles. In 1964, he was insulted when Harold Wilson offered him a life peerage and a junior ministry at the Board of Trade. He was also in some respects out of sympathy with the Labour Party his papers supported: his initial instinct had been to support Eden at Suez, he favoured hanging, and by early 1968 he wanted a national government of businessmen and technocrats which he invited Lord Mountbatten to head.

Although farcical, and anachronistic in that King was the servant of shareholders in a public company, the episode awakened memories of Alfred Northcliffe and Harold Rothermere.[20] Because he was a successful newspaper publisher, in touch with public opinion, King had become disillusioned with politicians and felt personally undervalued.

Personal frustration and excessive pessimism about the state of the nation led him to overreach himself: behaviour which would have seemed familiar to his uncles – how many times had Harold tried to get rid of Baldwin? – appeared unacceptable by the late 1960s.

On the day he was deposed King invited a relation, St John Harmsworth, a well-known London magistrate, to have lunch with him in the *Mirror* building. St John was surprised to find them lunching alone. He was treated well and they discussed the affairs of the country. He had not seen King for years when he got the invitation. On his way out he saw an evening paper placard, 'King Ousted at Mirror' and learned for the first time what had happened. Earlier in the day, when a reporter asked King what he was going to do next, he replied simply, 'I'm going to have lunch.'

For Esmond, Cecil King was, like Lord Beaverbrook, an awkward competitor. Beaverbrook, his father's good friend, tended always to better the *Mail* group: when he fired a number of *Mail* journalists in 1950 the Beaver was said to have exclaimed 'Hire the lot, boys!' With King, where the *Sketch* competed with the *Mirror* and the *Sunday Dispatch* did battle with the *Sunday Pictorial*, Esmond may have felt that not only were his papers getting the worst of it, but that the mantle of Northcliffe was at stake.

Many in the Harmsworth family disliked King because of the papers he ran, and because he made so little effort to hide his opinion that he was much cleverer than they were. What soured Esmond's relations with him, and drove other members of the family to fury, were volumes of his memoirs which they felt contained wounding inaccuracies. He had described his mother as a gorgon, many Harmsworths as drunks, Northcliffe as dying of syphilis, and an intelligent aunt as ignorant.[21] When challenged on such references he said he had put them in to make the story more interesting. Christabel Bielenberg, whom he invited to lunch with him at the Shelburne Hotel in Dublin, refused to sit down with him until he had apologised for remarks about her mother. 'I looked on the whole thing as a joke. If you won't take it as a joke, then I apologise,' he said.

King had encouraged Christabel Bielenberg to write her bestselling autobiography[22] which was subsequently televised. Other family members never quite knew what reaction they would get when they asked King for help. His first cousin Daphne, daughter of his godfather and uncle Cecil, Lord Harmsworth of Egham, got a rude postcard when she asked whether he could assist in finding a job for her Egyptian son-in-law who had been a diplomat but had fallen out with President Nasser.

On the other hand, when Madeleine Harmsworth, a granddaughter of the first Lord Harmsworth of Egham, wanted to start in journalism she felt she got a better hearing from Cecil King than from Esmond

Rothermere. Her father wrote first to Esmond, whom she found to be stiff and difficult. He then wrote to King, who also agreed to see her. King asked what she wanted, and she said she wanted a job. He asked why he should give her one – relations were always asking him, and anyway it was unfeminine for a young woman just graduating from Oxford to want to be a reporter. She said she hoped he would ask one of his editors to see her.

King passed her over to Hugh Cudlipp to see and, after some tribulation in abandoning her Oxford essay style in favour of *Sunday Mirror* prose – the *Sunday Pictorial* having undergone a name change – she embarked on a lasting career as film critic and letters editor. One of her major breaks came under Michael Christiansen, son of the *Express* editor, who had also suffered for his name. (When Lady King had been pressing Harold Rothermere for a job for Cecil, William McWhirter advised him to pass him on to his provincial editors, so that the young Cecil would have the satisfaction of feeling that he had earned his first job.)

There were enigmatic, unpredictable sides to King which were reminiscent of the previous generation. Once in Nigeria, where his company owned the *Nigerian Daily Times* a driver for the *Mirror* group subsidiary overturned his lorry at exactly the time when the great boss from London happened to be driving past; he was terrified of a rebuke, but King just said, 'Young man, you were driving too fast.' In 1959, when the *Mirror* group briefly owned the Cambridge evening paper, and he was shown over by the editor, the latter said dismissively, 'And these are just the subs.' At which point King jerked through the post-prandial cigar smoke, 'What do you mean? Subs *make* a paper.'

Esmond and his cousin were, of course, by no means the only stars in the Harmsworth firmament during his period of command. Cecil, the first Lord Harmsworth of Egham, who lived until 1948, provided a major centre for family hospitality at his London home, number 13 Hyde Park Gardens. It was a huge house, with ten attic bedrooms. Christabel Bielenberg, who stayed with him for a year in 1946 after leaving Germany, felt guilty about so much unused space when she was propositioned by Victor Gollancz, who was promoting a charity called Save Europe Now to help refugees and displaced persons. The charity was losing its premises in Covent Garden and wanted temporary accommodation.

Knowing that her uncle was anti-Semitic, and that he might well not realise what was going on several floors up in a big house, Christabel told Gollancz he could move into the attic but said nothing to her uncle. Save Europe Now arrived at a weekend when Lord Harmsworth was at his Egham home. Within three weeks they had found somewhere else. But at the last weekend, when they were moving out, Lord Harmsworth did not go down to Egham. Coming in from a walk in the park he caught Christabel and told her, 'There is a furniture van parked outside my house and a group who look like Balkan terrorists are taking all my furniture away. Do you know what's going on?' Christabel confessed and he just said, 'Don't ever do that again.'

The Burtons had been badly treated by both Northcliffe and Harold Rothermere. Esmond took the opportunity of some financial dealings over the Newfoundland interests to make recompense to his aunt Christabel. During his lifetime, too, Northcliffe's direct descendants by Mrs Wrohan resumed the name Harmsworth. Guy Harmsworth, son of Harold Wroham, was at Eton at the same time as Thomas Harmsworth, grandson of the first Lord Harmsworth and brother to Madeleine. At the instigation of Esmond's first wife, who realised that if legitimacy laws had not existed he might have been heir to the family firm, Guy was invited to the Ideal Home lunches. Someone who met Guy retaking A-levels after Eton remembers asking what his father did, and being told that he lived quietly off his investments.

There was one other Harmsworth who worked in the group, the eccentric and amusing Geoffrey Harmsworth who inherited his father Leicester's baronetcy in 1962. He was homosexual and every spring and autumn would travel to the West Country to inspect his interests – of which the chief was the *Western Morning News* in Plymouth – accompanied by a 'godson'. He was in a special position because it was through his brother and himself that these West Country papers, which Leicester had bought as an investment, joined the main Rothermere fold. He was also chairman of Harmsworth Publications, which included *The Field* and *Golf Illustrated* which were run out of Dickensian premises in Stratton Street, Mayfair.

Geoffrey liked to be paid as a journalist and contributor and once chided Noel Vinson, then editor of the *Western Morning News*, for paying him only ten shillings for an item. He also was the family historian, responsible for a weighty life of Northcliffe with Reginald Pound, and he kept in touch with Northcliffe's direct descendants. He built a substantial collection of family memorabilia which was taken to Canada after his death in 1980.

He was inclined to drink heavily and, while popular, was a subject of many stories. Once in a Torquay hotel, for example, he ordered a live lobster on a silver salver and then got up from his table and asked the waiter to follow him. Together they walked down to the sea where he threw it back into the water. On another occasion, outside the Ritz Hotel, he suddenly stood on tiptoes and kissed a senior male colleague full on the mouth.

In Esmond's time, the offices of Harmsworth Publications, over which Geoffrey presided, were unbelievably antiquated. When Vere took over and was shown them the managing director, David Hill, suggested that they should be left as a museum, with visitors charged for admission. In about 1971, when an advertisement manager timidly suggested that it might be time to invest in an electric typewriter Hill replied, 'There's only one snag, we're on gas. Get yourself a typewriter that works on gas!'

Compared with his uncle Alfred or his son Vere, both of whom had a thorough-going interest in all aspects of the business and wished to be involved even where they did not take all the decisions, Esmond's impact on the group seemed fitful. As in his father's era the group was dominated by management – a stratified management in which perks were carefully graded – and a group of directors and senior executives among whom there were always undercurrents of rivalry and creative tension.

Whereas both Northcliffe and Vere were inclined to see management as an obstacle to the successful development of the group – not always recognising that they themselves were part of it – Esmond was more at home with his managers, even as they jostled for his favour. Periodically there were convulsions. Once a managing director named Stanley Bell was ditched when the chairman sprung a vote of confidence in him which most of the Associated directors had been warned not to support; an unwary editor of the *Mail*, underbriefed as to what was going on, put up his hand for Bell and found himself out of a job too.

It was rare that a manager, like Don McClean, established an absolute ascendancy under Esmond: more frequently there were several people punching for the top jobs. In retrospect mistakes were made; Vere later thought that the loss of George Abel, a former guardsman who always wore a bowler hat and who left the firm when he was not made managing director after McClean, was a misfortune for the company. In the crisis period when Esmond handed over to Vere in 1970–1, both Duke Hussey and Mick Shields were negotiating to join Times Newspapers. When Hussey heard that Shields was also talking to the *Times* group he told Gordon Brunton of *The Times* management that he would accept his offer. Shields threw in his lot with Vere.

The head of an organisation who is not in the office seeing his staff every day inevitably has problems in knowing what goes on. Northcliffe always had his 'ferrets' – informants who would keep him up to date on everything from tittle-tattle to editorial or commercial developments of significance. It was said that switchboard girls would listen in on phone conversations for him. Harold Rothermere also had his 'trusties' who would not only do what he said, but keep him in touch.

Esmond broke with this tradition, relying rather on what his senior managers and contacts outside the firm told him. When an underling once wrote to him to say that a certain executive was useless he had the underling dismissed. While his approach was honourable, reflecting that public school code which punishes sneaks and perhaps reducing the feeling among his employees that everyone was watching everyone else, it could also leave him rather isolated and ill-informed. His wealth and background also made it difficult for him to understand how the rest of the population, including his own staff, were actually living. Whereas Northcliffe and his father, as self-made men, had their own experience to rely on, his comments sometimes seemed unreal. He once told Shields, who was suffering from a bad back, that he ought to do more swimming. 'You do have a pool, of course,' he added; at that time the number of London homes equipped with swimming pools, even those belonging to better paid businessmen, was tiny.

Whereas the managers had prestige, the editors were directly answerable to the chairman, and were expendable. Arthur Brittenden, Esmond's last editor of the *Mail*, once had his secretary check that, with six years in the editorial chair, he was second only to Tom Marlowe in longevity. The frequent changes of editor meant there was little consistency as editors tried going up-market and down-market, hiring and firing their journalists, passing on their own sense of insecurity to those around them. All the time they were bombarded with suggestions from the commercial executives so that even an editor who was popular with his journalists like William Hardcastle found himself tied up in administration.

Several editors whom Esmond employed were undoubtedly talented, among them Frank Owen, who had a weakness for drinking a glass of champagne as he interviewed his colleagues, Mike Randall, who carried out a clever redesign of the *Mail* but was sacked after sales fell following a price rise, and Brittenden himself. There were also some successful editors on the *Sunday Dispatch*, *Evening News* and *Sketch* (where David English began his lengthy career as an editor).

The frequent departures reflected Esmond's own uncertainty in editorial matters. It was noteworthy that the great proprietor-journalists who knew their own minds, Northcliffe and Beaverbrook, tended to hang on to their editors. Esmond was swayed by short-term movements of sale and balance sheet, and by what other people said to him. He once told Patrick Sergeant, the long-serving City editor at the *Mail* who had a considerable following in the City, that editors might come and go but that the chairman and the City editor could go on for as long as they liked.

He was always more at home with business as such than with journalism, and as critiques of Fleet Street gradually changed from complaints about the abuse of proprietorial power (a basis for the post-war Royal Commission on the Press) to attacks on managerial inefficiency and overmanning, he watched more closely. In 1966, after the Economist Intelligence Unit had published a series of tables which showed the *Mail* City office to be relatively overstaffed, he told Sergeant to get rid of some journalists. With this threat hanging over them Sergeant and his colleagues came up with the idea for a weekly section called 'Money Mail', a breakthrough in consumer journalism for savers.

In contrast with the *Mail* editors there were only three City editors, including Sergeant, over the sixty years following Northcliffe's death. They all had prestige. The first, a man named Meredith, helped in the merger of Enos and Macleans which created the Beechams toiletry business in the mid 1930s. He had won a special place in Harold Rothermere's heart in 1928 when, it is said, his proprietor had asked him, 'Meredith, do you know anything about Hungary?' He replied that he was, in fact, Hungarian. 'Good,' said his boss, 'because they have offered me the crown of Hungary, and I will make you my Finance Minister.'

Esmond's relationship with Sergeant, who had started in life as a dance instructor for Arthur Murray and ended up wealthy and knighted, was trusting and cordial. After 'Money Mail' had been going for a fortnight Esmond told Sergeant he knew it was a success, because half a dozen people had been in to claim credit for the idea. When in the late 1960s the growing Eurodollar market seemed to warrant a special journal, Sergeant met Esmond in New York – seated on a Central Park bench by the boating pool – and they agreed to launch *Euromoney*. It was set up with £6,200 capital, with half the equity supplied by Sergeant and the journalists. When it was floated as a separate company in the mid-1980s it was worth £92.5m.[23]

Esmond was not an interfering proprietor, indeed in at least one *Mail* editor could not recall a single occasion when he had asked either for the inclusion or the exclusion of a story. On the rare occasions when he did intervene there was usually a good reason. In 1968, the City editor of the *Evening News*, David Malbert, caught wind of the fact that Rupert Murdoch was going to buy the *News of the World*. John Gold, the editor, rang Esmond who said that it was not true and that the *News* must not run a thing. Although the editor expostulated that Malbert's sources were secure no report was carried. Shortly after, an announcement confirming the purchase came through.

Esmond then rang John Gold, the *Evening News* editor, to apologise for having misled him and asked that he pass on his congratulations to Malbert. He said that, exactly ten minutes before he had heard from his staff, he had Rupert Murdoch in his office explaining what he was going to do, and pledging him to total secrecy. Any article run by the *News* would have looked like a breach of trust.

In spite of the high turnover of editors Esmond greatly disliked having to sack people himself; wherever possible he passed the chore over to his managing directors or else – as in the case of William Hardcastle – sent departing editors off on a cruise or overseas trip from which they returned to find someone else in their place. It was probably a combination of personal kindness and a sense of the obligations of running a family business which made direct involvement in sackings so difficult. The prospect of having to enforce large-scale redundancies was almost certainly a factor in his decision to hand over the chairmanship of Associated Newspapers to Vere.

Looked at in the context of the family business, Esmond's long period of responsibility, thirty-four years from 1937, had seen a steady decline in the national newspapers which had made his family's name. At his own transfer of power there seemed only two options: either a creeping take-over by the *Express* group or drastic surgery and a fresh journalistic start. New developments threatened further to destabilise the group's national dailies, as Rupert Murdoch's purchase of the *Sun* for virtually nothing in 1969, followed by a rapid increase in sale, challenged the mighty *Mirror* and the vulnerable *Sketch*.

None the less, the family business, thanks originally to Harold Rothermere's philosophy, had long been more than the Fleet Street titles. It was a great deal stronger than the narrowly based Beaverbrook group. Under Esmond the provincial chain had been expanded and made more profitable and the process of diversification had, in addition to oil and television, extended into property, pizza parlours and magazines. Mick Shields, who had a mind which was described as being like a computer when it came to number-crunching, had been at the forefront of this expansion when he was managing Harmsworth Investments.

Shields had been responsible, via a series of mergers in Canada involving Price Brothers, Abitibi and Consolidated Bathurst, for parleying the original Anglo-Newfoundland Development Co. into a far more valuable shareholding in a much, much greater concern. It would have been quite possible for the Harmsworths to have walked away from Fleet Street in 1971 and done the same kind of thing: to have had a substantial holding in a merged *Express–Mail* group, with much less management anxiety, and a family investment business of major proportions. Whereas an exclusively Fleet Street focus made it appear as if Esmond's reign had been a process of retreat leading up to a crisis, a more rounded commercial history must suggest that the value of the enterprise he inherited in 1937 had fructified considerably under his stewardship.

Another major contribution was to reduce the high political profile of his newspaper group. Esmond's support for the Conservative Party was not in doubt, indeed it was a great deal more consistent than his father's. But, in the circumstances of the landslide Labour victory of 1945, there were voices calling for restraint on the power of the press proprietors; left-wingers, and also some Conservatives, recoiled with horror from the unbridled propaganda of Northcliffe, Harold Rothermere and Beaverbrook in the inter-war years. There were those who felt that power had been abused, and that the proprietors were partly to blame for the descent into war.

Esmond never sought to play the kind of political role reached for by the previous generation, in spite of his friendship for Churchill and his genuine interest in history and politics. The nearest he came to it was during the abdication crisis. In addition to working with Beaverbrook to keep material about Edward and Mrs Simpson out of all the papers, he proposed to Baldwin the concept of a morganatic marriage under which Edward could marry and keep the throne, but his children would not have inherited the crown. Although not keen on anything emanating from a Harmsworth, Baldwin felt obliged to consult the Cabinet and Dominion governments, but they turned the idea down.

Some continue to believe that the dominance of the Conservative press in the middle-brow market after 1945 greatly added to the hurdles facing the Labour Party, and that the imbalance here, particularly as living standards rose in the 'age of affluence', was an additional reason for regret at the death of the *News Chronicle*. But Esmond's own restraint reduced the political threat of possible regulation or divestment.

His personal qualities have been touched on already, but perhaps the most marked was his sense of loyalty. This, as in the case of Aidan Crawley, transcended political difference. Another example concerned an industrial correspondent on the *News*, R. J. Finnemore, who was an office-holder in the Communist Party. Arthur Deakin, right-wing general secretary of the Transport and General Workers' Union, complained about him to Esmond. None the less, Esmond, who was always anxious about Communists and used to ask editors of the *Mail* if they had any lurking about, refused to sack Finnemore. He even managed to get back on civilised terms with his ex-wives: at his 70th birthday party at Warwick House he was not only accompanied by the current Lady Mary Rothermere, but by both the others who had borne the title before her.

He was not a major philanthropist on the scale of his father or uncle, though he set up a scholarship fund which paid for six graduate students a year to come from Newfoundland to Britain. He also at one stage harboured the desire to leave Daylesford to the nation. But he could be extremely generous to individuals. For instance, when Mike Randall was editing the *Mail* his mother died in painful circumstances; Esmond heard one day and the next he sent him to stay in his suite at the Plaza Hotel, New York, to help him get over the shock.

Noel Barber, editor of the *Continental Daily Mail* and then a star writer for the *Mail* in the 1950s, was given a tax-free bonus of £10,000 by Esmond in 1957. He said, 'Put it down on a house.' Three years earlier he had suggested that Barber and his fiancée should marry from his house in Monte Carlo, but then sent them a telegram to say that he had forgotten a board meeting in London. Instead the Barbers got married from Warwick House at Caxton Hall registry office. No wedding photographs were taken because Esmond thought it could cause jealousy at the *Mail*

Barber was unusual in that he was an employee who became a friend – some felt that he would have made a good editor of the *Mail* – for Esmond had a shy and suspicious streak which did not let many get close to him. Once, on Barber's birthday, they went together to the Monte Carlo casino. Barber had been born on the ninth day of the ninth month in 1909 and he duly put 1,000 francs on the number nine on each of three tables. He won a large sum, and then wanted to wager it all. Esmond took the money from him, saying that he would be the only winner in Monte Carlo that night; he let him have only a relatively small sum, which Barber duly lost, and then he went home with his winnings.

Esmond often tried to avoid fuss, and did not exert the pull which he could have as a newspaper proprietor. He was once seen queueing for a seat in Radio City, New York, and although he made regular visits to the United States his staff felt he did not know a great many people there. Driving once from London to Florence with Barber he accidentally ran into a girl cyclist in Italy. Although it was her fault he asked Barber to pay her off because he was concerned about police involvement and delay. Barber gave her 20,000 lire to which his only reaction was, 'Couldn't you have got away with 10,000?'

He did, like his father, have a good nose for money. A characteristic story was told of one of his visits to his newspaper office in New York. A reporter, wanting to make conversation, asked whether he had had a successful visit. Yes, he said, he thought he had had a successful visit. He had made a million dollars on Wall Street. Well, said the reporter light-heartedly, he hoped the next time he came to America he would give him a tip. 'Young man, I'll give you the best tip you've ever had. If you hear of a good tip, keep it to yourself,' he was remembered as saying.

People found him difficult to talk to, though fellow directors managed to engage him on topics ranging from numerology to men's fashions. He was fond of history and, when Francis Chichester was nearing the end of his round-the-world sail in *Gipsy Moth*, he enjoyed throwing a trick question as to who exactly had knighted Sir Francis Drake at Greenwich. Even his interest in the British weather could sometimes pall. On the night of Harold Macmillan's speech about the wind of change blowing through Africa, he rang the *Mail* night news desk to find out about the editorial. An ill-informed reporter, who may only have seen the headline, told him it was about the weather. 'What, all of it?' he asked gruffly.

He was a good host, mixing a good Martini, and his hospitality had a genuinely aristocratic quality; he gave special parties for Churchill and Beaverbrook and, when an editor won a Journalist of the Year award, he threw a champagne reception at Warwick House. It was as though he had a duty to live up to Rothermere name.

But at the same time, like others in his family, he had a quizzical and lateral quality to his thinking. John Gold was brought back from the United States, where he had originally gone to escape asthma, to edit the *Evening News*; because it was then one of the few air-conditioned hotels in London, he was initially put up by the company at the Park Lane Hilton. One day Esmond asked him which floor he was on. He replied that it was the sixteenth. 'Have you seen any bees?' he was asked, to which at first he did not answer. Then he said he thought his employer had asked whether there were any bees, which there weren't, at which Esmond commented, 'No, you must be too high up there for pollen, you'd better stay there.'

The honesty of some of Esmond's remarks could make people catch their breath. When McClean died of cancer in his forties he told a colleague that yes, it was a terrible thing, because it made you realise what a dreadful thing it would be if it happened to oneself.

Although he was a different personality from his father or uncle, he too could cause awe and fear amongst his subordinates. Perhaps the reputation he had had for being a martinet at Eton was not totally unfounded. At his death, though there was much sadness, there were also one or two who felt that a weight had been mysteriously lifted.

In part this may have been because of his formality and reticence of manner. It was remarked that whereas Esmond, when he had a cup of tea, did not arrange for one for a guest, his son Vere would always offer a cup to a visitor. But on the other hand when Esmond invited someone to have a glass of sherry with him, he regularly sent out a glass to his secretary.

Towards the end his deafness made him seem more vague and standoffish. But at 6 foot 4 inches, with strong blue eyes, he really looked like a viscount. An old commissionaire put it like this to a new colleague, 'You've got to watch out for Lord Rothermere, he's your guv'ner.' But how would he know what he looked like, the other asked. 'Son, when you see Lord Rothermere, you'll know it's Lord Rothermere.' The third son of Alfred Harmsworth's closest brother had become a legend in his own right.

PART IV

Vere Rothermere

The Grandson

13
From Birth to 1971

Vere Harold Esmond Harmsworth, named after the uncle who was killed in the battle of the Ancre, was born three years too late to have known Northcliffe. His childhood was influenced by the fact that his parents split when he was about 5, and by the looming presence of his grandfather who died when he was 15. As the only legitimate male heir to a dynasty which had been a household name for three decades by the time he appeared on the scene in 1925, his existence and survival were extremely precious.

As the youngest of the three children, he seems to have been the most affected by his parents' separation. His mother took him initially into a suite at Claridge's, he lost a nanny who idolised him, and he never mentioned her again. He later had a French governess, whom the children thought was ghastly, and they moved around in their holidays between their father's base at Warwick House and their mother's in Dorset.

Like other children of broken marriages he had the experience of being shunted around and risked either being spoilt or suffering from benign neglect. He did not want to go to boarding school and cried on his way to preparatory school. As a little boy he preferred stories about real things, animals, trains and so on, to fairy stories. But he did have an imaginative side: when he and his sisters were playing by the River Piddle in Dorset they would pretend that they were exploring up the Amazon.

His school reports were not flattering, and when he was young he was not regarded as very strong (the Harmsworths were notoriously health conscious). But he was a fearless skier. At about the age of 9, when he was on a skiing holiday with his father at Kitzbuhel, he was very ill with jaundice and strained his heart. His mother, who was staying at St Moritz, had a telepathic feeling that something was wrong, came over to see him, and insisted on getting second opinions. Possibly because he was a poor student at school, some of Esmond's friends got the idea that he might be slightly retarded.

A further handicap to his self-image was the fact that he looked like his mother's family, not like a Harmsworth. He was teased about it, and rumour-mongers later tried to suggest that he might not be his father's son.[1] Like Esmond he was destined to go to Eton but he only had a year there before he was evacuated with Esme to Canada in 1940. It was not his first trip across the Atlantic because he had been over with Lorna in 1937. He and Esme travelled on the *Duchess of Bedford* in June 1940, arriving safely at Quebec City. They had been disappointed that their grandfather, Harold Rothermere, decided at the last moment not to take them with him because he wanted to split the risk from U-boats. In Quebec, where they met up with him, Vere was mistakenly assumed to be one of the war-wounded because his arm was in a sling after an accident on board ship.

It seems as if Vere was attached to his grandfather, and his death must have been a considerable blow. Over forty years later he was involved in battles to protect his reputation in the correspondence columns of *The Guardian*.[2] With his parents and Lorna still in England the presence of his grandfather in America, until he fell ill, must have been a real consolation.

Vere was sent to Kent School, Connecticut – a prestige school in the United States – and was cared for in the holidays by Frank Humphrey, his father and grandfather's business representative in the US. Esme had found the Humphreys difficult and Frank Humphrey[3] wrote to Esmond in 1940 in somewhat unflattering terms that his son was supremely good at three things – sitting, sleeping and eating. After nearly four years at Kent School he returned home just before D-Day.

Back in Britain he returned briefly to Eton, where one story has it that he fell foul of the authorities for chewing gum in chapel, but he did not take the Higher Certificate which was a requirement for university entry. He was not an academic boy and his education had been disrupted. But his father, who had never gone to university, would have liked him to go to Oxford, perhaps to Christ Church where there was a family connection.[4] After some inquiry it was generally understood that this ambition was unrealisable.

Instead he did military service, where he did not get a commission and it was said that his commanding officer would not even have him as a lance-corporal. Vere, as a private, had a spell in the Middle East. Esmond told a colleague that he thought being in the ranks had given Vere an inferiority complex. In a patriotic family, where his father and uncles had been commissioned and his uncles had been recognised for their gallantry, this would not have been surprising. However, his time with ordinary servicemen may have given him an insight into the way they thought and felt which his father's more privileged experience had denied him. Conscription, for boys from wealthier homes, was as good for social education as comprehensive schools could be in the 1960s.

After national service there was about a year in which Vere seemed to drift. He was very thin. Indeed he was described as emaciated in May

1948 when he had the pleasant duty of dancing with the film star Jean Simmonds, just back from filming *The Blue Lagoon* in the Pacific at the Daily Mail National Film Awards. His father worried about him. He said that Wright the butler could not get him out of bed in the mornings. Vere did not seem to have any vices, but nor did he have any initiative of any sort. Esmond wondered whether he ought to see a psychoanalyst, or whether he might be deficient in some gland.

He had girlfriends, but here again his lassitude seemed to hold him back. Late in 1947 he went with his father on one of his regular visits to New York. Exchange control was tight, Don Iddon, the *Mail* correspondent, acted as a kind of paymaster, and staff were amused to see Esmond and Vere racing each other out of cabs to avoid having to pay the fare. Vere stayed on with his sister Esme and his brother-in-law Lord Errington, who were working out there, and they celebrated Christmas Day with Noel Barber in the St Regis Hotel. Barber recalled later that Vere had not got up until after lunch.

The supposed purpose of Vere's stay had been so that he could make contact with a Spanish girlfriend; the idea had been that he would fly down to Mexico to see her. But he put it off and put it off. He was still staying with the Erringtons in January 1948 when his father came out to New York again. Esmond drew the conclusion that the affair was over, and they went down to the Bahamas in a small boat accompanied by Barber. There was a pretty girl who sang in the band on board, and both Vere and Barber made a play for her; Vere asked Barber whether he minded taking a walk for half an hour, to give him a chance to have her to himself.

In the Bahamas, Vere had a relaxed and lazy holiday, and then started talking about wanting to see his girlfriend again. By that time she had moved on from Mexico to Costa Rica. Again he postponed any action, while his dollar allowance dwindled. Esmond went back to New York, which seemed to stir Vere into life: he flew to Costa Rica, spent a day with the girl, flew on to New York, and then caught his boat back to Britain. No one knew how seriously to take the affair.

His life took a turn for the better in 1948 when, aged around 23, he joined the Anglo-Canadian Paper Mills in Quebec for a couple of years. It was the firm which had given rise to problems for his grandfather in 1930–2, when he owned the *Mirror*, and it was still supplying paper to the *Mirror* group when Vere worked for it. It was all a long way from London, but good practical experience, and an introduction to the raw material on which – as Northcliffe and Harold Rothermere had appreciated in 1902 – all publishing and journalism ultimately depended.

By the time Vere returned he seemed a much more confident figure. Apart from his experience in the paper company he had been involved in amateur dramatics, compering at parties, and had acquired skills which would come in useful when he had to speak in public later. (Although his grandfather had hated making speeches, Esmond was always rather good at them.) More subtly, the fact that he had spent a quarter of his first twenty-five years on the other side of the Atlantic must have been a formative influence. He liked North America – something which would be a common bond with David English, for example – and would have been struck by the greater dynamism and openness of its people.

Esmond told friends that it was difficult to bring his son into the *Mail* group; Vere, still very modest, said he would be happy to be a tea boy. In fact he joined Associated Newspapers in 1951 and over the next twenty years did a variety of jobs; although he had some satisfactions, he must also have been frustrated for much of the time. Basically, what he was up against was the fact that he was working in a family firm where power was centralised in his father and the other barons jealously guarded their position. He was not like anyone else, competing for advancement. He was insulated from much of the roughness associated with the lower and middle levels of the management ladder; yet in their hearts either his failures or his successes would be held against him by colleagues.

Moreover, there was no tradition for this kind of apprenticeship for the man who would in due course be the monarch. Esmond had started at the top, and his father and uncle had invented the firm. Also, Vere was alone in being special. Unlike other family firms, which sometimes employ a string of relations and let them fight it out so that the best candidate wins, the Harmsworths worked strictly by primogeniture. Esmond by the 1950s owned the controlling shares and could expect to pass them on to Vere. No one else was in anything like Vere's position; there was no colleague in whom he could fully confide. For someone who did not have a strong self-image anyway, it was a heavy burden to bear. However, Vere was good at mixing with people, having a drink in the Fleet Street pubs and happy to talk to telephonists and salesgirls at Christmas parties. In the late 1950s, he was attached to the *Sketch* on the management side, where David English had become Features Editor at the age of 25. Together they ran a successful promotion – 'Win a Pub' – which was fun and did some good for sales.

At a time when some others did not rate Vere, he and English hit it off together. This was to be of significance later when, after nine years on the *Express*, English came back to be editor of the *Daily Sketch* in 1969. Vere, although he did not seem to have a heavyweight role in the group, even when he became vice-chairman of Associated Newspapers in 1963, was quite observant. In particular he was concerned that the *Daily Mail* had become an inferior copy of the *Express* without a sufficiently strong and distinct identity of its own; further, although the *Sketch* might not seem a promising commercial prospect, it had a leanness and vitality which the senior paper often lacked.

In spite of the difficulties in Vere's situation – for deputy jobs have an intrinsic lack of authority from the US Vice-Presidency down – his potential did not go totally unnoticed. Lord Beaverbrook was once speculating with a trusted colleague on how his group might fare against the Rothermeres when his son Max Aitken had taken over from him, and Vere had succeeded Esmond. He feared that Vere would get the better of the contest.

In 1957, Vere got married. Whereas his father had married young, Vere was in his thirties when he fell in love with the actress wife of a racing driver, Mrs Patricia Evelyn Beverley Brooks. The fact that he married relatively late matched his slow-moving image, and may partly have been a reaction to his father's matrimonial misfortunes. But Pat was stunningly beautiful, under contract to the Rank film studios, and also intelligent.

More recently, the gossip columnists have turned her into a figure of fun, satirising her socialising and her outsize, outrageous dresses. That is only a partial picture of her now, and tends to obscure the person she was in the mid-1950s. The daughter of a Hertfordshire architect, John William Matthews, she had been brought up in the Church of Scotland. She spent a year in hospital as a teenager with rheumatic fever and later broke her spine in a riding accident.

She was only 18 when she first married. She had met Captain Christopher Brooks, a former Coldstream guardsman, at the Goodwood motor races.[5] Brooks himself was an exact contemporary of Vere's at Eton – they were both born in 1925 – where they knew each other. They married soon after they met, in 1951, and Patricia managed to combine having a baby, Sarah, with making a promising start in films.

Known as Beverley Brooks, she went to the Webber-Douglas drama school near their home in Chelsea, was spotted by a Rank talent scout, and was offered a seven-year contract after she performed on stage in the Edinburgh Festival. She thereby became a starlet in the celebrated Rank Charm School and began to get small parts in a number of films – in *Man of the Moment*, *Simon and Laura* and, as a flighty deb, in *Reach for the Sky*. She would have liked to have become a serious actress and has said that, after her marriage to Vere, Darryl Zanuck wanted her to go to Hollywood. But by then she realised it was a choice between Vere and Hollywood, and Vere won. Her Rank days, however, left a number of permanent marks: her clipped upper-class accent, rather like the Queen's; her delight in dressing up and partying; her pleasure in the company of actors and other creative people; her effortless and sometimes embarrassing skill as a performer; and her genuine gifts for friendship.

In her twenties she was extremely good looking, a subject of studies by Baron and Cecil Beaton. Vere met her either at a party or in a pub and they were soon smitten. He, too, was handsome, and in addition rich and heir to a viscountcy. But she has said since that she felt he was an underdog, in spite of all his apparent advantages. She thought there were hang-ups in his relationship with his father, and that she could help to promote him in society, and increase his self-confidence.[6]

Captain Brooks vainly told Vere to stop hanging round his house and, following the divorce, Vere and Patricia got married relatively quietly with a reception at the Hyde Park Hotel and a honeymoon in Florence. Curiously, just as had happened when his parents married, his father was not in attendance; Esmond had arranged to be in New York at the time of the wedding. This led some to believe that Esmond had disapproved of the match. But according to others he had at one point encouraged the relationship, as he believed that Patricia could help Vere with an alcohol problem. (In more recent years Vere has been a very light drinker, almost teetotal.) Patricia has since told an interviewer that she went through hell soon after she married Vere, finding him very withdrawn, and sensing his difficulties with his father; it was not an easy life being married to the heir to the Rothermere empire. But when she spoke frankly to Esmond he urged her to persevere, for if she left Vere it might break him. In an important paternal gesture, Esmond endowed him with £2.75m when they got married.

Within a year they had their first baby, Geraldine. Their second, Camilla, was not born until 1964, nearly eight years later. By that time the Honourable and Mrs Vere Harmsworth had established quite a presence on the London social scene and Patricia was already being seen as a major asset for charity occasions, with a vivacious smile and a talent for bringing together the bright and the beautiful. She was becoming a Rothermere hostess to match the celebrated Ann Rothermere, a friend of people like Andy Warhol, Patrick Lichfield and Princess Margaret as the swinging 'sixties got under way.

Both Vere and his wife were fond and proud of their children. They were to establish a country base at Stroods in Sussex, although Pat made it clear at the start of their marriage that she did not want to be cut off from her husband's London life, however much she enjoyed the countryside and thought it good for the children. From a dynastic viewpoint it was unfortunate that both their two first children were girls. A new complication in Vere's relationship with his father, and Pat's relationship with her father-in-law, arose in 1966 when Esmond married again; his new wife was only a few years older than Patricia who, on New Year's Day, 1967, got a letter from her new mother-in-law to say that she wanted Vere's wife to be the first to know that she was pregnant.

Vere had always been slightly in awe of his father. The possibility that, nearly 70, he might produce another son could have been galling. If Vere himself never had an heir the viscountcy, and control of the family concern, would in due course revert to such a stepbrother. Yet Pat and her baby had been very ill when Camilla was born and she had been advised not to have another child. However, Pat was determined not to be beaten. She read as many books as she could lay hands on and adopted the technique recommended by a Dr August von Borosini[7] for those who wish to choose the sex of their baby. She prayed. On 3 December 1967, she gave birth to a son, Jonathan. Although Esmond and Mary Rothermere had had their baby son six months before, Vere and Pat had their own son and heir.

The late 1960s must have been very difficult for Vere as he saw problems building up for the national newspapers, but his father kept control to himself and appeared to put more faith in his other executives. Yet it was Vere's heritage – and possibly Jonathan's after him – that was at risk. On the other hand, senior executives could get a negative impression of Vere. Esmond, for instance, would ask a senior director to join him when he knew his son was coming to see him, otherwise he said, Vere would stay for hours; others remember Vere ringing them up on the internal office phone system and talking inconsequentially for what seemed like half an hour, punctuated by long silences.

Vere's wife also began to cause irritation to the diary page and the backbench subeditors by ringing in with stories and gossip items. Arthur Brittenden as editor took the matter up with Esmond, who issued a directive that if any member of the family wanted to get an item in the *Mail* they should contact him first. Pat also sometimes got hold of the wrong end of the stick in reporting the views of his colleagues to Vere.

As the crisis over the profitability, or lack of it, of the national papers blew up in 1970 Vere still seemed rather on the sidelines. Duke Hussey and his teams were negotiating with their opposite numbers at the *Express*, and were answerable to Esmond. However, the outlines of an alternative solution to merger with the rival group did exist. McKinseys, the management consultants, had done some work on how it might be possible to convert the *Mail* into a smaller, tabloid newspaper. The idea seemed daring in Britain, although middle-market tabloid papers did exist in the United States. But apart from the *Evening Standard* the tabloid format in Britain was strongly associated with sledgehammer headlines, exaggerated prominence given to a single front page lead story, and a down market product. Yet the economics of a change from broadsheet to tabloid pagination were attractive: the same quantity of paper would produce more pages, giving readers an impression of better value, and yielding a higher income from advertisers.

Although Vere's go-it-alone strategy for the national newspapers was ultimately successful, it is easy to forget what a high risk gamble it appeared at the time. The old broadsheet *Mail*, what William Hardcastle had once called 'the popular paper for sensible people', had a long lineage and was well loved by its traditional, if ageing readership. It had some good journalists, of whom the most celebrated was perhaps Vincent Mulchrone, and with all its back-stabbing and intrigue it had a tough morale. Many reporters who were quite unmoved by its Tory politics felt honoured to work for Northcliffe's creation, and what was still seen as a good hard newspaper.

To merge the *Mail* and *Sketch* in a new middle-market tabloid seemed to many, journalists, managers and members of the Harmsworth family, a dangerous leap in the dark. Readers and advertisers could easily be lost. The *Daily Express* might easily mop up the wreckage. Furthermore, there could easily be the most drastic confrontation with the print unions. In 1970–1, the Fleet Street unions were almost at the apex of their power, enforcing high wages and duplication of labour. Threats of missed editions to a perishable product were imposed at short notice by anarchic chapels, as the local union branches were called. Although Harold Rothermere had cut journalists' salaries in the 1930s, the tradition of Northcliffe and Esmond Rothermere had been to sweet-talk the printers. On at least one occasion when Esmond had wanted to resist union wage demands, he found himself undermined by Beaverbrook who was ready to concede them. There was no doubt that a survival strategy for an independent *Mail* group would require huge redundancies, with bitter and unpredictable results.

Some in the Associated hierarchy were also aware that, during 1959–60 when their company had had an option to buy the *News Chronicle*, the Cadbury management had considered going tabloid. The *News Chron*'s problem was not so different from the *Mail*'s a decade later, with an insufficiently youthful, upwardly mobile and feminine readership. But the *News Chronicle* had decided against it.

The go-it-alone strategy also implied a clear-out at the top – editorial, managerial and above all dynastic. There had to be a new editor with a fresh policy for the tabloid *Mail/Sketch*. Duke Hussey, as the managing director who was convinced that there had to be a merger between Associated and the Beaverbrook group, would be in an impossible position if he stayed. And Vere would be taking over from his father.

This last seemed like the biggest question mark of all. With his known defects as a proprietor Esmond nevertheless had enormous experience; he could when he wished regale colleagues and staff farewells with stories of Northcliffe and his father; even in his seventies he seemed to represent the continuity of the firm. Vere, by contrast, appeared little known. He had been disparaged behind his back and had had little opportunity to give others much confidence in his judgement. His succession, at a time when jobs and the future of the national newspapers were at stake, was an additional cause of anxiety.

In an interview published in *The Tatler* in May 1986, Patricia, Lady

Rothermere has claimed that her intervention was crucial in psyching up her husband to take on the chairmanship of the group at such a difficult moment, and in persuading Esmond – in return for her promise not to desert Vere – to hand over to his son. Lady Harmsworth Blunt, Vere's mother, has told the author that she passed on to him a message from a psychic friend of hers that the founders of the business considered that it was right to convert the *Mail* into a tabloid.

As always success has many parents, while failure is an orphan. Among the crucial factors were Vere's own inner courage, the fact that he had a strategy and staff ready to implement it, and Esmond's loyalty to him once the die was cast. His father seems to have done all that he could to help, not only by slipping quietly away to South Africa to give Vere a clear run. He had also helped to hang on to David English, by indicating to him that he could expect to get the editorship of the *Mail*, and he seems to have smoothed the way for Duke Hussey to join Times Newspapers when it was obvious that his position would be untenable at Associated.

Vere also benefited from the loyalty factor which can be the secret ingredient in the long-term survival of family firms. There was a general sense of rallying round in a crisis with Mick Shields the new managing director supporting the new proprietor with tact and all his considerable ability; Vere's confidant Howard French, former editor of the *Sketch* and now editorial director, ready to take on the unpleasant duty of handing out redundancy letters to hundreds of journalists; David English working flat out, forgoing lunches and sleep to design a new and exciting product; Brittenden and Walter Terry on the old *Mail* trying to keep the show on the road until the transformation; and younger managers, like John Winnington-Ingram, son of a Bishop of London, who was brought down to help Shields from Manchester, extending every effort.

Vere's succession was far more dramatic than either of the two previous transitions. When Northcliffe died both the editor and chief manager at the *Mail* stayed in place. When Harold Rothermere handed over to his son Esmond the process was so gradual that people had difficulty in placing when exactly it had occurred. But Vere's coming into his inheritance, and his personal renaissance, had the unexpected quality of a rainbow in a stormy sky. The hour made the man.

14

From 1971 to 1981

Vere had a concept for the tabloid *Mail* from the start, and he and David English established an almost telepathic understanding which has become one of the legendary proprietor-editor partnerships in journalism. Vere's concept began from the idea that the *Mail* should become a new paper – his *Who's Who* entry describes him as founder of the *New Daily Mail* – and not a mere combination of the old *Daily Mail* and old *Daily Sketch*.

This was a risky approach. Most publishers and editors then and since have preferred to make changes in the way attributed to Woodbines cigarette packets – so gradually that the purchaser hardly knows the difference. But the experience of the *Mail* merger with the *News Chronicle* had shown that you cannot fool readers in matters of newspaper identity. If the tabloid *Mail* had been a boiled-down version of the broadsheet paper there was a great danger that the old readers would have been annoyed and few *Sketch* readers would have been attracted. Further, such a change would have done nothing to remove the structural weaknesses of the old *Mail*, which had an ageing readership and had not matched the growth in the middle classes.

Vere was looking for a well-written, well-laid-out paper with drive and sparkle. It would be something he could be proud of, and something that would amuse him. Of course, like its predecessor, it would support the Conservative Party, though he seems to have been less interested in politics than his father or his editor and never insisted that every column inch should reflect the party line. It would have a lot of journalistic talent in all departments. It would attract the newly affluent, the young, and those living in the Home Counties. Especially, it would attract women readers, a prized audience for advertisers: Vere was the inspiration for the celebrated campaign slogan, 'Every woman needs her *Daily Mail*.'

His journalistic partner in this adventure, David English, was aged 40 in the month the *Mail* went tabloid. He had fought his way up in Fleet Street from lower middle-class beginnings on the south coast and had worked for the three major popular newspaper groups – the *Mirror*, Associated and Beaverbrook. He had a reputation for being extremely sharp, extremely hard-working, and occasionally going over the top and taking unacceptable risks with good stories of doubtful accuracy.

Vere had kept in touch with him from 1960 to 1969 when he was at the *Express*, a background which did him no harm in Vere's eyes. He had fallen in love with America when he was chief US correspondent for that paper, and he also had an entrepreneurial capacity unusual in journalists. From his Chislehurst home, following his return from the United States, he had launched a chain of free newspapers, the *News Shoppers*, which he was able to sell at a handy profit.

English was the kind of journalist who was clearly destined for great things. He might have stayed in America; after he wrote a feature in *US Publisher*, a trade paper, he was offered a good job on the *Washington Post*. Back in Britain for the *Express*, there was an abortive move to bring him to the *Mail* as deputy editor, but Brittenden was not prepared to fire his existing deputy, Bruce Rothwell. When he was offered the editorship of the *Sketch*, a paper with a limited life expectancy, he consulted his proprietor, Sir Max Aitken. But Sir Max would not give him any immediate hope of editing the *Express*, where Derek Marks was in charge, and he took the *Sketch* offer.

English brought a valuable mixture of talents to the merger project, not just that he could write stories himself, lay out pages and edit articles. He had a real empathy with young middle-class people – proto-yuppies to use a later description. He was strongly hostile to Labour – Ted Heath's Conservatives had just ousted Harold Wilson after six years of Labour government – and quick to publicise how the customer suffered in virtually any strike. He was totally in favour of free enterprise and viewed the 1960s as a low dishonest decade in which a whole generation, which itself was living off the fruits of Britain's commercial and political achievements, had corruptly and self-indulgently attacked every establishment totem.

During the weeks of planning and activity surrounding the relaunch of the *Mail* English slept in the office and hyped up his journalists. He was also diplomatic with his proprietor, for whom this was the first chance to break out of the embrace of managers and to work closely with journalists in the Northcliffe tradition. It is said that Vere himself was laying out a couple of pages a night at one stage. English also put his organisational talents at the service of the venture, devising a critical path analysis for the switch.

Planning of the new paper went alongside a tremendous hostility from the old guard at the broadsheet *Daily Mail* which felt that Vere, Shields and English were stealing their paper from them. The *Mail* changed its size and nature in May 1971. Simultaneously, the majority of journalists on the old *Mail* and *Sketch* got the sack. There had been 650 editorial people on the *Mail* and 180 on the *Sketch*. This number was cut to a total of 320, and the 70 whom English had brought with

him from the *Sketch* tended to get the plum jobs. A further 1,200 jobs
went amongst the printers and assorted circulation, advertising and
management grades.

It was a bitter time, and the redundancies cast a shroud over the
appearance of the new *Mail*. Strong men wept when they got their
'French letters' of dismissal, one evening which was variously described
as 'the night of the long white envelopes' or 'the night of the thousand
knives'. Vere, Shields and English had their fill of union meetings. Vere
seemed monarchical. Shields sought to demonstrate mathematically
that without cuts on this scale no jobs would be safe. English argued
that with a different product what was left of the staff would win
through.

Vere revealed depths of courage and inspiration which astonished
those who had known him a long time, talking to ordinary members of
staff, encouraging Shields and English, and keeping up the size of the
new paper. When the sale fell, he did not lose his nerve. In fact Shields
negotiated the redundancies surprisingly quickly. The unions were
impressed that Associated was making a fight of it, had to recognise that
the cuts if the merger with Beaverbrook had gone through might have
been even more severe, and were not immune to the loyalty factor
aroused by the sight of Northcliffe's great-nephew struggling to save his
kingdom.

Patience was necessary, however, before it became clear that the
gamble had come off. Newspaper mergers often fail, and readers do not
necessarily appreciate it if a new product is pushed uninvited through
their front doors, even if it carries a familiar title. In the case of the new
Daily Mail sales dropped to 100,000 below what the old *Daily Mail*'s
alone had been, and it was not until 1973 that the loss was recouped.
From then onwards the *Mail* started a gentle circulation rise until it hit
1.94m in 1979, the year in which, much to its joy, Mrs Thatcher won the
election to start her long run as Conservative Prime Minister. But in
spite of winning journalism awards the *Mail* under English was never a
circulation success. It never recaptured 'the magic two million' which its
broadsheet predecessor had lost in the late 1960s.

This did not greatly matter. The more relevant comparison was with
the fate of the *Daily Express* which was selling some 3.5m copies in 1971
and around 1.6m copies eighteen years later: its descent in sale had been
steady in spite of going tabloid five years after the *Mail*, four different
owners, and the efforts of many editors. Crucially, the *Mail* had
acquired a younger readership after its relaunch which stayed with the
paper and was worth advertising to. In spite of occasional errors there
was a consistency about the new paper which gave it strength. It
developed its own stars, from Lynda Lee-Potter and Nigel Dempster to
Ian Wooldrige, and it was noticeable that with the passage of time good
journalists who had made their names elsewhere – people like Keith

Waterhouse, George Gale, Colin Welch or Ann Leslie – would turn up in its pages.

With hindsight, too, the continuity between the tabloid *Mail* and its predecessors over three quarters of a century was rather more obvious. Many of its political and social campaigns – such as the 'twelve Labour lies' onslaught on Labour in the 1979 election, or the campaign against the removal of Cleveland children from their parents in the late 1980s after questionable findings of child abuse – were ones that Alfred Northcliffe and Harold Rothermere might easily have endorsed.

Some things had changed. The *Mail* no longer carried the slogan 'For Queen and Commonwealth', a quiet casualty of Britain's desire to join the European Community. Nor was the restyled paper unaffected by the social and racial liberalisation set on foot in the 1960s. When it carried the story of Pamella Bordes, the prostitute who managed to get a job as a House of Commons researcher,[8] its revelations of sexual explicitness would have horrified the founder of the original *Daily Mail*. To its credit, but no doubt shocking for the racist early Harmsworths had they still been around, was the fact that the *Mail* made a star out of its black showbusiness writer, Baz Bamigboye.

In describing the rebuilding of the *Mail* group after Vere's take-over, it is important not to underestimate the contribution of Mick Shields which covered a wide ambit as managing director. Mick Shields – his full name was Ronald McGregor Pollock Shields – was four years older than Vere and had spent most of his life with Associated Newspapers. During the Second World War he began as a gunnery officer, was a major at 21 and ended up in charge of the police in the Control Commission in Trieste. Amongst other things he was responsible for keeping the Mafia in order. ('A good training for Fleet Street one might think,' Vere remarked sardonically at his memorial service).[9]

He was a grammar school boy who had gained an economics degree at London University and in 1948 he joined Associated. He worked his way up to become advertising director in 1963, was responsible for setting up National Opinion Polls as a market research firm, and became aware of the potential of computers. He first worked closely with Vere in setting up a software business. Somewhere in the 1960s, however, he fell foul of the office politics of the group, was dropped from the A team concerned with the newspapers, and sent off to use his good brain and judgement to earn money for Harmsworth Investments. This he did. Like Vere himself, therefore, in 1970–1, he knew a lot but was something of an outsider in the manoeuvres to bring the Associated and Beaverbrook groups together.

In the crisis of 1971 he proved his skill and mettle. At his memorial service in 1988 Vere credited his wife Pat for advising him that, whenever he became chairman, he must make Mick Shields his managing director. He described it as 'the best advice I ever got'. Not least of

Shields' achievements was that he forged a good working relationship with a new proprietor who was inevitably unsure of himself sometimes, and periodically lost his temper with 'management'. He deferred to Vere's opinion, even when colleagues thought his own line was wiser, and threw all his authority behind establishing Vere's. This was probably as important in 1971 as his ability in negotiation or finance. As well as his business gifts he was good at cheering people up and making them see the sunny side of life. Given that there were plenty of pessimists whispering that the end was nigh, this too was a help. For the travails of the group were not a private matter. There was a strong attack on the handling of the merger of the *Mail* and *Sketch* by Bernard Levin, by now writing for *The Times*, which led to successful litigation against himself and Times Newspapers.

By about 1973, as the revamped *Mail* began to make progress, other worries began to take over. For the Conservative press the economic and political picture seemed to darken dramatically in 1973–4 as the Barber boom petered out – Anthony Barber was a brother of the Noel Barber who some including Vere felt should have been made editor of the *Mail* in the 1950s – and the Heath government, which had done a U-turn into economic interventionism, stuttered into a three-day week and the miners' strike.

From a Tory viewpoint there appeared to be a combination of calamities: very high inflation, a property and secondary banking crash and the most dramatic Stock Exchange collapse since 1929, apparent victory by the National Union of Mineworkers in which the marxist Arthur Scargill with his flying pickets seemed to call the shots, and two elections in 1974 which allowed the distrusted Harold Wilson to form weak, minority Labour governments. As wealth-owners saw their assets written down on the Stock Exchange and in estate agents' windows, there was thinly disguised panic in surprising quarters, including *The Economist*: Britain was becoming ungovernable, and there might even be a revolution round the corner. Above all the Conservative Party had let its supporters down.

The *Mail*, of course, was firing on all cylinders over this period. One of its more memorable contributions was the 'Wigan alps' exposé – an attempt which was not entirely successful to demonstrate corruption in Wilson's kitchen Cabinet, as the brother of Marcia Williams, Wilson's powerful secretary, was supposed to have made a doubtful killing on a project to develop some slag-heaps near Wigan.[10] But in spite of rearguard actions of this kind, it was impossible to disguise the fact that the Conservatives had the worst of the argument in 1973–4; the conclusion drawn inside the *Mail* was that the Conservatives must try harder and try differently next time.

On the whole, election campaigns are good for newspapers which are willing to devote space to politics, but the sense of national crisis which reigned in the mid-1970s had other impacts on Associated and the Harmsworth family. For Associated the problem still lay with the London newspapers. Although the *Mail* had turned a corner, losses were beginning to pile up on the *Evening News*. The social and other factors which had begun to move against the *News* and to a lesser extent the *Standard* in the 1960s were still rolling forward. Heath's government had introduced commercial radio which had brought an extra layer of competition. London was the only city left which was trying to support two evening newspapers.

The economics of the *News* was entwined with the *Mail*, but even so to Mick Shields the *News* was beginning to look like an albatross. Vere had some sentimental attachment to the *News*, as his family's first foray into Fleet Street, but he had no clear idea as to its journalistic direction. In the early 1970s he was tempted by the accelerating success of the down-market *Sun* into thinking it could have a role in that area; in 1977, after failing to buy the *Standard* and being wounded by the propaganda about the *Standard*'s superior merits, it moved briefly up-market. Along the way it had changed from a broadsheet to a tabloid size, with no discernible impact on its decline. By 1975 Vere was warning that the *News* would need major cuts to survive.

The economic shivers had put a question mark against the *News*. They also led to a sudden dispersal of Esmond Rothermere's three children as, for reasons of capital transfer tax planning, they simultaneously moved into tax exile. Lady Lorna Cooper-Key settled in Spain. The Countess and Earl of Cromer established a base in Jersey from which the Earl continued an active business life, and where Countess Esme became involved in an orchid foundation.[11] And Vere adopted a nomadic live, in which homes in Paris and Manhatten were perhaps the most important of several. It was, of course, ironic that the head of a group which had historically stressed its British patriotism should be limited to ninety days a year in the United Kingdom. Even when Nigel Lawson, as Chancellor of the Exchequer after the 1987 Conservative election, lowered the top rate of income tax to 40 per cent, Vere did not resume British residence.

This change did not mean quite as much as it might have for another company. All three of his predecessors had exercised control while living a peripatetic existence. Initially, Associated executives were quite pleased to be invited over to Paris for a business conference with the chairman. Some were less pleased to be rung up in the middle of the night from Tokyo when he wanted to get an urgent message through. The degree of control by the proprietor hardly altered: executives and editors never forgot who was running the firm, and whose money was at risk.

What did alter, unavoidably, was the nature of Vere's family life. In Britain, he and Pat had an opulent flat in Eaton Square in addition to their home in Sussex. When he went into tax exile she, feeling that she ought to be with her children, stayed in Britain. Jonathan, the youngest, was coming up to prep school age when his father moved abroad. She gave him the option of going to schools abroad but he felt he was an English boy who would like to go to school where he was born. In fact he went to the American School in London and then to Gordonstoun in Scotland. His mother said he had a sensitive nature; other Harmsworths felt that he and his sisters had a rather rackety upbringing.

From the mid 1970s on, therefore, Vere and his wife 'lived together but apart', in the delicate phrase of a gossip columnist. It was from this period that Pat developed a public image as 'Bubbles' – a nickname given her by Nigel Dempster of the *Mail* writing in *Private Eye*, a description which she hated. The nickname derived either from her unashamed fondness for champagne – when she was a popular chairman of the Newspaper Benevolent Fund for a year there was always a bottle waiting for her at a function or old people's home – or from her mass of curly hair.

She developed a social life independent of her husband, throwing parties, attending charity occasions, habituating night clubs. She had homes in Mustique, New York and California, and was jet-setting as much as her husband. She was well liked, for her effervescent smile and hospitality, and her sense of humour. She crossed swords with *Private Eye*, getting an apology in 1975 for an allegation that she was having an affair with a designer and former restaurateur. Her dresses, fantasy creations for a full figure by Zandra Rhodes and other famous names, caused people to look at her wherever she went. She was famous for being famous and was eminently quotable. As long ago as 1960, when being prosecuted for speeding, she charmingly told the magistrates, 'My car is too fast for me.' She was a real asset for any charity she supported. In 1975, as president of the ball committee for the Pied Piper Ball for the NSPCC at the Dorchester Hotel, she persuaded the Duchess of Kent to be guest of honour and David Frost to help run the auction.

But journalists who reported her caught glimpses of a slim-thinking and sometimes sorrowful person behind the image of sunshine and glitz. She could not understand the osmosis of publicity which had turned her into good copy, and a figure of fun. She regretted a loneliness in her life, and that she was not able to live a conventional married existence with her husband. There were times, it appeared, when she would rather have given up her hectic lifestyle – worrying about the logistics of entertaining, air timetables, and how to eat successive courses of the same meal with different hostesses – if only she could have lived quietly with her husband and family in the country.

Inevitably she was photographed with other men, and Vere was seen with other women. When they were seen together in public, on charity, newspaper and similar occasions, it seemed an increasingly temporary kind of togetherness as the 1970s wore on. They were carefully correct in public references to each other. There was speculation as to why they did not get divorced. The reasons suggested for the fact that they never did – although there was an effective separation in the 1980s – were twofold: that they shied away from the expense and bad publicity that would ensue; and that each of them had a rooted objection to divorce in itself. Pat had a strong religious faith and considerable determination. Vere had seen the consequences of divorce in his father's generation, and it was significant that neither he nor his sisters followed that example.

During the 1970s there was one significant business development which distinguished Vere's management style from his father's. The firm did not pull out of North Sea oil exploration after a series of unproductive borings. The person administering the Daily Mail and General Trust investment on the Harmsworths' behalf argued that they would be throwing good money after bad. The story could have ended as a fiasco on the scale of Associated Rediffusion. However, Shields checked the seismic findings and recommended that the firm, which was within twenty-four hours of selling its investment, should hang on in. Vere backed him. The black gold was a lifeline well into the 1980s.

In 1976, Vere tried to buy *The Observer*. Had he succeeded he would have recaptured one of Northcliffe's papers and, by buying from the Astor family, would have won some late recompense from a family which had outmanoeuvred the Harmsworths over *The Times* after Northcliffe's death. The project never got far in 1976, and *The Observer* wound up in the indulgent ownership of an American oil company of philanthropic intent, Atlantic Richfield. The episode was interesting for two reasons. It signalled Vere's desire to run a Sunday paper – in effect to find a substitute for the departed *Sunday Dispatch* – even during the lifetime of the *Evening News*. And it brought to light the undying hostility in which the name Rothermere was held on the liberal and leftist side of British media. *Observer* journalists made it abundantly clear that Vere would be totally unacceptable as their proprietor.

Although the *Daily Mail* under English's editorship was playing a more effective partisan role than had been true in the 1960s, there was an element of irrationality in this opposition to Vere. It was as though the perceived sins of his grandfather and great-uncle were being visited on him. Those who knew him well were confident that a formula could have been devised and adhered to which would have protected the editorial tradition of *The Observer* – after all Northcliffe had left Garvin to his own devices. A Rothermere ownership could have been much less embarrassing than Lonrho's turned out to be later. But it was not to be, and the not enormous managerial cadre under Vere was spared involvement with a paper which had not been a great commercial success for many years.

Before the end of 1976, however, a more substantial prospect had come into view: a deal with Beaverbrook which this time would be very much on Associated's terms. Everything was coming unstuck for the Beaverbrook group simultaneously. It was running out of money; by 1977 it had an overdraft of £14m and the banks would be refusing to lend any more. Only the *Sunday Express* was making a decent return, and its daily sister had suffered a catastrophic loss in sale, losing almost a million purchasers in little more than five years. Above all the group was facing a dynastic crisis of succession: Sir Max Aitken was suffering from heart disease, was no longer able to be an active chairman, yet his son Maxwell was not old or experienced enough to be a plausible successor.

It was like a rerun of the 1970–1 crisis at Associated Newspapers, except that there was no Vere Harmsworth waiting in the wings, and there were no other significant investments or businesses to help tide Beaverbrook over. At Associated the only pressing need now, however, was to contain losses on the *News*. In early 1977, under the aegis of Lord Goodman, Mick Shields for Associated and Jocelyn Stevens for Beaverbrook devised a plan under which the *Standard* would be sold to Associated for £7.5m, and the combined evening paper would be printed on Beaverbrook's modern presses. Beaverbrook would get a useful cash injection and a continuing rental, and the possibility of further mergers was not closed.

The secret talks became public knowledge in April 1977 and all hell broke loose. Again, as at the death of the *News Chronicle*, the issue at stake was the identity of a newspaper. Again, as with *The Observer* chapel of the National Union of Journalists the year before, an undercurrent of suspicion of the Harmsworth dynasty started coming to the surface.

It might seem odd that the fate of a London evening paper, the *Evening Standard*, should come to seem so important. Its politics were little different from the *News* – they were both Conservative, with periodic criticism – and Lord Beaverbrook when he was alive had regarded it as his fun paper. But the *Standard* had a fanatically loyal staff and a strong and influential following. It was read by MPs (especially for Robert Carvel, its political editor), had an important financial readership in the City, had a major following in the arts world (thank to Sydney Edwards, Milton Shulman and Alexander Walker), was a significant advertising outlet for the West End stores and London employers, and was the preferred paper of middle-class commuters.

A howl went up at the thought that London might be deprived of the *Standard*. It somewhat bemused Vere and his colleagues at Associated, but a lot of people genuinely thought it was much superior to the *News*,[12] and the campaign was skilfully orchestrated by Charles Wintour and Simon Jenkins. Charles Wintour had edited the *Standard* for nearly twenty years and given it much vitality, even though its market was declining. Simon Jenkins, who had written an attractive lifestyle and environmental column, had been made a youthful editor when Wintour was promoted to be a Beaverbrook director.

To begin with Wintour and Jenkins were somewhat alone in a Beaverbrook hierarchy which could see little alternative to saying goodbye to the *Standard*. But the expressions of public and private support for the *Standard* as a paper gradually persuaded others to look for other options. Sir Max told Wintour that he did not wish to sell the *Standard*, least of all to the Harmsworths, and Stevens who had his own associations with the paper began to look for another solution. At the same time, it became increasingly apparent that the Beaverbrook group as a whole was on the rocks, and that the price of saving the *Standard* was that the Aitkens would have to sell out.[13]

The twists and turns of the saga were exciting at the time. When it looked as though Associated might win, Vere's father, Esmond Rothermere, flew in from Florida, ready to applaud the victory. A party for union leaders at the Bonnington Hotel on 28 April was actually arranged to celebrate Associated's take-over of the *Standard*, only to be told by Stevens that Sir James Goldsmith who owned a block of shares in Beaverbrook was seriously interested in buying the company and wanted a six week delay. There was talk of a combination of Goldsmith and Tiny Rowland's Lonrho. The unexpected dénouement was that Trafalgar House, a construction and shipping firm, bought out the Aitkens over the heads of the Harmsworths, and incidentally Rupert Murdoch.

It had been a noisy battle, and it had been revealing. The *Evening News* journalists were much more fed up with their proprietor and management than was the case at the *Standard*, where everyone was more obviously under threat. Possibly a backwash from the *Mail/Sketch* merger and Vere's unwillingness to talk to his own journalists when he was ready to talk to other papers covering the story were to blame. In fact, at an icy meeting at his London home over lunch – undercooked frozen food added little to the atmosphere – Vere, with David English and his *News* editor Lou Kirby beside him, had offered Wintour and Jenkins a deal under which 80 per cent of journalists on the merged paper would come from the *Standard*. But, loyal to Kirby, he insisted that he should be editor, and offered Jenkins only a deputy editorship, which he refused.

In retrospect it is easy to see in this 80:20 offer an echo of the terms on which journalists from the *Mail* and *Sketch* had come together. But on that basis Wintour and Jenkins were probably right to fear for the personality of the merged paper, for English and his seventy recruits from the *Sketch* had been dominant on the new *Mail*. None the less, there was a toughness in Vere's attitude in regard to his own employees,

and a willingness to concede defeat in the argument over the quality of
the two papers.

At the end of May the merger proposals fell foul of an unfortunately
timed own goal at the *Daily Mail* which raised all the ghosts of
Rothermere anti-socialist propaganda, going back to the publication of
the Zinoviev letter. On 19 May, it published a sensational but bogus
exclusive story under the heading 'World-wide Bribery Web by
Leyland' and 'Exposed – the amazing truth about Britain's state-owned
car makers.' This was the Ryder slush fund story – an allegation based
on a forged document that British Leyland, the nationalised car firm,
was operating an extensive system of bribery throughout the world to
promote the sale of its vehicles.

With a Labour government under James Callaghan in power, this
was a disaster. The government had powers to prevent newspaper
mergers. The *Standard* already had powerful friends in the Labour
government, going back to Lord Beaverbrook's maverick pleasure in
employing left-wingers: the most notable was Michael Foot, now a
senior minister, who had been an acting editor of the *Standard* for
Beaverbrook during the Second World War, and who had been a book
reviewer for the paper until quite recently.

The Ryder slush fund story had been leaked to the *Mail* by a Leyland
executive and was handled by Stewart Steven, a close associate of
English who had also worked with him at the *Express*. The *Mail* had
been having a good run of investigative stories and the fact that Lord
Ryder did not return phone calls, designed to check the authenticity of
the letter he was supposed to have signed, was taken as proof of his
guilt. The story goes that English asked a sub editor who had been given
this exclusive whether he had ever read anything like it before and he
answered with dangerous intuition, 'Yes, when I got given the Bormann
story at the *Express*' (Steven had been involved in the serialisation by
the *Express* of an imaginative account of the life of the Fuhrer's heir in
South America.)

When the storm broke over the Ryder affair English initially defended
the report, and is alleged to have extracted a promise from his
proprietor that Steven would not be sacked before he went on to explain
the background and offered to resign himself. Vere did not accept this
offer, apparently treating the imbroglio as one mistake to be set against
a string of successes. There was an expensive legal settlement and the
affair had a lasting impact in demonstrating that even the most
marvellous editors can slip up, and that final authority rests with the
proprietor. (Earlier in the relationship English had told colleagues that
he had to protect Vere from attempts to con him.)

The slush fund allegation showed up the weakness of an overtly
Conservative press group when Labour was in power. Having stayed
neutral hitherto in the Associated–Beaverbrook shenanigans, James

Callaghan then indicated that any deal between the two groups would have to be referred to the Monopolies Commission. Vere responded by saying that Callaghan's attitude to 'this deplorable but honest mistake' had followed closely on the furore over the appointment of his journalist son-in-law Peter Jay, to be British ambassador in Washington. This brought out the knives in a way not seen since the battles around the first Lord Rothermere. Charles Wintour could not resist exploiting the advantage which had opened up in relation to a Labour government which was instinctively hostile to the hereditary peerage. At an Automobile Association lunch on 25 May (actually held at the Royal Automobile Club), Wintour let fly:

> I had intended to say no more about the current situation in Fleet Street, but Vere Harmsworth's statement today calls for comment. On the exposure of the Ryder forgery David English honourably and immediately offered his resignation, Mr Harmsworth, rightly in my view, rejected it. But today Mr Harmsworth, in attempting to answer the prime minister's description of the *Daily Mail*'s conduct as contemptible and a display of political spite, drags up the appointment of Mr Peter Jay to Washington. In other words, he is smearing the charge of nepotism against the name of the prime minister.
>
> Why is Mr Vere Harmsworth chairman of Associated Newspapers? Why is he in a position to squander millions of his shareholders' money in an effort to force the *Evening Standard* out of business? Why has he been able to sell his evening paper at an uneconomic price, to offer cut rates to advertisers who switch from the *Evening Standard* to his own paper, to start up costly and uneconomic ventures in the suburbs, and to maintain an uneconomic circulation area – all, I believe, with the aim of compelling his competitor to surrender?
>
> May I suggest that the only reason why Mr Vere Harmsworth is chairman of Associated Newspapers is that he is the son of the second Lord Rothermere. And the second Lord Rothermere had the job because he was the son of the first Lord Rothermere. And the first Lord Rothermere had the *Daily Mail* because he was the brother of a real newspaper genius, Lord Northcliffe. Mr Jay is acknowledged by all to be a most brilliant man who is earning large sums entirely as a result of his own talents. Mr Harmsworth, however, is in a position to endanger the jobs of 1,700 people in Fleet Street purely through a mere accident of birth.

The fact that Sir Max Aitken owed his position equally to an accident of birth, and that the Beaverbrook group and *Standard* had been involved in many types of warfare against Associated over the previous half century were both conveniently forgotten. Staff and supporters of the *Standard* applauded this tirade, which was widely reported, and Michael Foot in a letter of congratulation to Wintour said it must have been the first time in months that Lord Beaverbrook in his grave could have had a night's sleep.

The failure to buy either the Beaverbrook group or the *Standard* alone meant that the ghost of a *Mail/Express* merger – which had been knocking around since the 1960s as the market for middlebrow newspapers appeared to decline – was definitely laid, but the problem of the losses on the *News* remained.[14] When in 1980 the *News* and *Standard* merged, on terms which effectively retained the identity and journalists of the *Standard* although Lou Kirby from the *News* succeeded Wintour as editor, it seemed much less controversial. This was because it was overshadowed by far more dramatic happenings. In the middle of 1979 Mrs Thatcher's Conservatives had been elected to office and the election was not reported at all by *The Times* which was in the middle of its year's shutdown, when the Thomson management tried unsuccessfully to break the power of the print unions. Both these events had far-reaching effects.

The *Mail* fought very hard for Mrs Thatcher in the 1979 general election, and although other Conservative newspapers were weighing in it is arguable that the *Mail* was particularly in sympathy with the policy for which she stood, and therefore particularly effective in motivating Conservatives and waverers to come out for her. The attack on the 'twelve Labour lies' allegedly being spread about what a Conservative government might do – the most telling concerned a rise in value added tax which Sir Geoffrey Howe promptly raised to 15 per cent when he became Conservative Chancellor – was only one element in a mix of news coverage and opinion formation which had run for months.

Vere had become the 3rd Viscount Rothermere of Hemsted, in 1978, when his father died and he had also become chairman of the Daily Mail and General Trust. He was, in his own way, a Tory grandee. But Mrs Thatcher's approach, with which the *Mail* so strongly empathised, was not about making the country safe for Etonians: it was claiming to give merit from all social levels a more generous financial reward, to cut back the size of government and the power of the unions, to support private enterprise in every way possible. It was a radical popular Conservatism which marked a clear breach with the spirit of the party for most of the post-war years, not least because it was pursued with determination and gathered confidence as it continued.

The strength of the combination of Vere as proprietor and David English as editor of the *Mail* was shown at this point. For English understood the well-springs of what soon became known as Thatcherism: the frustration with the prices-and-incomes policy and the corporatism of the Labour government among small businessmen and ex-grammar school boys; the desire to own your own council house; the loss of national pride as Britain was forced to accept an IMF loan and appeared to slip inexorably down the economic league tables of the nations; the nadir of a 'winter of discontent' in 1978 when even grave-diggers and dustmen went on strike and James Callaghan, returning from a summit in Guadeloupe, could ask airily why anyone could think there was a crisis.

Using the renegade socialist Paul Johnson as commentator and hitman, English not only slashed the record of the Labour government but also educated readers in what would be the Conservative alternative. Instead of prices-and-incomes policy and high taxation there would be control of the money supply and a switch to indirect forms of taxation. Instead of striking public employees, forever dissatisfied with their lot and trying to catch up with private sector wages, there would be ballots before strikes and a reduction in the size of the public sector. (In 1979, however, few dreamed of how far privatisation might progress in the course of successive Thatcher adminstrations.)

The *Mail*'s journalism was effective because it seemed to reflect movements of public opinion as much as to create them. Labour's vocabulary of compassion was looking shopworn when public employees seemed to disregard the interests of their clients and customers. The British were ready to accept more inequality in exchange for a greater opportunity to create and hang on to wealth, a greater competence in the delivery of services with more say for the customer, and a greater sense of individual liberty from the state. Most damningly the *Mail* with other Conservative commentators managed to paint the trade unions as self-centred interest groups, battening off the body politic, instead of associations to protect workers from the injustice of their employers.

The arrival of Mrs Thatcher changed the environment in which all companies worked. Basically the government was on their side; it would be successively more difficult to call strikes, as successive industrial relations acts came into operation; high earners could retain more of their income, without necessarily being paid more by their employers, through tax reductions; and new business opportunities opened up with deregulation and privatisation. For national newspapers it created a climate in which at last it would be possible to introduce computer-based print technology which had been spreading through the provinces over the previous decade, but which had been baulked by the Fleet Street unions.

It was against this background that Vere Rothermere, in 1980, first closed the *Evening News* and then actively tried to buy Times Newspapers, preferably the *Sunday Times*. Associated might simply have shut the *News*, which was estimated to have lost £38m by the time it departed, but the negotiating skills of Shields and the foresight of his proprietor enabled them to achieve a remarkably good deal out of an adverse competitive position. Although redundancies cost £6m and some more bad feeling amongst printers and journalists – which Vere himself was prepared to confront – Associated got 50 per cent of the shares in a new Evening Standard Company, with the option to buy if Trafalgar House ever wished to sell. (Vere appreciated that Trafalgar

House might not wish to retain a newspaper subsidiary, and that Victor Matthews, its executive in charge of the *Express* group, would retire before too long.)

At the time of the *News* closure, Vere said he might be interested in buying the *Sunday Times*, even though it was losing £15m a year: in fact that was a figure for the whole of Times Newspapers, weighed down by losses on *The Times*, but a useful way of talking down the price of the company. By 1980, the saga of the Thomson ownership of Times Newspapers had reached a predictable conclusion. After a long shut-down by the management, designed to get regular working from the unions and to open the door to new technology, production had resumed but had again been interrupted. In particular Kenneth Thomson, who was based in Canada and had taken control of the conglomerate Thomson Organisation following his father's death, was thoroughly disillusioned when *The Times* journalists went on strike after being paid throughout the shutdown. By October 1980, Times Newspapers were up for sale.

Vere had already been meditating starting his own Sunday paper; he had had a shot at *The Observer* four years earlier. Although there might have been a certain Harmsworth symmetry in becoming proprietor of *The Times* it was hard to see how that paper could be made profitable, while the *Sunday Times* was a potential goldmine if only the labour problems could be overcome. This was the chief attraction; a further advantage was that printing of the *Daily Mail* could be transferred to the Grays Inn Road presses of Times Newspapers, thereby releasing for profit the old Associated properties south of Fleet Street.

However, although Vere certainly wanted to buy, and was assumed to have been able to offer more money than his successful rival, Rupert Murdoch, he was beaten to it. There was a mixture of reasons, and in retrospect he probably benefited more from Murdoch's victory in early 1981 than if he had bought the group himself.

Murdoch wanted the group very badly, was preferred by the Thomson management, and was prepared to guarantee the uninterrup-ted publication of *The Times* which Associated was not. It was clear that Associated was more interested in the *Sunday Times* and there were divisions between Vere, who was keen to buy the group, and Mick Shields who was probably more influenced by the daunting managerial headaches they would be taking on. (The fact that Vere was based in Paris, while Rupert Murdoch was able to do his negotiating in person, was also a snag.)

Why Sir Gordon Brunton and the Thomson management preferred Murdoch, in spite of his ownership of the *News of the World*, and *Sun*, is an interesting question. It may have had to do with a view that Murdoch had the steel to discipline the printers and journalists, and memories of Vere and Shields which Duke Hussey had brought with him when he came from Associated to Times Newspapers. (Hussey as chief executive at Times Newspapers had been responsible for the failed closure tactic; people who remembered him at Associated recalled an 'up Guards and at 'em' figure whose troops might get levelled by machine-gun fire when he led them over the top.)

Although suspicion of the Rothermere name does not seem to have been quite so important for *Times* group journalists as it had been at *The Observer*, the journalists had been mesmerised by the possibility of running their own papers under a trust or consortium arrangement; fatally for their collective chances, the editors and journalists on the two papers were each looking for a separate salvation. Hence they were not terribly interested in the Associated offer and allowed themselves to be outgunned by Murdoch. The image of the Rothermere press at the time was firmly middle-brow and stridently Conservative: the first impression went down without much enthusiasm at *The Times* while the second raised little excitement at the *Sunday Times*, which was being edited in an investigative and unpartisan way by Harold Evans.

At the end of the day, it was impossible to believe that Associated was going all out to win. A late chance to upset Murdoch's apple-cart arose when the *Sunday Times* journalists approached the company for financial assistance to mount a legal challenge to the government's use of its powers to nod the Murdoch deal through, on the basis that the newspapers were losing money. Such a legal challenge could well have succeeded as the *Sunday Times* itself, it could be argued, was making money. If the courts had found against the discretionary decision by John Biffen, the Trade and Industry Secretary, the issue would have been referred to the Monopolies Commission and other solutions might have become possible.

However, Associated rejected the request from the *Sunday Times* journalists. It may be that Thomson's threat to close its papers in March 1981 if no sale had been agreed weighed with Associated's management. (It was always said that Esmond Rothermere had only taken over the *News Chronicle* when he was satisfied that there was no way of keeping it alive.) In the upshot, Murdoch's triumph prevented Vere Rothermere from establishing a dominant position in Britain's national press, and opened the way to Murdoch's dramatic move to Wapping in early 1986 of all the News International titles. That was a manoeuvre that Associated could never have undertaken, but from which it greatly benefited.

15
Towards the 1990s

Looking at the British press today Lord Northcliffe has two surviving progeny, the *Daily Mail* and *Daily Mirror*, and the first Lord Rothermere has one – the *Sunday Mirror* (née *Pictorial*). In 1982, Vere Rothermere made his bid to join the small number who, in the twentieth century, have started new national papers and gone on to see them flourish. He started the *Mail on Sunday* as a sister paper to the *Daily Mail*. It was nearly as big a disaster in its early weeks as Northcliffe's initial *Daily Mirror* for women and his drastic corrective action, followed by a patient process of nurturing over several years, give him one of his best claims to be regarded as a creative proprietor.

In spite of the jungle of industrial relations in Fleet Street, the late 1970s had produced a certain amount of talk about new newspapers; the existing choice seemed narrow and there was a belief that extra advertising could be found. Victor Matthews at the *Express* group actually launched the *Daily Star*, admittedly from a Manchester base, in 1979. Periodically, Vere remarked that he wanted to start a Sunday, most specifically when the *Evening News* shut down. After the *Sunday Times* possibility came to nothing in 1981 nothing stopped serious planning; he had already appointed Bernard Shrimsley, recently editor of the *News of the World*, to be editor-designate in the autumn of 1980.

The idea was Vere's alone, not taken up with much delight by his management, and David English was kept out of much of the preparatory work. There was a feeling that the proprietor would have liked to demonstrate that he could get a new newspaper off the ground without help from his celebrated editorial partner. Vere was, however, interested in every detail. Shrimsley made many dawn shuttles to Paris, conferring with him at the offices of the old *Continental Daily Mail*, at his exquisite apartment, or in restaurants where he would superfluously remind the head waiter, 'Je suis le Vicomte Rothermere.' In England, meetings were frequent in hotels and restaurants, at Annabel's, the night-club, and the Sussex family mansion; even on the day Prince Charles and Lady Diana Spencer got married, Shrimsley was summoned.

The task was not easy and not made any easier by postponements of the launch date. The difficulty on the editorial side was that Vere felt that the Sunday paper should be different from the daily – he thought the *Sunday Telegraph* had initially made a mistake in trying to be too like its daily – which meant that it was unwise for Shrimsley to try to use any of the *Daily Mail*'s existing stars. Further English vetoed the use of some people, like Patrick Sergeant and Ann Leslie (though he offered a book of Nigel Dempster's for possible serialisation).

On the production side the problem was that there were not enough trustworthy printing presses to get out up to 2 million copies. The group had a printing contract with *The People*, which meant that to produce its own new Sunday some ancient waterlogged machinery in the bowels of Carmelite House, which had seen service for Northcliffe, would need to be resurrected. Significantly, while Northcliffe himself had had plenty of dummy runs before he launched the *Daily Mail*, there were never any full dummy runs prior to the launch on 2 May 1982.

As far as marketing was concerned a bad decision was made to launch the tabloid *Mail on Sunday* without a colour supplement, yet at the same price as the broadsheet *Sunday Express* which had recently started one. The Associated management, which was worried that costs on the new paper could get out of hand, had ruled out a colour magazine. Any advertising agency which believed a colour extra was essential was cut out of the shortlist of agencies invited to pitch for the promotion of the launch.

At a New York meeting a few weeks before the launch David English, who by then had been given some supervisory powers over the project, discussed the dummy page layouts with Vere. Vere was worried, thought the paper would not succeed, and asked English to take over at once. English resisted. Both were exceedingly loyal when the first issue did see the light of day after a night of disasters. Vere told *Daily Mail* that it was 'the best first issue of a newspaper I have ever seen'.

English, who was knighted in 1982, had been positively fulsome on the eve of launch. 'A parent is too close to his child to be truly objective,' he wrote to Shrimsley.

> But, having seen your final pages and line-up yesterday, I think I can say (as a god-parent, grandfather or great uncle; whatever I am) that the *Mail on Sunday* is a beautiful, perfectly formed baby, and the Sunday newspaper reading public is going to fall in love with it.
>
> I am positive, Bernard, that you will be swamped by congratulations by Monday. I would like to send mine in advance. You can go into battle tomorrow feeling super-confident. Have the most wonderful day.[15]

For poor Shrimsley it was not a wonderful day at all, and the succeeding weeks did not get any better. The output of newspapers on the first night fell half a million short of target, a senior manager felt he ought to offer Vere his resignation, and Shrimsley could not get a copy from the newsagent at the bottom of his road for the first three weeks because it never arrived.

Journalistically, the paper was unexciting. Also, by an extraordinary fluke, it appeared when Britain was at war. Although the Boer War and the 1914–18 war had been good for the *Daily Mail*, the Falklands War did the *Mail on Sunday* no favours. Crucially, the *MoS* – its title had been adopted because of the prior existence of a *Sunday Mail* – failed to carry a report of the heroic death of Captain H. Jones in all but a few late copies. After ten weeks, with the sale down to 700,000 and falling, Shrimsley was fired. Characteristically, Vere broke the bad news to him in person. But by the time the ex-editor arrived back to tell the staff he found his secretary in tears, because English had posted a notice to say the Shrimsley had gone and he had taken direct editorial responsibility.

This change ushered in the toughest publishing struggle on which Vere had embarked since his relaunch of the tabloid *Mail*. Once again, the reputation of Vere Rothermere and David English was at stake. The logical accounting conclusion would have been to have cut the losses and closed the paper. Coming so soon after the shutdown of the *Evening News* that would have been a terrible setback. Instead Vere was absolutely staunch in the face of costs which terrified his managers.

The initial job was to stop the decline in sales which was hard because English and his task force of *Mail* veterans moved on to seven day working in the middle of the summer. They sought to put some snap into the *Mail on Sunday*, being paid double for their efforts. Vere also accepted that the paper would have to be expensively relaunched in October with another advertising blitz, a colour magazine, a cookery part-work, and an insert of comics for children and grown-up children. The comics and the cookery were his ideas. The total cost of the relaunch was estimated as more than the original launch, and when Stewart Steven, appointed as editor under English, went to a board meeting and heard for the first time from the finance director that the paper would lose £24m in the first year he feared for the jobs of all the staff.

However, Vere ignored all those who advised him to pull the plug, even when it was clear that losses in the second year would continue to be significant. The paper did improve, the sales began to climb. The *Mail on Sunday* began to pick up a new readership which was younger and less conservative in every way than the *Daily Mail*'s and the *Sunday Express*'s. Its advertising slogan, 'a newspaper not a snooze-paper', put over its spirit exactly and while it ran a Dempster gossip column like the daily it also had a different cast of columnists, ranging from Marcia Falkender to Julie Birchill. By 1989, it had not only overtaken the *Sunday Express* in sale but the *Daily Mail* as well. In

1987, it had come quite close to endorsing the Liberal–SDP alliance in the general election, until the squabbles between those parties caused it to back off.

Interestingly, although it had been the *Daily Mail* task force which had rescued the paper, Stewart Steven reached the conclusion after some years that if it had been a clone of the daily it would have had half the daily's sale. Many people want to read something different on a Sunday. There are no commuters. Looking back from safety at its tumultuous start he felt that, considering that there is hostility to as well as curiosity about new newspapers, the *Mail on Sunday* with its minimum sale of 700,000 had not really done so badly. It had been bedevilled by a shortfall of production. Compared with the Sunday disasters to come – *Sunday Today* and the *News on Sunday* – it had established quite a respectable beachhead before the autumn offensive.

None the less, the relaunched *MoS* was a much more skilful creation. An important part of its identity was provided by the *You* colour magazine, which quickly scored a hit with readers and advertisers. This combined good colour reproduction, a sense of fashion and glitz, a lot of varied features – none of them too long – and qualities of entertainment and consumerism. It was a world away from the challenging investigative colour magazine the *Sunday Times* had launched in the 1960s. Alfred Northcliffe would have liked it, though: its 'headliners' frontispiece, where cheeky captions were attached to pictures of the famous, would have appealed to his snobbery and humour; its lists of bizarre and amusing facts were in a straight descent from *Answers*.

The mid-1980s, when Thatcherism was at its apogee, found the newspaper world wrestling with a central question: when and how would Fleet Street introduce computer typesetting? In principle, it was possible to do away with several expensive layers of rigidly demarcated print workers, including typesetters, readers and layout hands, so that virtually nothing stood between the journalists and their computers and the rolling printing presses. This was the theory. To a greater or lesser degree it was already the practice in Britain outside London, in the United States and Canada, and surprisingly often in developing countries. Vere Rothermere, as president of the Commonwealth Press Union, knew well that papers like the *Daily Gleaner* in Jamaica and the *New Straits Times* in Kuala Lumpur had been computerised for years, while an ignorant London press continued to patronise their countries' backwardness. Indeed the scandal of outdated technology, restrictive practices and inadequate managements was preventing the British national press from being taken seriously. How could anyone, certainly not a Thatcherite Conservative, be impressed by the comments of an industry which had knowingly failed to bring its manufacturing process up to date?

For at least fifteen years Fleet Street collectively and its individual companies had been trying to find a way through. Associated, like the others, had its plans and had periodically discussed them with the unions. Before Eddy Shah launched *Today* and Murdoch moved to Wapping, both of which happened in 1986 when the dam burst, some agreements had been reached. But the obstacles had been the jealousy and particularism of the print union chapels, the latent threat of official and unofficial stoppages, and the huge price of buying out jobs which were being paid inflated wages. Associated had known the pain of crisis redundancies twice already – with the *Mail/Sketch* merger and the closure of the *News*. It was not in a position to be the hammer for the whole industry in the mid-1980s. Both Shah and Murdoch, in their different ways, had motive and opportunity. Shah, the victor in a battle against the print unions at Warrington, had the opportunity open to an outsider. Without putting any existing national papers at risk, he could try everything new – computer make-up and typesetting, non-union publishing, colour on every page, decentralised printing at regional plants, road rather than rail delivery, cheaper distribution deals, a seven day paper. If all turned out right, he claimed, his middle-brow tabloid would be viable with a sale of only 300,000.

For Murdoch the background was different. Feeling let down by the continued industrial unrest after he bought Times Newspapers from Thomson, he had to crack the problem if he was to gain the rewards of his investment. He had the ruthlessness, the resources and the expertise to make the overnight switch of four national papers from Fleet Street to Wapping, and then to withstand everything that the print unions could throw at him.

For Associated neither of these approaches was available. The Rothermere press could never have acted like Shah. It had too much at stake, was too much part of the newspaper establishment; its management tradition was too gentle, particularly in dealing with printers and wholesalers, and as the *MoS* had shown its senior staff could find it hard to make a go of new projects. Further, Associated could not emulate Murdoch's line at Wapping, for the same reasons and more. For a start it probably did not have the financial resources to build a large print hall at Wapping for £80m and then keep it idle for several years. Again, it did not have the expertise in road transport, for the lorries which ran the blockade at Wapping every night were crucial to the continuing distribution of Murdoch's papers. Murdoch, on the other hand, was a friend of the Australian, Sir Peter Abeles, who had built up the international TNT road freight business, who was an expert at lorry logistics.

Finally, there would have been a bigger political fall-out if Vere Rothermere had sought to copy Wapping. As it was, there was an ugly atmosphere between the Labour and trade union movement and the Murdoch press: Labour Party spokesmen were supposed not to speak to

Murdoch journalists for a while, and Labour councils stopped libraries from buying News International papers. If the name had been Rothermere, not Murdoch, a lot of ancient history would have been wheeled out going back to 'Hurrah for the Blackshirts!' and beyond. (Wapping was not far from Cable Street, where Communists, the Jewish community and others had famously stopped a Mosley march in the 1930s.)

The drama at Wapping quite overshadowed the launch of *Today*. When a new quality daily came out, *The Independent*, anticipated struggles with the unions never took place at all. Wapping may have shown that old-style print workers were not necessary, but a month before Murdoch's move there Robert Maxwell, the tough millionaire who had bought the *Mirror* group in 1984, had managed to cut a quarter of his print jobs and move the *Sporting Life* out of Fleet Street.

The whole balance of power between managements and workers had been transformed. After 1986 Fleet Street itself ceased to exist as the editorial and manufacturing centre of the national press. Cost-conscious managements, aware of the value of property so close to an expanding City financial district and the fact that printing could take place almost anywhere, dispersed their employees. The *Telegraph* group took journalists and what remained of their printers to the Isle of Dogs; the *Financial Times* and *The Guardian* did their printing in Docklands but kept their journalists in Southwark and Clerkenwell, respectively. The *Express* group abandoned 'the black Lubianka' – its listed black glass building in Fleet Street – in favour of a new home south of Blackfriars Bridge. Much that had seemed so difficult before – not only the new technology but run-of-the-paper colour printing and distribution by road instead of rail – suddenly became commonplace. Newspaper shares became more highly rated on the Stock Exchange. Management found the confidence to invest in new facilities. A climate was created in which it was possible to envisage not one but two new Sunday papers – the *Sunday Correspondent* and *Independent on Sunday* – in 1989–90.

Associated Newspapers was able to ride with the tide. By June 1987, Vere Rothermere attended a topping out ceremony for a new print centre in Surrey Docks, costing £27m and to be known as Harmsworth Quays. The building firm responsible was John Laing which had had a special relationship with his great-aunt Christabel. This was only part of a £200m modernisation programme which also included significant, phased redundancies and a move by the journalists to New Northcliffe House in Kensington. Significantly, a link with the past was maintained at these new premises: Room One – the expensively decorated if slightly gloomy mahogany office which Northcliffe himself had occupied at the *Mail* – was transferred thence in its entirety as a priceless heirloom. He had always believed that big rooms inspired big ideas in bigger men.

First to move was the *Evening Standard*, in December 1988; the *Mail*

on Sunday followed in July 1989; the last to cross were the *Daily Mail*
and the chairman himself. Journalists on the whole liked the atrium and
airy modern offices; one said that after Fleet Street they now felt they
had the theatre of London life on their doorstep in Kensington. Attentive readers spotted the occasional sign of their papers' new location, as
for instance when the *Standard* ran a piece about the malevolence of
dogs in Holland Park, allegedly inspired by the editor's wife.

One small but possibly unfavourable consequence of Eddy Shah's
Today was that Vere Rothermere missed the opportunity to strangle it
after its birth. A new middle-brow paper was in a way good news for the
Mail, since in the 1960s and 1970s the conventional wisdom was that the
press was polarising between quality and populars, with little room in
between. However, *Today* was also new competition. In fact, when
Shah ran into difficulties he sold to Lonrho; when Lonrho wearied with
the losses on *Today*, Tiny Rowland sold it to Murdoch in 1987. More
than once along this line there were talks with Vere Rothermere. But
although he might have been able to use *Today*'s printing there was
little that he wanted to do with the paper except to shut it. This was not
attractive to the vendors.

The potential danger in *Today* was demonstrated when, after
Murdoch had been persuaded to buy it by his editor of the *News of the
World*, the same David Montgomery succeeded in doubling the sale
within two years. Montgomery's *Today* had a younger feel than the
Mail by the late 1980s and if the rise and fall of newspapers is partly to
do with catching a demographic wave, this could become a threat. By
the end of 1989 there were still a million sales separating the *Mail* and
Today, but there was evidence that both the *Mail* and *Express* were
suffering from its growth. There was a risk that *Today* in the 1990s
could do in the middle market what the *Sun* in the 1970s had done in the
mass market.

Even if *Today* had got away, 1987 was also a year not only of Mrs
Thatcher's third election victory but of Vere's neatest, most individual
triumph as a newspaper publisher. Early in 1986, in circumstances he
had foreseen, he was able to buy out the remaining 50 per cent of the
Evening Standard which was sold by Trafalgar House. As far as readers
were concerned, there seemed no difference: the paper's identity, which
had seemed such an issue when he was worsted in 1977, proved safe in
Harmsworth hands. However, the undoubted prosperity of the *Standard* as an evening paper with a monopoly of the London market
attracted covetous looks from Robert Maxwell. He hired Charles
Wintour as editorial consultant and together they created a rival to the
Standard, the *London Daily News*. It was not just to be a rival to the
Standard; Maxwell wanted to make it a twenty-four-hour paper, with
morning editions which would compete with the London dailies at
breakfast as well.

The idea was a product of a fleeting moment in newspaper history when everything seemed possible to managements. It was probably flawed. But what killed the *London Daily News* was a brilliant stroke by Vere, the fact that Maxwell fell into a trap, and some good work by the *Standard* management and journalists. Vere's brainwave, which was launched within a week of his telephoned instruction from Tokyo, was to restart the *Evening News*. Preparations were carried out in secret, with some thirty-five *Standard* journalists and freelances detailed to get on with it, and the news only leaked out on the afternoon before its first appearance on a Tuesday, when a print chapel at the *Express* was informed. The revived *News* was priced at 10p, half the price of the *Standard* and Maxwell's *London Daily News*.

The reincarnation of the *News* was not entirely unexpected; Vere had mentioned it as a possibility at a conference in Paris some while before, and he may well have wished to experiment anyway. But the sudden apparition caught Maxwell completely off balance. He had already been enraged by steps which Bert Hardy and the *Standard* management had taken to shore up the loyalty of the street newsvendors, which had forced Maxwell into setting up an expensive and ineffectual selling system of his own.

Maxwell then cut the price of the *LDN* to 10p to match the *News*. The *News* promptly reduced its cost to 5p. What had happened had turned the *LDN*, which had the respectable aim of providing an up-market rival to the *Standard*, into a laughing stock. It never recovered, and Maxwell closed it after a few months. This conclusion was assisted by two other factors: Bert Hardy launched a brilliant house give-away competition, precisely tuned to the frustrations of the London housing market, while John Leese, a fresh editor of the *Standard*, gave it a sharper edge and successfully pinched the idea for a metropolitan arts and lifestyle section from the *London Daily News*. The episode proved once more the reserves of loyalty the *Standard* could call on. Just as in 1977, the threat to its existence seemed to increase its sale and advertising. But the outcome also proved that there was no longer a place for a second evening paper in London, even with reduced costs of production. The revived *Evening News*, which had started as a lark, could have become permanent. Kept alive for a while after the *LDN* had closed, its sales were a trivial 30,000 by the end.

The 1980s were good for the *Mail* group. In three years, from 1984–5 to 1986–7, the turnover of Associated Newspapers rose from £425m to £581m, and the profit almost doubled to £53m. Its interests continued their growth, from free magazines in Britain to newspapers for lawyers in the United States; it was involved in light fittings (Lumitron) and security services (Argus Shield) and box office services (Ticketmaster), but it remained at heart a media business. Late in 1989, in partnership with the Meredith corporation, it announced that it would bring out a British version of *Metropolitan Home*, a US magazine of stylish living.

Incidentally, of course, Vere Rothermere's personal fortune also grew. Just what it really was at any moment was as difficult to calculate as when Harold Rothermere had rung up the faithful Sutton at night to find out what he was worth. The *Sunday Times*, which periodically compiled lists of Britain's wealthiest men and women, had Vere down as worth £254m in January 1989 in its Business News, and £153m in April 1989 in its magazine.[16] Both figures were undoubtedly wrong, and the suggestion of a downward slide was certainly misleading. The problem was not only that every asset could be valued differently on a different day, but that trustee and personal holdings in the Daily Mail and General Trust were not easy to disentangle, and that Vere and his family could benefit from overseas trusts of which little was known.

However, in late 1988 he made a move which greatly increased the wealth of himself and the other family holders of Daily Mail and General Trust shares, when the DMGT bought out the 50.05 per cent of shares in Associated Newspapers which the trust did not own already. Other Associated shareholders got a price of 765p a share, over 50 per cent more than the Stock Exchange had shown the day before the offer. The DMGT, while still family controlled, remained a publicly quoted company and saw a welcome rise in its share price.

This financial coup had various causes and consequences. Because of the views of stockbrokers on investment trusts with a single indirect holding, the DMGT shares were somewhat undervalued; at the same time, Associated could not issue more shares without the risk of diluting the DMGT and family holding. An attempt to get round the capital gains tax bill which the DGMT faced on the sale of any assets had led the company to consider moving its tax residence to Holland; in 1987 and 1988, there was litigation by the DMGT in the British High Court and the European Court, which was ultimately unsuccessful.

By buying out the minority shareholders in Associated, however, Vere and his fellow directors at the DMGT not only improved the value of the DMGT shares and removed a structural weakness. They made the group almost invulnerable to outside take-over in all circumstances except where the family split or wished to bow out. And they made the Associated companies more central to the DMGT, which sold many of its listed investments to pay for the purchase.

By the end of the 1980s the *Mail* group was looking more solid financially than at any time since the heyday of Harold Rothermere in the 1920s. Vere was exploring the possibilities of satellite television. His peripatetic lifestyle enabled him to keep an eye on interests around the world and pick up new ones which seemed attractive. While the family business was not as large as Maxwell's or Murdoch's, and not driven by the same urges to make deals and expand, there would be many to argue that it was more coherent and firmly based than either of those.[17]

Two of his children, Geraldine and Camilla, were married. So was his stepdaughter, Sarah. The first to marry, in the early 1980s, was his eldest daughter Geraldine. She had been a model and she married David Ogilvy, heir to the Earl of Airlie, and a nephew of Princess Alexandra's husband, Angus Ogilvy. Lord David Ogilvy started out as a Sotheby's trainee, ran a night-club and launched his own record label. Later on the marriage hit difficulties. However, Geraldine, following her mother's example as a charity organiser, has played a significant role in events to raise money for rainforest conservation.

Camilla Harmsworth, who had trained as a teacher, married a commercial radio broadcaster seven years older then herself, in October 1989. With a sunny smile she was well liked in the wider family, and she married from the family home of Stroods in the village of High Hurstwood. (Stroods, which had burnt down some years before, had been lovingly rebuilt; it was as though both Pat and Vere had a commitment to maintain what they had inherited or acquired.)

His son Jonathan, tall and good looking, went to Duke University in the United States after his time at Gordonstoun, and began helping at the firm during vacations. Those who knew Vere well were sure that he hoped in due course that Jonathan would be a fourth generation Harmsworth controller of the group, and there was talk of him gaining experience in Australian newspapers.

Directly and indirectly Jonathan could expect to inherit a majority shareholding in DMGT. Should he form an alliance with Vere's young half-brother Esmond, they would have an overwhelming majority. The young Esmond was also at a US university, Brown, where he dropped art history to major in history, his father's great love. While his mother had once been heard to say that she hoped he would grow up to be rich, he himself seemed as uncertain of his future career as many students of his age. He was said to be bright. He had been brought up apart from his Harmsworth relations. No one knew whether he would develop a taste for publishing and, if so, whether he and Jonathan would click.

Vere himself guarded his privacy jealously. Indeed there was an amusing exchange of letters between himself and Stewart Steven, editor of the *Mail on Sunday*, in the pages of the *Financial Times* in early 1988 on this subject.[18] Steven had argued against an *FT* editorial which implied that intrusion into the privacy of the rich and prominent should be limited by the Press Council. He added, 'The truth is that in a democratic society those who have gained power, wealth and position must, sometimes, be prepared to pay the price for their good fortune.' Vere was not having that, if it meant that the right to personal privacy should diminish in direct proportion to the amount of property owned by an individual. 'As citizens succeed in this material world, they would be increasingly subject to the obscene inquisition of the current hypocritical journalism of the sensational press,' he wrote back to the *FT*. 'I have heard of some editors in Fleet Street who surely would not care to contemplate such a situation,' he added, for even the upright Mr Steven, if he had the seven year itch, might have a double page spread in the *News of the World* to look forward to.

Steven's published reply, which jokingly concluded, 'It is well known that all Fleet Street editors take a vow of chastity upon assuming office, and a vow of poverty too' did not remove a perception that his proprietor felt strongly about privacy, and had a real aversion to muck-raking. (The difficulty of laying down an ethical line in a competitive news situation was revealed during the libel case by Sonia Sutcliffe, wife of the 'Yorkshire Ripper' against *Private Eye*; Vere Rothermere had instructed that the *Mail* group should not make a payment to the wife of a convicted murderer, but his journalists found a way of getting money to her indirectly.)

The privacy issue was important to Vere, not only because of his beliefs and because he was a shy person. Malicious journalism could have threatened his own way of life for, since the late 1970s, he had acquired a regular companion in Maiko Lee. She was a beautiful and well-born Korean woman, whose family had moved to Japan. Maiko was his consort in Paris, where she organised a surprise party for him at the Ritz Hotel to celebrate his sixtieth birthday in 1985; his mother and Sir David English were among those who came over from England, there were a couple of Bourbon princes, and a chamber group from the Paris Conservatoire provided music. Vere and Maiko also attended the Seoul Olympics together in 1988, where she was popular with journalists, getting down on her knees on one occasion to explain to sports writers how they should eat Korean delicacies. Her part in Vere's life was quite widely known. There was an occasional indirect influence on the papers, as when the *Evening Standard* sponsored a photo exhibition on the Seoul Olympics, or ran a story on Hungary and South Korea establishing diplomatic and trade relations.

At the start of the 1990s, Vere remained something of an enigma even to those who worked closely with him. A quizzical raising of the eye, a humorous manner, went along with a strong sense that he was the last of the old-style British press proprietors from the family that had trade-marked the genus, and a confidence and authority born of success. As he grew older he looked more and more a Harmsworth, substantially built, with what an ex-editor described as 'an imperial head'. Mick Shields once said of him, 'The chairman is twice as clever as he looks, but only half as clever as he thinks.' But he was under no illusions that while the chairman enjoyed a good argument, he also liked to win. On another occasion, in a discussion of social class, Vere was asked how he would describe himself. 'I am a nobleman,' he said.

He had a clear view that it was journalistic talent that made newspapers successful, and that he wanted newspapers to go on being at the core of his family business. He once told a journalist on one of his papers that he wished he could do without management, so that there was nothing between the proprietor and his editors, a dream which had echoes of Northcliffe. His hostility to the management, which after all was his management, seemed to be carried to extremes, so that when a managing director met an editor for lunch to discuss the editor's pension, the former was anxious that Vere should not know they had met because he would disapprove.

Nevertheless, there was reason behind Vere's attitude. Newspaper managements can become a sort of bureaucracy, for whom survival, respectability and a quiet life become sufficient ends. There is a danger of short-term thinking and timidity. Vere may never have forgotten the way in which some of the Associated managers were ready to withdraw from the national newspapers in 1970. His own greatest triumphs were the product of an ability to think long-term, as when he captured the *Standard*, or sustained the *Mail on Sunday* until it turned the corner. Early in the 1980s, before *Today* appeared, he was calling for run-of-the-paper colour in his newspapers. He also rid the higher management of circulation people.

One of his strongest qualities, with both editors and senior managers, was his loyalty. This they repaid. It enabled a family group to retain a family feeling even when there were the usual disagreements. English turned down attractive offers to edit the *Express, The Times* and the *Sunday Times* out of loyalty to his proprietor. He and others were generously rewarded, both in prestige and financially. Both David English and Patrick Sergeant got knighthoods. While Sir Patrick Sergeant became a millionaire several times over through the success of *Euromoney* and its flotation, a number of other senior members of the group had also become wealthy through high salaries and stock options.

Although there was felt to be an element of divide and rule about the way Vere operated he was widely recognised as kind. There was not the ruthlessness or unpredictability of some newspaper publishers: substantial staff cuts only took place when there seemed no alternative within the economics of a competitive press, and senior individuals he discharged himself. He was, however, regarded as eccentric in a benign way. For example, he once told an editor that he thought there was some sexual racket to be uncovered in the small ads in *Private Eye* which advertised house removal firms in London. There seemed a lot of them; the editor said that young people were always moving their flats, why did he think there was something doubtful going on? On another occasion, following the sudden death of Colin Owen-Browne who had joined Associated from the Beaverbrook group as an advertising supremo, he implied to colleagues that his death was not due to natural causes.

His interest in psychic and paranormal phenomena led him to become a close friend of Patric Walker, the astrologer who lives on Rhodes, whose column was promptly transferred from the *Evening News* to the *Standard* when they merged. When 2 May was chosen as the date for the launch of the *Mail on Sunday*, Bernard Shrimsley was instructed by his proprietor to check with Walker that this was an auspicious date. In the late 1980s, when English would receive two or three phone calls a week from Vere when he was out of the country, astrology, comic strips and typography were some of his proprietor's main concerns. Colleagues were sometimes impressed by Vere's para-normal intuition. One story told how, following Mick Shields' death, Vere rang one of his London directors at home and spoke to his wife. The wife offered to get her husband, but Vere said he wanted to talk to her: he had had a visitation from Mick Shields who wanted to get a message to his surviving wife, Jacqueline. The message was that she was far more ill than she realised. In fact Mick Shields' widow died from cancer not very long after he did.

As he grew older people thought Vere became increasingly aware of his singular role as the last surviving, hands-on, newspaper aristocrat. He made significant gestures, as when he underwrote a memorial service for Sam White, the *Standard*'s inimitable Paris correspondent who had spent most of his life working for Lord Beaverbrook and his son. Whereas in 1961 it was said that, at a funeral service for his great-aunt Violet Wild, he had asked vaguely how she was related to him, by the 1980s he was regarded as knowledgeable and sympathetic on family matters. When someone wrote to say that a rather distant young cousin had expressed a desire to go into journalism, he was rapidly offered an interview on a provincial paper.

From a family viewpoint one of the most memorable events took place in 1989, when Vere Rothermere and a small party of *Mail* journalists including Sir David English visited Hungary as a guest of the liberalising Communist government. Vere had headed a sponsorship committee which had raised £230,000 for the Magyarok festival at the Barbican that autumn. The visit was a moving opportunity to retrace the steps of his father and grandfather.

At Szeged University he was shown that some of the radium given by his father to assist medical research was still there. He was shown where his father had stood in the Strangers' Gallery of the Hungarian Parliament in 1928, when the deputies had stood to cheer him. He was photographed next to the crown of St Stephen. And he gave a press conference on the exact anniversary of the publication of his grandfather's article, 'Hungary's Place in the Sun'. The party visited the Peto Institute, which had pioneered work with handicapped children, and Vere laid a carnation on the new grave of Imre Nagy, Prime Minister during the Hungarian revolt of 1956. The Minister of Culture teased him that amongst his wonderful gifts he could speak to horses in Hungarian – because Vere had succeeded in calming a frisky horse.

The visit had quite an impact in Hungary, which was not only preparing to move to a multiparty free enterprise system, but was concerned about the boundary issues which had inspired Harold Rothermere's campaign. But although the *Mail* publicised the Barbican festival and ran one or two articles about the evolution of events in Hungary, which included reference to the first Lord Rothermere, Vere's trip was not reported in Britain. English decided it was not newsworthy in itself. It was an interesting example of how news values, rather than proprietorial publicity, governed editorial coverage under the 3rd Viscount Rothermere.

16
Epilogue

A member once told the author that the Harmsworths were a very ordinary family. Pat, Lady Rothermere, once told a visitor who admired a painting on her wall and wondered why he could not have had it, that the difference was that he did not have a clever grandfather. What marks out the Harmsworths, who have controlled a family publishing business for over a century, is their staying power. Who, now, would like to bet that Robert Maxwell's grandson or great-nephew will be running a major firm that will include the *Daily Mirror*? Or that Rupert Murdoch – himself a second generation newspaper proprietor – will have an heir who successfully conserves his inheritance?

In spite of some awkward moments of transition down the generations, and huge changes in the media of communication, the Rothermere business has survived and prospered. Neither family incompetence, nor death duties, nor competition, nor social and political change have brought it down. It has, of course, marched with the times. Alfred Northcliffe, who was proud to have given the National Union of Journalists a helping hand at the start, might have been a little surprised to see Associated Newspapers seeking to withdraw recognition from the union in late 1989. He and his brother Harold, who made much of their British patriotism, would not have expected their descendants to become tax exiles, or that the Daily Mail and General Trust would seek to move its residence to the Netherlands.

Many other large British firms, started in the nineteenth century, had ceased to be family run and controlled by the last decade of the twentieth. ICI, Tate and Lyle, and Shell were no longer run by their families. The mortality in newspapers, with their especial pressures, had left the Harmsworths standing unique. For the passage of time tends to work against an active family control in any business, particularly the press. To begin with, successive members of the same family may not have the talent or desire to go into or survive in the same business: there is not only a temptation to try something else, but to opt out and live off an investment income. Again, a family firm may be outgunned by changes to its environment and market; or the need to raise fresh capital for the business may dilute the family's ownership.

Hence the achievement of Esmond and Vere in sustaining the firm as a significant newspaper enterprise was out of the ordinary. It was based on managerial skill and in Vere's case empathy with journalists and journalism. For there is always a danger that talented people will feel that they can never get to the top of a family firm, and that they must leave to get on. The family firm can also draw on reserves of affection not open to every public company. Christabel Bielenberg, when she was researching in the *Mail* library in the late 1980s, was impressed to meet staff who had made a pilgrimage to Totteridge, and found a genuine family awareness.

Family firms can also fall foul of their own sentiment, clinging on to habits and people that put them at a disadvantage. Somehow the Harmsworths managed to avoid this, while still appearing paternalist. It must have been a wrench on sentimental grounds to leave the Fleet Street area; but Vere remarked that the warren of Carmelite and Northcliffe buildings on the south side of the street held some bad memories, as well as the glorious ones. Destruction of the culture of Fleet Street, which had bound reporters, managers and printers in a common fraternity since the days of Northcliffe, was a break with press history.

The continuity of the Rothermere press has been based on a family continuity. The values of the *Daily Mail* have consistently supported the right and instinct of parents to provide for their children and grand-children. Yet there were ironies in this mainspring of private enterprise, for neither Northcliffe himself nor any of the Rothermeres were paragons of orthodox family life. And the heir to a title, a prominent name and more wealth than you can easily count, is also inheriting burdens. There are burdens of expectation; burdens of accumulated hostility caused by the actions of previous generations; burdens which can either paralyse the initiative or send someone flying off into tangents of self-indulgence or the butterfly life of a socialite.

For members of the wider Harmsworth family, who inherited wealth but were not involved at all in the business, their money was not always a source of happiness. The second Sir Hildebrand Harmsworth, son of the first baronet who was a younger brother to Alfred Northcliffe and Harold Rothermere, lived all his life on the income of a Canadian trust. He was the one, as a boy nicknamed Sonny, who had appealed to his uncle Harold. When he died in 1977, aged 76, he cut his estranged wife out of his will and left everything to his friend Valerie de Pass, with whom he had lived on and off for forty years. Inevitably, there was litigation over this will, initiated by his widow. Sir Hildebrand was described by a deputy High Court judge as 'a restless and self-centred man who could not bear to be alone, and whose life centred on his women friends, fishing, and his need for sun'. He had homes in New York, Florida and Surrey.

Central to the story of the Harmsworths in newspapers is, of course, the story of the *Daily Mail*. Newspapers have personalities and, in spite of the switch to tabloid make-up in 1971, there is a recognisable continuity to the *Mail* from the moment that Alfred Harmsworth told his mother that he had hit a goldmine to the present day. This was not just because particular themes and stances had a habit of reappearing in different guises: a love affair with the novelties of America; a fascination with the Duke and Duchess of Windsor; a fascination with flight, from air races to men on the Moon; an interest in Eastern Europe; a kind of Conservatism which stressed not just private enterprise but the interests of young people, women and the less well-off; a readiness to put the boot in on socialism and radical causes; a critical curiosity about rival media – films, radio and television.

All through its life a highly competitive spirit had been engendered inside the *Mail*, with different people vying for all the attractive jobs, two or three leader page features fighting every night for the privilege of the editor's approval. It was an atmosphere which could stimulate gossip, back-stabbing and jealousy all the way from the bars to 'Sunset Boulevard', as the executive floor was nicknamed. But with all that there was often a high morale, particularly stimulated by the obvious regard which Northcliffe and Vere Rothermere had for journalists. (After Northcliffe's death it is said that one of the problems for the accountants was to sort out the journalists' expenses, because Northcliffe had let them collect money without submitting records of expenditure.)

There was a fun side to all this. From Northcliffe on, the *Mail* had gone in for stunts and this tradition has continued to affect the journalists as well. David English, dressed as a Chinese coolie, once dragged a departing deputy down Fleet Street in a rickshaw; later, the Orient Express was hired for a champagne ride round the south London suburbs when another colleague left.

There was also a highly controversial side to the *Mail*, where those who disagreed politically or socially felt it could be grossly unfair. Northcliffe had been accused of bringing Randolph Hearst's yellow journalism to Britain. The first Lord Rothermere was often totally uninterested in journalistic aspirations towards balance and objectivity. More recently, the *Mail* has been criticised for showing a yellow journalistic streak, duffing up its opponents in print, and going for the jugular. Sometimes, as in the Zola Budd case, when it brought a young South African runner to Britain and used its influence to obtain her a passport so that she could represent Britain in international athletics, it has seemed to lack judgement.

However, a spice of controversy and an element of unpredictability are essentials in popular journalism. The *Mail* has also shown qualities of adaptation. In the 1970s, when investigative reporting was in fashion, it pioneered a clever approach of 'living the news', under which journalists or contributors spent time working in newsworthy situations – on a Vauxhall car assembly line, or teaching in a comprehensive school. It also imperceptibly moved up-market of the *Daily Express*, a product of good writing, elegant layout and consistency. On the other hand, some of its experiments did not work out, like its *Male and Femail* Saturday colour magazine.

If newspapers are rich men's toys it will already be clear that the various Harmsworths have each found their own pleasures in playing with them. Northcliffe was an editor-in-chief who could do anything, was interested in everything. Harold Rothermere intervened erratically in the editorial coverage, but was always interested in the balance of profit and loss. Esmond enjoyed the prestige of being a proprietor, changed his editors too frequently, but otherwise seemed distant from the content of his papers. Vere is interested in most things, periodically puts ideas to editors, but does not feed them constantly with stories in the Beaverbrook way.

Concern over the power of the press, and of the proprietors, has never been totally absent in Britain. Alfred Northcliffe and Harold Rothermere did much to stimulate such anxiety. But by the 1990s, with new newspapers appearing and a burgeoning of other media – from local radio to satellite broadcasting – the issues came to seem different. Although there was still hostility to the strength of Rupert Murdoch in the British national press – which was comparable to the influence of Northcliffe in 1914 – the worries were beginning to shift to specifics like a claim for a right of reply, protection of privacy and from obscenity, and the abuse of newspapers in multimedia companies to boost other house products.

The strengths and weaknesses of a family newspaper ownership appeared now in a different perspective. Many British newspapers were part of conglomerates in which the newspapers themselves could be of secondary importance. While chairmen and managing directors of non-family concerns might enjoy a bit of glamour from having press interests, their real concern was with profit rather than content, and they were as ready to dispose of their subsidiaries as to acquire them. Where there was a strong editor and corporate sense on a paper owned by such a conglomerate these attitudes might not matter. More frequently the result was demoralising: editors and newspaper managers might be changed for short-term reasons.

There were still risks in a family ownership, not least that the process of primogeniture was unlikely for ever to produce persons able to run a press group with success. But the Vere Rothermere experience showed the positive aspects: a willingness to look ahead, so that by planting acorns today one's grandchildren may enjoy the shade of the oaks; a willingness to take risks; the confidence to provide a stable environment, not only for editors; and a concern for employees which could sometimes be more akin to the big Japanese enterprises than to the run of British firms.

The problems are intrinsic. It is difficult to arrange a suitable apprenticeship for the heir who is to be the owner. A company may go downhill under an ageing chairman. A new owner may find it hard to establish authority. The sheer disparity in wealth between a dynastic press lord and his staff and readers may put him out of touch with their reality. As in all monarchies there are persistent hazards from flattery and court intrigue. But rather like the British monarchy the Rothermere dynasty has found new affection in the contemporary era. Pat, playing the character role of Bubbles, has been cheered on public occasions. Vere was praised to the *Sunday Times* by one of his editors, Stewart Steven, who said, 'Every night I'm on my knees thanking God that I have Lord Rothermere as a proprietor.'[19] If you are part of a working dynasty you are rather more confident than the most ebullient of self-made men, less ephemeral than the soap opera rich and the soap opera famous.

The first and last dynasty of the popular press is not just some surprisingly functioning antique. It embodies through the *Daily Mail* the ongoing commitment and relevance of a whole body of late Victorian beliefs – middle-class snobbery, entertainment, the joy of information, patriotism, the novelty of the everyday. The bursting Harmsworth household of north London towards the end of the nineteenth century had an archetypal quality, even when the money ran short. The way in which succeeding generations have used this psychological and intellectual capital has been as important as any financial inheritance in securing their future.

Notes

Further details of references cited in the Notes are to be found in the Select Bibliography.

Part I   Alfred Northcliffe: The Founder

1   The cartoon was published in the 27 April 1872 issue of *Punch*.
2   See Cecil Harmsworth, *Lord Northcliffe and Other Harmsworth Memorials*, p. 21.
3   In late 1889, £1 a week would be worth only £36.79p a week a century later, a telling indication of the rise in popular living standards in the twentieth century.
4   Quoted in Reginald Pound and Geoffrey Harmsworth, *Northcliffe*, p. 107.
5   W. H. Lapthorne in *Bygone Kent*, 1988.
6   Figures quoted by Pound and Harmsworth, p. 207.
7   Ibid., p. 282.
8   Northcliffe Papers, British Library.
9   Cecil Harmsworth King, *Strictly Personal*, p. 57.
10 See Philip Knightley, *The First Casualty*, p. 92 for a full account.
11 Alfred, Lord Northcliffe, *At the War*, p. 3.
12 Ibid., p. 46.
13 Ibid., p. 111.
14 Ibid., p. 257.
15 See Pound and Harmsworth, p. 566.
16 *Hansard*, 16 April 1919.
17 *British Medical Journal*, 19 August 1922.
18 Pound and Harmsworth, p. 228.
19 Pound and Harmsworth, p. 134.
20 Ibid., p. 792.
21 Martin Gilbert, *Winston S. Churchill*, Vol. IV, p. 790.

Part II Harold Rothermere: The Brother

1   Paul Ferris, *The House of Northcliffe*, p. 300. Further, various papers referring to the first Lord Rothermere, collected by Sir Geoffrey Harmsworth, became unavailable after Sir Geoffrey's death and correspondence exchanged between the first Lord Rothermere and his heir Esmond was stolen from the Paris flat of the third Lord Rothermere.
2   Reginal Pound and Geoffrey Harmsworth, *Northcliffe*, p. 94.
3   Paul Ferris, *The House of Northcliffe*, p. 40.
4   Cecil Harmsworth King, in *Strictly Personal*, pp. 79–80, states that Harold Rothermere also proposed to his first cousin once removed, Judith Wilson, after his wife's death in 1937.
5   Reminiscence by Lady Harmsworth Blunt, April 1989.

6 Northcliffe was also remembered in a similar way by the creation of a Lord Northcliffe Chair in English Literature at University College London.

7 The title derived from his property on the Kent–Sussex borders adjoining the River Rother.

8 In *Beaverbrook*, A. J. P. Taylor records that the *Sunday Express*, started at the end of 1918, cost Beaverbrook £2 million in its early years and only really became successful in the late 1920s.

9 Information supplied to the author.

10 She may even then have gone through a ceremony which was technically invalid; her wedding certificate on marrying Esmond described her as a spinster.

11 See *Memoirs of a Conservative* by J. C. C. Davidson edited by Robert Rhodes James, p. 135.

12 Beaverbrook Papers, 29 January 1914.

13 Ibid., between July and November 1921.

14 Cecil King, in *Strictly Personal*, p. 78, suggests that Harold Rothermere lost heavily in the Wall Street crash. However, other versions indicate that, in spite of his anxiety over the collapse in share prices, he personally benefited. Significantly, his business partner Beaverbrook had liquidated many investments just prior to the crash, and it is quite possible that he was publicly bullish to steady the nerves of the market after having sold on his own account.

15 Beaverbook Papers, 26 April 1923.

16 Ibid.

17 A full account, from the Hungarian viewpoint, of Rothermere's intervention was given by the private secretary of Jeno Rakosi in the 1 January 1933 issue of the Hungarian daily, *Pesti Naplo*. This stated that the Revisionist League came into being in response to the 'Place in the Sun' article, that Rothermere initially told Rakosi that he would accept the Hungarian throne, and that Hungarians saw him as a disinterested English humanitarian. (I am particularly grateful to Ferenc Szabo and Eugene Nadasy for their help on this episode.)

18 Lederer Papers.

19 Cecil Harmsworth King, *Strictly Personal*, p 77.

20 Other claimants to this title include the nineteenth-century Durham Report which led to self-government in Canada, Indian independence in 1947, and the setting up of the Commonwealth Secretariat in 1965.

21 Martin Gilbert, *Winston S. Churchill*, volume V, p. 387.

22 Letter in Lederer Papers.

23 Beaverbrook Papers, 7 May 1934.

24 According to Aidan Crawley, this aircraft was initially financed by Lady Hudson, Northcliffe's widow, and Rothermere came in after her. It is likely that his involvement fuelled the unjustified suspicion that his campaign for aerial rearmament was motivated by a financial interest.

25 Martin Gilbert, *Winston S. Churchill*, volume V, p. 636.

26 This was Cecil King's younger brother Bobby, drowned in 1918. His elder brother Luke (Lucas) had been killed in 1915 at Ypres, leaving their mother Geraldine distraught.

27 Beaverbrook Papers.

28 Alysia Nikitina, *Nikitina by Herself*, p. 66. Nikitina at one point asked Rothermere if he could get a job for her brother Vladimir as a tennis correspondent. Disingenuously he replied that he never interfered in editorial matters. He then asked why they did not start a sporting club in Monte Carlo which would feature tennis where Vladimir could coach. This was the origin of the Sporting Club de Monaco, where Bjorn Borg played in more recent times.

29 Martin Gilbert, *Winston S. Churchill*, pp. 1088–9. In this revealing letter, because it was so close to the outbreak of the war, Rothermere stressed that in conversation with him Hitler had said he would never take the initiative in resorting to

bloodshed and complained: 'I have never yet seen an authoritative statement made in England complimenting Hitler on his tremendous record of achievement in Germany.'

Part III   Esmond Rothermere: The Son

1   Aidan Crawley, *Leap Before You Look*, p. 127. The editor's name was W. L. Warden.
2   Correspondence between Harold and Esmond, subsequently stolen from Vere Rothermere, illustrated their divergences.
3   Conversation with author, July 1989.
4   His ex-wife also remarried twice.
5   POY's real name was Percy Fearon.
6   See Peter and Leni Gillman, *Collar the Lot*. The *Sunday Dispatch* was particularly vitriolic about 'the enemy alien menace'.
7   The story is told in Cecil King, *With Malice Towards None*, pp. 80–4.
8   Ibid., pp. 163–73. There had also been friction between Churchill and the *Mirror* group in early 1941 when the Prime Minister had written to King to complain of a spirit of hatred and malice against his government which was doing the work of the fifth column.
9   Ibid., p. 311. The letter was written on 18 April 1942.
10   *The Letters of Ann Fleming*, edited by Mark Amory, suggest (p. 37) that she had first fallen in love with Esmond on holiday in Austria, in August 1936.
11   *Time*, magazine, 5 June 1950.
12   Sanger Diaries, 18 January 1947.
13   Ibid., 19 May 1949.
14   Ibid., 8 February 1948.
15   Lederer named a son Randolph.
16   A full, but naturally one-sided account of the controversy was given in Randolph Churchill, *What I Said About the Press*.
17   An entertaining account of what must, at the time, have been tense incidents is given in Mike Randall, *The Funny Side of the Street*, pp. 8–10, 116–27.
18   Other newspaper families were to make just this transition. The Iliffes, the family who had given Alfred Harmsworth a chance in the nineteenth century, finally sold the *Coventry Evening Telegraph* in the late 1980s; but their investment vehicle, the Yattendon Investment Trust, emerged as the buyer of the Isle of Wight ferry company shortly afterwards.
19   From 'The Soldier', August 1914, the poem starting 'If I should die, think only this of me ...'
20   In particular it recalled a joke which went back to 1916, of Lord Northcliffe calling for the King ...
21   See Cecil King, *Strictly Personal*, especially pp. 51–92.
22   Christabel Bielenberg, *The Past is Myself*.
23   The annual accounts for the Euromoney group, published in December 1989, showed that by then Sir Patrick Sergeant's annual salary as chairman had reached £850,000. In January 1990, his shareholding was valued at £17m after selling 500,000 shares for £1.75m.

Part IV   Vere Rothermere: The Grandson

1   The late Godfrey Winn, a notorious gossip, told an informant of the author that Vere was not Esmond's son and the rumour also survived in the outer reaches of the

Harmsworth family. However untrue, it must have been a psychological burden for a young man, not made easier to bear by the fact that Esmond's second Lady Rothermere produced a baby fathered by Ian Fleming.

2   The correspondence was published in *The Guardian* in November/December 1982. Vere also pointed out that he was not the same Lord Rothermere as his grandfather, had been a child when Harold Rothermere took up with Oswald Mosley, and that grandchildren should not be assumed to share their grandparents' opinions.

3   Frank Humphrey also had a phobia about the British peerage.

4   Northcliffe's brother St John had gone to Christ Church, along with one of Leicester's sons and Cecil King.

5   Brooks also came from the relatively new aristocracy, being a son of the second Baron Crawshaw.

6   See article by Mario Amaya in *The Tatler*, May 1986.

7   August J. von Borosini, *Choosing the Sex of Your Child*, 1953.

8   Serialised in April 1989.

9   Vere gave the valedictory address on 1 March 1988 at St Bride's, Fleet Street.

10   In the 1980s Marcia Williams, by now ennobled as Lady Falkender, was writing a column for the *Mail on Sunday*.

11   The Cromers moved back to the British mainland, taking up residence not far from New Northcliffe House in Kensington, in December 1989.

12   The author, then Deputy Editor of the *Standard*, shared this view and rejected an approach – in the middle of the attempted take-over – to become Associate Editor of the *News*.

13   There are now various published accounts of this episode, including Lewis Chester and Jonathan Fenby, *The Fall of the House of Beaverbrook*, Andre Deutsch, London, 1979 and Charles Wintour, *The Rise and Fall of Fleet Street*, Hutchinson, London 1989 (see chapter on the third Lord Rothermere).

14   In the aftermath of the attempted take-over by Associated, Vere Rothermere received libel damages from the *Sunday Times* following an article in October 1978 which had alleged that Vere had been unable to reach a firm decision, and that it had been Associated company policy to wait for the Beaverbrook group to die. In general, Vere had a good record as a decisive proprietor, and his group had been supportive of a diversity of titles.

15   Message in the possession of Bernard Shrimsley.

16   *Sunday Times* Magazine, 2 April 1989; *Sunday Times*, Business News, 1 January 1989. By 8 April 1990 the *Sunday Times* Magazine valued Vere Rothermere at £308m – over twice the figure of the year before!

17   The nature of the Maxwell business changed drastically in the late 1980s, when Robert Maxwell pulled out of British printing and bought the American publishing firm Macmillan; the centre of gravity of the Murdoch enterprises appeared to shift from Australia to the United Kingdom and then to the United States, and in content from newspapers to TV and films.

18   The *Financial Times* published letters from Stewart Steven on 30 April and 18 May, and from Vere Rothermere on 25 May 1988.

19   *Sunday Times*, 29 May 1988.

Select Bibliography

Aitken Rudd, Janet, *The Beaverbrook Girl*, Collins, 1987.

Amory, Mark (ed.), *The Letters of Ann Fleming*, Collins, 1985.

Bielenberg, Christabel, *The Past is Myself*, Chatto & Windus, 1968.

Borosini, August J. von, *Choosing the Sex of Your Child: A Guide to Sex Predetermination*, Exposition Press, New York, 1953.

Boyle, Andrew, *Trenchard*, Collins, 1962.

Camrose, William Berry, Lord, *British Newspapers and Their Controllers*, Cassell, 1947.

Chester, Lewis and Fenby, Jonathan, *The Fall of the House of Beaverbrook*, Andre Deutsch, 1979.

Christiansen, Arthur, *Headlines All My Life*, Heinemann, 1961.

Churchill, Randolph, *What I Said About the Press*, Weidenfeld & Nicolson, 1957.

Clarke, Tom, *My Northcliffe Diary*, Victor Gollancz, 1931.

Cockett, Richard, *Twilight of Truth*, Weidenfeld & Nicolson, 1989.

Crawley, Aidan, *Leap Before You Look*, Collins, 1988.

Cudlipp, Hugh, *Publish and Be Damned*, Andrew Dakers, 1953.

Cudlipp, Hugh, *The Prerogative of the Harlot*, Bodley Head, 1988.

Evans, Harold, *Good Times, Bad Times*, Weidenfeld & Nicolson, 1983.

Ferris, Paul, *The House of Northcliffe*, Weidenfeld & Nicolson, 1971.

Fyfe, Hamilton, *Northcliffe: An Intimate Biography*, George Allen & Unwin, 1930.

Gilbert, Martin, *Winston S. Churchill*, vols III to VIII (The Churchill Biography) Heinemann, 1971–88.

Gillman, Peter and Gillman, Leni, '*Collar the Lot*', Quartet, 1980.

Gray, Tony, *Fleet Street Remembered*, Heinemann, 1990.

Greenwall, Harry J., *Northcliffe: The Napoleon of Fleet Street*, Allan Wingate, 1957.

Hamilton, Denis, *Editor in Chief*, Hamish Hamilton, 1989.

Harmsworth, Cecil (Lord Harmsworth), *Lord Northcliffe and Other Harmsworth Memorials*, unpublished, 1944.

Harmsworth, Cecil (Lord Harmsworth), *St John Harmsworth: A Brave Life*, Tonbridge Printers, 1949.

James, Robert Rhodes (ed.), *J. C. C. Davidson: Memoirs of a Conservative*, Weidenfeld & Nicolson, 1971.

Jenkins, Simon, *Newspapers: The Power and the Money*, Faber, 1979.

Jenkins, Simon, *The Market for Gory*, Faber, 1986.

King, Cecil Harmsworth, *Strictly Personal*, Weidenfeld & Nicolson, 1969.

King, Cecil Harmsworth, *With Malice Towards None*, Sidgwick & Jackson, 1970.

Knightley, Philip, *The First Casualty*, Quartet, 1975.

MacArthur, Brian, *Eddy Shah, Today and the Newspaper Revolution*, David & Charles, 1988.

Nikitina, Alysia, *Nikitina by Herself*, Allan Wingate, 1959.

Northcliffe, Alfred Harmsworth, Lord, *A Thousand Ways to Earn a Living*, Carr, 1888.

Northcliffe, Alfred Harmsworth, Lord, *At the War*, Hodder & Stoughton, 1916.

Owen, Louise, *Northcliffe: The Facts*, self-published, 1931.

Pemberton, Max, *Lord Northcliffe: A Memoir*, Hodder & Stoughton, 1922.

Pound, Reginald and Harmsworth, Geoffrey, *Northcliffe*, Cassell, 1959.

Quennell, Peter, *The Wanton Chase*, Collins, 1986.

Randall, Mike, *The Funny Side of the Street*, Bloomsbury, 1988.

Rothermere, Harold Lord (Foreword), *The Romance of the Daily Mirror, 1903–1924*, Daily Mirror Newspapers, 1924.

Rothermere, Harold Lord, *Warnings and Predictions*, Eyre & Spottiswoode, 1939.

Rothermere, Harold Lord, *My Fight to Rearm Britain*, Eyre & Spottiswoode, 1939.

Rothermere, Harold Lord, *My Campaign for Hungary*, Eyre & Spottiswoode, 1939.

Ryan, A. P., *Lord Northcliffe*, Collins, 1953.

Sendall, Bernard, *Independent Television in Britain* (vol 1, 1946–62), Macmillan, 1962.

Skidelsky, Robert, *Oswald Mosley*, Macmillan, 1975.

Steed, Wickham, *The Press*, Penguin Books, 1938.

The Times History, vols III and IV, *The Times* 1947 and 1952.

Wagner, Gillian, *The Chocolate Conscience*, Chatto & Windus, 1987.

Wintour, Charles, *The Rise and Fall of Fleet Street*, Hutchinson, 1989.

Index

abdication crisis 127, 152, 194
Abel, George 190
Abeles, Sir Peter 228
ACTT 171
advertising
  newspapers 25, 28, 58, 69, 79
  television 171
Ainsworth, Harry 169
aircraft 36, 47–8, 50, 68, 119
  campaign 112–14
  races 179
Air Ministry 41, 50, 53, 87–8, 112
Aitken, Jonathan 89
Aitken, Sir Max 179–81, 203, 209, 216–17, 219
Aitken, Maxwell 216
Aitken, William Maxwell *see* Beaverbrook, 1st
  Baron
Aitken family 98
Allied Control Commission,
  Budapest 162
Aly Khan, Prince 146
Amalgamated Engineering Union 149
Amalgamated Press 81, 172, 186
  Northcliffe and 37, 66
  sale 96, 126
Anglo-American Gazette 34
Anglo-Canadian Pulp and Paper 156, 201
Anglo-Newfoundland Development Co. 80,
  119, 156, 193
Anglo-Saxon, The 70
Answers (Answers to Correspondents) 8, 16,
  21, 24, 26, 63, 65, 71, 169, 227
  closure 170
  family involvement 19–20, 123
  growth 17
  launch 14–15
  Rothermere and 77–9
Answers Company Ltd 17, 77, 79
Answers Publications Ltd 30
anti-Semitism 70, 87, 111–12, 150–1, 163, 188
appeasement 112–14, 119, 127–9, 143, 147
army clothing department 41, 50, 86–7
Arnholz, Henry 7, 92–3
Asquith, Herbert 43–6, 48–9, 89
Associated Newspapers 58, 70, 90, 92, 140,
  158–9, 161, 179, 210–11, 213, 216–17
  Chronicle take-over 173–5, 206
  DGMT buy-out 232
  diversification 180, 231

Esmond Rothermere and 116, 134, 141, 166,
  181–2
  modernisation 228–9
  Northcliffe resignation 54
  and television 170–2
  Times bid 222–3
  turnover 231
  Vere Rothermere and 202
Associated Rediffusion 170–2, 215
Association of Cinematograph and Allied
  Technicians 171
Astor, John Jacob 94
Astor, Lord 122
Astor, Waldorf W. 36, 94
Astor family 215
Atlantic Richfield 215
At the War 47–8
Attlee, Clement 154, 163–4
Austin, Sapper C. D. 18
Australian Consolidated Press 174
Austro-Hungary 54–5

Baldwin, Stanley 88, 98–101, 136, 194
  and Rothermere 107–9, 127–8
Balfour, Arthur James 32, 50, 81
Balkans 102–3, 139
Bamigboye, Baz 211
Barber, Noel 158–61, 194–5, 201, 212
Baring, Lady Lorna 177
Barnetson, Lord 179
Bartholomew, Harry Guy ('Bart') 91, 117,
  154–5, 166, 184, 186
Bartholomew, Ivy 91
BBC 101, 126–7
Beaumont, Capt. and Mrs 14, 16, 20, 22–3, 78
Beaverbrook, William Maxwell Aitken, 1st
  Baron 104, 139, 154, 174, 187, 203, 206,
  216
  and Churchill 72, 152, 162
  Daily Herald 144
  Empire Free Trade campaign 107–9
  Express 86, 141, 166
  Ministries 54, 114, 119, 130
  and Northcliffe 49, 89
  and Rothermere 87–9, 96–100, 105–6, 108,
  110, 112, 116, 118, 127–8, 147, 194–5
Beaverbrook group 206, 208, 216–17, 219
Beer, George 38
Beerbohm, Max 29

Beeton, Sir Mayson 79, 95–6
Beit, Alfred 29
Bell, Moberly 34–5
Bell, Stanley 190
Belloc, Hilaire 40, 46
Benenden School 95
Benn, Tony 110
Bennett, Arnold 85
Berry, Gomer and William 96–8
Berry, Lady Pamela 157
Bethlem Hospital 105
Bevan, Nye 164
Bevin, Ernest 154, 164
Bhopal, Maharajah of 142
Bicycling News 11–12, 16
Bielenberg, Christabel 125, 161, 187–9, 239
  The Past is Myself 161, 187
Bielenberg, Peter 113, 125, 161
Birchill, Julie 226
Black, Peter 171
Black and White 80
Blackshirts 103, 110–12, 127–8, 141, 229
Blumenfeld, R. D. 34, 89, 96
Blyth, Jeffrey 176, 181
Boards of Guardians 136
Boer War 30–1, 40, 48, 70, 111–12
'booming' 25, 33, 127, 152
Borden, Sir Robert 53
Borosini, Dr August von 205
Bottomley, Horatio 83, 85, 134
Bracken, Brendan 152
British Electric Traction (BET) 170, 172
British Finance Act (1936) 156
British Gazette 100, 153
British Medical Journal 61
British Movietone News 126, 140, 143
British Union of Fascists 110–12, 127
British War Mission 50–4, 67, 72
Brittenden, Arthur 178–9, 181, 191, 205, 207, 209
Broadbent, Wilson ('Jack') 141, 151
broadcasting
  radio 101, 126, 213
  television 126, 167, 170–2, 176, 232
Broadstairs 21–2
Brooke, Humphrey 162
Brooks, Capt. Christopher 203–4
Brooks, Patricia *see* Rothermere, Lady Patricia
Browne's School 7
Brownrigg, Capt. Tom 170
Brunton, Sir Gordon 190, 222
Buchanan-Barker, Canon 137
Buckle, G. F. 34
Budapest 161–2
Budd, Misses 6–7
Bundles for Britain 119
Burton, Basil 184
Burton, Christabel 6, 29, 92, 118, 123–5, 141, 184, 189
Burton, John 118

Burton, Percy 62, 118, 141

Cadbury, Laurence 174
Cadbury family 173, 206
Caird, Sir Andrew 54, 60, 90, 92, 98, 100, 127
Callaghan, James 218–20
Cameron, Ewan ('Cammy') 138, 140
Campbell, Gerald 44
Campbell, J. R. 100
Camrose, William Berry, Lord 154, 157, 172
Canada 52, 72, 96, 119, 122, 126, 179, 193, 200
Cardozo, Harold 150
Carey, Robert 151
Carr, Dargaville 13–14, 20
Carr & Co. 13–14, 17, 77–8
Carvel, Robert 216
Cazalet, Thelma 182
censorship 40, 43–4, 153–4
Chamberlain, Joseph 26
Chamberlain, Neville 151
Charriere, Henri
  Papillon 179
Chichester, Francis 195
Chips 21
Chirol, Valentine 34
Chisholm, Hugh 38
Christiansen, Arthur 116
Christiansen, Michael 188
Chronicle group *see News Chronicle*
Church of Ireland Gazette 13
Churchill, Lady Randolph 70
Churchill, Randolph 115, 117, 143, 161, 167–9, 184
Churchill, Sir Winston 46, 49, 119, 127, 137, 139, 151, 154, 160, 163–5, 167
  and Esmond Rothermere 152–3, 160, 162, 169, 194–5
  and Harold Rothermere 82, 99–101, 107–8, 113–15, 129–30, 147
  and Northcliffe 31, 52, 58, 68, 71–3
  Prime Minister 152–3, 165
  The World Crisis 154
circulation 79, 116, 155, 166, 174, 178, 210
Comic Cuts 21, 66
commercial radio 213
  television 170–2
Commonwealth 108, 167
Commonwealth Press Union 227
communism 70, 99–100, 118, 127, 129, 147, 150, 194
computerisation 227–8
Conservative Party 108, 170, 212
  governments 94, 107, 165, 167, 171, 220
  Esmond Rothermere and 89–90, 98, 162, 164, 193
  Harold Rothermere and 88, 99–101, 128
  Northcliffe and 22, 24, 26–7, 32, 68–9, 81
  Vere Rothermere and 208
Continental Daily Mail 34, 55, 59, 66, 121, 158–9, 194, 224

Cooper-Key, Adrian 184
Cooper-Key, Lady Lorna 129, 137, 145, 157, 183–4, 200, 213
Cooper-Key, Neill 122, 157, 172, 184
Coote, John 179–80
Coven, Frank 172
Coward, Noel 159
Cowles, Victoria 158
Cowles, Virginia 143
Cowley, John 116, 155
Crawley, Aidan 141–3, 155, 158, 194
 Leap Before You Look 141
Crewe House 54–6
Cripps, Lady 154
Cromer, Earl of, *see* Errington, Lord Roland
Cromer, Countess of *see* Errington, Lady Esme
Csanky, Denes 162
Cudlipp, Hugh 117, 153, 168, 186, 188
 Publish and Be Damned 168
Cyclist, The 12

Daily Chronicle 38
Daily Courier 28
Daily Dispatch 174
Daily Express 98, 114, 127, 155, 167, 206, 209–10, 216, 241
 Beaverbrook and 88–9, 96, 119, 141, 166
 Express group 116, 147, 173, 179–80, 193, 224, 229
 Mail merger 173, 179–81, 220
 Rothermere holdings 97
Daily Gleaner 227
Daily Graphic 167–8
Daily Herald 116, 127, 144, 154–5, 186
Daily Illustrated Mirror 33
Daily Mail 32–3, 38, 58, 88, 124, 130, 141, 224, 226, 230, 239–42
 air campaign 112–14
 air races 179
 and Baldwin 107–9, 127
 Boer War coverage 30–1, 40
 and Churchill 162–4
 circulation 178, 210
 Daily Mail Exchange 42
 Empire Free Trade 107–8
 Esmond Rothermere and 146–8
 Express merger 173, 179–81, 220
 and fascism 110–12
 First World War 42–6, 48
 Harold Rothermere and 80, 83, 93, 99
 Ideal Home Exhibition 184
 launch 27–30
 Mail group 98, 116–17, 121, 166, 172, 231–2
 'Money Mail' 192
 munitions campaign 45–6, 69, 154
 National Film Awards 201
 News Chronicle merger 110, 173–5, 208
 1918 election 56, 70
 Northcliffe and 24, 27–31, 36, 69, 71, 240

 politics 98–101, 141, 143, 162–4
 post-war election campaigns 163–5
 relaunch 182, 208–9
 Ryder slush fund story 218–19
 Second World War 149–52, 154
 Sketch merger 181, 205–7
 social campaigning 70, 211
 tabloid 205–12
 and Thatcher 220
 Zinoviev letter 100
Daily Mail and General Trust 97, 99, 116–17, 166, 171, 233, 238
 Associated buy-out 232
 directors 96, 125, 184
 diversification 180, 215
 Esmond Rothermere and 143–4, 146, 182
 registration 95
 Vere Rothermere and 220
Daily Mirror 18, 36, 38, 45, 70–1, 91, 144, 147, 165, 168, 208
 Cecil King and 124, 171, 186–7
 and Churchill 153–4
 circulation 116, 155
 launch 6, 33–4
 Maxwell take-over 229
 Mirror group 117, 155, 166
 Rothermere buys 80, 83–4, 90, 95
 sold 117, 127
Daily News 49, 174
Daily Record 80–1
Daily Sketch 170, 178, 187, 202, 209
 Mail merger 181, 205–7
 pornography charge 167–9
Daily Star 109, 224
Daily Telegraph 28, 38, 154, 174, 229
Daily Worker 154
Davidson, J. C. C. 95
Davidson, Lilias Campbell 12
Dawson, Geoffrey 36, 38, 47, 51, 57
Daylesford 160, 176–8, 182–3, 194
Deakin, Arthur 194
Declaration of London 35
Dempster, Nigel 210, 214, 225–6
de Pass, Valerie 239
d'Erlanger, Leo 137, 143
Diaghilev, Serge 104, 129
Dickens, Charles 5–6, 174
Dolling, Father 22
Drayton, Harley 172
du Maurier, George 7
Dumont, Santos 68

Eade, Charles 166–8
Economist, The 212
 Intelligence Unit 191
Eden, Anthony 165, 171, 173, 186
 editors 191–2
Edward VII, King 31–2
Edward VIII, King 127, 152, 194
Edwards, Sydney 216

Elizabeth II, Queen 167
Ellerman, Sir John 65, 94
Ellis, Frank 179
Elmwood 21–2, 32, 50–1, 54, 89, 92, 134, 136
Empire Free Trade campaign 107–8, 127
Empire Paper Mills 155
Encyclopaedia Britannica 34
English, Sir David 179, 181, 191, 202, 207–10, 217–21, 224–6, 234–7, 240
English Review 85
Errington, Lady Esme 119–20, 137, 145, 157, 160, 171, 174, 184, 200–1, 213
Errington, Henry 138, 157
Errington, Lord Roland 157, 171, 174, 184, 201, 213
Euromoney 192, 235
Evans, Harold 223
Evans, W. J. 60
Evening News 36, 58, 60, 70, 79, 93, 116, 126–7, 169, 174–5, 179, 185, 213, 216
  circulation 141
  closure 221–2
  Northcliffe buys 24, 26
  relaunch 231
  Standard merger 180, 217, 220
  Star take-over 176
Evening Standard 97, 116, 176, 180, 213, 229–31, 234
  Mail bid 216–19, 235
  News merger 180, 217, 220
Evening Standard Company 221
Evening World 98
Express group *see Daily Express*

Falkender, Marcia 212, 226
Famous Breach of Promise Cases 13
Field, The 123, 189
Financial Times 152, 229, 233–4
Finnemore, R. J. 194
First World War 32, 38, 40–56, 70, 83–4, 103, 111, 133
Fish, Walter 105
Fisher, H. A. L. 135
Fleet Street 229, 239
Fleet Street Forum 184
Fleming, Ann *see* Rothermere, Lady Ann
Fleming, Ian 156–9
  Casino Royale 159
Foot, Michael 168, 218–19
Forbes, Alistair 158
Forever Amber 166
Forget-me-Not 23
Fowler, John 160
Freeman, John 164
French, Howard 181, 207
French, Sir John 45
'From War to Peace' 56–7
Fry, C. B. 101
Fyfe, Hamilton 44, 51, 54

Gale, George 211
Garrod, Norman 179
Garvin, J. L. 36
Gaulle, Gen. Charles de 162–3
general elections
  (1895) 26–7
  (1900) 42, 65
  (1918) 56, 88
  (1922) 100
  (1924) 100
  (1929) 101, 107, 115, 136
  (1945) 163, 193
  (1950) 164
  (1951) 164–5
  (1955) 171
  (1959) 174
  (1974) 175
  (1979) 211, 220
  (1987) 227
general strike 100–1, 107, 136, 139, 153
Genthon, Dr Istvan 161–2
George V, King 59, 89
George VI, King 152
Germany 32, 37, 40, 70, 72, 83, 103, 110–11, 113–14, 150–1
Gide, André 82
Gladstone, William 28
Glasgow Record 124
Globe, The 66, 89
Glover, Robert 58
Gold, John 192, 196
Goldsmith, Sir James 217
Golf Illustrated 189
Gollancz, Victor 188
Goodman, Lord 180, 216
Great Anti-Northcliffe Mail 50
Guardian, The 200, 229 *see also Manchester Guardian*
Gunn, Herbert 169

Haig, Gen. Douglas 87
Halifax, Lord 151
Hall, Edward Marshall 71
Hamilton, Florence 5
Hamilton, Fred 180
Hamilton Brothers 180, 185
Hammond, Bob 175, 177, 185
Hampstead & Highgate Express 5
Hardcastle, William 173–5, 191–2, 205–6
Hardy, Bert 231
Harmsworth, Alfred (Leicester's son) 123
Harmsworth, Alfred Charles William *see* Northcliffe, Viscount
Harmsworth, Alfred Snr 3–5, 9, 13–15, 17, 124
Harmsworth, Annie 66
Harmsworth, Camilla 204–5, 233
Harmsworth, Cecil (Lord Harmsworth of Egham) 6, 9, 12, 17, 42, 59–60, 78, 81, 123, 155, 187–9
  anti-Semitism 86–7, 112, 188

barony 62, 65
joins *Answers* 19
MP 50, 53, 134–4
New Liberal Review 66
Harmsworth, Charles 5–6, 64, 93, 123
Harmsworth, Christabel *see* Burton,
  Christabel
Harmsworth, Daphne 187
Harmsworth, Desmond 65, 121
Harmsworth, Esme *see* Errington, Lady Esme
Harmsworth, Esmond Cecil *see* Rothermere,
  Esmond, 2nd Viscount
Harmsworth, Esmond Vyvyan (Little Esmond)
  138, 178, 182, 184, 233
Harmsworth, Geoffrey 66, 104, 123, 189
Harmsworth, Geraldine *see* Ogilvy, Lady
  Geraldine
Harmsworth, Geraldine ('Dot') *see* King, Lady
  Geraldine
Harmsworth, Geraldine Mary 3–5, 17, 41, 59,
  62, 64–5, 82, 91–2, 105, 122
Harmsworth, Guy 189
Harmsworth, Harold (Leicester's son) 123
Harmsworth, Harold Jonathan Esmond Vere
  178, 205, 214, 233
Harmsworth, Harold Sidney *see* Rothermere,
  Harold, 1st Viscount
Harmsworth, Hildebrand ('Sonny') 118, 239
Harmsworth, Hildebrand Snr 6, 19, 62, 64, 66,
  89, 115, 122
Harmsworth, Jonathan *see* Harmsworth,
  Harold Jonathan
Harmsworth, Leicester *see* Harmsworth,
  Robert Leicester
Harmsworth, Lorna Peggy *see* Cooper-Key,
  Lorna
Harmsworth, Madeleine 187, 189
Harmsworth, Margaret ('Peggy') 84, 90,
  136–7, 144–5, 177, 207
Harmsworth, Mary *see* Northcliffe, Lady
  Mary
Harmsworth, R. L. St John 61
Harmsworth, Robert Leicester 6, 9, 14, 59–60,
  65–6, 80–2, 113, 122–3, 189
  baronet 62
  director of Daily Mail Trust 95
  edits *Home Chat* 25
  joins *Answers* 19
  MP 42, 135
Harmsworth, St John 6, 41, 62, 64, 66–7, 82,
  92–3, 122, 126, 137
Harmsworth, St John (magistrate) 187
Harmsworth, Sarah 5–6
Harmsworth, Thomas 189
Harmsworth, Vere 41, 47, 63, 67, 82–4, 133
Harmsworth, Vere Harold Esmond *see*
  Rothermere, Vere, 3rd Viscount
Harmsworth, Violet *see* Wild, Violet
Harmsworth, Vyvyan Jnr 41, 63, 82–4, 88, 96,
  133, 137

Harmsworth, Vyvyan Snr 6, 60, 93, 123
Harmsworth Blunt, Lady *see* Harmsworth,
  Margaret
Harmsworth Brothers Ltd 30
Harmsworth Encyclopaedia 34
Harmsworth Investments 193, 211
Harmsworth Publications 189
Harmsworth Quays 229
Harmsworth Self-Educator 34
Harrison, Austin 85
Hastings, Warren 160
Hawkins, Alfred 100
Head, Anthony 143
Hearst, Randolph 240
Heath, Edward 177, 209, 212–13
Henderson, James 10
Henley House School 7–9, 54
  Magazine 8–9, 15
Hill, David 189–90
Hillier, Lacey 12
Hitler, Adolf 56, 103, 110, 112–14, 129, 143,
  147, 149–50
Hohenlohe-Waldenburg, Princess Stefanie 103
Home Chat 25, 65
Home Notes 25
Honor and Generosity Lodge 5
Horder, Lord 60–1
Horsey Hall 82
House, Colonel 53
Household Words 5
Howarth, Mary 33
Howe, Sir Geoffrey 220
Hudson, Lady *see* Northcliffe, Lady Mary
Hudson, Sir Robert 48, 51, 60, 73, 86, 93
Hulton, Sir Edward 97
Humphrey, Frank 119, 156, 200
Hungary 101–3, 126, 128, 139, 161–2, 192,
  236–7
  Austro-Hungary 54–5
  Commission of National Property Abroad
  162
Hussey, Marmaduke 177, 179, 181, 190,
  205–7, 222–3

Iddon, Don 201
Ideal Home Exhibition 184, 189
Iliffe, William 11–12, 14–16
Iliffe technical press 186
Illustrated Chips 21
Illustrated London News 10, 85
Illustrated London News and Sketch Ltd 33
Independent, The 27, 38, 229
Independent on Sunday 229
Independent Television Authority 170–2
India 107–8, 142
Ingram, Sir William 33
International Publishing Corporation 173
investigative journalism 25, 240–1
Iran 164–5
Ireland 3, 38, 59, 70, 83, 135

Jay, Peter 219
Jealous, George 5
Jenkins, Simon 216–17
Johnson, Paul 221
Jones, Emrys 151
Jones, Kennedy 24, 28, 30–1, 38, 57, 59

Kemsley, Lord 158, 167–8, 170, 172
Kemsley Press 172
Kenealy, Alexander 33
Kensington Advertiser 6
Keynes, John Maynard 53
King, Alfred 118–19
King, Cecil Harmsworth 119, 121, 162, 166,
    184, 186–8
    Daily Mirror 91, 117, 124, 153–5
    and Esmond Rothermere 155, 186–7
    IPC 173
    memoirs 37, 60, 104, 123
    and television 170–2
King, Enid 64
King, Lady Geraldine 4, 6, 16, 19, 63–5, 92,
    105, 123–4
King, Lucas White 45, 62, 64, 96
Kipling, Rudyard 31, 109
Kirby, Lou 217, 220
Kitchener, Lord 43, 45, 154

Labour Party 110, 170–1, 186, 194
    Daily Mail and 56, 70, 100, 163, 165
    governments 101, 107, 128, 143, 218–19
    Murdoch and 228–9
    Rothermere and 99
    'twelve lies' campaign 211, 220
Lacon, Sir Edmund 129
Lacon, Sir Robert 137
La Dragonnière 42, 82, 89, 99, 104, 115
Laing, John 125, 229
Lane, Harry 141
Lansdowne, Lord 48
Laski, Harold 107, 163
Law, Bonar 87, 89, 94–5, 99
Lederer, Lajos 102–4, 161–2
Lee, Maiko 234
Leeds Mercury 90
Lee-Potter, Lynda 210
Leese, John 231
Legrady brothers 102
Leinster 118–19
Leslie, Ann 211, 225
Lever, Sir Samuel 95–6
Lever Brothers 36, 69–71, 80
Levin, Bernard 175–6, 212
Lewis, Blos 159
Liberal Party 42–3, 48, 54, 65–6, 81, 127, 164,
    227
    governments 69, 84
    News Chronicle 173–4
Libman, Dr Emanuel 61
Lipton, Sir Thomas 67, 86

Lloyd George, David 45, 48, 90, 92, 114,
    151–2
    coalition government 56, 68–9, 71, 88, 93,
        134
    and Northcliffe 37, 46, 50–9, 68–9, 71–2
    and Rothermere 86–8, 95, 98–9, 101, 127
London Daily News 231
London General Cab Co. 126, 157, 179
Lonrho 215, 217, 230
Lots of Fun 10

McClean, Stuart ('Donald') 141, 170, 172, 185,
    190, 196
MacDonald, Ramsay 100–1, 107
McDowell, Keith 174
McKenna, Reginald 89
Macmillan, Harold 175, 195
McWhirter, William 98, 105, 127, 158, 188
Maffett, Emily 65
Maffett, William 3
Magyarok festival 236
Mail group *see Daily Mail*
Mail on Sunday 86, 229–30, 234
    launch 224–5, 236
    relaunch 226–7
    You magazine 227
Malbert, David 192
Male and Femail 241
management 190–1, 235
Manchester Guardian 169 *see also Guardian*
Mander, Michael 179
Marconi affair 84
Marks, Derek 209
Markwick, Edward 13–14, 16, 20
Marlowe, Tom 36, 43, 51, 54, 70, 92–3, 98,
    127, 191
Matthews, John William 203
Matthews, Victor 222, 224
Maxwell, Robert 229–31
Meredith (city editor) 192
Meredith corporation 232
Mereworth Castle 138–9, 142, 146, 156, 160
Metropolitan Home 232
Milne, J. V. 8
Milner, Harry 13
Milner, Mary ('Molly') *see* Northcliffe, Lady
    Mary
Milner, Robert 13
Ministry of Information
    Advisory Council 152
    Beaverbrook's ministry 54
Mirror group *see Daily Mirror*
Mitchell, Leslie 143
Monopolies Commission 219, 223
Montgomery, David 230
Moore, Arthur 44
Morison, Stanley 158
Morning Post 31, 38
Morrison, Herbert 149, 154
Morton, Edward 10

Mosley, Oswald 103, 110–12, 229
Mossadeq, Dr 164–5
Mulchrone, Vincent 206
Murchison, Kenneth 177
Murdoch, Keith 46
Murdoch, Rupert 25, 46, 127, 217, 241
  News of the World 174, 192
  Sun 117, 167, 169, 193
  Times 222–3
  Today 230
  Wapping 228–9
Murray, George 175
Mussolini, Benito 102, 110, 143
Musson, Edward Coulson 7
My Fight to Rearm Britain 120

National Opinion Polls 179, 211
National Socialists (Nazis) 110–14, 128, 147, 150
National Union of Journalists 71, 216, 238
Newfoundland 33–4, 37, 58, 79–80, 126, 128, 189, 194
New Liberal Review 66
Newnes, George 11–12, 14, 17–18, 22, 27–8
  George Newnes Ltd 79
New Northcliffe House 229
New Party 110
News Chronicle 155, 194, 206
  Chronicle group 174
  Mail merger 110, 173–5, 208
News International 223, 229
News of the World 168, 174, 192
News on Sunday 227
Newspaper Benevolent Fund 214
Newspaper Proprietors' Association 152, 154, 168
newspapers
  certified net sales 79
  picture 33, 38, 85
  provincial 27, 32, 71, 80, 86, 90, 98, 193
  Sunday 86, 224, 229
Newsprint Supply Company 152–3
News Shopper 209
New Straits Times 227
Nicholson, Reginald 35
Nigerian Daily Times 188
Nikitina, Alice 104, 117–18, 129
Northcliffe, Alfred Charles William
  Harmsworth, Viscount 3–73, 78–9, 86–7, 109, 134, 238, 241
  At the War 47–8
  and Beaverbrook 49, 89
  British War Mission 50–4, 67, 72
  at Carr & Co 13–17
  childhood 4–7
  children 9, 32, 63, 92, 126
  civil aviation committee 50
  Daily Mail 24, 27–31, 36, 69, 71, 240
  death 60, 91–2, 95
  death duties 93, 96

Director of Propaganda 54–6
  education 6–8
  family 62–8
  First World War 40–56
  honours 31–2, 53
  ill health 23, 36–7, 49, 53–4, 56, 58–60, 72, 81, 89
  interests 9, 36, 47–8, 50, 68
  and journalism 25–6, 69, 240
  journalistic career 8–12
  magazines 14–23, 25, 30, 96
  marriage 15
  newspaper proprietor 23–4, 27
  origins 3
  parliamentary candidate 22, 24, 26–7
  personality 71–2
  philanthropy 22
  and politicians 68–9
  and popular press 69
  wealth 67
  will 92–4
  world tour 58–9
Northcliffe, Lady Mary 13–16, 31–2, 36, 42, 44, 47, 54, 59, 67, 73, 84, 86, 92–4, 157
Northcliffe Newspapers 98, 179
Northern Ensign 123
North Sea oil 180, 182, 185, 215

Observer, The 34–5, 86, 94, 102, 161, 215, 222
Odhams 186
Ogilvy, Lord David 233
Ogilvy, Lady Geraldine 204, 233
Ohrstrom, Mary *see* Rothermere, Lady Mary
Ohrstrom, Richard 177
One Eighty Nine trust 166
O'Neill, Ann *see* Rothermere, Lady Ann
O'Neill, Lord Shane 156, 158
Our German Cousins 40
Outhwaite, Ernest 104–5
Outing 14
Owen, Frank 157–9, 191
Owen, Louise 93
Owen-Browne, Colin 236

Packer, Sir Frank 174
Page, Walter Hines 51
Pandora Publications 21
paper-making 33–4, 37, 58, 79–80, 117, 126, 179
parliamentary candidates 22, 26–7, 42, 63, 65, 89–90, 94
Paterson, Peter 174
Pathé Frères 96
Pearson, C. Arthur 22, 25, 34
Pearson's Weekly 23
Pemberton, Max 9, 11, 20–1, 78
People, The 169, 225
Perrier 41, 66–7, 82, 122
Pesti Hirlap 102–3, 162
Phillips, Sir Perceval 142

Pollock, William 56
pornography 25, 69, 115, 167–9
Portsmouth 22, 26–7, 32, 71
Pound, Reginald 189
Powys, Rev. E. V. R. 10, 15
POY 149
Poynters Hall 41, 64, 91
Press Bureau 44
Press Council 233
printers 58, 181, 206, 221, 228–9
Private Eye 214, 234–5
Private Schoolmaster, The 13
propaganda 44, 46–7, 50, 54–6, 89
provincial papers 27, 32, 71, 80, 86, 90, 98, 193
Pulitzer, Joseph 34
Punch 7, 21

Quennell, Peter 158

radio 101, 126
    commercial 213
Rakosi, Jena 102
Randall, Mike 110, 175–6, 191, 194
Read, James Canham 26
rearmament 112–14, 120, 127–9, 147
Recreation 13
Redhead, Margaret *see* Harmsworth, Margaret
Redhead, Mrs 128–9
Redhead, Rita 82, 90, 104–5
Redhead, Robert 90–1, 141, 185
Redhead, William 137
Reith, John 101, 127
Repington, Colonel 43, 45
Rhodes, Cecil 26, 29–30
Riddell, Lord 49, 56
Robinson, George 9
Roe, A. V. 68, 112
Rothermere, Lady Ann 156–60, 183, 185
Rothermere, Esmond Cecil Harmsworth, 2nd Viscount 83, 94, 99, 102, 105, 127, 129, 133–96, 217, 239, 241
    and Cecil King 155, 186–7
    childhood 82, 133
    children 137, 145–6, 157, 184–5, 204
    and Churchill 100–1, 152–3
    death 182
    diversification 193
    divorces 144–6, 159
    family 184–90
    and journalism 144
    marriages 84, 122, 136, 156–8, 177, 185, 194, 204
    Ministry of Information 152
    MP 63, 89–90, 115, 124, 134–6, 139
    News Chronicle take-over 173–5
    newspaper career 98, 116–17, 121, 140
    personality 194–6
    philanthropy 194

politics 193–4
    pornography charges 167–9
    recreations 137–8
    relations with father 147
    retirement 181–2
    and staff 190–1
    Suez 173
    and television 170–3
    will 178
Rothermere, Harold Sidney Harmsworth, 1st Viscount 58–9, 62, 77–130, 137, 139, 141–2, 155, 241
    air campaign 112–14, 147–8
    Air Minister 41, 50, 53, 87–8
    art collection 161–2
    and Baldwin 107–9, 127
    and Beaverbrook 87–9, 96–100, 108, 112, 116, 118, 127–8
    childhood 4–7
    children 82–4
    and Churchill 82, 99–101, 107–8, 113–15, 129–30
    commercial skills 77, 126, 241
    death 120, 130, 155–6
    divestment 115–16, 140
    education 6, 77
    family 64–5, 118–25
    and fascism 103, 110–14
    First World War 41, 52
    honours 41, 82, 84, 88
    and Hungary 101–3, 161
    and Lloyd George 86–8, 95, 98–9, 101, 127
    magazines 17, 20, 23, 30, 77
    marriage 81
    newspaper publishing 24, 27, 36–7, 79, 84
    and Northcliffe 80–1, 92–4
    origins 3
    personality 103, 105, 117, 121, 128–9
    personal life 103–4
    politics 81, 98–101, 107, 118, 128, 141
    recreations 117, 130
    wealth 105, 116
Rothermere, Lady Lilian 41, 81–2, 91, 105
Rothermere, Lady Mary 176–8, 182–3, 185
Rothermere, Lady Patricia 203–7, 211, 213–15, 238, 242
Rothermere, Vere Harold Esmond Harmsworth, 3rd Viscount 137–9, 174, 180, 185, 199–237
    chairmanship 181, 193, 206–7
    childhood 119, 129, 145, 199
    children 177–8, 14, 233
    and computerisation 228–9
    education 157, 199–200
    and English 202, 207–9
    Evening News relaunch 231
    joins Associated Newspapers 184, 202
    and journalism 235, 239–42
    Mail on Sunday 224–7
    marriage 203–4, 213–15

and *New Daily Mail* 208–10
personality 233–4
tax exile 213–14
and *Today* 230
in USA 157, 200–2
wealth 232
Rothwell, Bruce 209
Rowland, Tiny 217, 230
Rowley, Annie 13
Royal Air Force 135, 139, 156
Royal Commission on the Press 191
Ruprecht, Crown Prince of Bavaria 55
Russian Ballet 104, 129
Ryder, Lord 218

Salisbury, Lord 26, 29
Sanger, Gerald 139–40, 158–9, 161, 166
Sapt, Arkas 33
Save Europe Now 188
Scarfe, Gerald 175
Schofield, Guy 176
Scott, Willie 20
Scraps 10
Second World War 118–19, 149–54
Selss, Albert Maximilian 6
Sergeant, Sir Patrick 191–2, 225, 235
Seton-Watson, R. W. 54
Shah, Eddy 228, 230
Share, George Wade 81
Share, Lilian *see* Rothermere, Lady Lilian
Shaw, George Bernard 29
Shawcross, Hartley 164
Shields, Mick 181, 183, 190–1, 193, 207,
    209–13, 215–16, 221–2, 234, 236
Shrimsley, Bernard 224–6, 236
Shulman, Milton 216
Simcoe, General 122
Simon, Sir John 46
Simpson, Mrs Wallace 127, 194
slump 97, 108, 166
Smith, Alfred Benjamin 9, 63
Smith, F. E., Earl of Birkenhead 44
Smith, Louisa Jane 9, 63
Snoad, Harold 59
social questions 70–1, 211
South Africa 181–2, 207
Southwood, Lord 154
Sphere 85
Sporting Life 229
Spring-Rice, Sir Cecil 51
Stanley, Henry M. 11
Star 169, 173, 176
Steed, Wickham 38, 47, 54, 57–61
Steevens, G. W. 29, 31
Stephens, Samuel 179
Steven, Stuart 218, 226–7, 233–4, 242
Stevens, Lord 169
Stevens, Jocelyn 176, 180, 216–17
Stevenson, R. L. 10
Stody House 84

Strand Magazine 14
Strobl, S. 104
Stroods 204, 233
Stuart, Sir Campbell 52, 54, 56–7, 94
Suez crisis 165, 170, 173–4, 186
Sullivan, Sir Arthur 29, 31
Sun 117, 168–9, 193, 213
Sunday Companion, The 26, 80
Sunday Correspondent 229
Sunday Dispatch 93, 116, 127, 141–2, 158,
    166, 170, 187
    closure 174
    pornography charge 115, 167
Sunday Express 86, 96, 141, 166, 179, 216,
    225–6
    Dispatch merger 174
Sunday Graphic 115
Sunday Mirror 188, 224
Sunday Pictorial 80, 98, 101, 108, 111, 116,
    124, 147, 153–4, 166, 187
    becomes *Sunday Mirror* 188
    Daily Mail Trust buys 95
    launch 85–6
Sunday Sport 169
Sunday Telegraph 225
Sunday Times 96, 158, 221–4, 227, 232
Sunday Today 227
Sutton, George 36, 53, 58, 60, 92–4, 97, 140–1
    Amalgamated Press 37, 51, 81, 96
    Associated Newspapers 116
    Daily Mail Trust 125–6
    joins *Mail* group 96
    Northcliffe's secretary 20, 22
Sutton Place 21, 31, 42, 44, 54
Sylvan Debating Club 4, 92
Szarvasy, Frederick A. 95–6

tabloids 33, 117, 144, 155, 168–9, 181, 210, 213
    Daily Mail 205–11
Tatler, The 206
tax exile 213–14, 238
television 126, 167, 176
    commercial 170–2
    satellite 232
Television Act 170–1
Terry, Walter 207
Thatcher, Margaret 210, 220–1, 230
Thomson, Kenneth 222
Thomson, Roy 25, 172
Thomson Organisation 173, 220, 222
Thousand Ways to Earn a Living, A 13
Thyssen, Baron von 182
Ticketmaster 231
Tildy, Zoltan 162
Time magazine 158
Times, The 51, 57–60, 81, 170, 190, 212, 215,
    223
    Book Club 34
    First World War 43-6, 48
    Murdoch take-over 222

Times, The cont.
  Northcliffe and 33–6, 38–9, 71, 92–4
  Rothermere and 94–6
  shutdown 220, 222
  sold 126
  Thomson buys 172
Times Newspapers 221–3, 228
Times Publishing Company 35
Tit-Bits 11–12, 15–17, 21
Today 228–30
Tracy, Louis 24
trades unions 221, 228–9, 238
  AEU 149
  NUJ 71, 216, 238
Trafalgar House 217, 221, 230
Trenchard, Sir Hugh 87
Treves, Sir Frederick 60

United Empire Party 107–8
United Newspapers 179
United States 72
  aircraft mission 119, 147–8
  British War Mission 50–4, 67, 72
US Publisher 209

Vanity Fair 66
Versailles 56, 90, 102, 113, 134
Victoria, Queen 31
Villa Rocque Fleury 105
Vinson, Noel 189
Volapuk Journal, The 13
Vorster, John 182

Walker, Alexander 216
Walker, Patric 236
Wall Street Crash 98–9, 107
Walter, Arthur 34
Walter, John 35, 57, 60, 92–4
Walter family 34–5, 60, 95
Wapping 223, 228–9
war correspondents 30–1, 43–6
Ward, Herbert 10–11, 67
Ward-Price, George 103, 108, 113, 115, 117, 130, 142–3, 150, 161
Wareham, Arthur 173

Warwick House 137–9, 156–7, 180, 182
Washington Post 209
Waterhouse, Keith 211
Weekly Dispatch 44
Welch, Colin 211
Wells, H. G. 20, 41, 54, 128
Western Daily Mercury 122
Western Morning News 66, 122, 189
White, Sam 236
'Wigan alps' exposé 212
Wild, Violet 6, 92, 96, 123, 236
Wild, Wilfrid 96, 122, 125–6
Willert, Arthur 51
Williams, Marcia *see* Falkender, Marcia
Willingdon, Lady 42
Wills, John Spencer 170, 172
Wilson, H. W. 46
Wilson, Harold 164, 186, 209, 212
Wilson, Judith 118
Wilson, Woodrow 52, 55
Winnington-Ingram, John 207
Wintour, Charles 216–17, 219–20, 230
Wollheim, Eric 112
women's journalism 25, 33, 69, 208
  suffrage 124, 136
Wood, Fred 77
Wooldrige, Ian 210
World (Newcastle) 98
World (New York) 34
World's Press News 184
Wrench, Evelyn 87
Wright brothers 37, 47, 72
Wrohan, Mrs Kathleen 32, 37, 59, 62, 92, 189
Wrohan, Alfred 32, 63, 68
Wrohan, Geraldine 32, 63, 68
Wrohan, Harold 32, 63, 68, 189

You magazine 227
Young Folks' Tales 10, 12
Younghusband, Peter 181–2
Youth 10

Zanuck, Darryl 203
Zec, Philip 154
Zinoviev letter 100